WILLIAM PITT AND THE FRENCH REVOLUTION

William Pitt and the French Revolution

1785–1795

Jennifer Mori

KEELEUNIVERSITY**PRESS**

First published in 1997 by
Keele University Press
22 George Square, Edinburgh

Typeset by Carnegie Publishing Ltd
18 Maynard St, Preston, England.
Printed and bound in Great Britain

ISBN 1 85331 137 5

Contents

Preface

This book started life as an undergraduate dissertation written long ago and far away at McGill University in Montreal, Canada. It then metamorphosed into a D.Phil thesis presented to Oxford in 1992 and has finally turned into a book. I owe academic debts to many people over the nine years since I started this project: to my undergraduate and postgraduate supervisors, Professor Hereward Senior and Dr Leslie Mitchell; to two examiners who kindly pointed out the failings of the thesis, Dr John Stevenson and Professor T. C. W. Blanning; and to Dr Paul Langford, who gave me advice on how best to prepare this for publication.

To my friends and family I owe a greater debt still for putting up with me and my obsession. The Middle Common Room at Worcester College, Oxford has been a source of friendship and support over the years and, of its members, I owe special debts to Mark Philpott and Karin Lesnik-Oberstein. Other Oxford friends who saved my sanity more than once during four years of doctoral research were Simon Burrows, Deborah Johnston and Khalid Siddique. After Oxford, the History Department at Lancaster University kindly gave me a job, a congenial environment in which to work and enthusiastic students and colleagues on whom to test my ideas. Particular thanks go to Stephen Constantine, Stephen Pumfrey and Sandy Grant. The University of Wales at Lampeter gave me an even greater blessing – the time to prepare this text for publication. To the personnel at Keele University Press, who have waited patiently for this manuscript, I am also greatly indebted. Space restrictions have resulted in the omission of a separate bibliography of secondary sources. Primary sources have been listed.

This book could not have been written without the help of archivists and librarians too numerous to mention. Acknowledgement and grateful thanks for permission to cite from manuscript collections go to the British Library, Public Record Office at Kew, Scottish Record Office, Trustees of the National Maritime Museum, Trustees of the National Library of Scotland, Syndics of the Cambridge University Library, Bodleian Library, John Rylands University Library, Pembroke College, Cambridge, William L. Clements Library at the University of Michigan (Ann Arbor), Sheffield City Libraries and County Record Offices of

Kent, Hampshire, Devon, Suffolk (Ipswich), and West Yorkshire. I also acknowledge and thank the Duke of Buccleuch and Queensberry, Earl Bathurst, Earl of Harewood, Viscount Melville, Viscount Addington, Board of Trustees of the Chevening Estate, Olive Countess Fitzwilliam's Settlement Trustees, Mrs G. Bence Jones, Mr Giles Adams and Mr Richard Head for permission to consult and quote from papers in their possession.

I wish to dedicate this book to my parents, who did not always support this project but, I think, always believed that I would finish it.

Jennifer Mori
Oxford, July 1995

Abbreviations

All books published in London unless otherwise stated.

Add MS: Additional Manuscripts (British Library)

Addington Life: G. Pellew (ed.), *The Life and Correspondence of the Right Hon. Henry Addington, 1st Viscount Sidmouth* (3 vols, 1847)

APLP: Association for the Preservation of Liberty and Property against Levellers and Republicans

Auckland Correspondence: Bishop of Bath and Wells (ed.), *The Journal and Correspondence of William, Lord Auckland* (4 vols, 1861)

BIHR: Bulletin of the Institute of Historical Research (now published as *Historical Research*), Senate House, London

BL: British Library

Bod: Bodleian Library

BT: Board of Trade

Burke Correspondence: A. Cobban and R. A. Smith (eds), *The Correspondence of Edmund Burke* (8 vols, 1967–9)

CJ: Journals of the House of Commons

Clements MS: Pitt Papers, William L. Clements Library, University of Michigan at Ann Arbor

Court and Cabinets: Duke of Buckingham and Chandos (ed.)., *Memoirs of the Court and Cabinets of George III* (4 vols, 1853–5)

CUL: Cambridge University Library.

DRO: Devon Record Office

Dropmore: Historical Manuscripts Commission, 13th Report, Part VII, and 14th Report, Part V, *The Manuscripts of J. B. Fortescue preserved at Dropmore* (10 vols, 1892–1927)

EHR: *English Historical Review*

FO: Foreign Office

FOP: Society of the Friends of the People

Fox Mem: Lord John Russell (ed.), *Memorials and Correspondence of Charles James Fox* (4 vols, 1853–6)

GLG: Castalia Granville (ed.), *Lord Granville Leveson Gower, Private Correspondence 1781–1821* (2 vols, 1916)

HJ: *The Historical Journal*

HO: Home Office

HRO: Hampshire Record Office

JBS: *Journal of British Studies*

KAO: Kent Archive Office (Centre for Kentish Studies), Maidstone

Keith Correspondence: Mrs Gillespie Smith (ed.), *The Memoirs and Correspondence of Sir Robert Murray Keith* (2 vols, 1849)

Kenyon: Historical Manuscripts Commission, 14th Report, Part VI, *The Manuscripts of Lord Kenyon preserved at Gredington* (1894)

LCG III: A. Aspinall (ed.), *The Later Correspondence of George III* (5 vols, 1962–8)

LCS Papers: M. Thale (ed.), *Selections from the Papers of the London Corresponding Society, 1792–1799* (Cambridge: 1983)

Life and Letters: Countess of Minto (ed.), *Life and Letters of Gilbert Elliot, First Earl Minto from 1751–1806* (3 vols, 1874)

Life of Stanhope: G. Stanhope and G. P. Gooch (eds), *The Life of Charles, 3rd Earl Stanhope* (1914)

Life of Wilberforce: R. I. and S. Wilberforce (eds), *The Life of William Wilberforce* (5 vols, 1838)

Malmesbury Diaries: 3rd Earl of Malmesbury (ed.), *Diaries and Correspondence of James Harris, Earl of Malmesbury* (4 vols, 1845)

Miles Correspondence: C. P. Miles (ed.), *The Correspondence of William Augustus Miles on the French Revolution, 1789–1817* (3 vols, 1890)

More Memoirs: W. Roberts (ed.), *Memoirs of the Life and Correspondence of Mrs. Hannah More* (3 vols, 1853)

MS: manuscript

n. d.: no date

NLS: National Library of Scotland, Edinburgh

NMM: National Maritime Museum, Greenwich

P&P: *Past and Present*

PH: W. Cobbett (ed.), *The Parliamentary History of England, from the Earliest Period to the Year 1803* (vols xxi–xxxv, 1806–15)

Pol. Mem.: O. Browning (ed.), *The Political Memoranda of Francis, 5th Duke of Leeds* (1884)

PR: J. Debrett (ed.), *The Parliamentary Register: or History, Debates and Proceedings of both Houses of Parliament* (45 vols, 1781–96), 2nd series; (18 vols, 1797–1802), 3rd series

PRO: Public Record Office, Kew

PRO 30/58: Dacres Adams Papers

Rose Diaries: L. V. Harcourt (ed.), *The Diaries and Correspondence of the Rt. Hon. George Rose* (2 vols, 1860)

Rutland: Historical Manuscripts Commission, 14th Report, Part I, *The Manuscripts of the Duke of Rutland preserved at Belvoir Castle* (4 vols, 1894)

SCI: Society for Constitutional Information

SRO: Scottish Record Office, Edinburgh

State Trials: T. B. and T. J. Howell (eds), *English State Trials* (vols xxiii–xxv, 1818)

TRHS: Transactions of the Royal Historical Society

Wickham Papers: W. Wickham (ed.), *The Correspondence of the Rt. Hon. William Wickham* (2 vols, 1870)

w.m.: watermark

WO: War Office

WWM: Wentworth Woodhouse Muniments, Sheffield Central Library

Wyvill Papers: C. Wyvill (ed.), *Political Papers, chiefly respecting the Attempt of the County of York ... to effect a Reformation of the Parliament of Great Britain* (6 vols, York: 1794–1802)

Introduction
The Pittite Legacy, 1806–1995

William Pitt the Younger, Prime Minister for eighteen years and wartime leader throughout what could be called the second darkest days in England's history, has long been, and will continue to be, a saint. A shining example of rectitude in a venal Augustan world, Pitt, having first taken the helm of the state in 1783, pursued a decade of enlightened fiscal, administrative and trade policies before the French Revolution emerged to threaten the intellectual, social and political status quo of western Europe. Pitt, having taken Britain to war against revolutionary France in 1793, resigned in 1801 after eight years of war when George III refused to countenance the admission of would-be Irish Catholic MPs to the united parliament created by the 1800 Act of Union between Britain and Ireland. Following the breakdown of the fragile Peace of Amiens at the end of 1803, Pitt returned to office to lead Britain once more in war against Napoleonic France. He died in poverty, a victim of overwork and suspected cancer, in 1806.[1]

Pitt's apotheosis as a saint began before his death. In 1802 his young disciple George Canning composed the verses that eulogized Pitt as 'the Pilot who weathered the Storm', and early nineteenth-century Tories revered the memory of a man who had become a martyr to the cause of public duty. Barely had Pitt's remains been interred in Westminster Abbey before a party of his personal followers emerged in the House of Commons, led by a ghost.[2] Its criticism of the 1806–7 All Talents coalition ministry led by Lord Grenville was based on what Pitt was supposed to have believed, had he lived. Said conduct would have horrified Pitt, a lifelong enemy of party, who defended his policies by reference to 'the principles settled at the Revolution' of 1688 and always called himself an 'independent Whig'.

Nineteenth-century dinners, clubs, scholarships and statues commemorated the life and works of the great man who had died in the odour of sanctity. According to close friends of Pitt – George Pretyman-Tomline, Bishop of Lincoln; George Rose, Joint Secretary to the Treasury; and William Eden, first Baron Auckland – Pitt had confessed his sins and taken the sacrament on his deathbed. His nephew, the fourth

Earl Stanhope, added that he expired with the words: 'my country, how I love my country'. Pitt's political legacy nevertheless posed certain problems for his heirs. The old broad-based Pittite 'national government' of the 1790s had broken up in 1801 when Henry Addington, Speaker of the House of Commons, became premier and William Grenville, Pitt's cousin and Foreign Secretary since 1791, went into opposition. Grenville did not rejoin Pitt in 1804, while Addington, who returned to Pitt's Cabinet as Lord Sidmouth, resigned within a year. Pittites and would-be Pittites had the option of attaching themselves to the Grenvillites, the Addingtonians or the younger generation of politicians who saw themselves as Pitt's heirs, amongst whom Canning, Lord Castlereagh and Spencer Perceval were the most prominent. More difficult was the definition of Pitt's 'true' political principles. A 'conservative' intellectual identity was strongly suggested by the policies of the 1790s, but embarrassing actions like the parliamentary reform bill of 1785, the resignation over Catholic Emancipation in 1801 and Pitt's consistent support for the abolition of the slave trade remained to be explained away. By 1832 this had, on the whole, taken place successfully and Pitt had been canonized as the founding father of the Tory Party.[3]

Three decades of haggling over Pitt's memory took some unusual forms. Pitt's receipt of the sacrament was one of them. Support for the Church of England was a pillar of conservative identity from 1760 to 1832 and Pitt's death became part of the 'Christianization' process by which Tories vindicated their reverence for Church and State. Pitt's political legacy was arguably '*the* main element in a developing early nineteenth century British conservative tradition'.[4] From 1806 to 1830 the term 'Pittite' was the unifying label for proto-Tories; the term 'Tory' itself was associated with the Jacobite treason of the early eighteenth century. For these reasons, Tomline was determined to make a devout Anglican out of his ex-pupil, claiming in his biography of Pitt, first published in 1821, that Pitt 'never omitted attending' chapel services, both 'morning and evening', as an undergraduate at Pembroke Hall, Cambridge during the 1770s.[5] The 'anti-Catholic' Tories used Pitt's memory to legitimate their opposition to emancipation, so contentious an issue in Tory ranks up to 1827 that no party line could be laid down on it. Tomline, for one, had been horrified by Pitt's conduct in 1801:

> I revere and love the King more than ever, for the union of steady adherence to his oath upon religious principles *at such a moment*, with the *affectionate attachment* to Mr. Pitt so very evident in his letters. I rejoice extremely that Mr. Pitt *did not intend unqualified toleration*, but I lament far more than I can describe the line of conduct he has adopted.[6]

George III's literal interpretation of the coronation oath that bound him to uphold the Anglican establishment as 'Defender of the Faith' scuppered many a toleration proposal from 1760 to 1810. Emancipation would have done away with the 1678 Test Act that required MPs to swear their loyalty to the state by abjuring key features of the Roman faith. Pitt had proposed to replace this with an oath of allegiance from which the sacramental elements were removed.

Catholic Emancipation and parliamentary reform were the two most problematic issues for the nineteenth-century Tories. Rose, a chief upholder of the sacrament myth, also claimed that Pitt had renounced parliamentary reform soon after 1785.[7] As late as 1830, however, J. W. Croker was telling the Pitt Clubs, ostensibly founded to preserve the principles of the great man, that 'the two most formidable objects of their apprehensions, Parliamentary Reform and Catholic Emancipation, were the measures of Mr. Pitt'.[8] Reform was easy to explain away, for Pitt had seemingly dropped the measure after the defeat of his 1785 bill in the House of Commons. Emancipation was not. Richard, Marquis of Wellesley and ex-Governor-General of India, who like Rose had been close to Pitt, wrote to the *Quarterly Review* in 1836 that the dead premier had 'received regular and systematic instruction in the principles of the Christian religion, and in the doctrine and discipline of the Church of England'. Pitt was 'not merely a faithful and dutiful, but a learned member of our established church' asserted Wellesley, who ignored what he had been told by Pitt's niece, Lady Hester Stanhope, who had kept house for her uncle from 1803 to 1806. Lady Hester declared that Pitt 'never even talked about religion, and never brought it upon the carpet'.[9]

Tomline's official *Life of Pitt* was greeted with howls of abuse in 1821. Seemingly compiled from excerpts of *The Parliamentary History of England* and the *Annual Register*, it was bad even by the standards of the nineteenth century. 'The worst biographical work of its length in the world' was Macaulay's verdict.[10] So negative were reviews of the first two volumes, which covered Pitt's life to the end of 1792, that the good bishop never published the rest. An additional fragment was printed privately in 1898 by Lord Rosebery. Tomline, as Pitt's literary executor, got most of the dead man's papers, with the exception of miscellaneous items kept at Walmer Castle, Pitt's official residence as Lord Warden of the Cinque Ports. These were absconded with by William Dacres Adams, Pitt's last private secretary, who detested Tomline.[11] The bishop, who saw himself as the custodian of Pitt's memory, is widely suspected of having destroyed some of the papers. He certainly suppressed others. When Lord Bute asked Tomline in 1823 to shed light on a rumour that Pitt had put together a scheme for tithe redemption, Tomline replied that 'Mr. Pitt never pursued a bill for the

Commutation of Tithes'. Pitt had first expressed interest in tithes in 1786, had sounded the Archbishop of Canterbury in 1791 on the possible replacement of tithes with a 'corn rent' – a proposal originating with Tomline – had reconsidered the subject in 1795–6 in the context of general enclosure, and had not only prepared a commutation bill in 1799, a copy of which still survives in Pitt's papers, but had demanded that the bill be placed before a panel of bishops for consideration.[12]

Catholic Emancipation had threatened to split the Tory Party in 1822 and this explains Tomline's unwillingness to complicate the debate on Pitt's attitudes to the Established Church by introducing another variable, tithe reform. Religion debates in Parliament since 1806 had witnessed the division of Tories into pro- and anti-relief camps, with Castlereagh, Canning, Palmerston and Huskisson acting as advocates of religious toleration in the Pittite tradition.[13] Other aspects of Pitt's 'liberal Toryism' were already receiving exposure from the Liverpool ministry which, following the end of the Napoleonic Wars, began to revive his fiscal policies of the 1780s.[14] From 1819 to 1822 the Liverpool Tories used Pitt's memory, the 'sacred' and 'immortal fabric' of Pitt, to vindicate a post-war economic reconstruction programme based on Evangelical Christian principles to which Pitt had never subscribed.[15]

No acceptable biography of Pitt could have been written before 1840, and no friend or associate, old or young, tried. The Grenvilles told no tales though they printed many of Pitt's letters. The younger followers of Pitt kept his memory alive in verbal forms which were as inaccurate as the official versions. Canning's repeated declarations that his foreign policy was based on 'the glorious system of Pitt' incensed Hester Stanhope at a distance of 3,000 miles.[16] The first critical analyses of Pitt's career came from the Whigs, for whom Pitt had been, since the days of Charles James Fox, the devil incarnate. Fragmented though the hagiography of Pitt had become over the three decades since his death, the demonology of Pitt was a coherent doctrine handed down to the Whig faithful on the Opposition benches by Holland House from 1807 to 1830.[17] In the Memoirs of the Whig Party in my Time, written by Fox's nephew, Pitt appeared as a toady of George III, a man driven by self-interest and the lust for power, an enemy of the people and their civil liberties; in short, living proof of the maxim that 'absolute power corrupts absolutely'. Pitt had taken Britain to war in 1793 to exacerbate divisions developing in the Whig Party since 1790; his persecution of radicals agitating for parliamentary reform from 1792 to 1794 was directed to the same end.[18] This unflattering portrait was touched up by Lord John Russell in the Memorials and Correspondence of Charles James Fox and The Life of Charles James Fox. Russell, in his determination to depict Fox's demon as a sheer opportunist, cast doubt on Tory received wisdom concerning Pitt's war aims during the 1790s.

According to Russell, Pitt was no supporter of ideological war as declared by Edmund Burke's *Reflections on the Revolution in France*:

> He [Pitt] was ready to admit that we had nothing to do with the internal government of France, provided its rulers were disposed and able to maintain friendly relations with foreign governments. He sought to confine France within her ancient limits, to oblige her to respect established treaties, and to renounce her conquests. He sought by expeditions to the West Indies an indemnity for the expenses of the war. In short, he treated Robespierre and Carnot as he would have treated any other French rulers, whose ambition was to be resisted, and whose interference in the affairs of other nations was to be checked.[19]

This hard-headed pragmatism was subservient to Pitt's greater goal of remaining in office and destroying the Opposition Whigs as a political force.

Philip, fifth Earl Stanhope and Pitt's grand-nephew, was appalled by these slanders. His *Life of the Right Honourable William Pitt*, which appeared in 1861, was a masterpiece of Victorian biography. Not only did Stanhope attempt to address major issues respecting Pitt's ideas and policies, but he printed much of Pitt's correspondence and had interviewed just about everyone still alive who had known Pitt personally. Stanhope defended Pitt's reputation as a parliamentary, fiscal and administrative reformer during the 1780s. He explained Pitt's opposition to the repeal of the Test and Corporation Acts from 1787 onwards as a response to the hostility of the Established Church, not a denial of civil rights to Protestant dissenters. Pitt's legal repression of the reform movement during the 1790s was more difficult to justify; this Stanhope explained as a product of longstanding anxiety about the social effects of the French Revolution which was translated into government policy in 1792 when British radical authors 'appeared to have no other view than that of the incitement of tumult and sedition'. By 1794 not only was treason seemingly real, but so were the demands of the public for 'a course of the most rigorous repression'.[20] The war with France was just and necessary, called for by Britain's obligation to protect the United Provinces, to which it had been allied since 1788, from French conquest.

Stanhope's *Life* established Pitt as an intellectual opponent of the French Revolution, if no advocate of Edmund Burke's ideas.[21] While this successfully discredited the Foxite interpretation of Pitt's motives, it left the intellectual foundations of Pitt's hostility to the revolution unclear. William Lecky broke with Stanhope by declaring Pitt indifferent to the revolution up to November 1792, when the United

Provinces, menaced by a French army on its borders, called for British aid and British advocates of parliamentary reform were sending addresses of support to the French National Convention. Faced with a combination of internal and external threats – one to Britain's public order and the other to the balance of power in western Europe – Pitt went to war with revolutionary France. While Lecky had some doubts about Pitt's commitment to both war and repression in 1792, by 1794 there could be no doubt that he was frightened of the threat that popular radicalism posed to the constitution and government of Britain.[22] Pitt did not share Burke's early fear of the French Revolution, but he had reached similar conclusions about the dangers it posed to western civilization.

By 1890 there were two schools of thought respecting Pitt. The first, described by the Liberal peer Lord Rosebery as 'the most common and least informed', was the Conservative Party legend that depicted Pitt as 'the great antagonist of the French Revolution'. So distasteful did Rosebery find this that he went out of his way to print Benjamin Disraeli's dissentient claim that Pitt's first decade in office 'was his title deed to be looked upon as a Tory minister'. Conservatism had come a long way since 1830. Disraeli, who still saw inspiration in Pitt's policies, praised 'Hostility to boroughmongering, economy, French alliances and commercial treaties', not the French war to which Sir William Harcourt's vote had gone. Pitt's memory was something that troubled Disraeli: 'in the more genial and less majestic days before 1874', wrote Rosebery, Disraeli had replaced the authorized Tory account of Pitt's death, the declaration of love for country, with the words; 'I think I could eat one of Bellamy's meat pies.' After 1874, when Disraeli became Prime Minister, it was *lèse-majesté* to make irreverent remarks about Pitt.[23] If Disraeli's meat-pie story was a personal attempt to popularize Pitt for a new generation of Tories, it failed miserably in its purpose. Rosebery, who in printing the Disraeli story may have been trying to update Pitt's image for the Liberals, killed off the sacrament myth for good.[24] In 1891 Pitt's legacy was still, as Rosebery acknowledged, a problematic issue in academic and political circles and would continue to be as long as Home Rule remained a festering sore in Anglo-Irish relations.

The second school of thought, represented by Lecky, was 'the more serious and scholarly ... which severely divides the life of Pitt into two parts'. Rosebery dismissed this division as artificial and did his best to claim Pitt for the Liberal Party: 'to the end of his life he [Pitt] called himself an independent Whig, a term which it must be remembered was then the only one to describe every shade of what we call Liberalism'.[25] This account of the 'liberal descent' was accepted by some *fin-de-siècle* Liberals who admired eighteenth-century Whiggism through rose-tinted spectacles. Winston Churchill, upon becoming First Lord of the Admiralty, insisted to George V on no less than three occasions that 'William Pitt' was an appropriate Liberal name for a battleship. The king, foreseeing the scatological nicknames that the navy would coin for any vessel named the 'Pitt', disagreed.

Outside the world of Westminster, a university consensus declared Pitt a Whig up to 1789. The process by which he came to embrace Toryism was still not resolved. The mystery was finally explained by John Holland Rose in the second volume of a biography that exemplified the scholarly approach to Pitt's life criticized by Rosebery.[26] *William Pitt and the Great War* stated that it was the emergence of popular radical reform societies at the beginning of 1792, not Burke's *Reflections*, that set Pitt against the French Revolution and all its works. The London Corresponding Society and its provincial associates were demanding democratic parliamentary reform, of which Pitt had never been an advocate. On 30 April 1792 he rose in the Commons to declare against reform. This set Pitt on the road to repression: the Royal Proclamation against Seditious Writings of May 1792; the suspension of habeas corpus in 1794 and 1798; the series of repressive public order enactments starting with the Traitorous Correspondence Act of 1793 and ending with the Corresponding Societies Act of 1799. War in 1793 was a product of French military and ideological aggression towards the Austrian Netherlands and United Provinces. The first fraternal decree of 19 November 1792, which offered French aid to all peoples striving to cast off the yoke of tyranny, was identified by George Stead Veitch as the cause of Pitt's transformation from liberal to conservative. Philip Anthony Brown agreed, but suggested that the domestic manifestations of Pitt's anti-Jacobinism, the repressive legislation of the 1790s, was a product of caution rather than conservative conviction.[27]

The 'caution vs. conviction' debate was not explored at length by historians because the Holland Rose account of Pitt's response to the French Revolution was subtly modified over the next half-century. The strange death of Liberal England heralded by the grant of Home Rule to Ireland in 1921 left Pitt to the Tories. Home Rule dissolved Pitt's 1800 Act of Union and, with it, the last bonds linking the dreams of the dead to the nightmares of the living. Soon after Pitt's ghost had been laid to rest at Westminster, G. M. Trevelyan placed Pitt at the head of the Tories in a two-party political system complete with safe seats, election funds and 'roots of affection in the great classes of the community'.[28] This kind of analysis did not stand up well to the critical research techniques pioneered by Sir Lewis Namier in *The Structure of Politics at the Accession of George III*. This denounced the concept of party as an anachronism imposed on the eighteenth-century Parliament by scholars intent on regarding England's history as a march towards parliamentary democracy. Namier's 'crooked taloned birds' went into politics motivated not by public duty, but by self-interest. Pitt, who refused to enrich himself by the spoils of office and wielded an axe around the Augustan jungle of places, pensions and sinecures, was not an appropriate candidate for Namierite analysis, but while Pitt's reputation as 'the Incorruptible' remained unscathed, the political world in which he lived did not. Pitt now presided over an independent House of Commons where 557 MPs jostled for position in complex permutations and combinations of factional and family groups.[29]

In 1924 Keith Feiling had identified Pitt as the leader of a Tory Party based on support for king, Church and the values of the independent country gentry. Pitt was the reluctant heir to a Toryism resurrected by Lord North during the 1770s. Although Feiling identified Pitt's parliamentary reform as cautious and conservative, he admitted that Pitt was difficult to class as a Tory until November 1792, at which date he succumbed to fears that Britain would follow France into revolution. From 1792 onwards his conservative side was increasingly in evidence. The Holland Rose analysis was still in force.[30]

On the other side of the Atlantic, Donald Groves Barnes was looking at Pitt's relations with George III. Pitt could not, contended Barnes, defy the king from 1785 onwards; the defeat of the 1785 parliamentary reform bill marked the end of any real autonomy on the part of Pitt. Some freedom, stated Barnes, was regained following the king's porphyria attack of 1788–9, but the resignation over Catholic Emancipation was prefigured by almost two decades of royal supremacy. No real disagreement between the two existed in the 1790s for both king and minister were united in their opposition to the anarchy that the French Revolution represented. Barnes, like Holland Rose and Feiling, dated the origins of Pitt's hardening attitudes to May 1792. Threats of revolution in Britain at the end of 1792 marked Pitt's complete conversion to Tory ideals.[31]

Despite these assaults, the bipartite assessment of Pitt's career laid down by Holland Rose remained current, though frayed at the edges. Further damage was done by the historians of the Opposition Whigs during the late 1960s and early 1970s, from whose studies Pitt's public order policies once more appeared as part of a campaign to split the Whig Party.[32] Pitt's Whig credentials were now very much in doubt and this scepticism was integrated into the work done by historians of radicalism and working-class movements. For those approaching parliamentary reform from a high political standpoint, Pitt did not fare too badly. He fared far worse at the hands of scholars addressing the democratic reform tradition.[33] In the early 1980s scholars began to question whether the popular radicals were as harmless as they seemed. When genuine revolutionary cells were identified in Ireland

and England, the government's domestic policies of the later 1790s, though by no means excused, began to bear some relationship not to illusion, but to reality.[34] The official measures of the early 1790s were still explained as products of Pitt's fear that the French Revolution would reproduce itself in Britain.

The appearance of John Ehrman's *William Pitt: The Reluctant Transition* in 1983 did not modify this picture. *William Pitt: The Years of Acclaim*, which came out in 1969, debunked old myths about Pitt's first decade in Downing Street. Pitt was no doctrinaire reformer pursuing theoretical objectives laid down by Adam Smith or Richard Price. He was reluctant to antagonize vested interests and could either modify or drop entire projects if faced by strong opposition. Parliamentary reform and the Irish Commercial Propositions of 1785 disappeared without a trace. Volume three was published in May 1996 and completes Ehrman's portrait of Pitt and his world. Exhaustive and meticulously researched, the Ehrman trilogy ought to have been authoritative, but left longstanding questions about Pitt's response to the French Revolution unanswered. His attitudes towards France from 1787 to 1792 did not receive much treatment, nor did the comparative importance of ideological and conventional objectives in diplomatic and military policy from 1793 onwards. Pitt, one gathers, was not much interested in French politics during the later 1780s and, having gone to war in 1793 to defend the United Provinces, was thereafter determined to make western Europe and Britain's maritime empire safe from future French aggression. This was a conventional war, so much so that the policies and principles of the enemy at any given time were of minimal importance. Pitt, we are told, was the possessor of a conventional mind, and his actions were increasingly governed by pragmatism during the 1790s and 1800s. In 1792 Pitt first recognized that popular radicals posed a potential threat to the constitution and government of Britain. By May 1794, when habeas corpus was suspended, this menace was regarded as actual. Where radicals were concerned, he displayed 'a readiness to associate sheep with goats'.[35]

The documentation on all these subjects is frustratingly patchy. So little remains that, in many cases, the scholar is forced to track Pitt at second or third hand through the Public Record Office and accounts of his thoughts and actions by friends and colleagues. This makes for very 'official' history. Ehrman's solution is to suggest possible influences upon Pitt, which are not always prioritized. The chapters on 'The Dimensions of Unrest' in volume two are particularly frustrating. This, one suspects, is deliberate. Ehrman's intention, stated in the closing pages of *The Consuming Struggle*, was to supply evidence 'which the reader can balance in the scales'. Ehrman nevertheless tends to dismiss Pitt's failures without assessing their long-term repercussions. Pitt, we are told, was easily disheartened by political – if not military – setbacks throughout the French Revolutionary Wars. Upon closer examination, one finds that he seldom dropped ideas or policies entirely, and seemingly abandoned projects appeared in new or modified forms throughout the 1780s and 1790s. Contrary to the claim of inconstancy made in 1798 by John Hatsell, Speaker of the House of Commons, Pitt seldom dropped ideas or policies entirely and seemingly abandoned projects cropped up in new forms throughout the 1780s and 1790s.[36]

On topics like sedition and treason, where one would be hard pressed to find more than a score of letters and memos in Pitt's handwriting for the years 1792 to 1795, it is necessary to turn to the parliamentary debates, a source to be used with extreme caution. Most scholars in search of a quick Pitt citation have gone to William Cobbett's *The Parliamentary History of England* in the past. John Debrett's *Parliamentary Register* is far more comprehensive and contemporary a source; it is also what Pitt regarded as the official version of the debates in the Lords and Commons. Having said this, Pitt's speeches were known by contemporaries to be 'miserably reported' and ought not to be cited unless consistent with supporting official and private documentation. Disentangling belief from ulterior motive is particularly difficult in the speeches of the 1790s, for Pitt was willing to use, if not accept, Burke's conservative doctrine that the principles of the French Revolution posed a universal threat to the existence of the old order throughout Europe. Pitt used this to justify the introduction of extraordinary public order measures and, in part, Britain's participation in the war against France. Much of this rhetoric sits uncomfortably alongside other statements often made in the same speech; it will be argued in this book that Pitt's willingness to recruit conservative voices at national and local levels reflected the ideological poverty of the official outlook during the 1790s. Ehrman is understandably reluctant to rely too heavily on the *Parliamentary Register* for this period of Pitt's life, useful though it is as a source of comparisons between Pitt's public image and private thoughts, but Ehrman did not concern himself with the relationship between the two. This book does, particularly in chapters 6 and 8, which deal with wartime domestic policy.

The metamorphosis from peace premier to war minister, with attendant policies, has been portrayed by Ehrman as a gradual response to the challenges, both foreign and domestic, faced by His Majesty's Government during the 1790s. All historians of Britain and the French Revolution accept that the changes in Pitt's political outlook were reactive and reluctant. The dating and causation remain controversial. 1792 was a firm favourite until Albert Goodwin's *Friends of Liberty* claimed that Pitt's opposition to Test and Corporation Act repeal in 1787 marked the point at which he turned against reform. This

suggested that the French Revolution had little to do with Pitt's attitudes towards the great 'liberal' issues of the later eighteenth century:
parliamentary reform, abolition of the slave trade and religious toleration. These are examined yet again in the first and third chapters of
this book.

Goodwin's point was taken up by historians of conservative thought,
who emerged in force during the 1980s. Ian Christie and Jonathan
Clark preferred to place Pitt within older eighteenth-century traditions
of cautious forward-looking policies rooted in preservative rather than
experimental principles. By 1790 patriarchalism and passive obedience
had been redefined through exposure to Enlightenment concepts rang-
ing from natural law to utilitarianism. It is to the intellectual flexibility
and social currency of such established beliefs that Christie, Clive
Emsley, H. T. Dickinson and Ian Gilmour have attributed Britain's
avoidance of revolution during the 1790s.[37]

Sympathy with, or recognition of, these pillars of British social and
political thought, widespread in the eighteenth century, did not necessarily produce a fearful defensive response in spectators of the French
Revolution, amongst whom we may include Pitt. An intellectual rejection of *liberté, égalité, fraternité,* as expounded by the French from 1789
onwards, is not enough to place someone in the new 'Tory' camp, for
to do so would leave Britain bereft of 'liberals'.[38] The chief determinant
of British opposition to the French Revolution was not reason, but
emotion – namely fear. As Frank O'Gorman has pointed out, the British
government, as a corporate body, did not spend the 1790s in a perpetual
state of acute apprehension about the potentially seditious and treasonable activities of a native reform movement inspired by natural rights
theorists.[39] Pitt's personal fears were not sustained at levels high enough
to warrant a permanent conversion to Toryism. John Derry has called
Pitt a 'conservative Whig', an analysis that strikes me as essentially
correct, though I see Pitt's 'conservatism' as a product of short-term
practical caution rather than long-term intellectual commitment.[40]

Pitt, in the words of the much maligned Tomline, was 'by no means
of a disposition to take premature alarm'.[41] Old insecurities were a far
greater influence on his thought and conduct than new threats, in the
identification of which the past decade of revisionist diplomatic history
is of much use. For revolutionary France from 1793 to 1795 Pitt had
little respect in fiscal and military terms. Bourbon France was another
matter, to which Pitt's pre-war attitudes are traced in chapters 2 and 3.
The success of British diplomacy during the 1780s was a process that
owed, and was seen to owe, much to a decline in Bourbon power as
the result of financial problems dating from the 1750s and exacerbated
by French involvement in the American War of Independence. By 1789
Pitt's fear of France was much reduced,[42] but it was in anticipation of

future Bourbon retaliation that the British government first declared itself neutral to the revolution.

Xenophobia was a powerful force defining Britain's national and international identity. At home its cultural and intellectual forms helped to legitimize Whig shibboleths about the superiority of the British constitution by running comparisons to the old, absolutist Catholic enemy. Abroad it gave shape and force to a foreign and colonial policy that originated in a century of overt and covert conflict for trade routes, forts, ports, and allies whose sympathies were seen to lie with Britain for a mix of strategic, economic and geopolitical reasons.[43] Estimates of French strength during the revolutionary decade were based on 1780s *ancien régime* estimates that predisposed Albion's leaders to see the revolution's impact on France in terms of 'guns and butter' rather than intellectual and social change.[44] In Pitt's case, this assessment was little altered by the events of the revolutionary wars. A counting-house spirit dominated Britain's military and diplomatic policy on the Continent and in the colonies. This is discussed in chapters 5 and 7.

When Pitt and his colleagues chose to consider the revolution in an intellectual and political context, which they did in private and, occasionally, in public, their perceptions were shaped, first and foremost, not by the headless phantoms of Burke's hysterical imagination or latent fears of social disorder, but by the 'ghost' of the French *ancien régime*, an intellectual, cultural, institutional, military and political entity that could not and did not disappear from western Europe overnight in 1789 or, for that matter, in 1793. In November 1792 Lord Grenville, defending the ministry's decision not to embark on a systematic campaign of seditious libel prosecutions, claimed that this could not be done 'without an expense equal to that of the old French police'.[45] Both the Bastille and the hated Bourbon police were no more by 1792 but the British government's official identity was still defined in contrast to the French system which had laid down the model for state-building in late early–modern Europe. The *ancien régime* survived in the minds of British statesmen as a static – if not sacred or inviolable – counterweight to a new revolutionary concept of nationhood.[46]

It is to the Opposition front benches, not to the Treasury, that one must look for the survival of anti-absolutism, a political doctrine highly reliant upon the memory of Charles James Fox. Although the nineteenth-century cult of Pitt was launched in response to the veneration of Fox, constructing a usable Pittite hagiography proved to be difficult because the dead saint had cultivated two personas in life. His public policies moreover encapsulated several contemporary and sometimes contradictory perspectives on war and revolution. Pitt's success in creating and maintaining a climate of consensus at Westminster bore testimony to the fact that men did not, on the whole, go into Parliament looking for rigorous intellectual consistency in their leaders. Had they done so, Fox and his friends, who launched repeated attacks on the ambivalent features of Pitt's policies, would not have seceded in despair from Parliament in 1797. By 1799, let alone 1806, Pitt's identity was already fragmented. When he died, it was not surprising that his legacy was fought over by his followers.

Notes

1. The most recent short introduction to Pitt is the article on 'William Pitt' by R. Thorne (ed.), *The History of Parliament: The Commons 1790–1820* (5 vols, 1986), ii, pp. 807–24. See my 'William Pitt' in R. Eccleshall and R. Walker (eds), *A Biographical Dictionary of British Prime Ministers* (forthcoming, 1997).

2. R. Pares, *George III and the Politicians* (Oxford: 1957), p. 81 and n. 1; A. D. Harvey, 'The Ministry of All the Talents: the Whigs in office', *HJ* 15 (1972), pp. 619–48; W. M. McCahill, 'The collapse of Addington's administration', *Parliamentary History* 6 (1987), pp. 81–94.

3. J. J. Sack, 'The memory of Burke and the memory of Pitt: English conservatism confronts its past', *HJ* 30 (1987), pp. 623–40.

4. J. J. Sack, *From Jacobite to Conservative: Reaction and Orthodoxy in Britain, c. 1760–1832* (Cambridge: 1993), p. 90.

5. J. C. D. Clark, 'Towards a theory of party: 1688–1832', *HJ* 23 (1982), pp. 314–15; Tomline, *Life of the Rt. Hon. William Pitt* (2 vols, 1828 edn), i, pp. 4–5. Tomline also claimed that Pitt's facility with Biblical quotations equalled his better-known fluency in Greek and Latin.

6. Sack, *From Jacobite to Conservative*, p. 88; Suffolk (Ipswich) Record Office, Tomline Papers, HA 119 T108/45, Tomline to Mrs Tomline, February 1801.

7. L. V. Harcourt (ed.), *The Diaries and Correspondence of George Rose* (2 vols, 1860), i, 17 September 1817, p. 37; Sack, 'The memory of Burke and the memory of Pitt', pp. 631–4; Rose also acted as a 'reader' of Tomline's *Life of Pitt*: HA 119 T108, Acc. 562, Rose to Tomline, 8 August 1816.

8. L. J. Jennings (ed.), *The Correspondence and Diaries of the Late Right Honourable John Wilson Croker* (3 vols, 1885), ii, p. 86.

9. Kent Archives Office, Stanhope of Chevening MS, Pitt Papers, U1590 S5 60/14, Wellesley to the editor of the *Quarterly Review*, 22 November 1836; unused clipping from Philip Stanhope's research for the 1861 *Life of Pitt*; R. R. Pearce, *Memoirs and Correspondence of the Most Noble Richard Marquess of Wellesley* (3 vols, 1846), ii, p. 406.

10. T. B. Macaulay, *Critical, Historical and Miscellaneous Essays* (2 vols, 1860), ii, p. 308.

11. The other executor was John Pitt, second Earl of Chatham. The Dacres Adams Papers (PRO 30/52) are now in the possession of Mr Giles Adams of Woodford Lodge, near Kettering, Northamptonshire. J. Ehrman, *William Pitt: The Consuming Struggle* (1996), p. 836.

12. HA 119 T108, Acc. 562, Tomline to Bute, 19 February 1823; E. J. Evans, *The Contentious Tithe: The Tithe Problem and English Agriculture 1750–1850*

(Leicester: 1976), pp. 76, 79–80; PRO 30/8/310, Draft bill for the redemption of tithes (w. m. 1796 but 1798–9), fos 72–92; CUL 69585, 1033, Pitt to Moore, 16 December 1791; PRO 30/8/195, Pitt to Dr John Moore (Archbishop of Canterbury), 9 January 1799, fo. 199.

13. G. I. T. Machin, *The Catholic Question in English Politics, 1820–1830* (Oxford: 1964), pp. 36–9; J. C. D. Clark, *English Society, 1688–1832* (Cambridge: 1985), p. 359; Sack, *From Jacobite to Conservative*, pp. 89–90.

14. J. E. Cookson, *Lord Liverpool's Administration: 1815–1822* (Edinburgh: 1974), pp. 116–29.

15. A. J. B. Hilton, *Cash, Corn and Commerce: The Economic Policies of the Tory Governments 1815–1830* (Oxford: 1977), pp. 162–3, and *The Age of Atonement: Influence of Evangelicalism on Social and Economic Thought* (Oxford, 1988), p. 223; B. Fontana, *Rethinking the Politics of Commercial Society: The Edinburgh Review* (Cambridge: 1985), p. 112.

16. *Court and Cabinets*: this is a collection of documents with ghost-written connecting text; [G. Meryon], *The Memoirs of the Lady Hester Stanhope in Conversation with her Physician* (3 vols, 1845), iii, p. 168.

17. L. Mitchell, *Holland House* (1980), pp. 47–50, 72–3; P. Mandler, *Aristocratic Whiggism in an Age of Reform, 1830–1850* (Oxford: 1987), p. 89.

18. Henry Edward, 3rd Baron Holland, *Memoirs of the Whig Party in my Time* (2 vols, 1852), i, pp. 13–15.

19. Russell, *Memorials and Correspondence of Charles James Fox* (4 vols, 1852), ii, p. 32. *The Life of Fox* was published in 1854.

20. [Philip], 5th Earl Stanhope, *Life of the Right Honourable William Pitt* (4 vols, 1861–2), ii, pp. 155, 170–2, 188–210.

21. This point had already been made by his aunt: *The Memoirs of the Lady Hester Stanhope*, ii, p. 74; Stanhope, *Life of Pitt*, ii, p. 189.

22. W. E. H. Lecky, *History of England in the Eighteenth Century* (8 vols, 2nd edn, 1887), v, pp. 64, 29–127.

23. [A.] Rosebery, *Pitt* (1891), Disraeli to Sir William Harcourt, 1873, pp. 278–9, appendix D, pp. 197–8.

24. This Rosebery did not once but twice: see *Pitt*, p. 254, and a *Monthly Review* article reviewing the last chapter of Tomline's unpublished *Life of Pitt* (12 August 1903, p. 14).

25. Rosebery, *Pitt*, pp. 193, 276, 278–9.

26. *William Pitt and National Revival* was published in 1909; *William Pitt and the Great War* came out in 1911.

27. Holland Rose, *Great War*, pp. 24–5, 76–7, 117; G. S. Veitch, *The Genesis of Parliamentary Reform* (1918), pp. 234–40; P. A. Brown, *The French Revolution in English History* (1918), pp. 130–3.

28. *History of England* (1926), p. 559.

29. Aeschylus, *Prometheus Vinctus*, 488–92, opening citation to L. B. Namier, *The Structure of Politics at the Accession of George III* (1929).

30. K. G. Feiling, *The Second Tory Party, 1714–1832* (Oxford: 1924) pp. 165–209.

31. D. G. Barnes, *George III and William Pitt, 1783–1801* (Stanford, Calif.: 1939).

32. F. O'Gorman, *The Whig Party and the French Revolution* (1967); L. G.

Mitchell, *Charles James Fox and the Disintegration of the Whig Party 1782–1794* (Oxford: 1971).

33. For representative examples of the first school, see I. R. Christie, *Wilkes, Wyvill and Reform: The Parliamentary Reform Movement in British Politics, 1760–1785* (1962); J. Cannon, *Parliamentary Reform 1640–1832* (Cambridge: 1973). For the second, see C. B. Cone, *The English Jacobins: Reformers in Late Eighteenth Century England* (1968); G. A. Williams, *Artisans and Sans-Culottes: Popular Movements in England and France during the French Revolution* (1968), which is relatively objective to Pitt; E. P. Thompson, *The Making of the English Working Class* (1968); M. Thomis and P. Holt, *Threats of Revolution in Britain, 1789–1848* (1977); A. Goodwin, *The Friends of Liberty: The English Democratic Movement and the French Revolution* (1979).

34. M. Elliott, *Partners in Revolution: The United Irishmen and France* (New Haven, Conn.: 1982), and 'French subversion in Britain during the French Revolution', in C. Jones (ed.), *Britain and Revolutionary France: Conflict, Subversion and Propaganda* (Exeter: 1983), pp. 40–52; R. Wells, *Insurrection: The British Experience, 1785–1903* (Gloucester: 1983).

35. Ehrman, *The Reluctant Transition* (1983), p. 400; Ehrman, *The Consuming Struggle*, pp. 849–54.

36. *Ibid.*, pp. 849, 435.

37. C. Emsley, *British Society and the French Wars 1783–1815* (1979); I. R. Christie, *Stress and Stability in Late Eighteenth Century Britain: Reflections on the Avoidance of Revolution* (Oxford: 1982); T. P. Schofield, 'Conservative political thought in Britain in response to the French Revolution', *HJ* 29 (1986), pp. 601–22; H. T. Dickinson, 'Popular conservatism and militant loyalism 1789–1815', in *Britain and the French Revolution, 1789–1815* (1989), pp. 103–25, and most recently in *The Politics of the People in Eighteenth Century Britain* (Brighton: 1995), ch. 8; I. Gilmour, *Riot, Risings and Revolution* (1992), ch. 19.

38. G. Claeys, 'The French Revolution debate and British political thought', *History of Political Thought* 11 (1990), pp. 59–80; J. Cookson, *The Friends of Peace: Anti-War Liberalism in England, 1793–1815* (Cambridge: 1982); A. V. Beedell, 'John Reeves' prosecution for seditious libel 1795–6: a study in political cynicism', *HJ* 36 (1993), pp. 822–3.

39. O'Gorman, 'Pitt and the Tory reaction to the French Revolution', in Dickinson (ed.), *Britain and the French Revolution, 1789–1815*, p. 36.

40. Derry, 'Governing temperament under Pitt and Liverpool', in J. Cannon (ed.), *The Whig Ascendancy: Colloquies on Hanoverian England* (1981), pp. 126–7. Of Pitt, Emsley writes: 'It is probably safe to say that he [Pitt] and his fellow ministers were as much prisoners of the rhetoric of English rights and liberties as everybody else', in 'Revolution, war and the nation state: the British and French experiences 1789–1801': M. Philp (ed.), *The French Revolution and British Popular Politics* (Cambridge: 1991), p. 114.

41. Tomline, *Life of Pitt*, ii, p. 618.

42. The decline in French power had been noted by all European statesmen: T. C. W. Blanning, *The Origins of the French Revolutionary Wars* (1986), and 'The French Revolution and Europe', in Colin Lucas (ed.), *Rewriting*

the French Revolution: The Andrew Browning Lectures 1989 (Oxford: 1991);
J. Black, A System of Ambition? British Foreign Policy 1660–1793 (Harlow:
1991), pp. 223–48, and British Foreign Policy in an Age of Revolutions,
1783–1793 (Cambridge: 1994), ch. 7.

43. J. Black, Natural and Necessary Enemies: Anglo-French Relations in the Eighteenth Century (1986), p. 68; L. Colley, 'Britishness and otherness: an
argument', JBS 31 (1992), pp. 31–2; G. Newman, The Rise of English
Nationalism: A Cultural History 1740–1830 (1987).

44. M. Duffy, 'British policy in the war against Revolutionary France', in
Jones (ed.), Britain and Revolutionary France: Conflict, Subversion and Pro-
paganda; 'British diplomacy and the French wars, 1789–1815', in Dickinson
(ed.), Britain and the French Revolution; Soldiers, Sugar and Seapower. The
British Expeditions to the West Indies and the War against Revolutionary France
(Oxford: 1986); P. Jupp, Lord Grenville, 1759–1834 (Oxford: 1985).

45. Court and Cabinets, ii, Grenville to Buckingham, 14 November 1792,
pp. 226–8.

46. C. B. A. Behrens, Society, Government and the Enlightenment: The Experiences
of Eighteenth Century France and Prussia (1985), pp. 201–5. For a general
discussion of state-building theory, see T. Ertman, 'The Sinews of Power
and European State Building Theory', in L. Stone (ed.), An Imperial State
at War: Britain from 1689 to 1815 (1994), pp. 33–51; J. Godechot, 'The
new concept of the nation and its diffusion in Europe', in O. Dann and
J. Dinwiddy (eds), Nationalism in the Age of the French Revolution (1988),
pp. 13–26.

Chapter 1

Reform Objectives Defined, 1779–1789

While many historians have questioned the strength of the Younger Pitt's interest in the 'liberal' political issues of the 1780s, few would deny that the public and private legislative initiatives that he supported before 1792 were significant enough to earn him a reputation as an 'improving minister'. Having risen to prominence in the Westminster of the early 1780s as a champion of fiscal, bureaucratic and parliamentary reform, the 'wonderful youth' went on to become First Lord of the Treasury at the age of 24. Within three years of taking office, he had presented bills to Parliament proposing to reorganize the administration of the East India Company, the tariff structure of Customs and Excise, the accounting practices of the Treasury and the mechanisms by which the nation's representatives were chosen to serve in Parliament. All but the parliamentary reform bill of 1785 became law.

Were one to judge by the policies of the 1780s alone, Pitt would go down in history as a man inspired by the political and economic thought of the Enlightenment. His second decade in office was not so illustrious. With the onset of the French Revolutionary Wars, Pitt seemingly turned his back on many of the causes he had once supported and, in the name of an ideological war against France, pursued a policy of domestic legal repression that subverted the civil liberties of the subject to the greater good of national security. So abrupt was this change in direction during the early 1790s that the causes of the transition from the liberal Whiggism of the 1780s to the defensive Toryism of the successive decade remain contentious.

There now appears to be very little that was innovative about what the Younger Pitt thought or did. The crusading zeal that he displayed in the realms of commerce, finance and administration now emerges as a cautious campaign for gradual change tempered by reluctance to antagonize established public and private sector interest groups.[1] The parliamentary reform bill of 1785 has been depicted as an effusion of youthful enthusiasm soon exhausted or a cynical gesture of appeasement intended to placate those voters who had carried Pitt to power in the 1784 general election. His refusal to revive the legislation after 1785 betokens no very great commitment to the measure and is believed to have resulted from a loss of interest, a decision to eschew contentious issues to keep his ministry afloat, or a decisive loss of a battle for supremacy with George III.[2]

Few would now call Pitt a liberal or even a Whig. Not only did parliamentary reform fall by the wayside, but Pitt's interest in the abolition of the slave trade was arguably on the wane after 1792. He could, moreover, be found consistently opposing measures of religious toleration in the House of Commons throughout the 1780s and 1790s. In defending the Church–State partnership, Pitt was displaying a conscious support for the Established Church and possibly for the social and political thought that the Church upheld. Tempting as it is to identify Pitt as a 'progressive Tory' before 1790, his political thought and actions during the 1780s defy such simple classification. Pitt's interest in reform causes was genuine and he did not abandon them easily or completely. His conduct in the high and low political debates on parliamentary reform, the abolition of the slave trade and religious toleration during the 1780s was based on intellectual conviction rather than political self-interest and, while Pitt would never qualify for a Whig pantheon, he upheld a code of beliefs in which tolerance and progress were principal features until 1792.

Parliamentary Reform Revisited

More ink has been spilled on parliamentary reform than on any other issue of the later eighteenth century and Pitt's conduct in relation to this issue has been hotly debated for two centuries. Pitt, the first premier to make reform part of an election platform (which he did in 1784), was also notable for allying himself with a grass-roots reform lobby, the county association movement led by the Reverend Christopher Wyvill, only to repudiate it in 1792. Pitt's 1785 attempt at reform, though unsuccessful, was the first to address major grievances in a bill that proposed to introduce practical remedies for the ailments thought to have enervated the British constitution. The 1785 bill, though still seen as too advanced for its time, is now regarded as a conservative scheme by which Pitt intended to make cosmetic changes to the composition of the Commons rather than overhaul England's system of parliamentary representation. When his 1785 request for Parliament's permission to bring in a reform bill was defeated, he decided that it was a liability, not an asset, to his fledgling ministry.

Although there is something to be said for parts of this analysis, Pitt's career as a parliamentary reformer has suffered from a failure to place the 1785 bill in its proper context. Not only was this one of six bills relating to the reform of Parliament that Pitt sponsored between 1782 and 1789, but it must be considered in relation not to his relationship with Wyvill and the extraparliamentary reform movement, but to a tactical campaign conducted in co-operation with personal friends inside Parliament.[3] Last but not least, insufficient attention has been given to Pitt's interest in the mechanics, rather than the principles, of representation and the electoral process.

Pitt's interest in reform predated his 1781 'election' as MP for Appleby-in-Westmorland. The Elder Pitt had been an advocate of parliamentary reform during the 1770s, though the extent of Chatham's commitment to this, like so many issues, is unclear.[4] His son, who matriculated at Pembroke Hall, Cambridge in 1773 and began to keep regular terms in 1775, was removed from his father's direct influence at the age of 16. Much has been made of Chatham's support for radical reform; the fact remains that the Elder Pitt, having taken up reform in opposition, never got much beyond the advocacy of triennial parliaments, the abolition of rotten boroughs and the creation of new county seats in the Commons. The second and third proposals Pitt found attractive; the first he never supported.

Chatham died in 1778, when Pitt was just 19. When the 'Great Commoner' passed away family sorrow was mingled with relief. Chatham had not been *compos mentis* for parts of the 1770s[5] and his death freed Pitt from what must have been a crushing burden of parental ambition. Pitt inherited little from his father but a lofty sense of public duty, a suspicion of the 'old corps' Whigs and an American colonial policy. More important by far for Pitt's development was the Whig education that he received at Cambridge. This, based on the rational logic of Locke and Newton, marked him for life. His tutor, George Pretyman-Tomline, was a mathematician as well as a clergyman who not only spent a great deal of time with Pitt between 1775 and 1780, but served as Pitt's private secretary from 1784 to 1787. Tomline was astonished by Pitt's rapid progress through Newton's *Principia*, noted that his pupil had no great interest in metaphysics and recorded that he 'had a pleasure in seeing theoretical rules exemplified and confirmed' in experimental philosophy.[6] Tomline's intellectual influence over his pupil was not great and, though the bishop remained a lifelong confidant of the premier, there is no evidence that Tomline's voice counted for much except in the realm of Church appointments.

Throughout 1779 and 1780 Pitt divided his time between London and Cambridge. In the 1780 general election he had stood unsuccessfully for Cambridge University and accepted the offer of Appleby from its 'owner', Sir James Lowther, only on terms of 'a liberal *Independent Footing*'. Pitt never enjoyed representing a rotten borough and, in the 1784 general election, he stood for Cambridge again, this time with success. He kept the seat for the rest of his life. Pitt, only 22 in 1781, was idealistic and ambitious, determined to make a splash in public life. Since 1779 he had been moving in a circle of Cambridge men who shared his taste for public affairs, most of whom were to remain his friends until death. Amongst them were Richard Pepper Arden, later Attorney-General and Master of the Rolls; Charles Manners, Lord Granby, later Duke of Rutland and Lord-Lieutenant of Ireland; Edward James Eliot, who married Pitt's sister Harriot in 1785; and, from 1780 onwards, William Wilberforce. It was amongst these men that Pitt's ideas and policies took shape. Having described Lord North, Prime Minister since 1770, as 'the Dictator' in 1777, he took his seat in the Commons with the Opposition, then led by the Rockingham Whigs.[7]

Rockingham and other critics of the government believed that North's abuse of power and influence since 1770 had destabilized the balance of power within the Holy Trinity of the British constitution: Crown, Lords and Commons. As Henry Dunning put it in 1780: 'The power of the Crown is increasing, has increased and ought to be diminished.'[8] Such power could be direct, as demonstrated by George III's supposed mismanagement of the war against the rebellious Thirteen Colonies, or indirect, as was suggested by the government's manipulation of state patronage in the armed forces, civil service and Parliament. For Rockingham and his Commons lieutenants, Burke and Charles James Fox, the 'secret influence' of the Crown and the personal prerogative of the king were inseparable. Pitt was an enemy of the former, but not the latter. The sovereign, he claimed, had important rights of mediation to exercise in the conduct of relations between the executive, legislative and bureaucratic branches of government. These royal powers, thought Pitt, were not only necessary, but sacrosanct.[9] For the Earl of Shelburne, the heir to the Chathamite tradition of patriot independence, the influence of the Crown encompassed the powers of the executive in all their manifestations.

Shelburne sought to rationalize and reform the finances and bureaucracy of the state. Pitt, taken up by Shelburne in 1781, shared these interests, if not the fanaticism of principle and purpose that characterized the Jesuit of Berkeley Square.[10] Pitt did not feel that Parliament had the right to scrutinize and control the inner sanctum of government; this remained, as William Blackstone had asserted, within the domain of the king's servants. In practice, Pitt proved reluctant to implement the findings of the Commission of Fees in the Post Office and dockyards, while at the Treasury he was far more flexible than Shelburne would have been in the reconciliation of reform objectives with the privileges of vested interests. Pitt's attendance upon Shelburne was motivated by a sense of duty rather than friendship. The two were never close and parted ways in 1783. Shelburne, excluded from the 1784 ministry, always believed that Pitt had stolen his best policies for later and incomplete implementation.[11]

After seven years of frustrating and unsuccessful war, Parliament was sympathetic to calls for economy and accountability. 'Economical reform' was therefore acceptable. Parliamentary reform was not, for it stood to destroy the privilege and prescription on which the Whig oligarchy of the eighteenth century was founded.[12] Equally damning were the historical and intellectual roots of parliamentary reform: the 'Levelling' republicanism of the English Civil Wars and, more recently, the democratic claims of American rebels and the London reform societies – most notably, the Society for Constitutional Information (SCI), headed by Major John Cartwright, author of the 1776 pamphlet *Take Your Choice!* This contained a six-point reform programme which included the secret ballot, universal manhood suffrage and annual parliaments. Moderate reformers, of whom Pitt was one, rejected natural rights theory but drew upon the old 'country' platform of the eighteenth century, according to which the independence of Parliament was jeopardized by government control of safe seats, rotten boroughs and those MPs whose loyalty had been purchased by the award of pensions, sinecures and places. All parliamentary reformers were economical reformers, but many of the latter, amongst them Burke, were enemies of the former.

When Pitt took his Commons seat in 1781, many of his friends were already active in the reform movement. Wyvill and his Yorkshire Association had emerged in 1779 to demand both economical and parliamentary reform; Wilberforce, who had been elected one of Yorkshire's two county members in 1780, was close to Wyvill. The Duke of Rutland was president of the Cambridge Association, one of the county associations formed on the Yorkshire model between 1780 and 1783. Lord Mahon, later third Earl Stanhope, was the husband of Pitt's sister Hester and president of the Kent Association, whose meetings Pitt began to attend in 1780. He did not, however, affiliate himself formally to any extraparliamentary reform group until 1783 and, when he did so, it was at Wyvill's invitation.[13]

On 7 May 1782 Pitt raised parliamentary reform as a discussion subject in the House of Commons. Ian Christie and John Ehrman have described this as an appeal for unity in a divided movement. Moderates and radicals were to disagree for the next fifty years on reform measures. The abolition of rotten boroughs competed for public attention with the shortening of parliaments, the extension of the franchise, the exclusion of placemen and pensioners from the House of Commons and Wyvill's pet proposal, the creation of new county seats to reinforce the landed interest. On 7 May 1782 Pitt declared himself in favour of no existing scheme of reform, but his speech displays a partiality not for the democrats, but for the moderates. Chatham's ghost was invoked to reinforce the point: 'That person was not apt to indulge in vague and chimerical speculations inconsistent with practice and expediency.' [14]

Pitt, having put himself forward as a potential mediator between the dissident schools of reform, attended a meeting of reformers at the Thatched House Tavern on 16 May 1782 as the spokesman of no reform organization. Here he first met Wyvill. The 1782 motion had been defeated by only twenty votes and in 1783 Pitt prepared three reform resolutions for the inspection of the Commons: the prevention of bribery and malpractice at elections; the disqualification of rotten boroughs when reported to Parliament for electoral offences; the creation of up to 100 new county seats. These were to be the foundations of the 1785 reform bill.[15] Wyvill requested an audience with Pitt on 4 May 1783. The meeting between them the following day initiated their partnership.

The 1783 resolutions, as Christie and Ehrman have noted, were consistent with the published aims of the Yorkshire Association, which in November 1782 had called for fifty new county seats in the Commons. According to Norris, the resolutions were drafted at Bowood, Shelburne's county seat, by Pitt, Dunning, Col. Isaac Barré and Shelburne in January 1782. The 1783 resolutions cannot be traced to a single source because they represented a synthesis of moderate reform opinion. As Pitt wrote to his mother, the debates of 1782 had been 'not without use'. Bearing in mind that he never got close to either Shelburne or Wyvill, the 1783 resolutions are more likely to have been drawn up in consultation with Mahon, Eliot and possibly William Windham Grenville. In 1782 Mahon and Eliot had presented a series of unsuccessful anti-bribery bills to the Commons. Joined by Pitt, they were to do so again in 1783.[16]

Never, announced Pitt during the debates on Mahon's bribery bill of 1782, 'would he connive at that madness and tumult which had rendered the elections in this country, for the most part, a farce'. As Mahon wrote on 22 June to Wyvill: 'Wm. Pitt spoke like an angel', and the anti-corruption resolution of 1783 was framed in support of Mahon's anti-bribery campaign. The second resolution, concerning the disfranchisement of corrupt boroughs, built upon George Grenville's Election Act of 1774, which had set up a Commons tribunal for disputed elections. To this his son William was committed, though neither the younger Grenville nor his brother, the future Marquis of Buckingham, were friends to franchise reform.[17] Wyvill was delighted by the third resolution, which could have come from Chatham, Shelburne or Mahon, and asked how the 100 new county seats were to be distributed.

Pitt, who had not worked out the details of his scheme, told Wyvill that additional seats would be created 'according to the importance of each county'. Fearful of conservative hostility to the resolutions, he 'did not care to touch upon the case of unrepresented persons' nor to raise the total number of MPs in the Commons.[18] The new county seats were to be counterbalanced by the abolition of fifty rotten boroughs. When Pitt confessed that no thought had been given to the creation of new urban constituencies, Wyvill declared that proposals to give new MPs to London suburbs and the provincial towns would bring Pitt the support of reform organizations outside Parliament.

7 May 1783 was a busy day for reformers. Not only were Pitt's resolutions to be debated but so too were three corresponding Mahon–Eliot–Pitt electoral reform bills dealing with bribery, 'the more convenient Attendance of Freeholders' at the polls and 'the better preventing Fraudulent Votes' in county elections. All were due for their second readings and the timing was not accidental. If some electoral reform were to be passed, Pitt could drop it from his programme.[19] His speech showed that he had given Wyvill's remarks some thought. While Pitt was now prepared to give MPs to unrepresented London boroughs, he denounced the reform ideas coming from the radical metropolitan clubs, the Westminster and Middlesex Associations: 'A spirit of speculation went forth, and a variety of schemes, founded in visionary and impractical ideas of reform, were suddenly produced.' Despite Pitt's best efforts to denounce actual representation, which he described as 'subversive of true liberty', the resolutions were defeated by 193 to 149 votes. Support from the Yorkshire Association began to look very attractive. When Wyvill proposed the creation of a 40s. copyholder franchise in the counties, Pitt listened. During the autumn of 1783, following his resignation from the Shelburne ministry, where he had served as Chancellor of the Exchequer and Leader of the House of Commons since March, Pitt had the freedom to promote reform as an independent MP. George Rose recalled that Pitt was a most persuasive spokesman for moderate reform. This Rose opposed, like many other MPs, on the grounds that any reform was the thin end of a democratic wedge.[20]

When Pitt was called to office as premier on 19 December 1783, parliamentary reform was put on hold though Wyvill was assured that a reform bill would be put together 'at the first seasonable opportunity'. Following the 1784 general election which returned Pitt to power with an impressive majority, he began to put his thoughts on reform in order and spent the winter of 1784–5 in consultation with Wyvill, Mahon and Richmond, all of whom were close to the grass-roots reform groups that were to send petitions in support of the bill to Parliament. Spectators were concerned by this alliance of high and low politics. Thomas

Orde, who could not decide whether Pitt was 'blessed or encumbered' with reform, suspected that the premier's ideas had been compromised by partnership with the county associations which had campaigned for Pitt during the 1784 general election. Orde nonetheless found 'nothing inconsistent in his [Pitt's] partial adherence to his original ideas, his delicacy on the point of consistency'.[21] Pitt, while willing to negotiate with the county movement, was less concerned about paying political debts than in devising a comprehensive bill that would command widespread acceptance. The 1785 reform bill, like the 1832 Reform Act, was to be the first and last reform of Parliament. It was a hybrid creation, some of whose features – the grant of the franchise to London constituencies, provincial towns and county copyholders – represented concessions to reform groups outside Parliament.

There were four pillars to the 1785 reform bill: the reduction of bribery and expense at elections; the addition of 40s. copyholders to the county franchise; the abolition of thirty-six rotten boroughs; the creation of replacement seats in the counties, metropolis and provincial towns. The voluntary disfranchisement of corrupt boroughs was a modification of the 1783 resolution demanding compulsory disqualification. Commons debates on Mahon's three unsuccessful bribery bills had made Pitt aware that his fellow MPs were no friends to legislation that banned the distribution of cockades, the provision of free drink to voters and the practice of transporting one's supporters to the polls. Even less popular was the recording of such offences in the Journals of the House of Commons, following which convicted voters, parliamentary candidates and entire constituencies lost the right to participate in the electoral process.[22]

Conservative though Pitt's arrangements were for the compensation of rotten borough patrons – £1m. was to be set aside in recognition of their proprietorial 'rights' – the Commons disfranchisement committee was to be selected 'in the same manner as the committee under Mr. Grenville's bill'. On 7 April 1785 Grenville had asked the Commons for leave to bring in a bill to amend the trial of controverted elections. Grenville, supported by Pitt, proposed to make certain modifications to his father's legislation: to prevent the submission of frivolous petitions of complaint by making the petitioners pay legal costs; to punish returning officers for misconduct; and to determine the rights of election in constituencies subject to election disputes.[23]

Pitt, who was not anticipating much opposition to his proposals, expected the seats to change hands without trouble. The transfer of voting rights to unrepresented regions was to take place in accordance with a schedule that gave 72 MPs to London and the counties. What Wyvill called 'the second part' of Pitt's plan would earmark an additional 28 seats for Manchester, Leeds, Sheffield and Birmingham, amongst other provincial urban centres.[24] Pitt, primarily interested in giving additional representation to the counties, not the towns, was by no means as committed to the second plan as to the first:

> The idea of transferring a certain proportion of representation from boroughs to counties (which is limited by the impossibility of more than a certain number being conveniently chosen by counties), and of providing that the boroughs which must continue to elect, shall be those best entitled to it, seems to include all the amendment that our constitution can admit of, in the frame of Parliament, unless some new principle were to be admitted, for which I see no reason.[25]

Pitt did his best to make these proposals palatable to the House of Commons. Of the 40s. copyholders he said: 'Their property was secure, and in some cases more so than the freeholders.' Town dwellers were to be qualified for the franchise by high tax assessments on land and luxury goods. Pitt insisted that the true spirit of representation lay in 'a community of interest between the representative and the represented', namely property.[26] By increasing the number of county MPs, the landed interest, which Pitt had described as 'the least susceptible to influence', would be reinforced.

Pitt's reform case was novel for its definition of representation. Parliament, whose origins he dated to the reign of Edward I, was a microcosm of England, an assembly whose composition reflected the interests of regional communities making active political, economic and social contributions to the nation. The House of Commons therefore mirrored the actual status of counties and boroughs. To do so effectively over time, stated Pitt, the concept of representation had to be flexible, not fixed. Retrospective constitutionalism was, in short, no more than a rhetorical device because the ancient principle of representation was anything but immutable.[27] It was by no means Anglo-Saxon or Gothic.

Pitt's historical relativism, though pragmatic, was not amoral. In the context of the 1785 bill, the grant of seats to provincial towns was justified by their financial, mercantile and manufacturing importance in the economy. Landed property, as has been pointed out by many commentators on the 1785 bill, was not the exclusive arbiter of liberty. The county copyholder franchise might enshrine land as the basis of active citizenship, but, by enlarging the electorate, it also guarded against the abuse of local influence by rural magnates. Rotten boroughs marked out for abolition were to possess electorates numbering less than 400.[28]

Pitt never revived the 1785 programme in its entirety. The opposition to the bill, which had been formidable, started with the Crown. In July 1783, when George III determined to rid himself of the hated Fox–

North coalition and sent Lord Chancellor Thurlow to sound out Pitt about the formation of an alternative ministry, Pitt refused to take office under the 'old system' – what Pitt saw as the institutionalized abuse of influence. When he announced that he needed a free hand to set up 'a permanent system based upon principle', Thurlow reminded Pitt that the king was an enemy to parliamentary reform. Pitt was reluctant to compromise: 'If the King did not wish for change, he would not agitate the measure, but that he was personally pledged to reform and, if he could form a strong ministry, would strenuously advocate it whenever he got the opportunity.'[29]

On 19 March 1785 Pitt asked George III not to interfere in the passage of his reform bill, declaring not only that the success of the bill was by 'no means improbable', but that the good name of the administration depended upon the fulfilment of personal electoral pledges. The king replied that 'out of attention to Mr. Pitt, I carefully avoid expressing my unalterable sentiments on any change in the Constitution'.[30] The monarch's reservations were shared by the Cabinet, in which only Earl Camden and the Duke of Richmond were friends to reform. The House of Commons was not enthusiastic about the proposal. Fox and the Whigs denounced it, while the back benches listened to Pitt 'with that sort of civil attention which people give to a person who has a good claim to be heard, but with whom the hearers are determined to disagree'. This was the response that Pitt had been dreading: 'it may have an effect upon the public opinion, fatal, I will not say personally to myself, but to the cause in which we are all embarked'.[31]

Public opinion had let Pitt down. Only eight petitions had come from the provinces in support of his bill. Having been, as Wyvill put it, 'shamefully deserted' by his extraparliamentary allies, Pitt dropped what he felt were the more contentious aspects of the 1785 bill.[32] The enfranchisement proposals, both of towns and persons, vanished. Wyvill, anxious to keep parliamentary reform in the public eye after the defeat of the 1785 bill, asked Pitt for permission to print the 'Head or Heads of a Bill or Bills for Amending the Representation', the memo that had been sent to Wyvill in April 1785. Refusal was given on the grounds that the 'Heads' did not represent Pitt's final statement on reform.[33] There was some truth to this, but, in the immediate aftermath of the bill's defeat, Pitt was more concerned about the possible misrepresentation and exploitation of his ideas by radical reform groups like the SCI. In January 1785 Pitt had notified Wyvill that he planned to pursue reform as 'a man and a minister', a phrase that was used freely in the Yorkshire Association's correspondence.[34] By April Pitt, who was alarmed by what he saw as Wyvill's quest for petitions of any and every description, was wishing that 'Mr. Wyvill had been a little more sparing in his use of my name'. By April 1785 Pitt was trying to distance himself from the county association movement. When the 'Summary Explanation of the Principles behind Mr. Pitt's Bill' was prepared by Wyvill, he was told to avoid 'any allusion' to the 'Heads'. Following the defeat of the 1785 bill, Pitt, who felt betrayed, decided not to bring forward parliamentary reform again unless there was '*a reasonable prospect of success*'.[35] He decided to concentrate not on the factious reform groups outside Parliament, but upon the more predictable responses of MPs in the House of Commons.

Having asserted that 'sooner or later something would be effected'[36] *vis-à-vis* parliamentary reform, Pitt affirmed his commitment to the cause throughout the later 1780s by supporting private members' bills which conformed in spirit to his 1783 and 1785 resolutions. The 'Heads' had involved more than one piece of draft legislation, most notably Mahon's bribery bills and Grenville's election tribunal regulations.[37] Pitt continued to support these proposals up to 1789. For twentieth-century historians, parliamentary reform involved the extension of the franchise; for Pitt, reform involved the entire electoral process.

Experience proved that parliamentary reform presented in the guise of economical reform was most likely to win the vote of the Commons. In March 1786 James Marsham proposed to disfranchise employees of the Ordnance and the navy on the grounds that Crown servants were subject to a conflict of interest at the polls. Disfranchisement legislation had been successful in the past, most notably in 1782, when Crewe's Act had disqualified revenue officers from exercising the right to vote. Pitt, who had voted for Crewe's Act, agreed that 'any influence whatever, remaining in the Crown in matters of election, might effectually be done away with', but cautioned the House against the wholesale disfranchisement of entire occupational groups within a borough, for to do so would reduce the size of the electorate and leave the remaining voters more susceptible to bribery.[38]

Marsham and his friends pointed accusatory fingers at Queenborough, a government safe seat in Kent, where it was claimed that the Ordnance had instituted public works projects for no other purpose than the control of the local workforce and, thence, the return of an MP. Did they who castigated such practices, asked Pitt, 'mean this as a step to parliamentary reform'? 'If they did, he should go with them hand in hand ... he should only regret that it was a limited, instead of a full remedy ... however, he might be dissatisfied at the trifling extent of the reformation, he should nevertheless embrace it as a beginning.'[39] If a borough's electorate was deemed too small, declared Pitt, the remedy was 'the extending, instead of contracting, [of] the privilege of voting, as in the case of New Shoreham'. This Sussex borough, pos-

sessing an electorate of approximately 100 voters, had been notorious
for corruption in the mid-eighteenth century. In 1771, following the
trial of a disputed New Shoreham election, the borough was enlarged
to include 40s. freeholders in the rape of Bramber. A similar remedy
had been applied to the borough of Cricklade in Wiltshire, whose
franchise had been extended in 1780 to incorporate the freeholders of
five neighbouring hundreds. 'Cricklade and New Shoreham' had been
given an honourable mention in Pitt's 'Heads'.[40] Both had been transformed from venal boroughs into mini-counties possessing electorates
of 800 and 1,000 respectively.

The radical Richmond, Master General of the Ordnance, was horrified by the accusation that his department was responsible for
corrupting the electorate and conducted a private enquiry into the state
of affairs at Queenborough. Soon after the debate on Marsham's bill,
Wyvill asked Pitt once more for permission to print the 'Heads'. 'The
idea seemed to meet your entire approbation', he wrote on 29 July
1787, but 'the attempt on that borough not having been renewed, no
opportunity has yet occurred to make the proposed experiment.' Franchise reform was acceptable to Pitt as a weapon against bribery and in
May 1788 he appeared once more as a supporter of Grenville's controverted elections bill. Of all the moderate efforts made to secure some
degree of reform, this was the only one to succeed.[41]

In May 1786 the long-suffering Mahon's county election bill was
brought before the Commons by Wilberforce and Henry Duncombe.[42]
From 1782 to 1785 three efforts had been made to clean up the conduct
of elections for knights of the shire by the proposed introduction of
electoral registers and multiple polls. All had been passed by the
Commons and rejected by the Lords. By 1786 Pitt, Eliot and Mahon
had concluded that direct anti-bribery legislation was a lost cause.[43]
Electoral registration was not, for it would end fraudulent voting: 'A
plan for registering voters which will simplify the proceeding in taking
the poll ... Different places of polling to be appointed in parts of each
County or District.' The bill also proposed to replace the land tax
assessment records, on which electoral qualification had been based,
with a genuine register of voters. On 12 May Pitt rose to defend the
county election bill in the Commons; it was thrown out by the Lords.
This Wyvill attributed to 'a formidable coalition of the King's Friends
and the Whig Aristocracy'.[44]

Wilberforce championed electoral reform once more in 1787, but,
owing to disputes with Stanhope over the content of the bill, it was
abandoned. In 1788 Edward Bearcroft was found to sponsor the legislation. Bearcroft's 'adopted child', as he called it, finally made it onto
the statute book, but not without a struggle: 'Fought through Lord
Stanhope's Bill', wrote Wilberforce. Pitt, who had worked behind the

scenes to mobilize the friends of reform in 1787, did so once more in 1788: 'I consider the object itself of diminishing the expense and trouble of elections as a very important public object.' Pitt spoke for the second reading: 'it was on hands agreed that some such bill was highly necessary; the sooner, therefore, it passed, the better'.[45]

Within a year twenty-two petitions calling for the repeal of the County Election Act had been tabled by the House of Commons. The bill's opponents, amongst them Grenville, had argued that its provisos would restrict the exercise of the vote and increase the cost of elections; by forcing voters to register their freeholds and by making electoral registration chargeable upon the county rates. Pitt had rebutted these objections in 1786:

> ... far from having the tendency of excluding from the power of voting those who were entitled to vote, and of increasing the expense of elections, it would operate in a directly opposite manner. It would confine the election to those only who were entitled to vote, except such as by their negligence in registering their freeholds, shewed themselves unworthy of the privilege. This, of all the faults to be found in the most unobjectionable part of the constitution of the House of Commons, would be effectually remedied; a blessing which he hoped the country would one time or another be able to obtain in every department of the representation.[46]

The county freeholders agreed with the bill's opponents. Not only would the expense and trouble of elections be much increased, but every freeholder would have to pay at least a shilling a year for the privilege of maintaining his vote. Stanhope's idealistic and well-intentioned legislation had not taken into consideration the reality of county electoral procedures.[47] On 12 March 1789 Thomas Stanley moved to repeal the County Election Act.

Pitt, Wilberforce, Duncombe and Bearcroft could hardly protest against the pleas for repeal coming from the nation. Pitt spoke on 27 March not to oppose Stanley's bill, 'but merely to lay his claim hereafter to defend the principle of the act of Parliament the present bill went to the repeal of'.[48] Neither the debate nor the claims on posterity were recorded by William Cobbett, editor of *The Parliamentary History of England* as published by T. C. Hansard in 1816. Pitt thought electoral registration 'a matter so important in itself' that he trusted the House would not repeal the County Election Act in its entirety. He fought for the principle of registration to the bitter end and, on 6 May 1789, voiced strong objections to the revival of 20 Geo. III, c. 13, the pre-existing legislation governing electoral registration which discriminated against 40s. freeholders, particularly those who, for various reasons, were exempt from paying the land tax. Stanley's repeal act received royal assent on 19 May 1789, as did the suspension of Bearcroft's act for six months, hastily put together by George Sumner, Pepper Arden, Bearcroft and Pitt. Two additional attempts were made before the 1790 general election to clarify the pre-existing law on county elections, which Pitt had described on 6 May as inadequate and 'in need of great alteration and amendment'.[49] The first bill was withdrawn after meeting heavy Commons opposition; the second, which made but cosmetic changes to the old electoral law, received royal assent just before the 1790 general election.

Electoral reform did not appear again on the agenda of the House of Commons. It did not appeal to Fox, Grey or any of the heirs to the Rockingham Whig tradition for it struck at the heart of aristocratic power.[50] Limited though Pitt's objectives were, he was prepared to go further than many of his contemporaries in the rationalization of electoral mechanisms and procedures, the reduction of bribery and the limitation of influence. His reluctance to revive the 1785 bill stemmed from a repudiation of specific measures, but not its overall spirit. There is no evidence to suggest that these moderate reform principles were abandoned during the 1790s. What did change after 1785 were Pitt's tactics.

Wyvill and his dying county association movement were left to Stanhope, Wilberforce and Duncombe. Pitt was still willing to act as a formal sponsor of Grenville's 1788 election tribunal regulations, but he supported Stanhope's county election bills as an MP, not as a minister. This conduct, though it ensured him the continued support of the back benches, should not be seen as mere self-interest. By 1785 Pitt had acquired a healthy respect for the independence of a House of Commons that could be persuaded, but was quick to resist any hint of coercion. Throughout the later 1780s he was careful to be neutral or guardedly supportive in public when potentially contentious bills which he privately liked were first presented to Parliament. This contrast between public circumspection and private enthusiasm was particularly apparent in his involvement with the campaign for the abolition of the slave trade.

The Abolition of the Slave Trade

The abolition of the slave trade, like parliamentary reform, was not a party or factional issue. MPs were free to vote according to conscience and, over the vociferous protests of West India planters, slave merchants, parts of the City of London and the Royal Navy, abolition was passed in principle by the House of Commons in 1792. From that date onwards, abolition fell foul of the French Revolution. The St Domingo slave insurrection of 1791 linked the end of the slave trade to anarchy in British minds, a point that was reinforced by the National Convention's abolition of slavery in 1795. Before the revolution, resistance to the measure had been couched in economic terms; from 1791 onwards, the spectre of slave revolt was invoked to prophesy the ruin of Britain's West Indian colonies.

Pitt, who spoke in favour of immediate abolition during the 1780s, changed his tune in 1792 and, thereafter, gave his voice and vote to the gradual abolition of the slave trade.[51] This suggests that he harboured reservations about the wisdom of abolition following the emergence of resistance to the old order in the West Indies, but there was no fundamental change in his position on the subject.[52] Pitt's consistent support for the measure was owed to personal conviction and his friendship with Wilberforce. The former consideration outweighed the latter, for when Wilberforce began to vote against the war with France in December 1794 the two men began to drift apart. This did not stop Pitt from voting for all the abolition motions of the 1790s.

In 1785 Wilberforce underwent a religious experience, following which he resolved to devote his life to the pursuit of godly reform causes. Pitt, who found this difficult to understand, nevertheless encouraged his friend to pursue the abolition of the slave trade in Parliament.[53] Wilberforce's devotion to the cause stemmed from a conviction that the trade in human flesh was morally reprehensible and unbecoming of a Christian nation. Pitt's support was based on humanitarian principles. Britain and its colonies, he believed, ought to renounce this degrading and exploitative form of commerce. Africans, he was to argue in the Commons, were not sub-humans incapable of understanding anything but violence, but represented a racial group capable of cultural, intellectual and economic achievements parallel to those of western Europe. 'The truth was, that we stopped the natural progress of civilisation; we cut off Africa from improvement; we kept down that Continent in a state of darkness, bondage, ignorance, and blood.'[54] What was seen as the violent behaviour of negroes, asserted Pitt, was a product of mistreatment at the hands of so-called civilized Europeans, who encouraged West African coastal tribes to make war on their neighbours in the interior to raise a supply of slaves for export. The situation was no better in the Caribbean, where the plentiful supply of incoming cheap labour gave planters no incentive to treat their slaves with decency.

Pitt's concern was genuine: 'It would delight you to hear Pitt talk on this question,' wrote Wilberforce to Wyvill.[55] In September 1787 Pitt gave Wilberforce access to Custom House records for the collection of statistical data on the slave trade. In October Wilberforce asked

William Eden, the negotiator of the 1786 Anglo-French commercial treaty and Pitt's personal envoy in Paris, to broach the subject of a joint abolition treaty to the French Foreign Ministry. Pitt admitted that the project might appear 'to some people chimerical, but which I really believe may, with proper encouragement, be made practicable'.[56] British planters and slave merchants were bound to challenge the renunciation of so profitable a commerce while other European states continued to trade in slaves, opposition which Pitt hoped to forestall by coming to some agreement with France.

Eden, who thought the project admirable if unrealistic, sent Foreign Minister Montmorin a *mémoire* on the subject in December 1787.[57] Pessimistic about the prospects for negotiating an embargo on the lucrative slave trade, Eden had couched his memorandum in terms of a partial or temporary settlement, to which Pitt and Wilberforce returned strong objections. Pitt felt a temporary abolition to be 'full of difficulty and inconvenience ... if the principle of humanity and justice upon which the whole rests is in any degree compromised, the cause is in a manner given up'.[58] He had been impressed by the conduct of French ministers during the 1786 trade talks and Montmorin's favourable response to Eden's *mémoire*. Enlightenment ideals, thought Pitt, governed the councils of France during the 1780s. 'I therefore trust you will find the French government in a disposition to concur with the measure in its fullest extent, in which I am persuaded it will not be found less practicable, and in which alone it can be effectual.' Approaches had been made to Spain and the United Provinces late in 1787. Pitt was still waiting for the answers.

No abolition motion was to be brought before Parliament until interested parties had been sounded out and a case constructed from empirical data: 'I am clear that much of our success in this country will depend on its being brought to a desirable issue before the discussion of Parliament be finally taken.'[59] Pitt and Wilberforce, though disappointed by the low turnout of petitions for the 1785 reform bill, still believed that extraparliamentary lobbying was a vital part of any reform campaign. 'For many reasons, and Pitt is of the same opinion; it is extremely desirable that petitions for the abolition of the trade in flesh and blood should flow in from every part of the kingdom.'[60] On 8 February 1788 Pitt presented a Cambridge University abolition petition to the House of Commons. Neither he nor Wilberforce expected to call upon twenty years of public support: 'We must expect that the flame that is kindled will die, and the public attention attracted by some new object.'[61]

Wilberforce was to become the public face of abolition, but the real research, organization and publicity behind the campaign to end the slave trade came from its association, founded on 22 May 1787.[62] Its most active member was the Anglican clergyman Thomas Clarkson. Abolition had, however, been brought to the attention of the public by the Society of Friends, the Quakers, for whom it had been a long-standing object. In 1783 they had formed a standing committee on abolition and in 1784 they began to promote the cause in earnest, with petitions, addresses, and reprints of contemporary abolition tracts.[63] The Abolition Committee set up by the Association for the Abolition of the Slave Trade was quick to carry on this good work. On 12 June 1787 Clarkson was authorized by the committee to gather data on the slave trade from the relevant ports. Without this research, no abolition bill could have been drawn up.[64]

By April 1788 no positive responses on the subject had come from Europe. Pitt, who felt that abolition could not compete with the impeachment of Warren Hastings for the attention of Parliament, told Wilberforce that the introduction of an abolition bill in 1788 was 'impracticable'. The abolitionists had planned to push through the bill in one session, which, Pitt thought, was unrealistic. He offered to air a notice of motion in the Commons, to which a depressed and ailing Wilberforce consented. Pitt took the conduct of abolition in Parliament 'as a trust from you to the whole extent you can wish'; he would hand it back to Wilberforce when the passage of an abolition bill seemed feasible.[65] Pitt told Granville Sharp, president of the Abolition Committee, on 21 April 1788 that he was acting for Wilberforce and, on 9 May, persuaded the Commons to hear an abolition motion in 1789.[66] This was passed in a swift and businesslike manner for Pitt had left the rhetorical fireworks at home. His caution succeeded in its purpose.

When Pitt presented the Cambridge petition to Parliament, Sir William Dolben said that his Oxford constituents were friends to 'the abolition of that disgraceful traffic'.[67] On 21 May 1788 Dolben, inspired by Pitt's example, introduced a bill to improve the living conditions of slaves being transported on the infamous Middle Passage from Africa to the West Indies. This involved the regulation of the number of slaves in relation to a vessel's tonnage. The bill, limited to a trial period of one year, passed the Commons with little trouble. Heavy opposition was encountered in the House of Lords. Pitt had told the Cabinet to vote for Dolben's bill but his colleagues ignored these instructions. Many were absent from the Lords debates; three spoke against Dolben's bill. 'I wonder how any human being can possibly resist', remarked Pitt, who, delighted by the positive response of the Commons, proposed to introduce an abolition bill in 1789 after receiving factual and statistical data from the Abolition Committee and the West Indies. The platform in 1788 was still based on 'general grounds, [rather] than any positive information'.[68] Pitt, though upset by resistance to Dolben's bill in the Lords, believed that it could be brought to vote for abolition through 'good management'.

Such confidence was short-lived for Lord Chancellor Thurlow spoke in strong terms against Dolben's bill and Pitt, who had been visiting his constituents in Cambridge, rushed back to London on 29 June 1788 determined to confront the recalcitrant members of his Cabinet: 'The opposers of it [Dolben's Bill] and myself cannot continue members of the same Cabinet and I mean to state this distinctly to the Cabinet before the House meets tomorrow.'[69] Bowing to this pressure, Pitt's colleagues held their tongues and Dolben's bill was passed at the end of June.

Pitt spent the rest of the summer waiting for European responses to fresh British queries on the subject of mutual abolition pacts. The Dutch refused to consider the proposal and the Spanish showed little interest. Pitt's hopes continued to rest with France and received a boost at the end of August 1788, when Louis XVI called the Swiss banker Jacques Necker to office as Director-General of Finance. In 1784 Necker had pledged himself not only to the abolition of the slave trade, but to a general European concert in pursuit of this object. Pitt, who raised the issue with the Marquis de Luzerne, the French ambassador in London, had been told that the Necker ministry would support abolition.[70]

On 12 May 1789 Wilberforce rose in the House of Commons to propose an immediate abolition of the slave trade. The case for abolition had been prepared by the Privy Council Committee of Trade appointed by Pitt late in 1787. Its report, published in March 1789, was 'irresistible'. The twelve resolutions presented to the Commons on 12 May were arguably more the work of Pitt and Grenville than Wilberforce. When handing over abolition to Pitt in April 1788, Wilberforce admitted that he was daunted by the amount of work involved in the drafting of an abolition bill, whereupon the empiricists Pitt and Grenville stepped into the breach. Pitt thought this might be 'best for the business'.[71] Wilberforce was suitably grateful: 'Pitt, with a warmth of friendship and principle that have made me love him better than ever I did before, has taken on himself the management of the business, and promises to do all for me, if I desire it, that, if I were an efficient man, it would be proper for me to do myself.'[72] By the summer of 1788 the Abolition Committee was becoming annoyed by Wilberforce's lack of action.[73]

MPs spent the Easter recess of 1789 studying the Privy Council committee report and, on 20 April, Wilberforce was invited to Holwood, Pitt's country house in Kent, to draft joint resolutions justifying abolition in moral and practical terms. Resolution three stated that European oppression obstructed 'the natural course of civilization and improvement' in Africa. The common humanity of man was the only true basis of trade. The Abolition Committee had identified alternative African products for European markets with which Pitt was much struck, particularly 'the manufactures of the natives in cotton, leather, gold and iron. These he handled over and over again,' recalled Clarkson, who showed them to Pitt in February 1788.[74] Ordinary commerce with Africa 'might reasonably be expected to increase in proportion to the progress of civilization and improvement'. Pitt had discovered a new market for British goods.

The slave trade, asserted the resolutions, was both inhumane and wasteful. Not only did vast numbers of British merchant seamen die from illnesses contracted on the Middle Passage but the West Indian colonies, argued Pitt and Grenville, would become more cost-efficient were a self-sufficient workforce to be established. Ending the trade would reduce slave hostility to the white minority in the Caribbean by forcing planters to improve the living conditions of slaves. 'I see no part of our case', wrote Pitt to Wilberforce, 'that is not made out upon the strongest grounds.' Not only had Pitt very much downplayed his role in bringing abolition before Parliament, but he had left the starring role in the Commons to Wilberforce. Despite brilliant supporting speeches from the Opposition the House of Commons did not pass Wilberforce's motion, preferring instead to commission its own abolition enquiry.[75]

The twelve resolutions had been drafted with two aims in mind. The first, the separation of planters from merchants by concentration on the economic interests of the West Indies, failed in its purpose. The second, a high political appeal to public opinion, was more successful. The Abolition Committee had already made abolition a national issue through its network of local associations, publications and addresses, correspondence with supporters and would-be supporters of the cause, deputations to MPs and peers, and meticulous research on the ill effects of the slave trade. Pitt, impressed by this tireless energy, hoped that the Commons debate on the Privy Council report and the twelve resolutions would give abolition the attention it deserved: 'Our idea is, that by bringing into one view all the leading points of the case, we shall bring on the discussion to great advantage, and insure making a strong impression on the public.'[76] In 1789 public opinion as expressed through an organized extraparliamentary lobby was still seen by Pitt as a positive political force. By 1792 his attitude to reform groups outside Parliament was to have undergone a change, for which the abolition campaign was to be partially responsible.

Test and Corporation Act Repeal

Pitt's commitment to reform always seems to have diminished in direct proportion to the degree of hostility displayed by institutional bodies. When faced in 1787 by a House of Commons neutral to Test and Corporation Act repeal, Pitt spoke and voted against the measure, taking the back benches with him. He consistently opposed such repeal motions from that date onwards. Pitt's reason for defending the supremacy of the Church of England, that of political expediency rather than principle, has left scholars divided over his attitudes to the Established Church.

For Goodwin and Jonathan Clark, Pitt's stand on Test and Corporation Act repeal encapsulates his true thoughts on the great reform issues of the late eighteenth century.[77] The legislation in question made all religious minority groups into second-class citizens by excluding them from public office and, in the case of Roman Catholics, Parliament. Fox became a campaigner for nonconformist civil and political rights in 1787. Pitt, willing to sponsor 'liberal' reform of some description, was not prepared to countenance any modification in the relations between Church and State, which, for some scholars, indicates that his commitment to reform was partial and conservative. Ehrman asserts that Pitt's interest in religious toleration was slight, which explains his perfunctory defence of the Established Church.[78]

Pitt, like most members of the Whig oligarchy, was nominally an Anglican, but he never displayed much interest in religion. The Elder Pitt had been a friend to the Protestant dissenters; in 1773 he had spoken in favour of the 1772 bill to abolish subscription to the Thirty-nine Articles. When the Younger Pitt emerged as an advocate of parliamentary reform during the early 1780s, the dissenters, who believed that this would lead to greater things, turned out in force to support him at the 1784 general election. When Pitt rejected Test and Corporation Act repeal in 1787, they transferred their allegiance to Fox.[79] Religious toleration was a recurrent issue in eighteenth-century English politics and Test Act repeal was mooted in 1786 when Protestant nonconformist leaders asked Henry Beaufoy, MP, to act as their spokesman in a bid to end the penalties prescribed by the 1661 Corporation Act and the 1673 Test Act.

Beaufoy began to canvass the opinions of his fellow MPs at the beginning of 1787. Religious toleration was another 'open question' whose fate was difficult to predict.[80] Pitt saw a delegation of dissenters on 19 January. They left Downing Street with the impression that, though sympathetic to repeal, he would not give them government backing. At the end of January Pitt asked Dr John Moore, Archbishop of Canterbury, to collect episcopal views on repeal. The bishops met on 10 February 1787 at Lambeth Palace. Only 16 of the 27 prelates made an appearance, but the vote was decisive – 14 to 2 against repeal.[81] The importance of this ruling in Pitt's final decision is difficult to assess. Repeal, wrote Moore, 'occasions much dilemma to the Minister' who, on 9 March, 'could not make up his mind' to support Beaufoy.[82]

Moore had been assured by John Hatsell, Speaker of the House of Commons, that Test and Corporation Act repeal would be 'rejected on the first motion'. Pitt suspected that the bishops who had not come to the 10 February conference would reject repeal.[83] The king's opinion must also be taken into account. The day before Beaufoy's motion was due to come before the Commons, George III wrote of repeal: 'my coronation oath, as well as my conviction of the temper ever shown by the Church of England will oblige me in the most public manner to shew it my discountenance.'[84] Pitt can not have been anxious to witness a repeat performance of the confrontation between Crown and Parliament that had brought down the Fox–North coalition of 1783. Regardless of Pitt's personal doubts, it was stupidity to oppose the king and the Church of England.

Pitt's arguments in the debate on 28 March 1787 were curiously ambivalent. Neither Church nor State was in danger from the principles or activities of the dissenter community, for which he professed a great respect. Pitt played instead upon eighteenth-century English fears of religious proselytism: 'there is a natural desire in sectaries to extend the influence of their religion; the Dissenters were never backward in this, and it was necessary for the establishment to have an eye to them.' He admitted that the vast majority of England's dissenters were loyal subjects but that it was impossible to admit moderates while excluding their 'violent' brethren; 'the bulwark must be maintained against them all'. The Church–State partnership was therefore 'necessary' as a social and political safeguard against potential future religious activism.[85]

Pitt's denial that the Test imposed a penalty for religious belief was reminiscent of Bishop William Sherlock's 1718 *Vindication of the Test and Corporation Acts*, reprinted in 1787 and reputedly 'read over' to Pitt by the Bishop of Lincoln before the 1787 debate on Beaufoy's motion.[86] This claim deserves some consideration, if only because the Opposition Whig Sir Gilbert Elliot wrote to his wife that the Commons had played to a full house of strangers on 28 March: 'dissenters with straight heads of hair, and persons with bushy wigs, and a number of bishops, among whom Dr. Prettyman sat under the gallery'.[87] Pretyman-Tomline, clearly concerned about the attitudes of the Commons to Test repeal, heard his ex-pupil tell the House: 'If I were arguing upon principles of right, I should not talk of alarm; but I am acting upon principles of expediency, and it concerns those for whom the well being of the state is intrusted, to take care that the church should not be rashly demolished.' Pitt may have seized upon Sherlock's *Vindication* as a convenient source of argument, but he did recognize that there was an abstract case for the civil, if not the political, rights of dissenters. On 8 May 1789, when Beaufoy moved once more for Test and Corporation Act repeal, Pitt repeated the arguments of 1787. He praised the informal recognition of equality accorded to nonconformists in all walks of life and asserted that exclusion from civil office was not a mark of discrimination or disrespect.[88]

The chief determinant of Pitt's vote against repeal was the opposition of the Established Church. Great was the power and influence of the national Church, capable of mobilizing local and national opinion against political issues of all descriptions. When Moore withdrew his support from the campaign for the abolition of the slave trade in 1792, the cause received a severe blow. In May 1794, before an Opposition Test repeal motion, Pitt warned a young George Canning that the Established Church made a powerful and dangerous enemy:

> I should, in *his* opinion, do well to reflect how very large a part of England the Church of England party were, how great a value they attached to this particular question – (which he confessed he thought comparatively speaking of very little importance) – & how rash it would be in a young man, just entering into political life, & likely to have and to continue a public character, – to do anything unnecessarily that might prejudice so large a party of the people against them.[89]

In 1792 Moore thanked Pitt for 'the able and effectual support which on all occasions you have given to our Church establishment', but the premier, at heart, had no real objections to Test repeal.[90] The Church–State marriage could be modified, if not dissolved.

Although Tomline and Pitt agreed to disagree on Test repeal, the bishop continued to act as Pitt's Church appointments adviser and to obey Downing Street commands on other reform bills. In 1792 Tomline was asked to 'Pray come down *if you profitably can*' to vote in the Lords for the abolition of the slave trade. Pitt liked enlightened clerics and, as an MP for Cambridge University, was well placed to identify them. Richard Watson, Regius Professor of Divinity and Bishop of Llandaff, was a prelate with Foxite principles whom Pitt once considered for the mastership of Trinity Hall, Cambridge. As Pitt put it: 'a Bishop is always something gained'.[91] A vote in the Lords was indeed an asset, especially if its owner voted for Test repeal, as Watson had done at Moore's Lambeth Palace conference in 1787.

Pitt was thought by the Grenville clan to display excessive favour towards Cambridge candidates for ecclesiastical preferment during the 1780s. Pitt took office determined to distribute posts equally between the two universities but the rota was upset in 1787 when two sees went to Cambridge men. The appointment of Pretyman-Tomline to Lincoln was tolerated with some grumbles, but when Hereford went to John Harley instead of the Grenville candidate, William Cleaver, the Marquis of Buckingham was half convinced that Pitt and his old borough patron Lowther, now Lord Lonsdale, intended to give a disproportionate number of senior Church posts to Cambridge.[92] Pitt was in fact sensitive to accusations of university nepotism and deferred the claims of his constituents when more suitable Oxford candidates presented themselves. 'It will not be supposed that it [Cambridge] will not have its equal share in the Long Run while it depends on me.'[93]

Another maverick clergyman connected with Lonsdale, William Paley, has recently been identified as *the* formative influence upon Pitt's political and social thought. In 1856 Lord Aberdeen, Pitt's ward, told Philip Stanhope that Paley, Archdeacon of Carlisle, had been described by Pitt as 'the best writer in the English language'.[94] *The Principles of Moral and Political Philosophy* was so widely admired that it became a standard Oxbridge examination text soon after its publication in 1785. Support for limited parliamentary reform and the abolition of the slave trade was not incompatible with Paley's ideas. He stopped at Test repeal, which, as Ehrman suggested, may have influenced Pitt's 1787 vote.[95] In 1986 T. P. Schofield put forward the suggestion that Paley's model of conservative social progress was attractive to Pitt. By 1993 Paley was described by James Sack as 'Pitt's favourite author'![96]

Before concluding that the *Principles* alone unlocks the door to Pitt's mind, some consideration ought to be given to his other literary favourites. Pitt's love of the classics was acknowledged by all contemporaries, and the writings of antiquity are likely to have shaped his political ideas. Cicero, Thucydides, Polybius, Plutarch, Pliny, Quintilian and Sallust were, claimed Tomline, Pitt's most admired authors. Cicero, though the best represented in Pitt's library at Walmer Castle, was not often cited in the Commons. That honour went to Thucydides, Livy and Sallust. Conyers Middleton's *Life of Marcus Tullius Cicero*, that manual of court Whig virtue, stood high on Pitt's list of English-language authors.[97] He also admired Bolingbroke, Hume and Robertson 'in point of style'. Therein lay part of Paley's appeal and, later, the work of Thomas Paine. Pitt did not like Johnson, Gibbon or the speeches and writings of Edmund Burke. In 1780 Pitt had remarked on the 'real beauties and ridiculous affectations' that characterized the former; fifteen years later he was making disparaging comments about the latter: 'in which there is much to admire and nothing to agree with'.[98]

Pitt's literary tastes point strongly to a court or establishment Whig identity though his choice of authors reflects the seemingly contradictory elements in his psyche. Bolingbroke, a Tory opponent of Walpole, was a neo-Harringtonian classical republican. Hume, accused of Toryism in his own day, called himself a 'sceptical Whig'. Paley is still claimed by historians of both liberal and conservative thought.[99] While it would seem that Pitt's intellectual lineage was straightforward – from the court Whigs through the Scottish Enlightenment to a conservative utilitarianism – his attacks on corruption and influence suggest a graft of country values, if not concepts, onto a court base.

Tomline referred to Locke's *Essay on Human Understanding* (1690) as the key text of Pitt's Cambridge education: 'He was a great admirer of this truly excellent work.' Locke and Paley had denied the existence of the 'innate', be it in 'Children and Ideots' or moral and political systems. Pitt agreed, so much so that he rejected Locke's 'notions on the origins of civil government', the original contract, as 'unfounded and as of dangerous tendency'. If no ancient past could set practical standards for the present, inspiration would have to come from other sources. According to the 'theological utilitarianism' advanced by Paley in the *Principles*, all social and political change was a relative expression of God's will. The divine spirit had been reduced to a mechanist force in a rational universe. Paley defined happiness as the state in which 'the amount or aggregate of pleasure exceeds that of pain'. This was utilitarianism. Progress could be traced through 'THE WILL OF GOD AS COLLECTED FROM EXPEDIENCY'.[100] Pitt gave little thought to God, but maintained a lifelong interest in the art of expediency.

Early Hanoverian Whigs had been obsessed with how best to harness the energizing and enervating powers of monarchy, aristocracy and democracy to create a balance between virtue and corruption. This debate, conducted up to 1740 in terms of classical civic values, was transformed by the Scottish Enlightenment's use of environmental determinism, as expressed in Montesquieu's *Esprit des lois* (1748), to construct new models of polite and commercial progress which incorporated social, as opposed to political, development into the historical process. The new history written by William Robertson and David Hume described civilization as a conflict between feudalism and commerce. From Hume came a depiction of the British constitution as the embodiment of an ideal balance between despotism and anarchy, or liberty and control, in which commerce could perform its civilizing and improving functions upon society as a whole.[101]

Paley's debts to Hume were, to put it mildly, considerable. Hume, nevertheless, was always uneasily aware that the 'mixed' constitution that he admired had mediated a temporary compromise between reason and passion. Paley, no advocate of parliamentary reform or Test repeal, was confident that the balance in society and polity that was embodied in and by the British constitutional monarchy was perfect. He did not, moreover, incorporate commerce into his discussion of civic values and stuck to the models provided by republics and aristocracies. Pitt, who did not accept that the constitution functioned perfectly, still saw the pre-commercial classical world as a model of private virtue. Man was a blend of reason and emotion. The two could never be reconciled, but each needed the other to temper its effects.[102]

Other factors were involved in the path of progress. France, as Pitt told the Commons during the debates on the 1786 Anglo-French commercial treaty, had been gifted 'perhaps more than any other country on earth with what made life desirable, in point of soil, climate and natural productions'. Soil and climate were the foundations of any society's development; 'there was nothing in the soil, climate and manners' of Africans, he told the Commons in 1792, apart from the barbarism enforced by the slave trade, to prevent Britain from promoting the 'general trade' that was the catalyst of civilization.[103] This account of history owed much to Robertson's *View of the Progress of Society in Europe*, but Pitt's faith in the great benefits of contemporary commerce came from Adam Smith, to whom Pitt is reputed to have said at one of Henry Dundas's dinner parties in 1787 that 'we are all your scholars'.[104]

For Pitt, dynamic *vertu* was the mainspring of progress in the public sphere. In its private and personal equivalent, civic *vertu* remained to govern the property owner's conduct. Expedient though it was to rely on a society's private vices, to do so only enjoined a particularly stringent public virtue upon the custodians of the realm. Property entailed civic duties for its owners, which, at their lowest level, involved the registration of one's 40s. freehold. This vision of society was prescriptive, but the concept of virtue was real and with it went a sense of balance. Self-interest produced corruption, which had become institutionalized, thought Pitt, by faction, the source of influence. The structures of the British constitution were sound, he thought, but there was scope for reform to be conducted in a contemporary spirit. Pitt's enmity to party, the enemy of consensus, was very real. Here lay the link to Bolingbroke. Pitt's friends and protegés were invariably younger sons of the aristocracy, gentry representatives and products of relatively new money. Though he later regretted his ennoblements, he enticed such people out of the backwoods because he found their political and social attitudes more congenial than those of the 'old corps' Whigs.[105] Pittism represented a revolt against aristocratic Whiggery.

Gifted though France was by nature and promising as the future of Africa might be, there was no doubt in Pitt's mind that Britain's society and polity represented the pinnacle of human achievement. The luxuries of France were 'produced with little cost and moderate labour', but Britain had overcome the obstacles of inferior soil and climate to give France and the world the unique manufactured goods that were its trademark. Montesquieu's *Esprit des lois* had described what looked suspiciously like Britain's government and society as products of human interaction with the physical environment.[106] With this analysis, Pitt agreed. From Britain's struggles against the elements of nature had come 'the happy freedom of its constitution, and the equal security of its laws, an energy in its enterprise, and a stability in its exertions, which had gradually raised it to a state of commercial grandeur'. The equilibrium that Pitt extolled was central to his definition of civil and political liberty. He was intensely preoccupied with maintaining it throughout the 1780s and 1790s.

Liberty was not a unique product of Britain's history. 'Monsieur, vous n'avez point de liberté politique', he told his host in Rheims during his one and only trip to France in 1783, 'mais pour la liberté civil vous en avez plus que vous ne croyez.' In depicting *ancien régime* France as a polite and commercial state with the potential to be fully free, Hume's essay *Of Civil Liberty* criticized the 'vulgar Whiggism' that portrayed Bourbon France as a despotic state. Pitt, though no admirer of absolute monarchy, possessed a 'polite Whig' outlook on French politics and society.[107] More importantly, he believed that all societies found their own routes to civilization. No series of events laid down any models or standards for universal change. This Pitt implied in another comparison between England and France which he made just before the two countries went to war in 1793: 'The situation of this country, he must, indeed, compare to the temperate Zone, which was the situation in every respect best fitted for health and enjoyment; and where, enjoying a mild, beneficient, regulated influence, the inhabitants were equally protected from the scorching heat of the torrid, and the rigorous frosts of the Frigid Zones.'[108] The subtext of this speech was that Britain would not succumb to revolution, because it was not *ancien régime* France. Utilitarian concepts of progress could, as they did with Pitt, result in a rejection of the due process inherent in the radical and conservative thought of the 1790s. The rights of man were not inalienable, but the revolution did not pose an apocalyptic threat to all forms of order. The French Revolution was a unique experience.

Pitt was to associate utility with policy during the 1790 Commons debate on Fox's Test repeal motion. 'The essence of policy consisted in the general good of the Public: where the rights and interests of individuals therefore came in competition with those of the Public, policy claimed precedence even of Justice.' In arguing for the supremacy of expediency Pitt endorsed Paley's definition of civil liberty: 'the not being restrained by any Law but what conduces in a greater degree to the public welfare'.[109] In the debate on Test repeal in 1787 Pitt had distinguished between civil and political liberty by a tortuous process of logic that eluded the note-taking skills of reporters in the Strangers' Gallery. The survival of the speech is unlikely to have been enlightening, for he concluded that it was 'impossible to separate the ecclesiastical and political liberties of this country', a statement difficult to square with his later remarks to Canning.

What does emerge from the Test repeal debates is Pitt's belief in liberty as a negative concept, involving the observation of duties rather than the assertion of rights. He was not, nevertheless, without sympathy for the dissenter case and was, as Moore recorded, clearly uncomfortable with the moral responsibility for defining the common good. Pitt saw the legislature as an impersonal body that existed to maximize opportunities for the individual and corporate pursuit of happiness. Here Pitt and Paley parted company. Paley had defined public virtue as 'doing good to mankind in obedience to the will of God'. The divine will was benevolent, paternal and collected from expediency. This justified the Test Acts.[110] Like Montesquieu and the young Jeremy Bentham, Pitt saw liberty as a form of security. The legislator could not predict the choices that a person might make in life. To maintain a climate conducive to the quest for happiness, the legislator was obliged to protect property, encourage trade and prevent misrule.[111]

Paley's liberty – the absence of restraint – ultimately confused liberty with utility. Were an individual to be imprisoned under a law framed for the good of society, he would lose his personal liberty but not his civil liberty. Pitt saw law primarily as a guardian of liberty. The British constitution united both in a 'mixed' government that, by the exercise of Montesquieu's much-vaunted checks and balances, defended Britons against the tyranny of arbitrary power and, as Pitt said in 1792, 'the violence of popular commotion', thus creating a balance between freedom and constraint in which a community could prosper. This system had been laid down by the Revolution Settlement of 1689–1714 and reinforced by the reign of the Hanoverian dynasty.[112] 1688 was a date contemporary enough to have some significance for Pitt, but his reference to the accession of George I in 1714 indicates that he saw the British constitution as a changing entity whose final form was yet to be determined. In 1783 he stated that the House of Commons would become the dominant chamber in Parliament and, by virtue of this, in the constitution.

By 1789 Pitt's reputation as a 'reforming minister' was established. He emerges from the 1780s with a record of consistent interest in the theoretical issues of the day. Though his commitment levels could have been higher, decisively so on the question of Test repeal,[113] Pitt showed himself ready to pursue parliamentary reform through several tactical routes and to push the House of Commons to the limits of its tolerance where electoral reform was concerned. His withdrawals from such causes were dictated by practical experience, both legislative and executive, but he was prepared to fight issues on another day. In 1785 Daniel Pulteney, one of Lord-Lieutenant Rutland's MPs at Westminster, had gloomily predicted an unstable future for the ministry: 'This system of Pitt's to act upon great general ideas or the propriety or wisdom of a measure without attending enough to the means by which it can be best and most happily introduced – I mean, knowing the general opinion of the House, must, I foresee, involve him in one or another of these difficulties.'[114] By 1787 Pitt had learned this lesson and, where the slave trade was concerned, his tactical advice was of great value to Wilberforce and the Abolition Committee.

Five years in office had left their mark on Pitt. By 1788 he clearly preferred Westminster to any other political arena; though willing to talk to delegations of petitioners, he preferred to leave negotiation between the world of politics inside and outside Parliament to others. Wilberforce was the chief link between Parliament and the Abolition Committee and, after the disappointment of involvement with Wyvill and the association movement of 1785, Pitt decided that never again would he compromise his reform ideas for the sake of extraparliamentary support. In 1789 Pitt's interest in the application of theory to practice was still strong. He welcomed Necker's return to office in 1788, because 'it would enable us to settle something about the slave trade', and in the 1789 Test repeal debate he paid tribute to a spirit of enlightenment that he felt was general throughout the civilized world: 'It was, he believed, pretty generally felt on the Continent, and was owing to the universal intelligence that had spread itself through all ranks of people, which had contributed to enlighten their minds, soften their hearts, and enlarge their understandings.'[115]

On 8 May 1789 Pitt could say that the 'age of reason' had arrived. His faith in its progress was based on solid court Whig foundations and informed by a critical country conscience. Whatever Chatham might have said, done or thought, his son was no heir to a 'Commonwealthman' intellectual tradition.[116] Pitt, whose political ideas and values were thoroughly contemporary, could perhaps best be described as a 'sceptical Whig', the term that Hume coined to describe himself. Pitt did not always live up to his own ideals, but this does not detract from the importance of their existence.

Notes

1. J. Ehrman, *The Years of Acclaim* (1969); J. R. Breihan, 'William Pitt and the Commission on Fees, 1785–1801', *HJ* 27 (1984), pp. 59–82.

2. Ehrman, *The Years of Acclaim*, chs. III and IX; J. Cannon, *Parliamentary Reform 1640–1832* (Cambridge: 1973), pp. 86–96; D. G. Barnes, *William Pitt and George III 1783–1801* (Stanford, Calif.: 1939), pp. 27–38.

3. An exception here is G. M. Ditchfield, 'The House of Lords and parliamentary reform in the 1780s', *BIHR* 54 (1981), pp. 207–25.

4. M. Peters, *Pitt and Popularity: The Patriot Minister and London Opinion during the Seven Years War* (Oxford: 1980) pp. 266–71; J. Black, *Pitt the Elder* (Cambridge: 1982), pp. 304–7; A. Goodwin, *The Friends of Liberty: The English Democratic Movement and the French Revolution* (1979), pp. 22–9, 49.

5. PRO 30/8/111, Pitt to Lady Chatham, 19 July and 21 August 1775, fos 178–9; 19 March 1777, fo. 132.

6. Ehrman, *The Years of Acclaim*, pp. 56–7, and *The Reluctant Transition* (1983), pp. 12–13; Tomline, *Life of the Rt. Hon. William Pitt* (2 vols, 1828 edn), i, pp. 8–10.

7. PRO 30/8/112, Pitt to Lady Chatham, 27 March 1780, fo. 160; A. M. Wilberforce (ed.), *The Private Papers of William Wilberforce* (1897), sketch of Pitt, p. 48; PRO 30/8/111, Pitt to Lady Chatham, 13 April 1777, fos 184–5; *PR*, ii, pp. 17–20.

8. A. S. Foord, 'The waning of the influence of the Crown', *EHR* 67 (1947), pp. 484–507.

9. *PR*, ix, 31 March 1783, pp. 550–2; I. R. Christie, 'Economical reform and the influence of the Crown, 1780', in *Myth and Reality in Late Eighteenth Century British Politics and Other Papers* (1970), pp. 296–8.

10. J. Norris, *Shelburne and Reform* (1963), pp. 240–2.

11. Breihan, 'William Pitt and the Commission on Fees', pp. 80–1; Ehrman, *The Years of Acclaim*, pp. 273–81, 319–26, 87–89; Norris, *Shelburne and Reform*, pp. 271–2; P. Brown, *The Chathamites* (1967), p. 101.

12. Cannon, *Parliamentary Reform*, ch. 4; H. T. Dickinson, 'Radicals and reformers in the age of Wilkes and Wyvill', in J. Black (ed.), *British Politics and Society from Walpole to Pitt* (1990), pp. 127–32.

13. Ehrman, *The Years of Acclaim*, pp. 74–5; I. R. Christie, *Wilkes, Wyvill and Reform: The Parliamentary Reform Movement in British Politics, 1760–1785* (1962), pp. 174–6.

14. *PR*, vii, pp. 1206–9.

15. C. Wyvill (ed.), *Political Papers, chiefly respecting the Attempt of the County of York ... to effect a Reformation of the Parliament of Great Britain* (6 vols, York: 1794–1802), iv, 'The substance of Mr. Wyvill's Conversation with Mr. Pitt on 5 May [1783]', pp. 2–5.

16. Ehrman, *The Years of Acclaim*, pp. 73–4; Christie, *Wilkes, Wyvill and Reform*, pp. 174–6; Norris, *Shelburne and Reform*, Shelburne to Camden, 26 January 1782, p. 146; [Philip], 5th Earl Stanhope, *Life of the Right Honourable William Pitt* (4 vols, 1861–2), i, Pitt to Lady Chatham, 15 May 1783, p. 121; Ditchfield, 'The House of Lords and parliamentary reform', p. 209.

17. *CJ*, xxxviii, pp. 1019, 1053; xxix, pp. 23, 383; *PR*, vii, 19 June 1782, pp. 247–8; York City Library, Wyvill MS, Mahon to Wyvill, 22 June 1782; specific reference was made to the 1774 Grenville tribunal in Pitt's

speech of 7 May 1783: *PR*, ix, p. 694; P. Jupp, *Lord Grenville, 1759–1834* (Oxford: 1985), pp. 17, 30.

18. Wyvill Papers, iv, Pitt–Wyvill interview, 5 May 1783, pp. 4–5; Christie, *Wilkes, Wyvill and Reform*, pp. 148–9.

19. The freeholders' attendance bill, a Mahon–Eliot production, had first been aired in June 1782 and was revived in 1783: *CJ*, xxxvii, p. 1053; xxxix, p. 408; Christie, *Wilkes, Wyvill and Reform*, pp. 174–80. Fraudulent votes, yet another Mahon–Eliot joint effort, had received its first reading on 5 May 1783: *CJ*, xxxix, p. 23. For bribery and expense, the long-suffering Mahon and Eliot were joined by Pitt: *CJ*, xxxix, p. 383.

20. *PR*, ix, 7 May 1783, pp. 689–96; Wyvill Papers, iv, Wyvill to Pitt, 23 May 1783, p. 6; Rose Diaries, i, pp. 32–3.

21. *Rutland*, iii, Orde to Rutland, 6 and 14 December 1784, pp. 157, 159.

22. When Mahon's first bribery bill came before the Commons, 'almost every clause occasioned debate': *PH*, xxiii, 12 June 1782, col. 102. The disqualification clauses were particularly unpopular: *PR*, vii, 21 June 1782, pp. 258–9. When Mahon and Pitt tried to bring bribery before the House once more in May 1783, it was attacked from all quarters of the House: *PR*, x, 6 June 1783, pp. 130–3; *CJ*, xxxix, p. 383.

23. Wyvill Papers, iv, 'Head or Heads of a Bill or Bills for Amending the Representation', Pitt to Wyvill, 15 April 1785, p. 104; *CJ*, xl, p. 814.

24. *PH*, xxv, 'Summary Explanation of the Principles behind Mr. Pitt's Bill', written by Wyvill, cols 445–8, n. 1.

25. A. Aspinall (ed.), *The Later Correspondence of George III* (5 vols, Cambridge: 1962–9) i, P. Yorke to Hardwicke, 22 March 1785, pp. 141–2, n. 1; *Kenyon*, Pitt to Kenyon, 20 March 1785, p. 519; Wyvill Papers, iv, p. 110.

26. *PH*, xxv (much the same as *PR*, xvi, pp. 42–59), 18 April 1785, cols 338–9; Wyvill Papers, iv, 'Heads', March 1785, pp. 103–9.

27. *PR*, xvi, 18 April 1785, cols 42–59.

28. *PR*, ix, 7 May 1783, p. 694; Wyvill Papers, iv, 'Heads', p. 105.

29. *Dropmore*, i, Pitt to Temple, 22 July 1783, pp. 215–16; Stanhope, *Life of Pitt*, i, George III to Pitt, 20 March 1785, p. xv.

30. *LCG III*, i, 182, Pitt to George III, and 183, George III to Lord Sydney, 19 March 1785, pp. 141–2.

31. *Rutland*, iii, D. Pulteney to Rutland, 19 April 1785, p. 202; PRO 30/29/384, Pitt to Lord Gower, 19 March 1785.

32. Wyvill Papers, iv, Wyvill to Stanhope, 17 December 1796, pp. 540–2.

33. *Ibid.*, Wyvill to Pitt, 29 July 1787, pp. 32–4. An additional draft of the 'Heads' can be found in U1590 S5 010/5.

34. *Private Papers of William Wilberforce*, E. Eliot to Wilberforce, December 1784, p. 6.

35. *Dropmore*, i, Temple to Pitt and Grenville to Temple, 31 July 1783, pp. 214–17. By this was meant respectable public support.

36. *LCG III*, i, P. Yorke to Hardwicke, 22 March 1785, pp. 141–2, n. 1.

37. P. Stanhope (ed.), *Correspondence between the Right Honourable William Pitt and Charles, Duke of Rutland, Lord Lieutenant of Ireland* (1842), Pitt to Rutland, 12 January 1785, pp. 76–7; Wyvill Papers, iv, 'Heads', pp. 104–7; Wyvill's account of the 'Explanation', pp. 63–4; PRO 30/8/198, Notebook

6, 'Parl. Ref^m – Scrutinies – Grenville's Bill. Ld. Mahon's Bill and Acts for Registering', [April 1785], fo. 172.

38. *PR*, xx, 30 March 1786, pp. 36–8; Christie, *Wilkes, Wyvill and Reform*, pp. 150–2.

39. L. Namier and J. Brooke (eds), *The History of Parliament: The Commons, 1754–1790* (1985), p. 314; Christie, 'Economical reform and the influence of the Crown', p. 302.

40. Namier and Brooke, *The Commons, 1754–1790*, pp. 34–5, 396–8, 409; Wyvill Papers, iv, 'Heads', p. 108; Christie, *Wilkes, Wyvill and Reform*, p. 220.

41. PRO 30/8/171, Richmond to Pitt, 7 April 1788, fos 104–5; Wyvill Papers, iv, Wyvill to Pitt, 29 July 1787, p. 37; *CJ*, xliii, p. 455.

42. Mahon had just gone to the Lords as the third Earl Stanhope.

43. *Life of Stanhope*, p. 86; Pitt's copy of Stanhope's bill can be found in PRO 30/8/134/2, fos 167–8. These bills can be traced through *CJ*, xxxviii, pp. 1019, 1053; xxxix, pp. 23, 383, 444, 458, 963; xl, pp. 635, 635; xli, p. 202; Christie, *Wilkes, Wyvill and Reform*, p. 220; Jupp, *Lord Grenville*, pp. 58–9.

44. *Wyvill Papers*, iv, 'Heads', p. 105; Wyvill to Stanhope, 17 December 1786, pp. 540–1; Wyvill to Pitt, 11 January 1787, p. 29; *PR*, xx, 12 May 1786, p. 212; *Life of Stanhope*, p. 70; P. Langford, *Public Life and the Propertied Englishman, 1689–1798* (Oxford: 1991), pp. 281–2; Ditchfield, 'The House of Lords and parliamentary reform in the 1780s', pp. 212–13.

45. *Life of Wilberforce*, i, Diary, 15 May 1788, p. 148; *Kenyon*, Pitt to Kenyon, 11 April 1788, p. 525, and Stanhope to Kenyon, 14 April 1788, p. 525; *PR*, xxiii, 7 May 1788, p. 580.

46. *PR*, xx, 12 May 1786, pp. 210–12.

47. Langford, *Public Life and the Propertied Englishman*, pp. 278–82.

48. *PR*, xxv, 27 March 1789, pp. 535–6, and *PR*, xxvi, 6 May 1789, p. 88.

49. *CJ*, xliv, pp. 161–3, 240, 340; xlv, p. 275; Ditchfield, 'The House of Lords and parliamentary reform', pp. 215–16.

50. E. A. Smith, *Lord Grey, 1764–1845* (Oxford: 1992), p. 39.

51. Ehrman, *The Years of Acclaim*, p. 387.

52. R. Thorne, 'William Pitt', in *The History of Parliament: The Commons 1790–1820* (5 vols, 1986), ii, p. 808.

53. *Life of Wilberforce*, i, Journal (28 October 1787), pp. 149–51.

54. *PH*, xxix, debate on abolition bill, 19 April 1791, col. 342.

55. *Life of Wilberforce*, i, Wilberforce to Wyvill, 25 January 1788, p. 161.

56. *Ibid.*, G. Rose to Wilberforce, 27 September 1787, p. 154; Auckland Correspondence, i, 20 October 1787, pp. 239–40, and Pitt to Eden, 2 November 1787, pp. 266–7.

57. PRO 30/8/102, Pitt to Eden, 7 December 1787, fo. 133; U1590 S5 01/5, Eden to Pitt, 13 December 1787.

58. Auckland Correspondence, i, Pitt to Eden, [7] January 1788, p. 301.

59. *Ibid*, Wilberforce to Eden, 5 January 1788, pp. 305–6.

60. *Life of Stanhope*, Wilberforce to Stanhope, 25 January 1788, p. 72.

61. *PR*, xxi, 8 February 1788, pp. 193–4; *Life of Wilberforce*, i, Wilberforce to Eden, 7 January 1788, pp. 305–6; S. Drescher, *Capitalism and Anti-Slavery* (Oxford: 1986), p. 65.

62. J. Walvin, *England, Slaves and Freedom* (1982), p. 25; J. R. Oldfield, 'London

opinion and the mobilization of public opinion against the slave trade', *HJ* 35 (1992), pp. 331–44, and *Popular Politics and British Anti- Slavery: The Mobilization of Public Opinion against the Slave Trade 1787–1807* (Manchester: 1995), pp. 49–50.

63. T. Clarkson, *A History of the Rise, Progress and Accomplishment of the Abolition of the Slave Trade* (2 vols, 1808), i, pp. 117–128, 256.

64. BL Add MS 21255, fos 5–9.

65. R. G. Wilberforce (ed.), *Pitt and Wilberforce* (1897), Pitt to Wilberforce, 8 April 1788, pp. 39–40.

66. BL Add MS 21255, fo. 12; *PR*, xxiii, 5 May 1788, p. 545.

67. *PR*, xxiii, 8 February 1788, pp. 162–3.

68. Ehrman, *The Years of Acclaim*, pp. 394–5; *Pitt and Wilberforce*, Pitt to Wilberforce, 28 June 1788, p. 41.

69. *Dropmore*, i, Pitt to Grenville, 29 June 1788, p. 342.

70. *Ibid.*, Pitt to Grenville, 29 August 1788, p. 353; *Private Papers of William Wilberforce*, Pitt to Wilberforce, 1 September 1788, pp. 23–4: 'I hope Necker's coming in will prove very favourable to this object.'

71. *Life of Wilberforce*, i, Pitt to Wilberforce, 10 April 1789, p. 215; *Pitt and Wilberforce*, Pitt to Wilberforce, 8 April 1788, pp. 39–40.

72. *Life of Wilberforce*, i, Wilberforce to Wyvill, [April] 1788, p. 170.

73. J. Walvin, 'Abolishing the slave trade: antislavery and popular radicalism 1776–1807', in Walvin and C. Emsley (eds), *Artisans, Peasants and Proletarians, 1760–1860* (1985), pp. 39–40.

74. The resolutions were printed in the 1789 *Annual Register*, cols 268–70; Clarkson, *History of the … Abolition of the Slave Trade*, pp. 472–4; BL Add MS 25154, fos 39–40.

75. *Pitt and Wilberforce*, Pitt to Wilberforce, 20 April 1789, p. 41; Ehrman, *The Years of Acclaim*, p. 397; *Court and Cabinets*, ii, W. Young to Buckingham, 22 April 1789, pp. 148–9.

76. *Life of Wilberforce*, i, Pitt to Wilberforce, 10 April 1789, p. 215.

77. Goodwin, *Friends of Liberty*, pp. 76–95; J. C. D. Clark, *English Society, 1688–1832* (Cambridge: 1985), pp. 340–2.

78. Ehrman, *The Reluctant Transition*, p. 67; I. Gilmour, *Riot, Risings and Revolution* (1992), p. 387.

79. J. Cookson, *The Friends of Peace: Anti-War Liberalism in England, 1793–1815* (Cambridge: 1982), p. 17.

80. *Rutland*, ii, Pulteney to Rutland, 10 March 1787, p. 377.

81. W. Belsham, *Memoirs of the Reign of George III*, iv (1795), p. 127; Moore MSS, Lambeth Palace Library, 17, Minutes of Episcopal Conference, 10 February 1787, and Moore to Pitt, 12 February 1787, cited in Ehrman, *The Reluctant Transition*, p. 65.

82. Auckland Correspondence, i, Moore to Auckland, 9 March 1787, p. 405.

83. *Rutland*, i, Pulteney to Rutland, 19 March 1787, p. 379.

84. A. Aspinall and E. A Smith (eds), *English Historical Documents, 1783–1832* (1959), 472, George III to Pitt, 27 March 1787.

85. *PR*, xxi, 28 March 1787, pp. 525–6, 567–8; G. M. Ditchfield, 'The parliamentary struggle over the repeal of the Test and Corporation Acts, 1787–1790', *EHR* 89 (1974), pp. 553–4, 559–60.

86. Herbert McLachlan (ed.), *Letters of Theophilus Lindsay* (1920), p. 64.
87. *Life and Letters*, i, Elliot to Lady Elliot, 29 March 1787, pp. 142–3.
88. *PR*, xxvi, 8 May 1789, pp. 126–8.
89. West Yorkshire Record Office, Canning MS, 29 dii, Diary [12 May 1794], fos 74–5.
90. PRO 30/8/161, Moore to Pitt, 19 January 1792, fo. 10.
91. HA 119 T108/42, Pitt to Tomline, 26 June [1792] and 25 September [1789].
92. *Dropmore*, i, Buckingham to Grenville, 8 November 1788, p. 289. James Lowther, first Baron Lonsdale, had given Pitt his Appleby seat in 1781 and was a product of 'radical' Peterhouse under the mastership of Edmund Law, Bishop of Carlisle: Clark, *English Society*, p. 312.
93. HA 119 T108/42, Acc. 240, Pitt to Tomline, 27 May 1791.
94. Ehrman, *The Years of Acclaim*, p. 396. As Ehrman pointed out, this remark was made long after Pitt's death.
95. I. R. Christie, *Stress and Stability in Late Eighteenth Century Britain* (Oxford: 1982), pp. 199; Ehrman, *The reluctant transition*, pp. 62–3.
96. T. P. Schofield, 'Conservative political thought in Britain in response to the French Revolution', *HJ* 29 (1986), p. 60; J. J. Sack, *From Jacobite to Conservative: Reaction and Orthodoxy in Britain, c. 1760–1832* (Cambridge, 1993), p. 84; J. A. W. Gunn, *Beyond Liberty and Property: The Process of Self Recognition in Eighteenth Century Political Thought* (Kingston and Montreal: 1983), p. 252.
97. Ehrman, *The Years of Acclaim*, p. 14; HA 119 562/21, 'Catalogue of the Library Belonging to the Right Honble. Wm. Pitt at Walmer Castle' (compiled by Tomline), 12 February 1806; Stanhope, *Life of Pitt*, i, p. 18.
98. Tomline, *Life of Pitt*, i, p. 10; Ehrman, *The Reluctant Transition*, p. 80 and n. 4; R. Browning, *Political and Constitutional Ideas of the Court Whigs* (Baton Rouge, La.: 1983), pp. 222–5; Stanhope, *Life of Pitt*, i, Pitt to Lady Chatham, 14 March 1780, p. 38; Auckland Correspondence, iii, Pitt to Auckland, 8 November 1795, p. 320.
99. H. T. Dickinson, *Liberty and Property: Political Ideology in Eighteenth Century Britain* (1977), ch. 4: Browning, *Political and Constitutional Ideas of the Court Whigs*, chs. 7–8; I. Kramnick, *Bolingbroke and his Circle: The Politics of Nostalgia in the Age of Walpole* (Cambridge, Mass.: 1968), pp. 24–8; D. Forbes, 'Sceptical Whiggism, commerce and liberty', in A. Skinner and T. Wilson (eds), *Essays on Adam Smith* (Oxford: 1970), pp. 179–201; J. G. A. Pocock, 'The varieties of Whiggism from exclusion to reform', in *Virtue, Commerce and History* (Cambridge: 1985), pp. 250–6, and (with L. Schwoerer and G. Schochet), *The Varieties of Political Thought in Early Modern England 1500–1800* (Cambridge: 1993), p. 313; Christie, *Stress and Stability*, pp. 160–4; Schofield, 'Conservative political thought', pp. 605–12; J. W. Burrow, *Whigs and Liberals* (Oxford: 1988), pp. 54–5.
100. Tomline, *Life of Pitt*, i, p. 9; W. Paley, *The Principles of Moral and Political Philosophy* (2 vols, 10th edn, 1794), i, Book I, chs. v–vi; ii, Book VI, ch. iii. Paley fell out of favour with Pitt during the later 1790s: Ehrman, *The Consuming Struggle*, p. 828, n. 5.
101. Browning, *Political and Constitutional Ideas of the Court Whigs*, pp. 225–30;

Pocock, *Virtue, Commerce and History*, pp. 250–1. See essays by N. Phillipson and J. Robertson in I. Hont and M. Ignatieff (eds), *Wealth and Virtue: The Shaping of Political Economy in the Scottish Enlightenment* (Cambridge: 1983).

102. T. H. Green and T. Gross (eds), *The Philosophical Works of David Hume* (4 vols, 1885–6), iii, 'Whether the British Government inclines more to an Absolute Monarchy or a Republic' and 'Of Commerce'; Paley, *Principles*, ii, Book VI, chs. vi–vii; S. Burtt, *Virtue Transformed: Political Argument in England 1688–1740* (Cambridge: 1992), ch. 6.

103. *PR*, xxi, 12 February 1787, p. 178.

104. E. C. Mossner and I. S. Ross (eds), *The Correspondence of Adam Smith* (4 vols, Oxford: 1977), iii, Dundas to Smith, 21 March 1787, p. 302 and n. 5. The remark is apocryphal; Pitt's admiration of Smith was not.

105. [G. Meryon], *The Memoirs of the Lady Hester Stanhope in Conversation with her Physician* (3 vols, 1845), iii, p. 163.

106. C. Montesquieu, *The Spirit of the Laws* (Cambridge: 1989), pp. 242–3, 286–88, 326–32.

107. *Life of Wilberforce*, i, [2–5] October 1783, p. 38; Hume, *Works*, iii, 'Of Civil Liberty'; D. Forbes, *Hume's Philosophical Politics* (Cambridge: 1975), pp. 145–72; J. Robertson, 'The Scottish Enlightenment at the limits of the civic tradition', in Hont and Ignatieff (eds), *Wealth and Virtue*, pp. 179–202.

108. *PR*, xxi, p. 178; xxxiv, 1 February 1793, pp. 385–6.

109. *PR*, xxvii, 2 March 1790, pp. 160–1; Paley, *Principles*, ii, Book VI, ch. v.

110. Paley, *Principles*, i, Book I, ch. vii.

111. Montesquieu, *The Spirit of the Laws*, p. 157; F. Rosen, *Bentham, Byron and Greece: Constitutionalism, Nationalism and Early Liberal Political Thought* (Oxford: 1992), pp. 35–6.

112. Paley, *Principles*, ii, Book VI, ch. vii; Montesquieu, *The Spirit of the Laws*, pp. 157–66; Hume, *Works*, iii, 'Of the Protestant Succession'; *PR*, xxi, 12 February 1787, p. 178; *PH*, xxix, 17 February 1792, cols 816–18.

113. Ehrman, *The Reluctant Transition*, p. 67.

114. *Rutland*, iii, Pulteney to Rutland, 11 April 1785, p. 198.

115. *Dropmore*, i, Pitt to Grenville, 29 August 1788, p. 353; *PR*, xxvi, 8 May 1789, pp. 126–8.

116. C. Robbins, *The Eighteenth Century Commonwealthman: Studies in the Transmission, Development and Circumstances of English Liberal Thought from the Restoration of Charles II until the War with the Thirteen Colonies* (Cambridge, Mass.: 1959), pp. 274–6, 323.

Chapter 2

Revolutionary France in British Foreign Policy, 1784–1789

When the younger Pitt came to power in 1783, Britain's international reputation was at an all-time low. The Thirteen Colonies had just separated from Britain, an event superintended by a France now revenged for the humiliations of the Seven Years War. Spain and the United Provinces, as eleventh-hour entrants, had shared in the French triumph. Britain, stripped of its most valuable colonies and saddled with a colossal war debt, had not a friend in Europe. The 1783 Treaty of Versailles left British statesmen and diplomats in a state of insecurity and paranoia that was to focus on Bourbon France for much of the 1780s. British xenophobia respecting its cross-Channel neighbour, nothing new in the eighteenth century, was reinforced by the part played by France in the loss of America, which strengthened official and public fears that the servants of the French Crown plotted, both independently and in collusion with other powers, to undermine Britain's power and influence on a global scale.[1]

William Pitt shared the sentiments of his countrymen, but his distrust of France did not, as was the case with his first Foreign Secretary, the Marquis of Carmarthen, manifest itself in an aggressive and hostile foreign policy. This, felt Pitt, was impractical, risky and expensive in the immediate aftermath of the American war. Conscious that Britain was bankrupt and dangerously isolated in Europe, he preferred to work on a reduction of international animosity to Britain while steering clear of involvement in disputes between other states.[2] Pitt, uncomfortable with foreign affairs during his early years in office, was content with isolation when he took office. From 1786 onwards he began to involve himself in the direction of Britain's foreign policy, in which he acted primarily as a restraining influence upon the hawkish Carmarthen, the chief advocate of British interventionism in Europe.[3]

Of all eighteenth-century ministerial portfolios, the Foreign Office was the most restrictive for its incumbent. Poor communication was a fact of life in early modern Europe, for travel was regularly delayed by bad roads and weather, particularly during the winter months. During the 1790s the progress of French arms was further to disrupt the routes of couriers. All diplomats and ministers in the courts and Cabinets of Europe based their decisions on what was often outdated information. The workload of a Foreign Secretary was crippling; second-guessing the course of events overseas relied upon an intimate knowledge of any given state's finances and internal affairs, court intrigues and past centuries of dealings with its neighbours. Carmarthen was, by the admission of his own under-secretaries, a lazy and under-informed Foreign Secretary. His successor, Grenville, was not.[4] When Pitt and Carmarthen came to power in 1783, neither was familiar with the conduct of foreign policy. Their experience was limited to domestic spheres, where other traps lay for a Foreign Secretary.

All major decisions needed the approval of the king, the Cabinet and, in some cases, Parliament. An ambitious Foreign Secretary had, at worst, to overcome the prejudices of his countrymen in Closet, Cabinet and Commons. Judging by Carmarthen's lacklustre performance as government leader of the Lords in 1790–1, the management of Parliament was not something for which he had much talent. It was something that Pitt ignored at his cost. In disputes within the ministry's senior ranks, Carmarthen was often worsted by Pitt, who, irritated by Carmarthen's persistent efforts to mobilize royal, ministerial and official support for his ideas, tried at least twice to oust Carmarthen from the Foreign Office. Carmarthen had not been Pitt's first choice for the job. Lord Grantham, who had spent nine years in Madrid as ambassador and served as Foreign Secretary under the Earl of Shelburne, had refused the Foreign Office in December 1783. George III and the king's friends, Lord Chancellor Thurlow and Hawkesbury, President of the Board of Trade, could be relied upon to resist any hasty measures, a conservatism that frustrated Carmarthen and, on occasion, Pitt. Richmond and Grenville, who were close to the premier, could occasionally persuade him to change his mind, but not necessarily in Carmarthen's interest.[5] Although the relationship between Pitt and Carmarthen was uneasy throughout the 1780s, there was no disagreement about general objectives: the reinstatement of Britain as a first-rank power and, inseparable from this, the reduction of France as a military and diplomatic threat. Little agreement could be reached on the methods and timing of the diplomatic revival, a division that reflected more deepseated differences in opinion about the direction and purpose of British foreign policy.

Unsplendid Isolation

Before any British government could exert itself abroad, it had to be strong at home. Throughout 1783 and much of 1784 the Pitt ministry rested on insecure political foundations and, more importantly, was perceived to be unstable by continental observers. Carmarthen, alarmed by his country's isolation and low status in Europe, hoped to mask Britain's military and fiscal weaknesses by alliance with one or more of the continental powers.[6] Pitt, who believed that international influence was based upon a nation's real military and economic strength, thought that Britain was in no position to play power politics. In June 1784, following the landslide general election victory that had, felt Carmarthen, given the ministry the mandate to assert itself in Britain and Europe, the Foreign Secretary proposed that Britain join forces with northern or central Europe. Two alliance systems were proposed: a Baltic triangle involving Prussia, Russia and Denmark; and a central European union encompassing Austria, Prussia and Denmark. The latter configuration was vastly preferable to the former, for Austria, the linchpin of such a network, had long shared Britain's interest in curbing French expansion in Europe. Attractive as the 'old system' of the 1730s and 1740s was in principle to British ministers and officials, Austria had been allied to France since 1756 and was also joined to Russia, whose territorial ambitions in eastern Europe were regarded with distaste by the British government. In 1784 Austria was soliciting the support of France for the Bavarian Exchange – the Habsburg withdrawal from the Netherlands, modern Belgium, in preference for the overlordship of Bavaria.[7] The British government, since 1713 the defender of an Austrian Netherlands as a barrier to French expansion in northwest Europe, was concerned. Carmarthen, who admitted that Austria was not likely to abandon France for Britain, suggested the formation of the Baltic ring as a check on Bourbon–Habsburg designs.[8]

The Foreign Secretary's hatred of Bourbon France was so strong that he saw plots against Britain in every action of French diplomats on the Continent. Carmarthen had good reason to be insecure. France, allied by marriage or treaty, sometimes both, to Spain, most of south Italy, Austria, Russia, the Ottoman Porte (Turkey) and, from July 1784, Sweden, was the most influential state in Europe. The very existence of this alliance network was worrying to an isolated British government. Pitt, who saw the attractions of an opposing alliance system 'in order to counterbalance the House of Bourbon', also believed that the acquisition of British influence required its active defence in military or diplomatic terms were any long-term gains to be realized. These were commitments that Pitt was not prepared to make:[9] 'The great difficulty is how to lay the foundations of such Connections, keeping clear at the same Time of being too soon involved in the Quarrels of any Continental Power. Whatever can be done, consistent with this Caution, towards forming a System of Alliance, cannot, I think, be done too speedily.'[10] For Pitt, isolation was vastly preferable to confrontation and British diplomats in Europe were instructed to promote their country's interests in as conciliatory and inexpensive a manner as possible. This was not at all to the taste of Carmarthen or Sir James Harris, British ambassador at the Hague, who complained about the lack of direction he was receiving from London.

Carmarthen, though hamstrung by the Cabinet's lack of interest in an interventionist European policy, was determined to reassert Britain's influence in Europe.[11] The United Provinces looked like the most likely route, but, despite Harris's best efforts to resurrect the old friendship between Britain and Holland, it was apparent by the end of 1784 that the Dutch were on the verge of signing a defensive alliance with France. Carmarthen, realizing that Britain's links to the Continent were not likely to be renewed via the United Provinces, decided instead to turn to Austria, who, on behalf of its subjects in the Netherlands, was embroiled in a dispute with the Dutch government over navigation rights in the river Scheldt. The 1648 Treaty of Munster had given the United Provinces control over the estuary with disastrous results for the commerce of the Netherlands.[12] Supporting Austria's claims as presented at the Brussels Conference of 4 May 1784 – free navigation in the Scheldt and the return of the fortress of Maestricht, then a Dutch enclave surrounded by the Prince-Bishopric of Liège – would, hoped Carmarthen, pave the way for an Anglo-Austrian *entente*.

In 1792 the British government was to act as the champion of Dutch sovereignty in the Scheldt, 'according to the maxims which this country has upheld for a century'.[13] In 1784 Carmarthen wrote to Sir Robert Murray Keith, ambassador in Vienna, that support for an open Scheldt would bring Austria into alliance with Britain. Pitt, who did not see his court as a potential arbitrator in the Austro-Dutch dispute, felt that the services of France would be more acceptable to both parties. An appalled Carmarthen nevertheless asked Keith to promote Britain's good offices to the Austrian government, going so far as to advocate a personal approach to Joseph II.[14] Keith's efforts to woo the emperor were ultimately fruitless, for which George III's Hanoverian servants were responsible.

In July 1785 the *Fürstenbund*, a friendship pact intended to promote German unity in the Holy Roman Empire, was signed by Prussia, Hanover and Saxony. As a manifestation of German concern about Habsburg policy in eastern Europe, particularly Bavaria and Poland, the *Fürstenbund* challenged the authority of Austria within the empire. The Austrian government, believing that Hanover's policy was at least known to, and probably directed by, George III's British ministers, was not impressed by Keith's professions of friendship. The Pitt ministry, however, knew little of what was going on in the king's Hanoverian councils. In April 1785 Pitt spoke for his colleagues when he declined to comment on the *Fürstenbund*: 'I feel myself at present much too ignorant of it.'[15] Carmarthen, blissfully unaware of imperial suspicions about the connections between George III's Britannic and electoral policies, hoped throughout the summer of 1785 that the *Fürstenbund* would act as a friendly but separate lobby in opposition to the Bavarian Exchange. This was seen by the *Fürstenbund* in the east as a dangerous accession of Austrian strength and by the British government in the west as a prelude to the French conquest of the Netherlands.[16] So much faith did Carmarthen place in the persuasive powers of the *Fürstenbund* that he not only defended it to the Austrian ambassador, Count Kageneck, but hoped to capitalize on the goodwill it had created between George III and Frederick the Great to propose the signature of an Anglo-Prussian alliance. Carmarthen also wanted to appeal to Russia for a formal protest against the Bavarian Exchange. This, declared Pitt, was too forceful a step for the British government to take: 'I should be inclined to Confine the Communication rather more to a Recital of our General Sentiments on the Necessity of concerting a solid system to counteract the restless projects of France.'[17] This was not the first time that Pitt had restrained Carmarthen, who was becoming irritated by the premier's excessive caution. On 5 July, nevertheless, both men told Count Vorontsov, the Russian ambassador in London, that the chief bar to an Anglo-Russian alliance was the Austrian link to France. Carmarthen wanted a binding mutual defence alliance, but Pitt was only looking for closer ties with Russia. When Vorontsov, whose court was afraid that the *Fürstenbund* would operate against Russian interests in the empire, asked the Pitt ministry to protest against the German pact, Carmarthen replied that the British government had nothing to do with Hanover.[18] When the *Fürstenbund* was received in eastern Europe as another example of Albion's perfidy, Carmarthen was stunned but powerless to reverse events: 'Austria I now look upon as disposeable'. When he began to concentrate on Prussia as a potential alliance partner, Pitt was so lukewarm towards this project that an exasperated Carmarthen considered resignation.[19] The premier, who had declared himself in favour of a security system in principle, was rejecting every practical proposal for its creation.

The Foreign Secretary was also dismayed by Pitt's interest in European trade, to which Carmarthen believed that his leader was sacrificing the 'real' interests of Britain, namely the distribution of political, military and territorial power. Carmarthen's outlook on international affairs was narrowly conventional and he paid no attention to the commercial and cultural aspects of European diplomacy. Pitt alone supervised the negotiation of the 1784–6 trade treaties with France and Portugal and the unsuccessful 1786–8 Anglo-Spanish commercial negotiations. Carmarthen regarded these initiatives with suspicion and contempt, none more so than the Eden Treaty of 1786. These pacts, he felt, were poor substitutes for treaties of defensive alliance and only drew attention to Britain's status as a supplicant in Europe.[20] This perception was shared by Parliament and many British diplomats. Carmarthen's Francophobia was so strong that he did not see any sincerity or goodwill in the conduct of the French government during the negotiation of the 1786 commercial treaty.

This distrust of France was shared at a much lower level by Pitt, who was 'much struck by the goodwill shown by the French government' on trade issues, but 'could not listen but with suspicion to their professions of friendship'.[21] Had it not been for the willingness of Foreign Minister Vergennes to seek better relations with Britain, it is unlikely that the treaty would have been signed, let alone negotiated within two months. Pitt was startled.[22] When he told the Commons that France was not to be considered a natural enemy of Britain, this was an international public relations statement, not an article of personal faith. Pitt believed that Anglo-French hostility could never be eliminated entirely. His 'free trade' pacts, devised to defend the established market position of British merchants on the Continent, did not herald a new era of *laissez-faire* international relations. The commercial treaties consolidated an already favourable British balance of trade; as such, they did not justify Carmarthen's accusations that national interest had been overruled by political economy.[23] Pitt shared Shelburne's interest in the new diplomacy of the Enlightenment and wished to improve Britain's international image during the 1780s by recourse to it. This policy, and the Eden Treaty in particular, has been denounced by Jeremy Black as a risky, idealistic and potentially disastrous venture for Pitt. Whether a coincidence of idealism and good luck makes for bad statesmanship is a moot point;[24] while the 1786 treaty did not change the direction of Britain's foreign policy, its swift and amicable negotiation made a great impression on Pitt, who, convinced that 'Enlightenment diplomacy' was effective, tried to launch a Europe-wide initiative to end the slave trade between 1787 and 1789.

After the failure of the 1784–5 Austrian alliance venture, Carmarthen moved to contest the growth of French influence in the United Provinces, a trend which the British government had encouraged by its support of Austria's claims in the Scheldt. A Franco-Dutch alliance had been signed on 8 November 1785 and, worse still, the French government was actively supporting the Dutch Patriot Party, a body of 'pure' republicans intent on removing the hereditary Stadtholder of Holland, the Prince of Orange, from his post as governor of the United Provinces. Harris, though no admirer of William V, was determined to prevent the United Provinces from becoming a French satellite. His recommendation since taking up his post had been that the British government should subsidize the 'loyal' Orange Party and mobilize public opinion against the ratification of the French treaty.[25] Here he and Carmarthen were faced once more by Pitt's lack of interest. The Foreign Secretary, prodded by an alarmed Harris, tried to awaken Pitt to the parlous state of the United Provinces, but met with no success. In October 1785 Pitt remarked that Dutch affairs 'seem in truth too mysterious to form any conjecture'. On 6 December Pitt finally authorized the grant of a Secret Service allowance to Harris for his pet project, but this was not enough for the ambassador or the Foreign Secretary.[26]

In December 1786, upon Carmarthen's advice, Harris wrote to Pitt with details of Patriot preparations for a French-backed *coup d'état*. This was alarming enough to get Pitt's attention. Having successfully roused the premier to a state of genuine concern, Harris was urged to '*keep it up*, and not allow Holland to be sacrificed to lawn and cambric'.[27] Carmarthen had been angered by the signature of the 1786 Anglo-French trade convention without reference to British interests in Europe and overseas.[28] Pitt, however, had not turned a blind eye to French designs on the United Provinces and, through Eden, had a private source of information about French politics and policy. This partially explains Carmarthen's intense dislike of Eden, who always saw himself as responsible to Pitt first, as did all the commercial envoys employed during the 1780s.[29] Eden pandered to Pitt's personal tastes, sending him French financial and political pamphlets in addition to draft treaties and political gossip. These predisposed Pitt to think that France was in no position to support a Patriot rising in the United Provinces, an analysis with which Carmarthen agreed; the first meeting of the Assembly of Notables, he claimed, was security for the short-term good conduct of France.[30]

In mid-May Harris was recalled to London. On 23 May 1787 he asked the Cabinet to fund the Dutch legitimists. Pitt displayed no enthusiasm for an armed confrontation with France in support of the Orangists, to which the British government might be forced by a French mobilization in favour of the Patriots. Britain, claimed Pitt, could contest France through trade, not arms. Over dinner with Harris on 24 May, Pitt was brought to agree that financial support of the Orange Party, if not armament, was acceptable. On 26 May 1787 the Cabinet voted to give £70,000 to Harris. Pitt and Carmarthen lobbied the king for the money from the Civil List: 'The circumstances of the French finance make it highly improbable that they should embark on hostile operations; and unless they should march an army to the support of Holland, there seems at least an equal chance of a favourable issue to the present contest.'[31] George III, unwilling to be drawn into confrontation with France, nevertheless gave his consent. As Pitt pointed out, Britain was by no means committed to hostilities. This, indeed, was what he was dreading and explains his reluctance to move against France over the summer of 1787. When the Patriots kidnapped Wilhelmina, Princess of Orange, on 28 June, the British government encouraged her brother, Frederick William II of Prussia, to intervene, but did nothing to commit itself and would continue to do nothing until the sentiments of the other powers, Austria in particular, were known.[32] The British government was not going to send military assistance to the United Provinces without support from at least one other major power.

Harris had maintained since May that France would not go to war for the Patriots. Despite these assurances, every rumour of French military action was greeted with consternation by Pitt, who spent the summer of 1787 in a state of nervous anxiety. The Dutch crisis of 1787 was resolved by the armed intervention of Prussia, not the diplomacy of Britain. Pitt sought to avoid war by negotiation on two occasions. On 27 July Britain and France agreed to disarm the half-dozen or so ships that both had mobilized. Pitt, banking on French political instability and financial disarray, sought confirmation of both from Charles de Calonne, the ex-Comptroller General of France, in September.[33] When fresh rumours of French mobilization in support of the Patriots reached London, Pitt sent Grenville to Paris on 21 September to broach the subject of joint disarmament: 'We have adopted this measure as furnishing the best prospect of avoiding extremities.'[34] Pitt was intent on thwarting the plans of France without jeopardizing the uneasy post-war accord between France and Britain.

> It will certainly be our interest and our Wish to bring about such a Settlement with as little appearance as possible of mortifying the feelings of the French Government; and we should be ready to concede whatever points we can (without giving up the substance) in order to satisfy their friends in Holland, and save to a certain degree their honour.

Having already learned from Grenville, who had been sent to the United Provinces in July to report on the Orange Party's prospects of success, that the Patriots were in disarray, Pitt could afford to salve the wounded feelings of the French government.[35] This was in marked contrast to the trenchant diplomacy advocated by Harris and Carmarthen and suggests not that Pitt exercised indecisive leadership during the Dutch crisis of 1787, but that he had not yielded to the pursuit of the anti-French policies advocated by Carmarthen and Harris.[36] By 4 October France had given up all pretence of support for the Patriots of the United Provinces and, on 26 October, both nations agreed to disarm.[37] France, humiliated by the showdown, was to withdraw by degrees from the theatre of continental diplomacy over the next two years. Britain, on the other hand, was now set to re-enter Europe.

The Triple Alliance, 1788–1789

The Triple Alliance of 1788, the series of mutual defence treaties binding England, Prussia and the United Provinces, was a partial realization of Carmarthen's dream. Pitt's interest in the project arose from the urgency of issues raised by the Dutch crisis of 1787.[38] Mutual interests in the United Provinces had drawn England and Prussia closer together over the summer of 1787 though this had not been a product of Pitt's diplomacy alone. Frederick William II, who had just succeeded his uncle Frederick II as King of Prussia, was interested in improving relations with Britain and had seen co-operation in the United Provinces as a possible route.[39] On 8 October Pitt discovered, through Grenville, that France was trying to rouse Russia and Austria against Britain and Prussia.[40] Internally divided though France might be, its diplomatic network was still largely intact and the Pitt ministry feared that this call upon the friends of France was a preliminary to more overt attacks upon Britain. Such apprehensions were confirmed a few days later by the news that a French expeditionary force was preparing to set out for the East Indies. No less than ten expeditions were to be sent to India and its environs from 1785 and 1789, which ensured that the British government's fear of French power in the Indian Ocean remained strong up to 1790.

France, though clearly reluctant to go to war for the Dutch Patriots, could intimidate Britain where it was most vulnerable. The British government was always worried about the security of communication links with its overseas possessions and Pitt had therefore been considering the merits of an Anglo-Dutch East India pact since 1785.[41] The Dutch East Indian empire was perceived in London to be weak and British officials were haunted by the fear that France, having undermined the first British empire in the west, would turn its attention to the east. The Pitt ministry, believing that the Dutch shared its concern about France in the East Indies, was intent on reinforcing its hold on India against the anticipated French attack.[42] On 2 August Pitt had warned Lord Cornwallis, Governor-General of Madras, that any war with France as a result of the Dutch crisis would be global: 'I trust the effects of your Administration have already been such that we have nothing to fear for those Possessions in the Event of a War.'[43] On 13 October orders were issued to assemble British ships and men for both East and West Indies. Pitt was now eager to open alliance talks with the United Provinces 'and eventually with Prussia'.[44] The Anglo-Dutch

East India treaty that was to lead to a fully fledged mutual defence pact had now become a vital priority.

Britain signed the Triple Alliance to safeguard its hard-won influence in the United Provinces and protect itself from French attack in Europe and the colonies.[45] Fears of hostile French action in India were still prevalent in January 1788, so much so that Harris, engaged in nego-tiating the Anglo-Dutch arm of what was to become the Triple Alliance, urged Carmarthen to accept and ratify the defence treaty without waiting for its East Indian counterpart.[46] At the same time, the French government called for a joint Anglo-French guarantee of the Dutch republican constitution and invited the Pitt ministry to participate in mutual arms reduction talks. This appeal, arriving two months after French denials of involvement in the Dutch Patriot rising, disgusted Pitt and Carmarthen by its seeming hypocrisy. Pitt was interested in an East Indian agreement and went so far as to propose the grant of Mauritius to France, but replied disparagingly on the subject of a wider alliance: 'I have great doubts whether the idea of an engagement and concert between the two countries, in view of securing the general tranquillity in the extent to which you seem to state it, can ever be attempted with any hope of success.'[47] On mutual defence, Carmarthen stated that no settlement could be reached unless 'something were settled about India'.[48]

The British government's unwillingness to discount the military resources of France and the guile of its diplomats produced a six-month delay in the negotiation of the Prussian alliance treaty. French attempts to coalesce with the imperial powers were renewed in 1788 and, whilst Pitt and Carmarthen thought it unlikely that Austria and Russia would join a quadruple alliance with France and Spain, neither man wanted to antagonize France or its allies without good cause. Austria and Russia had gone to war in August 1787 with the Ottoman Porte, yet another old ally of the French Bourbons. This, stated Pitt with satisfaction, was 'very embarrassing' for a France powerless to interfere. With imperial sights fixed firmly on the Crimea, the Balkans and Asia Minor, it was unlikely that Russia or Austria would join a French-sponsored quadruple alliance with western interests.[49] British anxiety about the strength of France's connections with Russia and Austria drew the attention of the Pitt ministry to the east, where Prussia was looking like a far from ideal ally. Seizing upon this sudden display of British interest in eastern Europe, the Prussian government proposed the submission of a joint Anglo-Prussian mediation offer to Russia and the Porte.

Carmarthen, wary of commitment in a region where British policy was ill-defined, was nevertheless longing to entice Austria, Russia or both into alliance with Britain. Pitt preferred to keep Prussia at arm's length and had cooled towards Russia. From 1784 to 1786 Pitt had looked favourably upon the forging of Baltic links with England, a union made attractive by the prospect of trade talks with the northern powers.[50] In 1786 Britain had failed to renegotiate its 1756 trade treaty with Russia and by July 1788 Sweden was allied to a Turkey at war with Russia. Pitt now had no desire to get embroiled in northern politics. In December 1787 Sweden had submitted plans for the formation of a quadruple alliance to the British government. This would have involved Sweden, Prussia, the United Provinces and Britain. Carmarthen was ecstatic; when he demanded that Russia be admitted to the system, the Swedish government was not.[51]

Britain and Prussia began to discuss alliance terms in December 1787. The dispatches sent home from Berlin by Joseph Ewart revealed that the two states had little in common. Prussia looked for Britain's diplomatic support in its eastern quarrels, while Britain sought Prussian military assistance to forestall French threats to the United Provinces and Austrian Netherlands, not to mention the East and West Indies.[52] Ewart warned his superiors in London that Frederick William II's interest in the eastern war between Russia and the Porte was nothing more than a determination to weaken the Austrian empire and, more specifically, to wrest Galicia from the emperor's grasp. This was the pet project of Frederick William's favourite, Ewald von Hertzberg, and involved the grant of Turkish lands to Austria, the cession of Galicia to Poland and the gift of Thorn, Dantzig and Great Poland to Prussia. Neither Pitt nor Carmarthen liked the Hertzberg project, but both realized that, were Ottoman territory to be ceded to either imperial power as an outcome of the eastern war, Prussia was not likely to rest until it had received its due.[53] In May 1788 the British government admitted, in the name of Anglo-Prussian harmony, that any peace settlement involving Turkish concessions to Austria and Russia 'should, if possible, be counterbalanced by a proper equivalent to the King of Prussia'.[54] The Porte might be reconciled to this arrangement by an Anglo-Prussian guarantee for its remaining lands and future membership in Carmarthen's grand alliance. 'I am not afraid of France', he wrote to Harris, 'but shall be happy to have our Connections well secured with other Powers, if only for the purpose of *strutting* about Europe with an Air of Consideration unknown to us for some time.'[55]

This bravado was hollow. When it was rumoured that Prussia, in addition to Russia, was contemplating alliance with France, Harris was sent to the King of Prussia by an alarmed Cabinet. On 13 June he signed a provisional treaty with Frederick William II.[56] France was powerless to respond, but the British government was intent on isolating it from all potential sources of support. It was at this point that Pitt became interested in a wider alliance network. Any lingering hopes of a Baltic addition to the Triple Alliance disappeared in July 1788, when Gustavus III declared war on Russia. Although Russia was now fighting on two fronts, no British diplomat saw the northern war as an equal contest. In early August, following a series of military and naval defeats, the Swedish government asked Prussia to act as a mediator in its peace talks with Russia. On 28 August the Danes offered to join their good offices to those of Prussia and Britain. Carmarthen was delighted: 'The Consequence of so friendly an Interference would naturally be a grate-full and lasting Impression of the Obligations Sweden must in such Circumstances owe to those Powers which had saved her from Des-truction.'[57] Following the cessation of hostilities, he declared, Sweden could be brought into the Triple Alliance and thus prevented from 'returning to her former System of Dependence on France'. Carmar-then was not expecting any interference or protest to come from a distracted France, but Pitt, who preferred to be cautious, recommended that both Bourbon courts be invited to join the mediation. On 29 August the British government received the news that Necker had replaced Lomenie de Brienne, Archbishop of Toulouse, as chief min-ister of France. Pitt, who thought Brienne incompetent, expected that the popular Necker, for whose abilities he had a high regard, would introduce a programme of reforms that would leave France in a strong position to retaliate against Britain: 'I think we may expect from Nec-ker's character that he will set himself in earnest to put their finances in real order, if the thing is possible; and will probably be glad to avail himself of the necessity of a free constitution.'[58] Pitt's response to Necker's appointment was mixed. Although France stood, under his leadership, to become a more formidable opponent of Britain, Pitt also thought that *ancien régime* France was long overdue for constitutional reform. From this perspective, Necker's appointment was 'probably the best thing that could happen for that country'.[59] It would also improve 'our chance for settling something about the slave trade'.

Grenville, fast becoming a confidant of Pitt, did not share his cousin's apprehensions about a possible revival of French militancy. Necker's reliance on public support, claimed Grenville, made it imperative for France to avoid unpopular wars. With these speculations Pitt tended to agree.[60] The parameters of French politics were changing and the British government, drawing on experience, could predict some of the revolution's developments. By bypassing established constitutional pro-cedures – namely the placement of new legislation before the *parlements* for registration – and the attempt to give legitimacy to reform proposals via the approval of extraordinary representative bodies – the two Assemblies of Notables – the French crown was inviting the public to comment not only on the measures themselves, but on the institutions and practices of the *ancien régime*. On 1 September 1788 Richmond predicted that Louis XVI would be forced to call a meeting of the Estates General.[61]

On 5 September the British government learned that the Estates General was indeed to meet for the first time since 1614. No British Cabinet minister now expected France to display any diplomatic initiative: 'The state of France, whatever it may produce, seems to promise more than ever a considerable respite from any dangerous projects, and there seems scarce anything to regret on our own account in the condition of foreign countries, except the danger that the King of Sweden may suffer too severely for his kindness.'[62] Pitt could now concentrate on the Baltic mediation and the prevention of Sweden from 'becoming totally Insignificant or dependent upon Russia'. This struck him as 'an essential Point'.[63] On 30 August Ewart had sent Carmarthen particulars of a Prussian peace package based on the status quo *ante bellum* in the Baltic. These proposals, endorsed by the British government, were presented at all the northern courts for approval. Denmark, which found them unsatisfactory, invaded Sweden in October, after which the Prussian government sent 15,000 troops to its western borders and called for a naval squadron from Britain. The Pitt ministry, which made enquiries about Hanoverian soldiers for Prussia, refused to send a fleet to the Baltic.[64] Little could be done for Prussia, because George III was opposed to a British armament. Pitt, inspired by the success of intimidatory tactics against France in 1787, saw little to fear from Sweden and Russia, which he classed as a pair of third-rate naval powers: 'There seems in the present situation of France great reason to expect that an object very important in itself may be secured with very little inconvenience or hazard.' Britain, he stated, was responsible for preserving 'the Balance of Power in the North'.[65] George III, suffering from the initial symptoms of a porphyria attack, was in a state of mental depression and did not relish the prospect of war. The king advised Pitt to rely on diplomatic pressure alone. France and Spain, when asked by the British government, had declared themselves in favour of Sweden, but were unwilling to commit themselves further.[66]

At the beginning of November Prussia asked once more for British naval succour, but, by that date, George III was seriously ill and the foreign policy of his government was in limbo. No fresh instructions could be sent to British diplomats abroad pending the resolution of constitutional debates at home about the true seat of executive authority. This was a state of affairs that lasted until the king's recovery in February 1789 and Pitt, embroiled in parliamentary battles to save some dignity for an ailing monarch, had little time for foreign affairs. Carmarthen's frustration with the impotence of the British government was apparent in his private and official correspondence, as was the habitual paranoia that Britain's paralysis only enhanced.[67]

Eden, now stationed in Spain, reported in January 1789 that France had resurrected the quadruple alliance project with the imperial powers. The moment that George III recovered the use of his faculties an alarmed Carmarthen asked Eden to sound out the Spanish government on the subject of an alliance with England. Eden registered strong objections: 'I do not conceive that it would be possible for Us, under any Events, to form a regular and avowed system of Alliance with this Country – Religious Prejudices and general Bigotry maintained here by the Influence of Princes at the height, would prevent such an Alliance even if the Family Compact was out of the way.'[68] He thought, however, that an improvement in Anglo-Spanish relations would 'prevent the weight of Spain from being thrown into an Adverse Scale'. Balance of power, as a geopolitical concept, operated at several levels in British foreign policy. It imposed an artificial order upon the network of rivalries that dominated international relations; it was in this context that the term was most frequently used by diplomats, officials and ministers.[69] As a guiding principle for action, it was dangerous. The recognition of an imbalance between two or more powers did not dictate that the British government or its servants should move to assert a correcting influence, still less to defend the rights of the state or states seen to be placed at a disadvantage by the actions or intrigues of any power.

Pitt, who saw an equilibrium in power between the major participants in European politics as an ideal, was nevertheless too wary during the 1780s to accept the responsibility for maintaining it if, by doing so, Britain's present or future freedom of action was compromised. A balance was therefore to be maintained with as little effort as possible. Carmarthen, though also sensitive to the dangers of entanglement in, and consequent commitment to, the affairs of states in distant parts of Europe, was intent on exercising the international influence which he thought was his nation's due.

From 1788 to 1791 the British government saw France as a state that was fast losing its status as a great power in Europe. British diplomats told each other with glee that French influence was on the wane all over Europe. On 17 April 1789 Carmarthen dropped the Spanish alliance upon learning from Eden that Madrid, while sympathetic to the plight of the French Bourbons, was not prepared to go to war for the counter-revolution.[70] The courts of Spain and Austria were seen in London as barometers of French intrigue and influence in Europe; as nobody could foresee the downfall of the *ancien régime*, a wary eye was to be kept on both governments up to 1792. Austria, preoccupied with the Turkish war and its own financial problems, was seemingly unconcerned by events in France during the early months of 1789.

Throughout the Regency crisis Carmarthen had entertained grave misgivings about Prussia's management of the Baltic situation. Anglo-Prussian mediation in the northern war had been accepted by Russia in January 1789. The earlier proposal relating to the eastern conflict was turned down. Gustavus III, however, refused to make peace without his Ottoman ally. Carmarthen, confronted by this deadlock, hoped that the Porte would sue for peace on its own. Receipt of Prussia's peace proposals for both theatres dampened British spirits even further. In the north the Prussians still wanted a British fleet to intimidate the Danes in addition to the establishment of an Anglo-Prussian peace lobby in Stockholm to argue the merits of a status quo peace. In the east the Prussian government intended to stiffen the resolve of the Turks against any peace not presided over by Britain and Prussia. Any Austrian attempt to annex Turkish lands was to be met with the threat of Anglo-Prussian armament.[71]

Carmarthen withheld his comments because Denmark, now a target for possible recruitment to the Triple Alliance, was best approached through Prussia. Pitt and Carmarthen were now actively pursuing the Baltic system first mooted in 1784. Despite Frederick William II's determination to cow Denmark into neutrality, the Prussian government was eager to welcome it into the alliance. When Denmark disarmed at the beginning of June 1789, the Pitt ministry finally ventured a few remarks on the Prussian peace terms. The objectives of Britain's ally, Carmarthen stated wryly, seemed to be the expulsion of Austria from Galicia, the limitation of Austrian gains at the expense of the Porte and the acquisition of Polish lands for the Prussian Crown. These, thought Carmarthen, were not acceptable: 'The operations ... go so much beyond the Spirit of our Treaty of Alliance, which is purely of a defensive Nature, and by which, of Course, we cannot be bound to support a System of An Offensive Nature, the great End of which appears to be Aggrandisement rather than Security.'[72] The Prussian proposals, noted Carmarthen, were unlikely to detach Russia from Austria and, from thence, into union with Prussia and England. The June dispatches appear to have been composed by Carmarthen rather than Pitt, who doubtless saw them before they left the Foreign Office, but made no recorded contribution to their contents. He would have stressed the importance of security as the principal objective of Austro-Prussian joint action in the east but the preoccupation with new alliances is characteristic of the Foreign Secretary. Pitt took no personal interest in eastern affairs until 1790. Carmarthen's dispatch of 24 June 1789 was poorly received in Berlin. British attempts to separate the Baltic war from its Ottoman counterpart were resisted by a Prussian government which protested that Britain had both recognized Prussia's right to indemnification as an outcome of the mediation, if not necessarily in Poland, and agreed that the fates of northern and eastern Europe were connected. 'We certainly consider it as more desirable, if possible,' replied Carmarthen, 'to effect a General rather than a Separate Peace.' The two theatres were, nonetheless, to be treated separately 'with a View to any other Measures than those of negotiations'.[73]

After twelve months of alliance with Prussia, the Pitt ministry found itself partnered with a militant and expansionist ally intent on dragging Britain into eastern European politics. This was the last thing Pitt had wanted; Carmarthen was more upset about the exploitation of Britain for Prussian ends.[74] As Jeremy Black has pointed out, Britain operated at a disadvantage in Europe during the 1780s because it was a satiated and conservative power with no territorial ambitions on the Continent.[75] Security systems, as defined by the British, explicitly forbade major alterations to the territorial status quo, be it *post* or *ante bellum*. This was deeply frustrating to a Prussian ally always seeking the best return from its partners. Britain, already disillusioned with Prussia, was to become even more so by the end of 1789.

France in Revolution

France had not played its usual demonic role in British assessments of Europe since March 1789, when the Bourbon–imperial quadruple alliance project had once more reared its head. British apprehensions on this front related to the infrastructure and mechanisms of French diplomacy rather than French foreign policy *per se*. The British government was never to be a wholehearted supporter of the *ancien régime* Bourbon restoration because the existence of a Bourbon family with cadet branches throughout southern Europe meant that France possessed a ready-made alliance system to lead and exploit. As the French Crown declined in strength from 1787 onwards, France was to become increasingly marginalized in British foreign policy.

Bread prices rose in Paris throughout the spring and early summer of 1789 and political tensions followed suit. On 25 June Necker made a personal appeal to Pitt for supplies of British corn. The two had met in 1783, when Pitt made his one visit to France, and both had been impressed with each other – Necker so much so that he had offered Pitt his daughter's hand in marriage. The British government suspected that a request for grain was coming for England too was subject to grain price rises in 1789.[76] Under the Corn Laws, wheat was barred from export until domestic prices dropped to stipulated levels. Necker, hoping that Pitt's *laissez-faire* principles would prevail, was asking him to overrule these restrictions.

Pitt, who gave the matter some consideration, approached the Board of Trade for data on English corn stocks. According to the board, in consultation with London corn factors, native stores of wheat were low.[77] By October 1789 British merchants would be scouring the Continent in search of surplus wheat. The bad French harvests of the 1780s were shared by other European states and the board's ruling against exportation was sensible. Wilberforce, who hoped to reverse the board's decision and send grain to France as a humanitarian gesture, raised the question in the House of Commons on George Rose's advice. The House voted on 9 July to uphold the board's decision. On 16 July 'The news came of Necker's being out, and of insurrections, firings etc.'[78] The French Revolution had 'begun': 'Our neighbours in France seem coming to actual extremes, the King having suddenly dismissed M. Necker and appearing to support his [Louis XVI's] authority against the National Assembly. This scene, added to the prevailing scarcity, make that country an object of compassion, even to a rival.'[79] As France was bound to be inactive on the international scene for some time to come, compassion was a luxury that Pitt could afford. He was nevertheless disappointed to find that the consultative process between Crown and Assembly had broken down and that royal authority had been reasserted.

The French government, faced by domestic anarchy and foreign impotence, soon began to blame Britain for all its problems.[80] Despite Pitt's best efforts to reassure the French that his refusal of Necker's request was not the product of malice aforethought, Gallic politicians remained convinced that 'Pitt's gold' was employed in the subversion of revolutionary politics.[81] On 27 July 1789 Britain's ambassador, the Duke of Dorset, was accused of fomenting disorder in Paris, an insinuation which Dorset and Leeds promptly denied. Leeds, concerned about the safety of British tourists in France, warned the embassy that it should inform visitors that indiscreet statements and action might place their lives and the credit of the British government in danger.[82] This represented the British government's first official declaration of neutrality towards the French Revolution. Britain was to remain neutral until the outbreak of war with France in February 1793.

The Leeds statement was no reflex action. In September 1791, subsequent to the release of the Pillnitz Declaration by Austria and Prussia, Lord Grenville remarked that careful thought had gone into the ministry's original neutrality declaration.[83] In July 1789 the British government expected Bourbon authority to be restored in France. A defence of the *ancien régime* was out of the question but support, either overt or covert, for constitutional change in France was bound to provoke future Bourbon retaliation. As for the French critics of the old order, already split into several camps by 1789 and quarrelling amongst themselves, the odds for survival, let alone success, were poor. The Pitt ministry saw no need for interference in the Constituent Assembly, for France had already been rendered impotent by its own politicians. In Britain, so often on the receiving end of French-backed rebellions in Ireland, Scotland and America during the past century, the sponsorship of political dissidents was also regarded with great distaste. In 1789 Pitt felt that a noncommittal stand on the revolution was the best way of keeping the peace in Europe. Sensitive British projects were afoot in the east and he wanted no complications to arise from independent developments in the west.

British caution soon bore fruit. In August 1789 the Spanish government made a tentative attempt to reopen the trade talks suspended the previous year. As France grew weaker, an isolated Spain sought to forge ties to Britain, the nation with whose trade and colonial concerns it identified most.[84] The distinction between a community and conflict of interests was slender and the Pitt ministry soon learned that Spanish enthusiasm for an English connection was inversely proportional to the strength of the 'pure' royalist party in Paris. When the Austrian Netherlands burst into revolt in July 1789, the insurrection was not blamed on the French Revolution.[85] It was suspected that the Belgian rebels had received some encouragement from Paris but French attempts to stir up trouble in the Low Countries were nothing new. The Flemish revolt moreover was led not by democrats, but by the clergy and aristocracy of Flanders, Brabant and Hainault in protest against Joseph II's 'enlightened despotism', the abolition of provincial privileges and proposals to reform the Church. As Pitt noted on 28 August, a weak and independent Netherlands was a prelude to a French Netherlands. The French government was, however, ill-placed to give any effective aid to the Belgian rebels. On 10 September Pitt wrote that 'everything seems to be going on very well for Us at Home and Abroad'.[86]

Habsburg outrage at the treatment of the French royal family, already in evidence, was regarded in London as a positive development separating Austria from the new France, which would not be asked to help Joseph II restore order in the Netherlands. On 26 September 1789 the National Assembly refused to recognize the independence of the Netherlands; revolutionary France had, as yet, no desire for war with Austria. The motives of *ancien régime* France were more devious and British diplomats could not be too smug about the supposedly poor state of Franco-Austrian relations. Upon discovering from Keith that the Comte de Noailles, the French ambassador in Vienna, was trying to dissuade the emperor from sending troops to the Netherlands, Pitt and Leeds were alerted to the possible existence of an independent royalist foreign policy.[87]

When the Duc d'Orléans, Louis XVI's first cousin and a supporter of the French Revolution, appeared in London in October to question

British intentions *vis-à-vis* the Netherlands, the Pitt ministry was confronted with a French Bourbon seeking to undermine Habsburg authority in Brabant.[88] Upon enquiry, the French Foreign Ministry categorically denied that Orléans was an accredited diplomat with an official brief. Philippe Égalité was sent back to Paris, having been told that Britain would support whatever policy the Austrian government saw fit to implement in its rebellious provinces.[89] Matters were complicated in December 1789 when the Comte d'Artois, Louis XVI's second younger brother, appeared in London to ask for support for the restoration of the *ancien régime* monarchy, in the pursuit of which the Bourbons were prepared to grant colonial concessions to Britain. George III, though unwilling to commit Britain to any declaration in favour of the counter-revolution, told Pitt in March 1790 that there would be no harm in assuring Artois that Britain 'would not prevent the French constitution from being re-established on terms conformable to the sentiments of the Comte d'Artois'.[90] Pitt, that advocate of a 'free constitution' for France, did not entirely agree.

Orléans had also been misled as to British plans for the Netherlands. Pitt and Leeds, who did not want the emperor's position in western Europe to be strengthened, called for the establishment of qualified rule. Here the British government was worried about arms and commerce. Britain's balance of trade with the Netherlands was impressive, only surpassed by its credit with Germany and the United Provinces.[91] Despotism without a leavening of local tolerance, averred Pitt and Leeds, would inflame the inhabitants of the Netherlands against Austria and predispose them towards a union with France.[92] Emissaries of the French Revolution were seemingly pushing the Netherlands in this direction. Independence of any description was not acceptable[93] because it would only hasten the process of alignment with, and eventual absorption by, France. Habsburg absolutism would, however, render the Netherlands a threat to Britain and the United Provinces if Joseph II were to pursue hostile military or economic policies in the west. Constitutional autocracy was therefore the answer:

> The main object which the allies ought to pursue appears to be the preventing the Result of the present troubles in the Netherlands from raising up in that Quarter a Power formidable to our System, which might arise to the Emperor, supposing that Prince to succeed in overturning the Constitution, or to France, in case the Independence of those Provinces was established in any mode, which should connect them with that Kingdom.[94]

The government of the United Provinces, a passive member of the Triple Alliance in Europe, if not the East Indies, was content to follow

Britain's lead. Frederick William II, eager for an opportunity to humiliate Austria, was not. Prussia not only sought to arm in support of
the Belgian insurgents, but tried to make Triple Alliance approval for
the re-establishment of Habsburg power in the Netherlands conditional
upon the cession of Galicia to Prussia.[95] The Pitt ministry was horrified.
The Belgian question, Leeds wrote tartly on 14 December, was 'perfectly distinct from any other'.[96] The Prussian government, exasperated
by Britain's attitude towards Austria, was beginning to lose heart for
the Triple Alliance. Britain and the United Provinces finally persuaded
a reluctant Prussia to support a restoration of Austrian rule in the
Netherlands at the Hague Convention of 10 December 1790.

By the end of 1789 the Pitt ministry, though provided with fresh
evidence of Prussia's shortcomings as an ally, found little to complain
of in Europe. Austria and Russia were still at war with the Ottoman
Porte, in whose direction British eyes would turn now that France had
been neutralized by the revolution. From 1789 onwards Pitt moved
with far more confidence to exploit the power vacuum in the international arena that the withdrawal of France had created. Pitt had not
been controlling all aspects of Britain's foreign policy in Europe from
1784 to 1787, but he was effective in modifying and blocking Leeds's
initiatives when he found them too aggressive. From 1784 to 1786 Pitt
was far less interested in conventional diplomacy than in its enlightenment counterpart, if only because Britain was in no position to act
decisively in international politics. When Pitt took the helm at the
Foreign Office in 1787, he showed no great enthusiasm for trenchant
diplomacy because it called for decisive action on the basis of information which he regarded as inadequate. Pitt did not like to make
educated guesses without comprehensive data at his disposal; he used
personal agents like Eden and Grenville to collect that material because
he was alarmed by Leeds's confrontational foreign policy. Pitt found
political – as opposed to commercial – diplomacy deeply frustrating at
times. As Pitt became better informed about foreign affairs, Leeds
found himself marginalized.[97]

   In 1787 Pitt asked Eden to give him detailed particulars of the French
finances. It was on these estimates that he judged whether or not the
French government was serious in its professions of 'a sincere disposition to peace': 'I should be very glad ... to learn for how many years
their loans are to be repeated, what Taxes are fixed upon, and whether
the Reforms really go on. I also wish to know on what grounds of
Calculation the Annual Income and Expense is stated, whether on the
last year, or any part Average or future Estimate.'[98] A literal 'counting-
house spirit', as Edmund Burke was to call it during the 1790s, was
already in evidence. Because France possessed formidable military,

diplomatic and economic resources that might well be regenerated by public credit, Pitt was reluctant to dismiss France from the ranks of the great powers up to 1791. Burke's political economy of the French Revolution was metaphysical. Commerce was dependent on feudal manners and public credit had destroyed the chivalric order.[99] In 1789 the French Revolution was regarded in London as a temporary if major dislocation in French politics. The Pitt Cabinet could predict several possible outcomes to the revolution but none involved the ruin and reconstruction of the French state. The neutrality declaration of July 1789 was a direct reflection of British uncertainty about the future of France. So unwilling was the ministry to have anything to do with the revolution that the Paris embassy, the jewel in the Foreign Office crown of diplomatic postings, was downgraded in 1789 to what has been called a 'listening post'. As an ambassador, the indolent and cricket-loving Duke of Dorset had been no prize. In 1790 he was replaced by Earl Gower, a 34-year-old government MP with no record of foreign service.[100]

The British government's reluctance to deal with France in 1789 did not stem from any fear of the revolution. The rhetoric of French revolutionaries was not regarded as an intellectual or social threat in its own right. Identification as such awaited the publication of Edmund Burke's *Reflections on the Revolution in France* in 1790. The diplomatic uses to which subversive ideas might be put abroad had been made explicit by the American War of Independence. To Pitt, who had known the Bourbon Treasury to be embarrassed since 1781, subversion in the United Provinces in 1787 was a form of French warfare on the cheap. The call for Anglo-French arms limitation talks in December 1787 only confirmed this analysis: 'With respect to Holland, I think we have scotched the snake, not killed it', wrote Carmarthen. When Dorset was accused of subversion in Paris, the new Duke of Leeds was not surprised: 'The French find, I suspect, or at least wish to have it supposed that we have done to them what they would have done to us in similar Circumstances.'[101] Diplomacy was war by other means.

As France lost power and status in Europe over the 1780s, it was perceived in Britain as relying increasingly upon secret diplomacy for the assertion of influence. This lay at the roots of British apprehension respecting the French quadruple alliance project of 1787–8 and the care with which the diplomatic conduct of Spain and Austria was monitored by British diplomats throughout the later 1780s. The events of late 1789 suggested that there were at least three French foreign policies operating in western Europe. The National Assembly did not wish to antagonize Austria and was, as a corporate body, neutral to the Netherlands rising. The Orléanists were supporting the *révolutions de Brabant*. Spanish trade flirtations with Britain during the summer of

1789 indicated that the Family Compact, though weakening, was still operative. To make matters worse, there was no wholesale recall of French diplomats in 1789 and, as ministers and political factions rose and fell in Paris, it became increasingly difficult for the British government to ascertain whether French ambassadors and envoys accredited to the Court of Versailles were true representatives of His Most Christian Majesty and what value was to be given to such credentials. Under such circumstances, neutrality was the safest course of action for a British government determined to preserve its freedom of action in Europe.

Notes

1. J. Black, *Natural and Necessary Enemies: Anglo-French Relations in the Eighteenth Century* (1986), pp. 100–3, and *A System of Ambition? British Foreign Policy 1660–1793* (Harlow: 1991), pp. 223–4.

2. P. Stanhope (ed.), *Correspondence between The Right Honourable William Pitt and Charles, Duke of Rutland* (1842), Pitt to Rutland, August 1785, pp. 110–11.

3. J. Black, 'The Marquis of Carmarthen and relations with France, 1784–1787', *Francia* 12 (1984), p. 302.

4. T. C. W. Blanning, *The Origins of the French Revolutionary Wars* (1986), p. 48; J. Black, *British Foreign Policy in an Age of Revolutions, 1783–1793* (Cambridge: 1994), pp. 54–6; M. Duffy, 'Pitt, Grenville and the conduct of British foreign policy', in Black (ed.), *Knights Errant and True Englishmen: British Foreign Policy, 1660–1800* (Edinburgh: 1989), pp. 154–6.

5. J. Ehrman, *The Years of Acclaim* (1969), pp. 186, 537; BL Add MS 28064, Leeds to Pitt, 27 July 1789, fo. 180; I. R. Christie, 'Lord Grantham and William Pitt, 12 December 1783', *HJ* 34 (1991), pp. 144–5. Thurlow's inertia, though distasteful to Pitt, was not always a liability and Richmond prodded the Prime Minister to take an interest in the United Provinces.

6. Black, 'The Marquis of Carmarthen', p. 289, and *British Foreign Policy ... 1783–1793*, p. 21.

7. This project had been partially thwarted by Prussia during the 1778–9 War of the Bavarian Succession. The 1779 Peace of Teschen gave Austria the province of Innvertiel in south-east Bavaria, but this was not enough for Joseph II: O. Browning (ed.), *Despatches from Paris, 1784–1790* (2 vols, 1909–10), i, Dorset to Carmarthen, 17 February 1785, p. 42.

8. BL Egerton 3498, Carmarthen to Pitt, 9 June 1784, fos 36–7; *Pol. Mem.*, Account of a conversation with Pitt, May 1784, p. 101; BL Add MS 28059, Leeds Memo, 11 June 1784, fos 40–1.

9. *Pol. Mem.*, p. 101.

10. BL Egerton 3498, Pitt to Carmarthen, 24 June 1784, fo. 40.

11. Black, *British Foreign Policy ... 1783–1793*, pp. 73–4; BL Egerton 3498, Carmarthen to Pitt, 28 September 1784.

12. T. C. W. Blanning, '"That horrid electorate" or "ma patrie germanique": George III and the Fürstenbund in 1785', *HJ* 20 (1977), p. 320.

13. *PR*, xxxiv, Grenville to Chauvelin, 31 December 1792.

14. Blanning, '"That horrid electorate"', p. 316; BL Add MS 28059, Leeds Memo on state of Europe, 20 April 1785, fos 60–1.
15. BL Egerton 3498, Pitt to Carmarthen, 27 April 1785, fo. 108.
16. Blanning, '"That horrid electorate"', pp. 325–7; FO 7/10–11, 4 and 5, Carmarthen to Keith, 8 April 1785, 15 July 1785; BL Egerton 3498, Carmarthen to Richmond, 20 May 1785, fo. 219; BL Add MS 28059, Minute of a conversation with Count Vorontsov, 14 June 1785, fos 88–9.
17. FO 7/10, Memo of conference with Kageneck, 26 May 1785; FO 64/7, Carmarthen to Joseph Ewart, 17 June 1785; BL Egerton 3498, Pitt to Carmarthen, 25–8 June 1785, fo. 118.
18. Black, British Foreign Policy ... 1783–1793, pp. 86–8; BL Egerton 3504, Carmarthen to Vorontsov, 5, 7 August 1785, Minute of conversation with Vorontsov, 14 June 1785, fos 88–9; Vorontsov to Carmarthen, 6 August 1785, fos 83–7; Egerton 3498, Pitt to Carmarthen, 8 August 1785, fo. 122.
19. Blanning, '"That horrid electorate"', p. 329; BL Add MS 28059, Carmarthen to Harris, 11 November 1785, fo. 475; PRO 30/8/151, Carmarthen to Pitt, 13 November 1785, fo. 31; Malmesbury Diaries, i, Memo in Harris to Carmarthen, 9 September 1785, p. 151.
20. Carmarthen's dislike of the 1786 commercial treaty included its negotiator: BL Add MS 28061, Carmarthen to Harris, 14 February 1786, fo. 29; Ehrman, The Years of Acclaim, pp. 493–4; Black, British Foreign Policy ... 1783–1793, pp. 104–5.
21. Auckland Correspondence, i, Pitt to Eden, 10 June 1786, pp. 126–7; Black, 'Marquis of Carmarthen', p. 289.
22. Opposition to the treaty within the French government was considerable: M. M. Donoghay, 'The Maréchal de Castries and the Anglo-French commercial negotiations of 1786–7', HJ 22 (1979), pp. 295–312.
23. W. O. Henderson, 'The Anglo-French commercial treaty of 1786', Economic History Review, 2nd series, 10 (1957–8), pp. 104–12; Ehrman, The Years of Acclaim, pp. 493–4; M. M. Donoghay, 'The exchange of products of the soil and industrial goods in the Anglo-French commercial treaty of 1786', Journal of European Economic History 19 (1990), pp. 377–41.
24. F. Gilbert, 'The new diplomacy of the eighteenth century', in History, Choice and Commitment (Cambridge: 1977), pp. 323–49; H. M. Scott, British Foreign Policy in the Age of the American Revolution (Oxford: 1990), pp. 324–5; Black, British Foreign Policy ... 1783–1793, pp. 27, 101.
25. S. Schama, Patriots and Liberators: Revolution in the Netherlands, 1780–1813 (1977), pp. 64–94; A. Cobban, Ambassadors and Secret Agents: The Diplomacy of the First Earl of Malmesbury at the Hague (1954), pp. 121–8.
26. Auckland Correspondence, i, Pitt to Harris, 13 October 1785, pp. 156–7; BL Egerton 3498, Pitt to Carmarthen, 6 December 1785, fo. 149; Auckland Correspondence, i, Carmarthen to Harris, 6 December 1785, p. 258 (£9,000 was not enough, as Harris complained in May 1786).
27. Malmesbury Diaries, i, Carmarthen to Harris, 12 December 1786, p. 258.
28. Ibid., ii, Pitt to Harris, 26 December 1786, p. 263; Auckland Correspondence, i, Carmarthen to Eden, 26 April 1786, pp. 112–13.
29. For example, see PRO 30/8/110, Eden to Pitt, 8 August 1786, fo. 70, on

the subject of the United Provinces and the East Indies; BL 28061, Carmarthen to Harris, 1 December 1786, fo. 392.

30. PRO 30/8/310, Pitt to Eden, 3 October 1786, fo. 162; PRO 30/8/151, Carmarthen to Pitt, 8 January 1787, fo. 39; *Pol. Mem.*, Memorandum for Cabinet, January 1787, pp. 117–18; BL Add MS 28062, Carmarthen to Harris, 20 March 1787, fo. 127.

31. Malmesbury Diaries, ii, Account of Cabinet meeting, 23 May 1787, p. 305; *LCG III*, i, Pitt to George III, 26 May 1787, p. 297, and Minute of Cabinet, Carmarthen to George III, 26 May 1787, p. 296; PRO 30/8/103, George III to Pitt, 26 May 1787, fo. 262.

32. Six British warships had put to sea at the beginning of June as a precautionary measure, an event that much alarmed the French: BL Add MS 34425, Pitt to Eden, 15 June 1787, fos 51–2; FO 64/11, Carmarthen to Ewart, 26 June 1787, fo. 100; BL Add MS 28059, George III to Carmarthen, 30 June 1787, fo. 137; *LCG III*, i, Pitt to George III, 17 July 1787, pp. 311–12; Black, *British Foreign Policy ... 1783–1793*, pp. 144–6.

33. PRO 30/8/102, Pitt to Cornwallis, 2 and 28 August 1787, fos 77–8, 84–5; [Philip], 5th Earl Stanhope, *Life of the Right Honourable William Pitt* (4 vols, 1861–2), i, Pitt to Lady Chatham, 19 September 1787, p. 346; Black, *British Foreign Policy ... 1783–1793*, p. 147.

34. J. Holland Rose, *Pitt and Napoleon: Essays and Letters* (1912), George III to Pitt, 16 September 1787, p. 218; *Courts and Cabinets*, i, Grenville to Buckingham, 19 September 1787, pp. 326–7; BL Add MS 28059, Pitt to George III, 19 September 1787, fo. 154; Auckland Correspondence, i, Pitt to Eden, 21 September 1787, pp. 198–9; Stanhope, *Life of Pitt*, i, Pitt to Lady Chatham, 22 and 29 September 1787, pp. 346–8.

35. Auckland Correspondence, i, Pitt to Eden, 14 September 1787, pp. 194–6; *LCG III*, i, Pitt to George III, 8 October 1787, p. 340; *Dropmore*, iii, Carmarthen to Grenville, 27 July 1787, Grenville to Pitt, 31 July and 1–4 August 1787, Harris to Grenville, 18 August 1787, pp. 408–16; J. Holland Rose, 'The missions of William Grenville', *EHR* 24 (1909), pp. 285–7.

36. As suggested by Black in 'The Marquis of Carmarthen', pp. 295–6, and *British Foreign Policy ... 1783–1793*, p. 122.

37. Browning, *Despatches from Paris*, i, Hailes to Carmarthen, 4 October 1787, pp. 244–7.

38. BL Egerton 3498, Carmarthen to Pitt, 6 December 1785, fo. 147; Malmesbury Diaries, ii, Harris to Carmarthen, 15 September 1786, pp. 232–3.

39. Blanning, *Origins of the French Revolutionary Wars*, pp. 52–3; Black, *British Foreign Policy ... 1783–1793*, pp. 144–52.

40. Auckland Correspondence, i, Pitt to Eden, 8 October 1787, p. 217; Browning, *Despatches from Paris*, i, Dorset to Carmarthen, 18 October 1787, pp. 253–5. For continuation of rumours, see BL Add MS 28062, Eden to Pitt, 27 December 1787, fos 496–8.

41. PRO 30/8/102, Pitt to Cornwallis, 2 and 28 August 1787, fos 77–8, 84–5.

42. Ehrman, *The Years of Acclaim*, pp. 424–5; Black, *Natural and Necessary Enemies*, p. 155.

43. PRO 30/8/102, Pitt to Cornwallis, 2 August 1787, fos 84–7.

44. Auckland Correspondence, i, Pitt to Eden, 14 October 1787, p. 229; PRO

30/8/103, George III to Pitt, 12 October 1787, fo. 262; *LCG III*, i, 407, Minute of Cabinet (West Indies), and 408, Pitt to George III (East Indies), 13 October 1787.

45. FO 64/12, 24, Carmarthen to Ewart, 2 December 1787, 'Terms of a Triple Alliance'; BL Add MS 28063, Carmarthen to Harris, 11 May 1788, fo. 170.

46. *Dropmore*, iii, Harris to Carmarthen, 4 January 1788, pp. 442–3.

47. Browning, *Despatches from Paris*, 1784–1790, ii, Dorset and Eden to Carmarthen, 6 January 1788, pp. 4–7, Dorset to Carmarthen, 17 January 1788, pp. 9–11; PRO 30/8/102, Pitt to Eden, 7 January 1788, fo. 115; Auckland Correspondence, i, Pitt to Eden, 8 January 1788, pp. 301–2.

48. Auckland Correspondence, i, Carmarthen to Eden, 17 December 1787, p. 291; G. C. Bolton and B. E. Kennedy, 'William Eden and the treaty of Mauritius, 1787–1788', *HJ* 16 (1973), pp. 681–95.

49. HA 119 T108/39, Pitt to Eliot, 8 September 1787; FO 64/11, 25, Carmarthen to Ewart, 2 December 1787.

50. BL Egerton 3498, Pitt to Carmarthen, 10 September 1784, fo. 54; BL Add MS 28060, Pitt memo on Anglo-Russo-Danish alliance, 13 October 1784, fos 166–70.

51. FO 64/11, 26, Carmarthen to Ewart, 25 December 1787; FO 64/13, 1, Carmarthen to Ewart, 14 March 1788.

52. No sooner had they received the alliance proposals than the Prussians began to complain about the colonial defence stipulations: BL Add MS 28063, Carmarthen to Harris, 11 May 1788, fo. 170; J. Black, 'Britain's foreign alliances in the eighteenth century', *Albion* 20 (1988), p. 592.

53. FO 64/13, 18, Ewart to Carmarthen, 15 March 1788.

54. *Ibid.*, 4, 5 and 8, Carmarthen to Ewart, 2 April, 14 May 1788.

55. BL Add MS 28063, 29 April 1788, fo. 156.

56. Ehrman, *The Years of Acclaim*, pp. 541–2; *LCG III*, i, Cabinet Minute, 31 May 1788, p. 375.

57. CUL 6958,3 520, Pitt to Ewart, 14 July 1788; FO 64/14, 55, Ewart to Carmarthen, 26 August 1788, 18, Carmarthen to Ewart, 29 August 1788.

58. *Dropmore*, i, Pitt to Grenville, 29 August 1788, p. 353.

59. Stanhope, *Life of Pitt*, i, Pitt to Lady Chatham, 29 August 1788, pp. 381–2.

60. PRO 30/8/140, Grenville to Pitt, 1 September 1788, fo. 34; BL Add MS 58906, Pitt to Grenville, [5 September] 1788, fo. 47.

61. CUL 6958,3 536, Richmond to Pitt, 1 September 1788.

62. Rose Diaries, i, Pitt to Stafford, 6 September 1788, p. 85.

63. *Dropmore*, i, Pitt to Grenville, 29 August 1788, p. 353; Holland Rose, *Pitt and Napoleon*, Pitt to George III, [18 October] 1788, p. 219.

64. BL Add MS 28063, W. Fraser to Carmarthen, 18 October 1788, fos 292–3; FO 64/14, 24, Carmarthen to Ewart, 26 October 1788.

65. *LCG III*, i, George III to Pitt, Pitt to George III, 19 October 1788, p. 396; Holland Rose, *Pitt and Napoleon*, Pitt to George III, [19–20] October 1788, p. 219; Kent Archives Office, Pratt Papers, U269 c. 182, Hawkesbury to Dorset, 23 October 1788.

66. Stanhope, *Life of Pitt*, ii, Appendix, George III to Pitt, 20 October 1788, pp. iii–iv; on 19 October France had announced that it would not interfere in the northern war.

67. FO 22/10, Carmarthen to Ewart, 5 December 1788, fos 472–3.
68. FO 72/14, 21, Eden to Carmarthen, 9 March 1789.
69. For a discussion of the concept, see P. Schroeder, *The Transformation of European Politics, 1763–1848* (Oxford: 1994), pp. 5–11.
70. FO 65/17, 4, Whitworth to Carmarthen, 9 January 1789; FO 72/14, 30 and 9, Eden to Carmarthen, 30 March 1789, Carmarthen to Eden, 17 April 1789.
71. FO 65/17, 1, Carmarthen to Whitworth, 23 January 1789; FO 64/15, 5, Ewart to Carmarthen, 28 January 1789.
72. FO 64/15, 8 and 10, Carmarthen to Ewart, 10 April and 24 June 1789.
73. FO 64/16, 41 and 16, Ewart to Leeds, 12 July 1789 (Carmarthen succeeded to the dukedom of Leeds at the end of June 1789), and Leeds to Ewart, 14 September 1789. The Baltic war dragged on for the next two years.
74. BL Add MS 28064, Leeds to Ewart, 20 September 1789, fos 274–5.
75. Black, *British Foreign Policy ... 1783–1793*, p. 17.
76. KAO U269 c. 168(68), Leeds to Dorset, 15 May 1789; PRO 30/8/161, Necker to Pitt, 25 June 1789, fos 23–4.
77. J. Ehrman, *The Reluctant Transition* (1983), pp. 42–5.
78. *Life of Wilberforce*, i, Journal, 2–14 July 1789, pp. 227–8; PRO 30/8/102, Pitt to Luzerne (French ambassador in London), 3 July 1789, fo. 180.
79. Stanhope, *Life of Pitt*, ii, Pitt to Lady Chatham, 14 July 1789, p. 38.
80. Black, 'Anglo-French relations in the age of the French Revolution, 1787–1793', *Francia* 15 (1987), p. 231.
81. This myth was finally exploded in A. Cobban, 'British Secret Service in France 1784–1792', in *Aspects of the French Revolution* (1971), pp. 192–224.
82. Browning, *Despatches from Paris*, ii, Dorset to Leeds, 27 July 1789, p. 250; FO 27/32, 14, Leeds to Dorset, 31 July 1789; BL Add MS 28064, Leeds to Lord Robert Fitzgerald, 31 July 1789, fos 188–9.
83. *Dropmore*, ii, Grenville to Dundas, 14 September 1791, p. 192. George III claimed to be the author of the policy in 1792: *LCG III*, ii, George III to Prince of Wales, 17 February 1792, p. 583.
84. FO 72/14, 22, A. Merry to Leeds, 10 August 1789; FO 72/15, 21, Leeds to A. Merry, November 1789.
85. This was despite long-standing rumours that French troops were destined for the support of the Flemish rebels: BL Add MS 58906, Pitt to Grenville, 22 September 1788, fos 51–2.
86. J. H. Clapham, *The Causes of the War of 1792* (Cambridge: 1899), pp. 37–41; Pitt memo of 28 August 1789, cited in A. W. Ward and G. P. Gooch (eds), *The Cambridge History of British Foreign Policy, 1783–1919* (3 vols, Cambridge: 1922), i, p. 188; Devon Record Office, Sidmouth Papers, 152M 1789/OZ 1, Pitt to Addington, 10 September 1789.
87. FO 7/18, 2, Leeds to Keith, 10 October 1789.
88. Browning, *Despatches from Paris*, ii, Fitzgerald to Leeds, 15 October 1789, pp. 266–9; FO 27/33, Fitzgerald to Leeds, 6 November 1789; FO 7/18, 4, Leeds to Keith, 13 November 1789; *Pol. Mem.*, Leeds to George III, 30 October 1789, pp. 145–6; FO 27/33A, Leeds to Fitzgerald, 30 October 1789, fo. 207; Black, *A System of Ambition?*, p. 235.
89. Black, *British Foreign Policy ... 1783–1793*, pp. 211–12.

90. J. Holland Rose, 'The Comte d'Artois and Pitt in December 1789', *EHR* 30 (1915), pp. 322–4; CUL 69586, 782, George III to Pitt, 28 March 1790.
91. M. Duffy, 'British war policy and the Austrian alliance, 1793–1801', D.Phil. thesis (Oxford, 9171), p. 5.
92. FO 64/16, 22, Leeds to Ewart, 14 December 1789.
93. FO 7/18, 14, Keith to Leeds, 4 November 1789.
94. BL Add MS 28059, Cabinet Minute, 30 November 1789, fo. 266; *LCG III*, i, 564, George III to Leeds, 1 December 1789, p. 451.
95. FO 64/16, 55, Ewart to Leeds, 5 September 1789.
96. *Ibid.*, 22, Leeds to Ewart, 14 December 1789.
97. Black, 'The Marquis of Carmarthen', pp. 284–5.
98. Auckland Correspondence, i, Pitt to Eden, 19 April 1786, pp. 105–6; BL Add MS 34425, Pitt to Eden, 15 June 1787, fos 51–2.
99. J. G. A. Pocock, 'The political economy of Burke's analysis of the French Revolution', in *Virtue, Commerce and History* (Cambridge: 1985), p. 199; J. M. Walsh, *Edmund Burke and International Relations* (Basingstoke: 1995), pp. 92–109.
100. Black, *British Foreign Policy ... 1783–1793*, pp. 344–5.
101. Auckland Correspondence, i, Carmarthen to Eden, 30 October 1788, p. 262; BL 28064, Leeds to Dorset, 31 July 1790, fo. 194.

Chapter 3

A Studied Neutrality, 1790–1791

For much of 1789 the French Revolution was an object of great British interest and speculation. France had long been an object of love–hate fascination, in conscious opposition to which – or admiration of – Britain's cultural, intellectual, political and diplomatic identity had taken shape over the eighteenth century. For Englishmen celebrating the centenary of the 1688 Glorious Revolution and the recovery of George III's sanity, the fall of the Bastille, almost as much a symbol of tyranny in England as in France, and the metamorphosis of the Estates General into the Constituent Assembly seemed to represent a movement for liberty defined in traditional terms.[1]

William Pitt and his colleagues participated at private levels in this orgy of English self-satisfaction. In public, their neutrality towards revolutionary France was scrupulous and complete. Gower and his Paris embassy were passive spectators of events in Paris from 1790 to 1792. British diplomats elsewhere on the Continent were ordered not to pass judgement on French political developments in any public capacity. The standards for this conduct were set by a Cabinet in London that made anodyne statements about the revolution in its dispatches and speeches. So deafening a silence bears testimony to the fear and respect in which pre-revolutionary France had been held in England, not to mention the British government's determination to minimize any retaliatory response from the French Bourbons and their friends in Europe. By January 1790, nevertheless, the Pitt ministry was aware that the French Revolution was becoming an important political and intellectual issue at national and international levels.

The first expressions of English collective interest in the French Revolution came from the societies that were 'leftovers' from the hundredth anniversary of the Glorious Revolution. The Society for Constitutional Information (SCI), moribund since 1785, was given a new lease of life in 1788 by an upsurge of patriotism which led to the formation of the London Revolution Society and other mutual-admiration 'revolution' groups. These were joined in their early admir-ation of the French Revolution by the older cultural and intellectual societies of the provincial towns, the products of middle-income genteel subscription to the ideals of the Enlightenment. The congratulatory addresses sent to the National Assembly in 1789 and 1790 gave the Pitt ministry no cause for concern. More worrisome to the government by late 1791 were those British grass-roots bodies with less respectable intellectual and historical antecedents. As magistrates and friends of the ministry were quick to point out, dissenter groups, active in the 1789 and 1790 campaigns for Test and Corporation Act repeal, brought the Norman yoke and the seventeenth-century commonwealth back into political use.[2] Pitt, however, had taken no notice of dissenter propaganda and activities in his 1789 speech against repeal. The time was yet to come when innovation was confused with tradition.

British hostility to the French Revolution at the beginning of 1790 was most noticeable in the ranks of the Opposition Whigs. Edmund Burke, defender of the Church–State partnership, and Richard Brinsley Sheridan, advocate of religious toleration, had first disagreed over Test and Corporation Act repeal in 1787. This schism, attributable less to differences in political perspective than to competition for the affections and attention of Charles James Fox, became more pronounced at the time of the Regency crisis, when a disgruntled Burke found himself marginalized while Sheridan acted as the intermediary between Fox and the Prince of Wales.[3] From Pitt's perspective, these rifts on the Opposition front bench had been healed by the Regency crisis, experience of which had given him a taste of the strength and influence of the Whig Opposition inside and outside Parliament. In 1790, a general election year, he was to become reacquainted with public opinion, a political force that was to intrude increasingly upon Pitt's consciousness over the next two years.

The General Election of 1790

Pitt had thought about going to the country as early as August 1788, when he, Grenville and Rose had estimated that a general election would return 298 government MPs and 153 Opposition supporters.[4] This margin was too close for comfort. By the end of the 1788 parliamentary session the omens for victory were not good. The repeal of the shop tax had been a major defeat for the ministry in the country and, with both the abolition of the slave trade and repeal of the Test and Corporation Acts on the Commons agenda for 1789, Pitt decided to delay the dissolution for twelve months.[5] He began, nevertheless, to organize for an election in earnest during the autumn of 1788.

Pitt, by no means displeased by the 1788 regeneration of public interest in extraparliamentary organizations, gave his blessing to the formation of the Constitutional Club, a London society set up to promote the principles of the Glorious Revolution. This, unlike the

Whig Club, was not socially exclusive in its membership. Enrolment was conditional upon the swearing of an oath and the purchase of the club costume: 'Our uniform goes on well. Several people have told me they will put it on. Today in the House we were a pretty knot of orange capes. Pitt, Lord Mornington, Lord Bayham, Lord Belgrave, Villiers, Addington and myself.'[6] James Bland Burges, Under-Secretary of State at the Foreign Office, thought the dress of the Constitutional Club more tasteful than 'the Buff and Blue of our opponents'. This is a moot point; the Prince of Orange's colours were certainly more conspicuous than those of George Washington. It was hoped that the club would attract young Oxbridge men to the ministry: '[It] should prove a good political net to catch young men just launching into the world from College.'[7] The Whig Club served this purpose 'and something was wanted to counteract'. No dissolution of Parliament took place in 1789, for government back-benchers had begun to defect to the Opposition during the Regency crisis and Pitt wanted what Grenville called 'messieurs les rats' to return to the government vessel.[8] By January 1790 Pitt was telling the Attorney-General that 'we shall not only not lose, but actually gain'.[9] Government election data is scanty, making reconstruction of Pitt's strategy difficult, but the Constitutional Club seems to have been an important secondary election headquarters for the ministry. During a summer of frantic canvassing for the general election, Burke wrote that many of the Constitutional Club's members were the Whig Club's 'rancorous enemies'.[10]

Pitt's opposition to reform bills during the spring of 1790 must be assessed in the light of the forthcoming election. He did not intend to stand as 'a reforming minister', as had been the case in 1784, planning instead to rest on his laurels. When parliamentary reform and Test repeal came before the Commons in March 1790, three months before the end of the session, Pitt was suspicious. Fox, the spokesman for religious toleration, had made a tactical alliance with the dissenters and expected to make electoral capital out of Test repeal.[11] Henry Flood, the author of a parliamentary reform bill, was an equally well-known opponent of the Pitt ministry. Once prominent in the Irish volunteer reform movement of the early 1780s, Flood was close to the Opposition in Dublin and London. He was no favourite of Pitt's, having criticized and opposed the 1785 Commercial Propositions.[12]

Flood's parliamentary reform bill came before the Commons on 4 March 1790. Based loosely upon Pitt's 1785 bill, it proposed to add 100 county MPs to the Lower House, an increase in numbers to be counterbalanced by the abolition of fifty rotten boroughs. Flood's new county members were to be elected by 'resident householders' paying at least 50s. in tax per annum. His supporting speech praised his would-be electorate and sought to distinguish it from 'the rabble'.

When he denounced virtual representation in favour of its actual alternative, the conservative instincts of the House were roused. Pitt, whose name had been invoked by Flood and, indeed, every other parliamentary reformer since 1785, rose immediately to deny that 'his [own] ideas of reforming the representation of Parliament were founded upon wild theory and visionary speculation'.[13] Moderate though Flood's reform proposals appeared to be, the implications of universal suffrage in his advocacy of actual representation were unacceptable to Pitt, who voiced contempt for the Irish MP's 50s. household franchise: giving the vote to all 'who paid 50s scot and lot ... would not answer any purpose'. In 1785 Pitt had attempted to reinforce the relationship between liberty and property and, while recommending that new borough MPs be selected by 'substantial householders', he had also stipulated that these electors should be qualified by a high tax assessment.[14] Flood, who claimed to have grounded voting rights in property, 'or as nearly commensurate to it as possible', had identified his prospective electorate in anything but prescriptive terms. Pitt's franchise had never been based on a universal contribution to the national revenue.

Having identified the intellectual inconsistencies in Flood's reform proposals, Pitt told the Commons that there were no anomalies in the representation which required immediate redress. The words 'general election' were, needless to say, not uttered. He reminded the House that his 1785 bill had been rejected because it had been associated with radical reform: 'He thought that those who argued the case were mistaken.' Pitt promised to make another attempt at reform when a favourable opportunity arose and moved the order of the day to get rid of Flood's bill. On the last day of the session the 1788 County Election Act was replaced by Berkeley's Act, which purported to 'explain and amend' 20 Geo. III. Pitt did not play any recorded role in the passage of this bill but one suspects that he deplored the repeal of legislation forcing the Treasury to raise its election budget from the £20,000 spent in 1784 to £40,000 in 1790.[15]

The debate on Flood's bill took place two days after Fox had aired his motion for the repeal of the Test and Corporation Acts. This had been preceded by a controversial publicity campaign that aroused the hostility of the Established Church. By this date prominent dissenters like Richard Price and Joseph Priestley had openly expressed their approval for the French Revolution – in the light of which, their claims for political equality cast sinister shadows over the minds of a British public made apprehensive by the revival of old religious debates.

Pitt, referring to the dissenters' extraparliamentary campaign for Test repeal, which had involved 'forming associations throughout the whole country', declared that the dissenters, 'who were undoubtedly a respectable body', might still 'exercise their power to the subversion of the present establishment'. Pitt's distaste for enthusiasm was real. One cleric's prospects for preferment depended partly on whether he was not 'too much of a Methodist'.[16] The Established Church was, however, told to confine itself to spiritual matters: 'to cultivate peace and good order; to instil into the minds of the Public a rational love of Christian morality ... to have no competition than that recommended by the Gospel'. Both sides had been chastised.[17]

Parliament was dissolved on 10 June 1790. According to calculations in *The History of Parliament*, the ministry was not worried about its prospects for victory at that time. Final estimates drawn up by Grenville postulated a return of 351 friends of government against 207 opponents. Independents had been classed according to general voting preferences. 92 of the 247 constituencies were contested in 1790, which is where the government made most of its gains. Final returns were 340 for the ministry to 188 for the Opposition. 29 MPs remained independent.[18] Some of the contested constituencies were subject to pairing arrangements. The borough of Westminster is a case in point:

On the 15th of March 1790, Lord Lauderdale and Mr Pitt held a Conversation on the Subject of the Westminster Election. Mr Dundas present.

They agreed that each Party should propose and support only one Candidate respectively at the first general Election and during the whole of the next Parliament, so long as either the D. of Portland or Mr Fox on the one Part, and Mr Grenville or Mr Pitt on the other are alive, and including any other Contingency of Death, Vacancy or changes in Administration.[19]

This may have been either an attempt to make amends for the 1785 Westminster Scrutiny or a tactical concession to the Whig Opposition made with good grace. When the ministry put up two candidates for Westminster in 1788, it had only succeeded in splitting the ministerial vote.[20]

By the time George III's thirty-sixth parliament met, Burke had published his *Reflections on the Revolution in France*. This was an object of immediate attention: 'Burke and Calonne's books have been and are the subjects of universal conversation, talked of forever in private and daily discussed in the public newspapers.' Pitt did not like the *Reflections*. Wilberforce, recording the table talk from one of Dundas's dinner parties, noted that there was 'much talk about Burke's book. Lord Chatham, Pitt and I seemed to agree, contra Grenville and Ryder.'[21] Grenville had become a strong anti-Jacobin, but his admiration for Burke did not equal that of William Windham, who described the

Reflections as 'a work that may seem capable of overturning the National Assembly, and turning the stream of opinion throughout Europe'. Fox did not agree.[22]

Windham, speaking during the Commons debate on Flood's motion, had asked the rhetorical question: 'would he recommend you to repair your house in the hurricane season?'[23] In 1791 this was what Pitt was proposing to do to the religious establishment. On 25 February 1788 he had given an audience to a Roman Catholic delegation seeking the repeal of recusancy statutes dating from the sixteenth century. Pitt stated that the government would support their claims for redress, but counselled the Catholics to delay the launch of their publicity campaign until 1789. Premature action, he stated, 'would prevent Government from preparing the minds of some of the leading interests in the country previous to the bringing of an issue of such importance'.[24] The most important of these was the Church of England. After three years of consultation, Sir John Mitford had agreed to bring Catholic relief before Parliament in 1791.

With the failure of Beaufoy's 1787 Test repeal motion fresh in their minds, the Roman Catholics did not seek 'to hold any of the offices of the Law or any other Civil Office of Employment'. What they wanted was the repeal of the recusancy statutes, an end to irksome legal obligations complicating the sale and transfer of property, and admission to His Majesty's armed forces, the legal profession and the medical profession.[25] What the Catholics got from Mitford was slightly different: the repeal of some stipulated statutes, permission to enter the professions, the right to give their children a religious education in England, and the freedom to stand for some, though by no means all, civil offices. The legislation would not give Catholics full religious or political equality. New oaths were required to qualify these 'dissenters' for limited toleration, and here the Catholic relief campaign ran into opposition from the Catholics themselves.

The friends of religious toleration, fearful of bigotry, had advised the Roman Catholics to debunk old myths respecting papists without reviving Protestant prejudices. Stanhope told Charles Petre 'to give to the world not an account of what they do believe, but an explicit disavowal of what they do not believe'.[26] At Pitt's request, the committee wrote to the theology faculties at the universities of Paris, Louvain, Douai, Salamanca and Valladolid to ascertain whether a foreign power, the papacy, could overrule a domestic secular authority or whether the Roman Church could absolve English Catholics from an oath of allegiance.[27] Firm denials were returned to these queries but Lord Chancellor Thurlow refused to remove the disavowals of transubstantiation and papal authority from the oaths. Appalled Catholics protested to Pitt:

We are ready to give every possible proof of our allegiance to
Government and of our attachment to our Sovereign which does not
trench upon the Spiritual Power of the Head of the Catholic Church
and of its other Pastors. But that the oath in its present form,
containing things contrary to the Catholic Faith, and involving questions foreign to civil allegiance, cannot lawfully be taken by members
of the Roman Catholic Church.[28]

Pitt, who possessed the backing of the Established Church and probably
the king, demanded that the Lord Chancellor alter the oaths. Thurlow
refused and Pitt stepped in. He was involved in drafting a new oath
and lent his weight to Mitford's bill in all stages of its passage.[29] Pitt,
who baulked at Test repeal, was willing to support Test amendment.
He viewed the two as distinct and separate issues, regretting in January
1791 that Catholic relief could not be brought forward 'without a
possibility of its being confused with the question of the Dissenters' in
the public mind. Striking outdated legislation from the statute book
was not an admission of religious equality.[30]

The Catholic relief bill passed its three Commons readings without
a division during the first week of April. It was supported in the Lords
by the Established Church. On 18 April Wilberforce rose to introduce
his bill for the abolition of the slave trade. Pitt gave his 1789 arguments
another airing. Abolition, he claimed, would improve labour relations
on the sugar islands and thereby their value to the empire.[31] Leading
Opposition members once more joined the abolitionists in debate but
Wilberforce's motion was decisively defeated. With heads bloody but
unbowed, the Abolition Committee marshalled its forces for yet
another propaganda campaign. It soon found that public opinion at
all social levels was becoming much less sympathetic to abolition. By
1790 the Abolition Committee had built up a network of local English
associations to distribute literature and organize petitions, a development which was deeply disturbing to some MPs, who foresaw the
adoption of such organizational tactics by other political lobby groups.[32]
Wilberforce was becoming uneasy about the strong links between
abolition and dissent, now associated in the English mind with the
French Revolution. When Clarkson, president of the Abolition Committee, attended a Bastille Day dinner at the Crown and Anchor Tavern
in 1791, a horrified Dundas, no friend to abolition, warned Wilberforce
of the irreparable harm that association with radical dissent would
do the cause: 'Clarkson called – warned him about French Revolution.'[33] Pitt too was dismayed, not by the reawakening of 'innovation'
per se, but by the encouragement that it gave to intolerance, a far
stronger feature of the eighteenth-century British political persona. By
the end of 1791 the polarization of public opinion into 'radical' and

'conservative' camps was to become more pronounced at all social and political levels.

From Nootka Sound to Ochakow

During the early months of 1790 the Pitt ministry's eyes were fixed on eastern and central Europe. Britain's interest in the fate of the Netherlands had been repaid by Joseph II at the end of 1789; on 12 January 1790 Leeds had wistfully turned down an alliance proposal which had come from Vienna. Attractive as an Austrian alliance had always been to Leeds, the emperor's insistence on admitting Russia to any English alliance made the plan unacceptable. The Austrian overture not only revived Leeds's hopes for the resurrection of the 'old system', but suggested a course of action by which to end the eastern war and outmanoeuvre a troublesome Prussian ally.[34] Frederick William was demanding that the Triple Alliance support the cause of Belgian independence or make its consent for the re-establishment of Austrian authority in the Netherlands conditional upon the grant of Polish lands to Prussia. When the ministry learned that Prussia was trying to sell the Hertzberg project to Russia as part of the allied mediation package, Leeds was swift to act. On 30 March 1790 new British armistice proposals were sent to Austria, Russia, Prussia and Turkey. Britain now offered to act as an intermediary between any two powers in search of peace.[35] Because Frederick William and Catherine the Great were seemingly intent on reciprocal guarantees for their respective prospective acquisitions in Galicia and the Crimea, the British government gave special consideration to the position of Austria. Were Joseph II to respect Anglo-Dutch wishes on the future of the Netherlands, the maritime powers would support moderate Austrian claims for indemnification from the Porte.

After two years of vacillation, the Pitt ministry had finally committed itself to the principle of a modified status quo in the east. Encouraging Austria to make a separate peace would, thought Pitt and Leeds, leave an isolated Russia disinclined to impose punitive terms on the Ottoman empire. The Austrians, however, were unwilling to abandon the Russians or to involve the Prussians in the peace talks. The proposals sent on 30 March were rejected, but not, as Keith reported, decisively. Chancellor Kaunitz insisted that Austria would take no action without Russia, while Foreign Minister Cobenzl claimed that the emperor was attracted to 'the very kind and beneficient proposition' of Britain.[36] When Keith explained the strength of his masters' hostility to the Hertzberg project, Joseph II's advisers grew more co-operative. On 23 May Pitt drafted new instructions for Keith and Ewart. The Prussians

had accepted the peace terms suggested in March, ostensibly a call for
an immediate status quo armistice between any two powers. In the
dispatch bound for Vienna in May Leeds denounced the Prussian
indemnification deal with Russia but urged Joseph II to make some
minor Polish concessions to Prussia.[37] This missive crossed paths with
two dispatches from Keith listing details of Austria's compromise offer.
Prussia could be bought off with land from the Porte rather than
Austrian Galicia. This the British government accepted, believing that
Turkey could be compensated for its losses by 'future Connections
with the Allies, both political and commercial'.[38] By 27 July 1790 the
Reichenbach armistice had been signed by Austria and Turkey. The
peace talks were then removed to the Bulgarian town of Sistovo.

France had hovered as a shadow in the background throughout these
transactions. The chief reason why Joseph II clung so tenaciously to
Russia was that France, the western mainstay of Austria's security
network, was impotent. This explains in part the Austrian approach to
Britain at the end of 1789. As the Constituent Assembly embarked
upon its 1790 session, Pitt ventured a few comments on the French
Revolution.

> The present convulsions in France must sooner or later terminate
> in general harmony and regular order, and though such a situation
> might make her more formidable, it might make her a less objec-
> tionable neighbour ... Whenever her system shall become restored,
> if it should prove to be freedom rightly understood, freedom resulting
> from good order and good government, France should stand forward
> as one of the most brilliant powers in Europe.[39]

Freedom for Pitt conformed to a British model, the 'mixed constitution',
under which a legislative assembly representing established interest
groups worked with a Crown subject to restrictions upon its royal
power. Pitt could afford to be generous to France; indeed, so little fear
did British diplomats display towards their ancient enemy that the
Prussians, hoping to reawaken English hostility towards the Bourbons,
reported that France was preparing to send troops to the assistance of
Jacobin emissaries in the Netherlands. The British government, having
already investigated these rumours and disgusted by Prussia's eagerness
to emancipate the Netherlands, replied that France was in no position
to give military or financial aid to the rebels. Pitt and Leeds added that
the French Revolution was likely to frighten the Belgian clergy and
nobility into obedience rather than insurrection.[40] The Pitt ministry,
unlike William V of Holland, was not concerned about possible French
interference in the Netherlands. According to Lord Fitzherbert, the
departing British ambassador at the Hague, William was panicking

about 'the immediate formation of a Batavo-Gallic National Assembly ... an insurrection of the Dutch Patriots within the republic ... or an invasion of those who are now supposed to be assembling in the Bishopric of Münster'. Leeds stated that such apprehensions were 'purely nervous'.[41]

British fears of secret deals within the Family Compact dictated the extreme delicacy with which France was treated throughout the Nootka Sound crisis of 1790. In May 1789 British merchant settlers based on Vancouver Island had been forcibly evicted from their base by the Spanish navy following the seizure of three British merchant vessels. On 26 February 1790 Leeds delivered the first of several ministerial remonstrances to Count del Campo, the Spanish ambassador in London. Pitt, unhappy about Leeds's determination to browbeat Spain, had toned down a strongly worded demand for the release of the British ships and crews, compensation for British losses in Nootka Sound and a recognition of Britain's trade and settlement rights in the Pacific north-west. All that Pitt demanded in the first instance was release and reparations.[42]

Repeated British demands for explanations and compensation were met by stony silence from Madrid. According to Anthony Merry, the senior British resident in the Madrid embassy, the Spanish government was afraid that the French Revolution would cross the Pyrenees and was therefore keeping France at arm's length. There seemed little to fear from an isolated Spain until its government ordered a naval review in April and resurrected the quadruple alliance project with France and the imperial powers. The Pitt ministry began to consider decisive action. The quadruple alliance was, reported Merry, a brainchild of the French ambassador in Madrid, 'always studious to increase the Jealousy of Spain with respect to England'. The Spanish government, he claimed, planned to use the Nootka quarrel with Britain as a pretext for a war in truth intended 'to re-establish the Royal authority in France'.[43] On 30 April the Cabinet voted to arm the fleet and, on 5 May, Alleyne Fitzherbert was appointed to the Madrid embassy.

Fitzherbert was ordered to travel to Spain via Paris, where he was to explain that the British government was seeking nothing but justice for its merchants. The new ambassador, in partnership with Lord Robert Fitzgerald, who was in charge of the Paris embassy pending Gower's arrival, was also to ascertain whether France intended to give Spain the military aid stipulated by the 1761 Family Compact. On 15 May Fitzherbert wrote that the French Foreign Ministry had offered to mediate between England and Spain.[44] Louis XVI had also armed fourteen sail-of-the-line. The French offer was refused. Acceptance would have constituted a renunciation of neutrality towards the revolution, placed Britain under an obligation to the new France and only encouraged any secret diplomacy taking place between Paris and Madrid.

Fitzherbert sent home an assessment of revolutionary politics that confirmed Merry's account of royalist Anglophobia. The *aristocrate* lust for war with Britain supposedly formed part of a sinister plot to dethrone the Necker ministry and reverse the process of political change in France.[45] The populist parties, observed Fitzherbert, hoped to foil the royalist international conspiracy by holding public debates on the executive powers of the Crown as they applied to the Family Compact treaty: 'It seems to have been principally with a view of guarding against such designs that the latter have chosen the present moment for carrying into Execution their plan of transferring the Power of making War and Peace from the Crown to the National Assembly.' The mediation offer from Foreign Minister Montmorin made a striking contrast to what Merry described as French-inspired Spanish defiance. As had been the case in October 1789, the British government was seemingly confronted with two French foreign policies.

Pitt had been following French and Spanish affairs with interest. Judging by his amendments to – and drafts of – the outgoing dispatches, he had been directing British foreign policy since January 1790. It was Leeds, however, who decided to call the Spanish bluff at the beginning of June.[46] The Spanish government, now willing to discuss trade and settlement, still refused to grant compensation to the British merchants. Pitt and Leeds had always insisted that an admission of liability precede any conference on trade and settlement. Although a French naval armament was preparing at Brest, the British government thought it unlikely that it would put to sea.[47] By 27 June 1790 Leeds had persuaded the Cabinet to vote for war. Pitt, who as usual had been the voice of caution, 'hardly knew how to conjecture on the possibility of peace or war', though he was committed to it in principle.[48] On 5 July full and immediate compensation for British losses at Nootka was demanded from Madrid.

The goodwill of the French Assembly would determine whether or not Spain received naval assistance. On 1 July the Assembly was still haggling over the royal power to make war and peace, whereupon Pitt and Leeds began to consider negotiation with French reform groups in the National Assembly. Fitzgerald had written on 7 May that the 'popular party' was consistently successful in debates 'where the power of the Crown is to be diminished'. On 15 July Pitt sent William Augustus Miles to Paris as a special envoy. Miles, a freelance journalist with a sideline as a Foreign Office spy, was asked to tap his network of French contacts for information on the future direction of the revolution. Stationed in Paris for ten months, he did little but convince the French government that he was Pitt's personal spy.[49]

Spain agreed in principle to compensate the dispossessed Nootka merchants on 24 August 1790. On the 26th the Assembly annulled the mutual defence clauses of the Family Compact and Leeds was relieved to find that separate negotiation with French politicians had not been necessary.[50] The French, however, continued to arm as a gesture of support for Spain, while Gower warned Leeds that the royalist party was still hot for war. The new ambassador told his superiors not to underestimate the naval strength of France: 'I firmly believe that nothing but want of discipline could prevent this country from sending to sea a fleet of 1 and 20 sail of the line immediately if it were thought necessary.'[51]

The Spanish government, appalled by the National Assembly's proposal to transform the Family Compact into a National Compact, proposed to ally with Britain instead. A delighted Pitt started to draft defence and commerce treaties. Leeds, though pleased, suspected that Spain was playing for time and, on 2 October, a British ultimatum demanding immediate compensation for the Nootka merchants was sent to Madrid.[52] The British government had been insisting since August that Spain drop its claims to an exclusive sovereignty over commerce and settlement in the north-west Pacific. By 16 October Pitt was more than half-convinced that Spain would fight for its self-declared monopoly. Richmond advised Pitt to make Trinidad and New Orleans the targets of a West Indian winter campaign.[53] Having succumbed once more to apprehensions that France was arming in earnest, Pitt sent Hugh Elliot, former ambassador to Denmark, on a secret mission to Paris.

By 20 October Spain had conceded Britain's right to set up and man outposts on the west coast of North America, with which Pitt was delighted. Elliot's mission was still rendered necessary by the French naval preparations and the appointment of a new Fayettist ministry in Paris.[54] Elliot, not the most discreet of diplomats, had received a sharp rap on the knuckles in 1789 for having, without clearance from London, brokered an armistice between Sweden and Denmark during the Baltic crisis of 1788–9. He had gone to school in Paris, however, and was on friendly terms with the Comte de Mirabeau, amongst other revolutionary notables. Elliot, authorized to treat with the Comité Diplomatique, was nevertheless to tell the Fayettist ministry that Britain remained strictly neutral to the revolution, eschewing alliance with France or any of its political parties.[55] Any French offer to intercede in the Anglo-Spanish dispute was to be declined politely but firmly. On 26 October 1790 Elliot reported to Pitt that both Mirabeau and the Fayettists wanted to ally with Britain. These overtures were ignored by Pitt, who was relieved to find that the new French government was not hostile to Britain.[56] Any further dealings with France or its politicians were cut off by the receipt of news on 4 November that Spain was to disarm, having admitted the justice of Britain's claims.

The Nootka crisis of 1790 strengthened Pitt's resolve to have as little to do with revolutionary France as possible. The British government was by no means disappointed with the direction that the revolution had taken. Necker's resignation confirmed that Louis XVI's ministers had little power either at home or abroad. Equally interesting to British observers were the French Assembly's debates on the future of the Family Compact. These stunned British ministers, not accustomed to a legislature's refusals to ratify treaties, let alone propose modifications to them.[57] The British government, while alarmed by the politicization of French diplomacy, was nevertheless in a unique position to assess its repercussions for European politics. It was all too familiar with the presentation of treaties to Parliament, the voting of ordinary and extraordinary supplies, the conduct of negotiations amongst factional groups and the manipulation of public opinion. Were France to set up a public finance system on the Anglo-Dutch model, as Pitt had feared in 1788 that Necker might, France would indeed become 'a more formidable enemy'. To counterbalance this, the 'secret diplomacy' that had made *ancien régime* France an international force to be feared and respected – and of which treaties like the 1761 Family Compact were exemplars – was now on the way to supervision by a regulatory authority promising to be more powerful than Parliament. Subject to such limitations upon its freedom of action, France would become 'a less objectionable neighbour'.

For the moment two types of diplomacy, the public and the private, were at loggerheads in France. Pitt's use of personal agents (Miles and Elliot) reflects his frustration with the threat of war looming over Britain, what he saw as the Foreign Secretary's slapdash belligerence and the inadequacy of the information coming from Paris. Pitt did not have the stomach for gunboat diplomacy nor was he comfortable with the introduction of so many unpredictable, if not entirely unknown, variables in French politics and government. By the autumn of 1790 the British government, wary of antagonizing the French government, Assembly or people, was unwilling to be associated with the French Revolution in any capacity.

Protest and Public Order

In May 1791 Pitt had finally taken notice of the English intellectual debate on the French Revolution. Of radical publications, he had told the Commons that 'he did not venture to think that there might be no danger arising from them', but that 'he could not think the French

Revolution or any of the new constitutions, could be deemed an object fit for imitation in this country by any set of men'.[58] Pitt left no recorded objections to – or approval of – the new French constitutional monarchy, the Civil Constitution of the Clergy or the administrative and judicial reforms taking place in the French provinces from 1789 onwards. None of them, he thought, was appropriate for introduction in England and he thought that this conviction was shared by the majority of his countrymen.

Such views received negative confirmation in July 1791, when a Bastille Day dinner staged by Joseph Priestley and his fellow Birmingham dissenters ended in a 'Church and King' riot. Pitt had little to say about popular disturbances before 1791, but what comments he left to posterity are negative. At the beginning of 1779, when England was threatened by a Franco-Spanish invasion following the entry of both states to the American War of Independence on the side of the Thirteen Colonies, Admiral Augustus Keppel was court-martialled for a supposed dereliction of duty after failing to pursue a slightly superior French naval force that had been met and briefly engaged off Ushant. When news of Keppel's acquittal reached London on 11 February, impromptu riots broke out in the capital and the provinces:

> I rejoice to hear that the good people of England have so universally exerted their natural Right of Breaking Windows, Picking Pockets, &c. &c. and that these Constitutional Demonstrations of Joy are not confined to the Metropolis ... I begin to fear that the Clamour may subside and the King still be blest with his present faithful servants.[59]

The Keppel riots have yet to be placed in the list of 'admirals as heroes' tradition of popular political protest. Keppel was the darling of the Rockingham Whigs and his acquittal, as Pitt observed, was seen at all political and social levels as a severe blow to the North ministry. Pitt saw no distinction between 'legal' and 'illegal' riots. The former definition was applied by many to victory, food, wage and, occasionally, election riots. Pitt knew that rioting was seen by the lower orders as a sort of right, a concept which he disliked, though he had remarked on the 'Peaceable Temper of the Mob' in the Keppel riots.[60] His comments on the Gordon riots illustrate his disapproval for the politics of popular protest. These demonstrations, instigated by the mad Lord George Gordon and a London mob enraged by the passage of Catholic relief legislation in 1780, terrorized the metropolis for a week. Pitt had joined the Lincoln's Inn volunteer corps to repel the crowd: 'we may at last sleep in a Christian country,' he observed with sarcasm to his mother after the violence had subsided.[61]

With these attitudes, it is not surprising to find Pitt supporting the London and Westminster police bill of 1785, which proposed to establish stipendiary magistrates' bureaux in metropolitan parishes. The bill was defeated on its first reading, on which occasion Pitt confessed 'himself not to be perfectly master of the subject'.[62] The London and Westminster police bill was the brainchild of John Reeves, ex-Chief Justice of Newfoundland and later to be famous as the founding father of the loyal association movement in 1792. A pared-down version of the London police bill was passed in June 1792. By then Pitt's belief in the utility of a London police force had been reinforced by the Birmingham riots of 1791 and he gave 'Mr. Reeves – Police Money' during the autumn of 1792.[63]

The government was aware that supporters of the French Revolution would gather to celebrate the fall of the Bastille. When riot warnings arrived at the Home Office on 9 July 1792, they were greeted with derision. 'Is it possible that any man can entertain serious apprehensions of disturbance on 14 July?', asked an incredulous George Rose, who traced these tales to 'the Partizans of M. de Calonne's fortunes or to Imaginations terrified by the Phantoms of Mr Burke'.[64] On 10 July a Plymouth magistrate reported that the locals were uneasy about dissenter preparations for Bastille Day and, on the 11th, Home Secretary Henry Dundas received a hearsay account of a plot to free the inmates of the King's Bench prison during the 14 July festivities. The Birmingham Friends of Liberty had begun to prepare for their annual French Revolution dinner on 9 July and handbills were distributed to publicize the event. The official advertisement was innocuous enough, but this could not be said of all the publicity material:

Is it possible to forget that your own Parliament is venal? Your Minister hypocritical? Your Clergy legal oppressors? The reigning Family extravagant? The Crown of a certain Personage becoming every day too weighty for the head that wears it? Too weighty for the People that *gave* it? Your taxes partial and excessive? Your representation a cruel *insult* upon the sacred rights of property, religion and freedom?

Sent to London by the Birmingham magistrates John Carles and Thomas Spencer, this was described by Francis Freeling, Superintendent of the Post Office, as 'the most treasonable and seditious Handbills that ever saw the light [of day]'.

I rec'd by the post this morning the favour of your letter inclosing a very Criminal Handbill, which had been found at a public house in Birmingham ... you will, I am persuaded make use of all proper means to endeavour to discover any persons who may be concerned in circulating papers of this nature and it will be desirable that you should send an early account in order that his Majesty's Law Servants may consider in what means it may be proper to proceed.[65]

This was evidently seditious libel prosecution material.

The Home Office made preparations for disorder in London but 'our day passed very quietly ... a most sovereign contempt was displayed for French politics'.[66] Midlands opposition to the Bastille Day celebrations took the form of religious bigotry and, on 16 July, three units of the 15th Regiment of Dragoons were sent to Birmingham. Within twenty-four hours the Home Office was scrambling for reinforcements. By 19 July magistrates in Coventry and Wolverhampton were asking for military aid to keep a troubled populace in check.[67] Despite the dispatch of regular troops, the rioters in Birmingham continued to attack the houses and property of dissenters; the Bastille Day dinner staged by Priestley and his friends had given locals the opportunity to vent their resentment against the nonconformist community in general: 'From the long continuance of these riotous proceedings, and the danger of their spreading to other places, Mr Dundas, having advised with Lord Grenville and Mr Pitt, has thought it expedient to send further reinforcements to Birmingham and its neighbourhood.'[68] Pitt drew up a list of troop detachments for the Midlands, some of which were from bases as distant as Salisbury and Chichester. Dundas warned the High Sheriffs of Worcestershire, Staffordshire, Oxfordshire and Shropshire to take action against 'any mischief which may be meditated'.[69] The government was perplexed and alarmed by the severity and duration of the Birmingham riots, so much so that Pitt conducted a national defence review during the autumn and winter of 1791–2. By 20 July 1791 Birmingham was reputed to be quiet although requests for troops were still coming in from Bristol and Sheffield. Riot reports from Birmingham and its environs could not explain the extent and violence of the riots but their authors agreed that hostility towards the dissenters had been the principal cause. Prosecution instructions were dispatched to the Treasury solicitor on 21 July, for Dundas was determined to see the 'speedy Trial and Punishment of any such offenders as may appear to be Objects for public Example'.[70]

The Home Office is not to blame for the failure of Birmingham magistrates to act against the rioters, nor for the trials in which only a handful of offenders were convicted. Riot control was a local responsibility and the ministry could do little but respond to regional demands for central assistance. Neither premier nor Home Secretary was happy with the handling of the Birmingham riots. In May 1792 Dundas told the Commons that prospects for the conviction of Birmingham magistrates on charges of misconduct were poor. He also stated that such trials would hold up dissenter claims to parliamentary compensation for the losses they had suffered.[71] This was no fiction. So dissatisfied were Pitt and Dundas with the riot reports reaching the government from Birmingham that, by 17 July, they were in search of additional data from acquaintances and local notables.[72] Pitt, Dundas and Grenville were appalled by the violence: 'I do not admire riots in favour of the government much more than riots against it,' observed Grenville. Pitt, when questioned about the Birmingham riots by Fox in the Commons, replied that all public disturbances, 'whether proceeding from fanaticism, republicanism or any other cause', would be dealt with 'in the most effectual manner'.[73] This suggests that Pitt held the dissenters responsible for initiating the violence but he was not blind to their sufferings. In August 1792 his financial connections in the City of London were instrumental in facilitating the release of parliamentary compensation to the Birmingham dissenter community.[74] Inadequate though this was, it was better than nothing.

The Birmingham riots only confirmed Pitt's poor opinion of the lower orders. After three campaigns for the repeal of the Test and Corporation Acts, British intolerance towards Protestant nonconformists had been revived with a vengeance. The government learned several things from the Birmingham riots. Not only was popular bigotry a force to be reckoned with, but fear of the French Revolution and its principles was now widespread in the higher social orders. Gregory Farquharson pitied the dissenters, but was glad that their proselytizing activities in support of the revolution had been checked: 'I have recently returned from the North of England, where I found the Doctrines alleged to have been propagated by Mr Paine, are known to many of the lowest people – nor are they unknown to many of our Soldiers.'[75] Oliver de Lancey thought that the Birmingham experience had strengthened the hands of the magistracy and weakened the appeal of British Jacobinism. George III was pleased that Priestley had met his comeuppance.[76]

The ministry had heard something, though not much, of Paine and part I of *The Rights of Man*, written in response to Burke's *Reflections*, before July 1791. During the Commons debates on the Royal Proclamation against Seditious Writings on 21 May 1792, Dundas said that *The Rights of Man* and other radical writings had become the targets of seditious libel prosecution as soon as their principles had been adopted by the Manchester Constitutional Society (MCS) and other provincial reform groups. The MCS, an organization founded in 1790, was representative not of the lower orders, but of the middle orders, and it is unlikely that the government saw much to fear from its activities in 1791. *The Rights of Man* was not declared a seditious libel until the publication of part II in February 1792, by which date, as Dundas told the Commons, provincial political societies were beginning to discuss democratic parliamentary reform.[77]

By August 1791 the Birmingham riots had alerted the Cabinet to the inflammatory effects of French ideas, both on radicals and conservatives. Pitt, however, did not believe that English radical violence would be inspired by the French Revolution. In January 1792 he said of riots in general that 'moderation and perseverance were the best means of getting rid of such disorders'.[78] These convictions were not shared by his colleagues, nor by the statesmen of Europe, whose attention was to focus on revolutionary France during the summer of 1791.

From Ochakow to Pillnitz

At the end of 1790 the British government was still considering the merits of a Spanish alliance, the value of which depended entirely on the outcome of the revolution in France. Two scenarios presented themselves: the restoration of the *ancien régime* in all its glory, in which case the Family Compact was likely to become a much stronger bond between France and Spain; or the survival of a constitutional monarchy, under which the new France would probably be hostile to the old blood allies of the Bourbons. The first development could be forestalled by the signature of an Anglo-Spanish alliance but Britain was best served in the second instance, particularly in the West Indies and Canada, by not signing an agreement with Spain, for Pitt had already identified America and post-revolutionary France as allies in North America.[79] The British government did not pursue the Spanish alliance, nor, by the end of 1790, was the court of Madrid enthusiastic about the project. Spain, though anxious to avoid isolation, was not likely to abandon France 'as long as there remains any prospect of a re-establishment of the Royal authority on its former footing'.[80] The Pitt ministry decided that, with France prostrate, Spain was not worth an alliance in the short run.

As France was now the leper of Europe, the British government felt confident about widening its interests, burning its fingers badly in so doing in 1791. In December 1790 Pitt and Leeds received the news that Catherine the Great proposed to keep the Black Sea port of Ochakow and its surrounding territory as a modification of a status quo peace in the east. Ochakow would not have been of any interest to Pitt, had not he, Joseph Ewart and Daniel Hailes, the senior British resident in Warsaw, sought to find an alternative supplier of hemp, timber and wheat from Poland. Russia, Britain's traditional source of naval supplies, had repeatedly refused to renew a 1756 trade treaty with

England on favourable terms despite Ambassador Sir Charles Whitworth's best efforts. For Pitt, committed to an expensive naval rebuilding programme, finding a new and reliable supplier whose economy did not compete with that of Britain was a major priority.[81]

Pitt had been interested in Poland as a potential trade partner since May 1790 and, when Ewart came home on leave in November 1790 with Prussian proposals to ally with Poland, Pitt considered its addition to the Triple Alliance. Prussia had signed an alliance with Poland in March to put a check on Russia's westward expansion.[82] The chief obstacle to be overcome was Prussian insistence on the acquisition of Thorn and Dantzig, a proposal unacceptable to the Polish Diet. By January 1791 the Poles, lured by promises of Anglo-Prussian military protection and very favourable trade terms, had agreed to let the port of Dantzig go. The importance of Ochakow lay in its command over navigation on the rivers Bug and Dnieper, through which the trade of Poland's richest provinces was carried to the Black Sea.[83] By the spring of 1791 Pitt was committed to the maintenance of Ochakow in Turkish hands and future Ottoman membership of the fast expanding Triple Alliance. He had always seen a federative alliance network in commercial as well as diplomatic and strategic terms.

When Anglo-Prussian threats of armed intervention, made from 8 January 1791 onwards, failed to intimidate Catherine the Great into abandoning Ochakow, the Cabinet voted for war on 22 March. Pitt was not anticipating trouble with Parliament; on 19 February Auckland had written to Keith that: 'Nothing can be more brilliant than our position in England.' Faced by a divided Cabinet and an unsympathetic House of Commons during debates on the mobilization of the fleet against Russia, Pitt decided on 10 April to compromise with Russia. His colleagues agreed on 12 April. Leeds, unable to accept this, resigned on 21 April.[84] The Prussians, though dismayed by Pitt's volte-face over the projected naval armament, continued to believe that some British pressure would still be applied to Russia. New peace terms sent to Berlin on 19 April had proposed that the Russians demilitarize Ochakow or keep the fortress without the surrounding territory that gave it strategic and commercial significance. On 24 May the British government received a request for a British Black Sea squadron to back up the new proposals.[85] Pitt and the new Foreign Secretary, William Grenville, replied in the negative: 'The same circumstances that compelled our departure from the original line adopted, operate with at least equal force against our recurring partially to it.' Pitt stated that 'the obvious effect of our persisting would have been to risk the existence of the present government and with it the whole of our system at home and abroad'.[86] Pitt still wanted Poland, Austria and Turkey to be added to the Triple Alliance.

Pitt's fears were very real. The Opposition Whigs had not only sown the seeds of dissent in the Commons, but had taken the question of war with Russia to the country. The Foxites were vocal and persuasive pacifists: 'I fear Opposition is too busy & too successful in spreading insidious reports all over the Country, in order to alarm the Public.'[87] Vorontsov was also active in the public relations campaign against war, buying up twenty newspapers and a small army of hack writers. Pitt was severely shaken by 'the prospect of not being cordially supported by Parlt. or the people'.[88]

The Prussians, disgusted by the conduct of an ally towards whom they had been growing lukewarm since 1789, decided to pursue an independent connection with Austria. Frederick William II, who had sent Colonel Bischoffswerder to Vienna in January 1791 to negotiate an alliance which England and the United Provinces would later be invited to join, revived this scheme at the end of May. Leopold II had given his preliminary consent to the project on 25 February 1791. Frederick William was anxious to get Austrian support for the new eastern peace terms proposed by Britain and to protect Poland against Russian expansion, all the more important as the Warsaw revolution of 3 May was inviting external intervention in Polish affairs. Pitt was alive to the importance of an independent Poland as a buffer state: 'The Establishment of a Solid and Permanent Government in that Country [Poland] would be advantageous to the General Interests of Europe, and might operate as a substantial check on the Ambition of Russia in any enterprise that she might hereafter form against the Porte.'[89] The British government was, nevertheless, unwilling to contract new obligations in a European theatre where Parliament had stated so strongly that it had no role to play. Leeds had originally wanted both imperial powers to be included in the Triple Alliance after the Russian threat in the east had been neutralized. Pitt, not enthusiastic about the prospect of a Russian alliance, favoured the forging of an Austrian link. Joseph II had died in March 1790 and the ministry had resolved on an approach to his successor, Leopold II. In November the young and inexperienced Lord Elgin had been sent to attend upon the Grand Duke of Tuscany, whose official coronation as Holy Roman Emperor would not take place until September 1791. When Bischoffswerder returned to Vienna at the beginning of June, Elgin was pushed aside. On 8 July he was recalled by Grenville.[90]

Although the British government was getting little in the way of confidential and detailed information about the Austro-Prussian talks, what it did learn made it uneasy. Particularly alarming was the interest that Frederick William and Leopold were taking in the fortunes of the French Bourbons. Pitt, who had hoped that imperial hostility to the revolution would bring Austria into an alliance with Britain and

Prussia, was determined to avoid involvement 'in any degree to any-thing, which can show any disposition to interfere in the internal affairs of France'. He was dismayed to find that 'The restoration of affairs in France is the Chief Spring of His Imperial Majesty's System.'[91] The Comte d'Artois, Louis XVI's youngest brother, had been taking a counter- revolutionary begging bowl around Europe since late 1789. He received plenty of sympathy, but no cash. Leopold, by no means deaf to the appeals of his sister, Marie Antoinette, had tried to dissuade Artois from precipitate action at the beginning of June. Three paths of action, said the emperor, were open to the friends of the French Bourbons:

> The allowing the fermentation to subside of itself
> A general interposition of Foreign Powers –
> An Invitation from the Royal Party; for a manifesto from the King (if he could be released from his captivity) addressed to the Sovereigns connected with the Royal Family of France to assist in forming their Constitution, and re-establishing a calm in their Affairs.[92]

Louis XVI's abortive flight to Varennes focused the attention of Europe on France: 'We are all anxious spectators of the events in France,' wrote Pitt to his mother.[93] The British government was in no position to do anything but watch, for its diplomatic status continued to sink over the summer of 1791 and, by August, Pitt and Grenville were anxious to extricate Britain from its eastern commitments.

William Fawkener had been sent to St Petersburg as the special envoy appointed to ensure that Russia did not keep Ochakow, its fortifications and its surrounding territory. The Prussians, who saw themselves as having been deserted by the British, left the negotiations to Fawkener and Whitworth, who did not succeed in enforcing their masters' modifications to the status quo. To add insult to injury, Robert Adair, an Opposition MP planning to speculate in British government securities, appeared in St Petersburg at the end of July to collect information on war and peace.[94] Not only was he shown some con-fidential documentation by the Russian court, but, in sending the news home, he implicated Fox in his dealings when his letters were inter-cepted by the Post Office.

Pitt, who kept copies of the correspondence with the intention, later abandoned, of impeaching Adair, was led to believe that Fox was conducting an alternative foreign policy in order to discredit His Ma-jesty's Government. Fox's contacts with France were already suspect. 'What do you think of Fox's letter to Barnarve?', wrote Grenville to Auckland 'Is not the idea of Ministers from Opposition to the different Courts of Europe a new one in this country?'[95] Fox's thoughts on

France, as Adair explained to the Russians, gave the ministry some cause for concern:

> I made no Difficulty in assuring them and that so decidedly as to preclude any return to the Subject, that the only Advantage you would ever take of the Distractions of France, was that which you had recommended to Mr. Pitt in Parliament, namely a Reduction of our Debt and a System of Alliance as far as Circumstances might render them practicable, and further that I was convinced if our Ministers at home entertained any Design of Employing the Forces of England in any hostile Attempt against France, you would oppose it with as much Earnestness as you had done that against Russia, and I made no doubt with as much Success.[96]

Pitt had no intention of going to war with France, but he did not want to see Britain's neutrality compromised by a shadow foreign policy. Opposition links with France were well-established, so much so that the French government saw Pitt as Fox did, as the servant of George III.[97] In the aftermath of Ochakow, an insecure ministry sought nothing more than isolation.

While Grenville admitted that imperial interference in France 'may be productive of consequences advantageous to the Allies', he was not going to support any Austrian venture on behalf of the Bourbons: 'We are not without good hopes of being able to put things in such shape … as will restore to us full confidence, and make our adversaries feel that all their expectations derived from the occurrence of last spring, will totally fail them.'[98] From June to August 1791 the Pitt ministry was plagued by the European courts for a new statement on the French Revolution. As Artois had been told by the emperor, England 'was much more directly concerned in these affairs'. Because the British government was in no position to exercise any moral or diplomatic leadership in Europe, Grenville stated that nothing could be said pending the end of the Sistovo talks on peace in the east. He was also waiting to see whether anything remained of Britain's security network, the future of which lay in Prussian hands.

On 25 July Austria and Prussia signed the preliminary articles of their alliance. From Ewart, the Foreign Office discovered that Austria insisted upon Russian membership in the new system, while Prussia, turning a blind eye to the voice of Parliament, wanted Poland and the Porte to join: 'I leave it up to your Lordship and His Majesty's other Ministers', wrote Ewart, 'to judge what could be expected from such a combination.'[99] The British government, hamstrung by its enthusiasm for a federative alliance, was now looking for escape from a coalition seemingly framed for the pursuit of eastern expansion: 'Can we guarantee to her [Russia] the Crimea by a defensive alliance? Can we, on the other hand, refuse the accession of any of the great powers without breaking in upon our avowed and ostensible principle?' Poland looked safe for the moment, as indeed it was, but Ewart warned his superiors on 4 August that a second partition was mooted by Russia, in which 'this country might be under the necessity of concurring, as it could not prevent its execution'.[100] On 19 September the British government cited unresolved commercial differences with Russia as its excuse for not joining the eastern alliance.

On 4 August the Austrians and Turks finally came to an agreement at Sistovo. This, as Grenville put it, 'has removed every difficulty which there was in our speaking out, and avowing our most scrupulous neutrality in the French business'. Pitt was relieved to be free from further embarrassment: 'Our different Business on the Continent is on the whole tolerably well over.'[101] The ministry withdrew into isolation to lick its wounds. Pitt pointed with satisfaction to 'a very promising Revenue' and was planning tax cuts for 1792 which, he hoped, would restore the confidence of the public in his government. Anxious eyes were now fixed on France, where Austrian intervention was looking increasingly likely: 'We are all extremely anxious for the presentation of the French Constitution,' remarked Grenville on 31 August.

When the 1791 constitution was accepted by Louis XVI and Leopold II, the British government decided that the Pillnitz Declaration of 27 August was an empty threat. Leopold and Frederick William pledged themselves to restore royal order and good government to France, but were not committed to any specific measures. Pitt was concerned enough about Pillnitz to consult Burke, whose attachment to the French royalist cause was so strong that his son Richard was sent to the *émigré* camp at Coblentz to learn what he could of French and Austrian intentions. When Dundas found out from Mercy d'Argenteau, via Burke senior, that '*neither the Emperor nor any other Power in Europe would take any part in the affairs of France until they were apprised of the dispositions of this Court and Ministry*', Pitt was relieved. Burke was mortified.[102] Of the Pillnitz Declaration, in which Leopold and Frederick William II had threatened armed intervention in the revolution on behalf of Louis XVI, Grenville remarked: 'these great princes are desirous of saying much, and appearing to have a great influence on the course of events, but ... they are quite determined to do nothing'. Dundas agreed.[103]

On 14 October the British government acknowledged the 1791 constitution.[104] By then Britain's withdrawal from Europe was almost complete, barring the revival of a prospective Anglo-Spanish alliance, which Burges described as 'a thing very much wished for by us all'.[105] This had been mooted once more by an uneasy Spanish government after the flight to Varennes and was embraced by a London ministry by no means happy about its exclusion from continental politics. In a return to the commercial diplomacy of the early 1780s, Pitt was determined that no alliance be signed without the corresponding commercial treaty, 'which we have so long looked for in vain'. Although the ministry was not desperate enough to seize any alliance that offered itself, Grenville and Auckland were concerned about Britain's isolation in Europe. Both men were worried about the security of the Austrian Netherlands. Should insurrection break out in Flanders and Brabant once more, 'It would, I fear, be very difficult to prevent the flame from spreading to Holland. If it did, France would play the same game there as in the Netherlands.' Were the French to resort to these tactics, in self-defence 'We must interfere'. On 1 May 1791 Grenville had hoped that Britain would be able to stop subsidizing the Hessian mercenaries hired in 1788 to prevent the Dutch Patriots from rising once more, either alone or in conjunction with their French or Flemish friends. By August 1791, with Austro-Prussian hostility to the revolution so clearly in evidence, he was afraid that moral and diplomatic pressure alone would drive the French to the active pursuit of subversive retaliation. Worse still, should war break out in the name of the revolution, thought Grenville, its ideas would be transmitted to neighbouring states through the soldiers who went to fight in or against France.[106]

This was not a fear shared by Pitt. At another of Dundas's dinner parties, held on 14 October: 'They talk much of Burke – particularly Grenville – and against Lafayette, who rather defended by Pitt'. The *ci-devant* Marquis de Lafayette, commander of the Paris National Guard, had sat at the feet of George Washington in the 1770s and was an aristocratic liberal of neo-Whig principles. 'Not all the French islands are worth one year of the peace and tranquillity we are enjoying', stated Grenville, for whom British diplomatic neutrality was a shield against French intellectual infection. Pitt did not share these sentiments. When warned by Burke of the universal danger that the French Revolution posed to the old European order, his answer was: 'Never fear, Mr Burke: depend on it we shall go on as we are until the Day of Judgement.'[107]

Notes

1. J. Black, *Natural and Necessary Enemies: Anglo-French Relations in the Eighteenth Century* (1986), pp. 180–6; D. Jarrett, *Begetters of Revolution: England's Involvement with France 1759–1789* (1973), pp. 233–4.
2. HO 42/19, W. Heywood to W. Russell, 27 October and 25 November 1789, fos 8–11.
3. L. G. Mitchell, *Charles James Fox and the Disintegration of the Whig Party 1782–1794* (Oxford: 1971), p. 85.

4. PRO 30/8/338, Grenville's election forecast, [August] 1788.

5. Auckland Correspondence, i, J. Hatsell to Auckland, 6 October 1788, pp. 233–4.

6. J. Hutton (ed.), *Selections from the Correspondence of James Bland Burges, Bart* (1885), Bland Burges to Ann Burges, 11 January 1789, p. 126.

7. *Court and Cabinets*, i, Sir W. Young to Buckingham, 10 August 1788, p. 418.

8. *Ibid.*, ii, Grenville to Buckingham, 4 December 1788, p. 32.

9. R. Thorne (ed.), *The History of Parliament: The Commons 1790–1820* (5 vols, 1986) i, pp. 111–14.

10. Burke Correspondence, ii, Burke to Fitzwilliam, 29 July 1790, p. 128; D. E. Ginter, 'The financing of the Whig Party organization 1783–1793', *American Historical Review* 71 (1966), pp. 421–40.

11. *History of Parliament*, i, p. 116.

12. E. Ashbourne (ed.), *Pitt, Some Chapters of his Life and Times* (1898), Pitt to Rutland, 20 August 1785, pp. 146–7.

13. *PR*, xxvii, Flood, 4 March 1790, pp. 201–6; for Pitt, see pp. 209–10.

14. *PH*, xxv, 'Summary Explanation of the Principles behind Mr. Pitt's Bill', 18 April 1785, cols 446–8; Wyvill Papers, iv, 'Heads of a Bill', p. 109.

15. *CJ*, xlv, p. 275; *History of Parliament*, i, p. 114.

16. HA 119 T108/42, Pitt to Tomline, [9 December 1790].

17. *PR*, xxvii, 2 March 1790, pp. 155–61; G. M. Ditchfield, 'The parliamentary struggle over the repeal of the Test and Corporation Acts, 1787–1790', *EHR* 89 (1974), pp. 559–60, and 'The debates on the Test and Corporation Acts 1787–1790: the evidence of the Division Lists', *BIHR* 50 (1977), pp. 69–81.

18. *History of Parliament*, i, pp. 114, 117; HA 119 T108/39, 293, Pitt to E. J. Eliot, 9 July 1790.

19. PRO 30/8/157, note by Dundas, fos 96–7.

20. Addington Life, i, Pitt to Addington, 15 July 1788, pp. 55–6; *Court and Cabinets*, ii, Lord Bulkeley to Buckingham, 25 November 1788, pp. 14–16.

21. Auckland Correspondence,. i, A. Storer to Auckland, 28 November 1788, p. 377; *Life of Wilberforce*, i, Diary, 22 November 1790, p. 284.

22. Mrs Baring (ed.), *The Windham Diary* (1866), 7 November 1790, p. 213; *Life and Letters*, ii, Elliot to Lady Elliot, 4 December 1790.

23. *PH*, xxviii, col. 467.

24. C. Butler, account of interview with Pitt, cited in B. Ward, *The Dawn of the Catholic Revival in England* (2 vols, 1909), i, pp. 128–9.

25. PRO 30/8/310, 'Observations on the Purport, Grounds and Effects of the Intended Application of the English Catholics to Parliament for Relief', fos 215–16.

26. *Life of Stanhope*, Stanhope to Petre, 14 November 1788, p. 80.

27. CUL 6958/3, 525, W. Fermor to Grenville, 24 July 1788; Kent Archives Office, U840 Z4, queries to Catholic universities, with their answers.

28. CUL 6958/4, 913, T. Weld to Pitt, 18 February 1791.

29. Ward, *Dawn of the Catholic Revival*, i, ch. 5; P. Langford, *Public Life and the Propertied Englishman 1689–1798* (Oxford: 1991), pp. 98–102; *PR*, xxix, 1 and 8 April 1791, pp. 53–4, 78–9: Thurlow was still complaining in June

1791; *Dropmore*, ii, Grenville to Thurlow and Thurlow's reply, 4–5 June 1791, pp. 89–91; PRO 30/8/135, W. Fermor to Pitt, 19 June 1791, fo. 75.

30. *Ibid.*, Pitt to Grenville, 11 January 1791, p. 13.

31. *PR*, xxix, 18 and 19 April 1791, pp. 239–40, 288–95.

32. R. Furneaux, *William Wilberforce* (1974), pp. 106–9; J. R. Oldfield, 'The London Committee and the campaign for the abolition of the slave trade', p. 333.

33. *Life of Wilberforce*, i, Dundas to Wilberforce, 18 July 1791, p. 344, and Journal, 25 October 1791, pp. 316–17.

34. BL Add MS 28065, Leeds to Fitzherbert, 12 January 1790, fo. 25; FO 7/19, 6, Leeds to Keith, 12 January 1790; Bodleian Library, Dep Bland Burges 30, fos 11–12, Bland Burges to Auckland, 16 March 1790; J. Black, *British Foreign Policy in an Age of Revolutions, 1783–1793* (Cambridge: 1994), pp. 217–20.

35. Pitt appears to have drafted most of the dispatches: FO 64/17, 10, Leeds to Ewart, 30 March 1790, and FO 7/19, 6 and 7, Leeds to Keith, 16 and 30 March 1790.

36. FO 7/20, 47, Keith to Leeds, 17 April 1790, and 53, 24 April 1790.

37. *Ibid.*, 11, Leeds to Keith, 23 May 1790.

38. *Ibid.*, 63, Keith to Leeds, 26 May 1790, 73, 11 June 1790, and 13, 8 June 1790; FO 64/17, 12, Leeds to Ewart (drafted by Pitt), 21 May 1790; FO 65/18, 4, Leeds to Whitworth, 15 June 1790; FO 7/20, 15, Leeds to Keith, 25 June 1790.

39. *PH*, xxviii, debate on the army estimates, 9 February 1790, col. 351.

40. FO 64/17, 13, Ewart to Leeds, 18 February 1790, and 4, Leeds to Ewart, 26 February 1790 (amended by Pitt).

41. BL Add MS 28065, Fitzherbert to Leeds, 16 March 1790, fos 198–9, and Leeds to Auckland, 29 March 1790, fo. 227.

42. PRO 30/8/102, Pitt to Leeds, 23 February 1790, fo. 170; FO 72/16, Leeds to del Campo (almost completely rewritten by Pitt), 26 February 1790, fos 136–7.

43. FO 72/16, 11, Merry to Leeds, 4 February 1790, 26 and 28, Merry to Leeds, 5 and 12 April 1790.

44. FO 72/17, 1, A. Fitzherbert to Leeds, 15 May 1790.

45. O. Browning (ed.), *Despatches from Paris, 1784–1790* (2 vols, 1909–10), ii, Fitzgerald to Leeds, 14 May 1790, pp. 311–16; FO 72/27, 2, Fitzherbert to Leeds, 20 May 1790.

46. Pitt's drafts and amendments appear in the Austria, Prussia and Spain files; H. V. Evans, 'The Nootka Sound controversy in Anglo-French diplomacy', *Journal of Modern History* 4 (1974), p. 615; J. M. Norris, 'The policy of the British Cabinet in the Nootka Crisis', *EHR* 70 (1955), pp. 562–80; PRO 30/8/151, Leeds to Pitt, 2 June 1790, fos 31–5.

47. FO 27/35, 2, Leeds to Gower, 7 June 1790.

48. Evans, 'The Nootka Sound controversy', pp. 615–16; PRO 30/8/119, Camden to Pitt, 29 June 1790, fo. 162; BL Add MS 28066, Leeds to Pitt, 5 July 1790, fos 67–8; PRO 30/29/384/1/15, Pitt to Stafford, 27 June 1790.

49. H. V. Evans, 'William Pitt, William Miles and the French Revolution',

BIHR 43 (1970), pp. 190–213; Browning (ed.), *Despatches from Paris*, ii, Fitzgerald to Leeds, 18 June 1790, pp. 326–9; Miles Correspondence, i, Miles to Buckingham, 15 July 1790, p. 150; Evans, 'The Nootka Sound controversy', pp. 617–19.

50. Bod, Dep Bland Burges 37, Leeds to Burges, 29 August 1790, fo. 25; FO 65/19, Leeds to Whitworth, 6 August 1790, fo. 43.

51. O. Browning (ed.), *The Despatches of Lord Gower, 1790–1792* (1885), Gower to Leeds, 10 September 1790, p. 32, and 5 October 1790, p. 36.

52. FO 72/19, 26, Fitzherbert to Leeds, 16 September 1790; FO 72/19, 19–20, Leeds to Fitzherbert, 2 October 1790, 21, Leeds (drafted entirely by Pitt) to Fitzherbert, 2 October 1790.

53. CUL 6958/4, 857, Richmond to Pitt, 16 October 1790.

54. HA 119 T108/39, 273, Pitt to E. J. Eliot, 3 September 1790; PRO 30/29/1/15, 97, Pitt to Stafford, 20 October 1790.

55. Evans, 'The Nootka Sound controversy', pp. 626–8; Black, *British Foreign Policy ... 1783–1793*, pp. 349–51; [Philip], 5th Earl Stanhope, *Life of the Right Honourable William Pitt* (4 vols, 1861–2), ii, Pitt to Elliott, [24] October 1790, pp. 56–9; *LCG III*, i, Pitt to George III, 25 October 1790, p. 498.

56. PRO 30/8/139, Elliott to Pitt, 26 October 1790, fos 123–6.

57. G. C. Gibbs, 'Laying treaties before Parliament in the eighteenth century', in R. Hatton and M. S. Anderson (eds), *Studies in Diplomatic History* (1970).

58. *PR*, xxix, May 1791, pp. 351–2.

59. HA T108/39, 112, Pitt to E. Eliot, 16 February [1779]; R. Reilly, *Pitt the Younger* (1978), pp. 46–7.

60. K. Wilson, 'Empire, trade and popular politics in mid-Hanoverian England: the case of Admiral Vernon', *P&P* 121 (1988), pp. 74–109; G. Jordan and N. Rogers, 'Admirals as heroes: patriotism and liberty in Hanoverian England', *JBS* 28 (1989), pp. 201–24; PRO 30/8/12, Pitt to Lady Chatham, 13 February 1779, fo. 56.

61. G. Rudé, 'The Gordon riots of 1780', *Transactions of the Royal Historical Society*, 5th series, 6 (1956), pp. 93–112; PRO 30/8/12, Pitt to Lady Chatham, 8 June 1780, fo. 180.

62. *PH*, xxv, 29 June 1785, col. 907; PRO 30/8/170, Reeves to Pitt, 18 July 1785, fos 211–12.

63. S. H. Palmer, *Police and Protest in England and Ireland, 1780–1850* (Cambridge, 1988), pp. 89–91; PRO 30/8/135, J. Featherstone to Pitt, 25 March 1791, fo. 1; PRO 30/8/198, Notebook 4, fo. 108.

64. HO 42/19, Rose to Dundas, 9 July 1791, fo. 86; J. Campbell to Dundas, 10 July 1791, fos 89–90; T. Parker to Dundas, 11 July 1791, fo. 97.

65. *PR*, xxxii, 21 May 1792, pp. 76–7; HO 33/1, F. Freeling to Rose, 13 July 1791; CUL 6958/5, 969, Pitt to Carles and Spencer, 12 July 1791.

66. Bod, Dep Bland Burges 48, Burges to Auckland, 15 July 1791, p. 251: some rowdiness was seen at the Bastille Day festivities in London.

67. HO 42/19, J. Wilmot to HO, Coventry, 18 July 1791, and W. Beto Taylor to HO, Wolverhampton, 19 July 1791, fos 154, 178.

68. *LCG III*, i, Dundas to George III, 18 July 1791, p. 551.

69. HO 42/19, Pitt's troop list, [19] July 1791, and Dundas to High Sheriffs, 19 July 1791, fos 68, 183.

70. *Ibid.*, Lord Ailesford to Dundas, 19 July 1791, fos 164–6, and Dundas to W. Chamberlayne, 21 July 1791, fos 210–11. See also accounts printed in *LCG III*, i, 17–21 July 1791.

71. *PR*, xxxiii, 21 May 1792, p. 80.

72. HO 42/19, Dundas to Lord Ailesford [drafted by Pitt], 17 July 1791, fos 121–2.

73. *Dropmore*, ii, Grenville to Auckland, 22 July 1791, pp. 135–6, and *PR*, xxxi, debate on the Address of Thanks, 31 January 1792, p. 39.

74. PRO 30/8/174, W. Russell to Pitt, 24 August 1792, fos 183–4.

75. J. Bohstedt, *Riots and Community Politics in England and Wales, 1790–1820* (New Haven, Conn.: 1983), pp. 23–4, 204–5; J. B. Rose, 'The Priestley riots of 1791', *P&P* 18 (1960), pp. 78–81; G. M. Ditchfield, 'The Priestley riots in historical perspective', *Transactions of the Unitarian Historical Society* 20 (1991), pp. 3–16; HO 42/19, Farquharson to Dundas, 29 July 1791, fos 286–7.

76. HO 42/19, de Lancey to Nepean, 20 July 1791, fos 191–2; *LCG III*, i, 662, George III to Dundas, 20 July 1791, and de Lancey to W. Fawcett, 21 July 1791, pp. 552–4.

77. *PR*, xxxiii, debate on the May proclamation, 25 May 1792, pp. 176–7.

78. *Ibid.*, xxxi, debate on the Address of Thanks, 31 January 1792, p. 39.

79. FO 72/19, Pitt memo, On a Defensive Alliance with Spain, [October] 1790, fos 139–65.

80. FO 72/21, 7, Fitzherbert to Leeds, 29 January 1791.

81. P. C. L. Webb, 'The rebuilding and repair of the Fleet 1783–1793', *BIHR* 50 (1977), pp. 194–209; J. K. Laughton (ed.), *The Letters and Papers of Charles [Middleton], Lord Barham, 1758–1813* (2 vols, 1909), ii, Barham to Pitt, 31 December 1785, pp. 197–208.

82. Ehrman, *The Reluctant Transition* (1983), pp. 9–10; Black, *British Foreign Policy ... 1783–1793*, pp. 259–62, 280–3; FO 64/17, Leeds to Ewart, 21 May 1790, fos 249–53; CUL 6958/5, 808 and 842, J. Durno to Pitt, 26 May, 3 August 1790; PRO 30/8/133/2, Ewart to Pitt, 16 and 24 November, 2 December 1790, 1 January 1791, fos 67–71, 72, 75.

83. R. H. Lord, *The Second Partition of Poland* (Cambridge, Mass.: 1915), pp. 153–70; FO 64/20, Leeds to Francis James Jackson, 8 January 1791, fo. 23; PRO 30/8/195, Turkey and Russia, fos 48–53; FO 7/24, A. Straton to Leeds, 9 February 1791, fo. 88.

84. Keith Correspondence, ii, Auckland to Keith, 19 February 1791, p. 377; *LCG III*, i, Cabinet Minute, 22 March 1791, p. 523; CUL 6958/5, 919, Richmond to Pitt, 27 March 1791; *Pol. Mem.*, Leeds Diary, 31 March–10 April 1791, pp. 154–61; P. Jupp, *Lord Grenville, 1759–1834* (Oxford: 1985), p. 127.

85. FO 64/21, 2, Ewart to Leeds [Grenville], 3 May 1791; FO 7/23, 1 and 2, Grenville to Ewart, 19 April 1791; E. D. Adams, *The Influence of Grenville on Pitt's Foreign Policy, 1787–1798* (Washington, DC: 1904), pp. 11–13; Jupp, *Lord Grenville*, pp. 122–7; M. Duffy, 'Pitt, Grenville and the conduct

of British foreign policy', in J. Black (ed.), *Knights Errant and True Eng-lishmen: British Foreign Policy, 1660–1800* (Edinburgh: 1989), pp. 152–4.

86. PRO 30/8/102, Pitt to Ewart, 24 May 1791, fos 121–6; *Dropmore*, ii, Grenville to St Helens, 19 April 1791, pp. 52–4; FO 64/21, 8, Ewart to Grenville, 31 May 1791; T. C. W. Blanning, *The Origins of the French Revolutionary Wars* (1986), pp. 83–5.

87. Bod, Dep Bland Burges 33, Ewart to Burges, 5 April 1791, fos 142–3.

88. Lord, *The Second Partition of Poland*, pp. 186–7; *Pol. Mem.*, 4 April 1791, p. 160.

89. FO 64/21, 12, Ewart to Grenville, 31 May 1791; FO 7/23, 4, Grenville to Elgin, 23 May 1791.

90. FO 64/21, 11, Grenville to Ewart, 14 June 1791; FO 7/28, 7, Grenville to Elgin, 8 July 1791.

91. Elgin Papers, Broomhall 60/2/16, Pitt to Elgin, 23 May 1791, cited in Black, *British Foreign Policy ... 1783–1793*, p. 328; FO 7/23, private, Elgin to Grenville, 26 May 1791.

92. J. H. Clapham, *The Causes of the War of 1792* (Cambridge: 1899), p. 81; FO 7/23, 26, Elgin to Grenville, 11 June 1791.

93. Stanhope, *Life of Pitt*, ii, Pitt to Lady Chatham, 2 July 1791, p. 126.

94. PRO 30/8/337, Adair to Messrs Ransom, Moreland and Hammersby [his bankers, copy], 28 July 1791, fo. 36; *Dropmore*, ii, Whitworth to Grenville, 17 June 1791, p. 100, and Fawkener to Grenville, 18 June 1791, p. 103; L. Mitchell, *Charles James Fox* (Oxford: 1992), pp. 117–18; A. Cunning-ham, 'Robert Adair's 1791 mission to St Petersburgh', *BIHR* 55 (1982), pp. 154–65.

95. *Dropmore*, ii, Grenville to Auckland, 29 July 1791, pp. 144–5.

96. PRO 30/8/337, Adair to Fox [copy], 28 July 1791, fos 49–50.

97. J. Black, 'Anglo-French relations in the age of the French Revolution, 1787–1793', *Francia* 15 (1987), pp. 417–18.

98. FO 64/22, Grenville to Ewart, 26 July 1791, fos 47–9; Addington Life, i, Dundas to Addington, 7 August 1791, p. 87. For the background to the ministerial stance on Adair and Ochakow, see Ehrman, *The Reluctant Transition*, pp. 34–41.

99. FO 64/22, 34, Ewart to Grenville, 17 July 1791.

100. *Dropmore*, ii, Grenville to Auckland, 22 July 1791, pp. 135–6; FO 64/22, 41, Ewart to Grenville, 4 August 1791; BL Add MS 58906, Pitt to Grenville, July 1791, fos 98–9.

101. *Court and Cabinets*, ii, Grenville to Buckingham, 17 August 1791, pp. 195–6; *Dropmore*, ii, Grenville to Auckland, 23 August 1791, p. 171; HA 119 T108/42, 237, Pitt to Tomline, 24 August 1791; William L. Clements Library, University of Michigan at Ann Arbor, Pitt Papers (no foliation), Pitt to Rose, 10 August 1791.

102. Burke Correspondence, vi, Burke to R. Burke, 1 [September] 1791, p. 377.

103. *Dropmore*, ii, Grenville to Dundas and Dundas's reply, 15 September 1791, pp. 142–3; Burke Correspondence, vi, Dundas to Burke, 20 September 1791, p. 404.

104. FO 27/37, Gower to Grenville, 14 October 1791.

105. FO 72/21, 15, St Helens to Grenville, 23 July 1791; Bod, Dep Bland Burges 46, Bland Burges to St Helens, 26 August 1791.
106. *Dropmore*, ii, Grenville to Auckland, 1 May and 26 August 1791, Grenville to St Helens, 26 August 1791, pp. 63, 176–7.
107. *Ibid.*, Grenville to Dundas, 15 September 1791, p. 192; DRO 152M C1791/OZ 11, Addington to Hiley Addington, 27 September 1791; Addington Life, i, account of a dinner party attended by Grenville, Burke, Addington and Pitt, p. 72.

Chapter 4

Action and Reaction: The Road to War in 1792

1792 was the year in which the British government turned publicly against the French Revolution. When metropolitan and provincial clubs sympathetic to the revolution began to show a real interest in parliamentary reform at the beginning of 1792, the ministry was concerned. Part II of Paine's *The Rights of Man* was officially condemned as a seditious libel within a week of its publication in February 1792. On 30 April a national reform campaign was launched by the Foxite Whig, Charles Grey, in the House of Commons. Three weeks later a royal proclamation against seditious writings was issued, in which Home Secretary Dundas denounced all parliamentary reformers as potential revolutionaries.[1]

These actions were – and continue to be – seen as expressions of official anxiety about the intellectual and social dangers of the revolution, thereby compromising the ministry's diplomatic neutrality towards France. On 20 April the National Assembly declared war on Austria, and the Pitt ministry's public statements against radicalism and reform have been read as indirect commentary on the issues of the revolution.[2] British involvement in the war began to look increasingly likely from the autumn of 1792 onwards. After a dismal start, French forces went on the offensive against the Austro-Prussian armies in September, a turnaround greeted with rapturous enthusiasm by British radicals. So vocal was native support for the revolutionary war effort by November that many Britons feared the outbreak of mass rebellion in their own country. On 1 December another royal proclamation called out two-thirds of the militia in selected English counties to save the nation from the purportedly imminent threat of insurrection. By the end of 1792 the foreign and domestic arguments for resistance to the revolution seemed inseparable and in February 1793 Britain joined the war against what had become the First French Republic.

To what extent was the ministry driven by conservative intellectual motives to embark upon repression at home and war in Europe?[3] Government statements about the intellectual and social threats of revolutionary principles led the general public to believe that sedition and subversion were as important as any conventional military dangers facing Britain or its Dutch ally. Oddly enough, the British government imparted an ideological tone to its policies to avoid war, not provoke it. In an atmosphere of intense intellectual, political and diplomatic tension, the Pitt ministry appealed to national unity in the belief that, by doing so, it could regain some direction over events at home and abroad.[4] It was thereby drawn unwillingly into armed confrontation with revolutionary France.

Throughout the 1780s British foreign and domestic affairs had been governed by a spirit of tolerance fast undergoing erosion by the escalation of European hostility towards France. In international terms, this could be measured by the movement of Austria and Prussia towards war with revolutionary France during the early months of 1792. Closer to home, the emergence of hostility to 'liberal' ideas was reflected in two ways: the disintegration of the old Whig opposition into two camps; and the independent efforts of new reformers to appropriate old issues – the reform of Parliament, the abolition of the slave trade and religious toleration – in the service of an explicitly radical political ideology.

These activities had a destabilizing influence on an already uneasy political order. Traditional codes of conduct were under threat in Britain and Europe, a scene viewed with grave misgivings by a premier whose strength had lain in the politics of equilibrium. From 1789 to 1791 the British government had been unwilling to take a stand on events in France, because its leaders did not want to jeopardize a fragile consensus in domestic and foreign theatres. The decision to climb off the fence was taken in the perception that the balance of national and international opinion was tilting against the Pitt ministry. The government's public reactions to the events of 1792 did not, however, imply that its leaders accepted the foundations and logic of the conservative case against the revolution.

An Uneasy Neutrality

Nowhere was British impotence and uncertainty about the revolution more apparent than in the diplomacy of 1792. So cold were relations between Berlin and London after the collapse of the Anglo-Prussian alliance in 1791 that almost nothing could be learned of German attitudes towards France. The Foreign Office could do no more than monitor events in Europe for much of 1792.[5] Frustrating though this situation was, British ministers remained convinced that war was unlikely. Austria and Prussia, bound by little but mutual suspicion, were unlikely to *agree* upon military and diplomatic objectives, let alone pursue them amicably.[6] On 10 February Whitworth wrote home of an

imminent tripartite division of Poland between the three eastern
powers. Grenville found this impossible to believe.[7]

The ministry's disillusionment with Prussia was complete by the
spring of 1792. Grenville, determined to find out what was going on
in Europe, decided to approach Austria, whose financial problems were
reputed to be so severe that the outbreak of hostilities against France
seemed unlikely. At the end of 1791 the Foreign Secretary, concerned
about the fate of the Netherlands, had again asked the Austrians to
ratify the 1789 Hague Convention. When this request was refused,
Dutch and British observers began to question the strength of Austria's
commitment to the status quo in western Europe.[8] By 1792 Pitt and
Grenville knew that the chief bones of contention between France and
Austria were the presence of royalist *émigrés* in the Rhineland, the
restoration of German feudal rights in Alsace-Lorraine which had been
curtailed by the Constituent Assembly in 1789, and the French repa-
triation of the Comtat Vénaissin. None of these, thought Pitt and
Grenville, justified war. They had learned that Prussia's spoils for
victory over France would consist of Jülich and Berg. Austria's gains
were supposedly to come from French Flanders.[9]

Leopold II of Austria died on 1 March 1792. Francis II, a far stronger
opponent of the revolution, began immediately to prepare for war. On
7 February Austria and Prussia signed the long-awaited alliance treaty
heralded by the Pillnitz Declaration. On 10 March the treaty was
published with a declaration of imperial unity and invitations for Russia,
Saxony, the United Provinces and Britain to join the counter-revolutionary crusade. This came as a severe shock to the London Cabinet,
which had not anticipated war so soon, if at all. Grenville was appalled
by the implicit affirmation of Habsburg absolutism in the Netherlands
in article 8 of the treaty, which guaranteed the constitutions of the
imperial states. This, he thought, 'cannot even be discussed without
Reference to the Affairs of France'.[10]

French paranoia, already strong, intensified as war drew nearer. Late
in 1791 the Feuillant administration began to look for allies. When
Prussia rejected these overtures, England was next on the list.[11] In
mid-March French requests for a loan and a defensive alliance were
turned down by a ministry which promised to remain neutral in any
armed conflict. Pitt and Grenville were relieved that the French approach had been made, if only because it reassured them that their
government had not been blacklisted by all the powers of Europe.[12]
Grenville hoped that France would solicit British mediation to stave
off war or arrange a peace. Gower was told to stand by in readiness to
receive such a request.

Between 10–23 March the Feuillants were replaced by a hawkish
Girondin ministry whose representatives had been making warlike

noises in the National Assembly since late 1791. The British government was familiar with the royalist call to arms. The militant defence of the revolution espoused by the Girondins was a new development. Upon learning of the change of ministries in Paris, Grenville wrote that 'a war will be inevitable'. On 20 April war was declared on Austria.[13] France was to be portrayed as the aggressor throughout Europe for the next decade, but, in truth, Pitt and Grenville laid the blame for the outbreak of hostilities at the doors of Austria and Prussia. Neither man expected the French constitutional monarchy to survive the onslaught of the combined powers and, following its defeat, Austria and Prussia were unlikely to supervise the establishment of a French government sympathetic to British strategic or diplomatic interests.[14] Under such circumstances, neutrality became doubly important. At the end of March the Dutch were warned off a *rapprochement* with Austria and all British diplomats were told that 'England has little concern in what is going forward on the Continent'.[15]

When the news of war reached London, Parliament was preparing to hear Charles Grey air a reform motion in the House of Commons. The Society of the Friends of the People (FOP), founded on 14 April, had joined forces with the London Corresponding Society (LCS), the Society for Constitutional Information (SCI) and several provincial reform groups to sponsor a reform bill which, on 30 April, Grey told the Commons he would bring forward in 1793. The prospects for the passage of Grey's notice of motion were not ideal. Although the Commons would pass Pitt's resolutions for the gradual abolition of the slave trade on 1 May, MPs and peers were becoming apprehensive about the advocacy of old reform measures by new popular societies like the LCS. The Established Church, once a friend to abolition, now thought that 'the Dissenters wish for a Revolution and that the Abolition of the Slave Trade is somewhat connected with it'. More damaging to the fortunes of abolition was the St Domingo slave revolt of August 1791. A dismayed Pitt voiced doubts about the wisdom of going ahead to the Abolition Committee.[16]

Despite these reservations, Pitt spoke brilliantly in support of an abolition motion presented to Parliament by Wilberforce on 2 April: 'with the improvement of internal population, the condition of every negro will improve also ... His liberty will advance, or at least he will be approaching a state of liberty.' Such statements should not be seen as a call for emancipation. Pitt's ideal plantation community was one in which slaves would have 'a common interest with their superiors in the prosperity of the whole'. This brought them closer to the status of British subjects. The Commons would not accept the immediate abolition demanded by Pitt and Wilberforce, but it passed the gradual abolition amendment put forward by Henry Dundas.

Dundas, the friend of the planters, resisted Pitt's pleas to vote for immediate abolition. In anticipation of the Home Secretary's intervention, Pitt announced during the debate on 2 April that he would support a gradual motion that led to complete abolition. This was a tactical measure, for on 23 April, when the Dundas resolutions were under debate, Pitt vehemently opposed their passage: 'If there was a moment lost in determining upon the propriety of an immediate abolition, more than was absolutely necessary for discussing so important a question, even that would be too gradual an abolition.'[17] Dundas proposed to end the foreign trade in slaves immediately. The imperial trade would continue until 1800. When the House voted on 25 April for Lord Mornington's amendment to abolish the colonial trade by 1796, Dundas abandoned his proposals. These were rescued by Pitt, presented to the House once more on 1 May and passed. Here Grenville jumped ship, telling Wilberforce that he thought persistence in the cause was 'an excess of zeal'.[18] The House of Lords stalled for time by setting up its own slave trade commission. This disbanded in 1794, having produced no report.

Wilberforce, though dismayed by the Commons rejection of immediate abolition, accepted Pitt's contention that the introduction of gradual resolutions was the only way forward: 'Some vote against abolition not to encourage Paine's disciples.' Both men were disinclined to abandon abolition, despite the hardening of public opinion against all reform causes. 'I see much reason', wrote Wilberforce in October 1792, 'to admire his [Pitt's] integrity, public spirit and magnanimity in despising unpopularity.' Aware that he stood to lose the support of back-bench MPs, Pitt nevertheless continued to defend abolition for the next decade.[19]

On 30 April Pitt spoke and voted against Grey's notice of motion. This came as a surprise to the House. British reformers, claimed Pitt, had adopted France as a model and any reform proceeding from the 'impracticable' principles of the revolution could only end 'in a wild state of nature'. The defeat of Grey's motion was followed on 21 May 1792 by a royal proclamation warning the nation about the inflammatory social effects of 'divers seditious and wicked publications'. These, referred to in general terms by Pitt on 30 April, were claimed by the proclamation to drive the people to riot.[20]

Two centuries on, the Royal Proclamation against Seditious Writings remains difficult to explain. Radical tracts had caused no riots, nor was any magistrate suggesting that they would. The speed with which the ministry moved against Part II of the *The Rights of Man* suggests that, by the end of 1791, Part I had been condemned in official circles as a specimen of seditious libel *par excellence*. In the absence of evidence to justify the May proclamation on public order grounds, it – and the anti-reform speech that preceded it on 30 April – have always been identified in part as indications of Pitt's hostility to the ideas of the French Revolution. As Portland, Burke and the leading conservative Whigs were consulted on the composition of the proclamation, Pitt's actions have also been presented as part of a long-term strategy to split the Whig Party. The proclamation has been described in its own right as a negative tribute to the impact of Paine's *The Rights of Man* and as a 'loyalty test' imposed by a government seeking information about the nation's attitude to radicalism, reform and revolution.[21]

Pitt was protesting not against Paine's principles *per se*, but the uses to which these might be put by political troublemakers. He accepted that public opinion had a role to play in British politics but regarded it as a volatile and ignorant force more capable of harm than good. When Grey and the FOP, undeterred by the defeat of 30 April, proposed to appeal to the nation on 1 May, Pitt was concerned: 'with regard to the Association', wrote Edward Eliot, '& the plan of sounding the People as they phrase it, I believe the Government is disposed to take a pretty decisive line and all the better part of Opposition to support them in it.'[22]

The aristocratic FOP had been established to lead a national reform campaign uniting the aims of high and low political organizations. Pitt, all too aware of the pitfalls awaiting any would-be mediator between reform groups, saw little hope for Grey's mission. Unity of sentiment and purpose, as Pitt observed on 30 April, were absent from the resolutions submitted in the FOP petition to the House of Commons. Grey's speech condemned rotten boroughs and electoral corruption, but did not propose any concrete measures for their reduction or elimination. This Pitt very much regretted. The petition demanded 'freedom at elections', but also called for more frequent parliaments and 'a more equal representation of the people'.[23] This Pitt saw as intellectual inconsistency. It is unlikely that he saw the popular radicals as a serious threat. Whilst he denounced their principles, contrasting them unfavourably with the moderate ideas of the 1780s, he also observed that the radicals were small in numbers. Affirming that an 'identity of interest' and 'conformity of sentiment' underlay the true spirit of representation, Pitt denied the existence of this consensus in the spirit and substance of Grey's motion.

In the absence of any concrete reform objectives, Pitt was afraid that the Opposition Whigs were mobilizing public opinion in the pursuit of more devious ends. Fox had gone on a successful public tour of the north during the summer of 1791, seemingly capitalizing on popularity gained during the Ochakow crisis. On 25 May Dundas had read out the resolutions of the Sheffield Society for Constitutional Information, described as 'subversive of the constitution and government of the country'. Of the FOP he said that 'it could do no good whatever, but might do much mischief'. Lord Loughborough and Earl Fitzwilliam agreed: 'Whatever is the Measure which is to be attempted by a show of public opinion, the Intrigues used to obtain that exhibition of opinion should be early opposed.'[24] These were bound to be humiliating in their consequences for the ministry.

Pitt continued to be uneasy about the shadow foreign policies of the Foxite Whigs. At the beginning of 1792 he was still thinking about Adair's impeachment. Opposition links to the French embassy were known to be strong, particularly through Fox, Sheridan and the Marquis of Lansdowne. On 19 January 1792 Gower had written to Grenville that all French diplomats came to England with a mandate for espionage and subversion. The entire staff of the French embassy was placed under strict surveillance. By April French agents had also been identified in Dublin. On 14 May Pitt told the Portland Whigs that 'he had undoubted information of many foreigners who are employed to raise sedition in England and that money from France is sent to assist in this attempt'.[25] This was not mere scaremongering. When the London police magistrates 'lost' the French ambassador, the Marquis de Chauvelin, in August, Pitt and Grenville were concerned.

On 19 June Grenville wrote to Auckland that any move away from official neutrality might upset 'the prevailing disposition for peace which reigns here'. The government, acutely conscious of its impotence in Europe, did not want its freedom of action further circumscribed by any native or foreign efforts to generate sympathy for or against the revolution in Britain. Pitt and Grenville were aware that political developments at home affected the ministry's status in Europe. On 15 May Dutch official concern about the British radical movement was expressed through Auckland.[26] There was thus an international dimension to the May proclamation. It presented an image of British strength and unity to the world, thereby giving a conservative slant to a formal neutrality perceived to have been undermined by events beyond the government's control.

There can be no doubt that Pitt sought to strengthen his position. Lord Holland, who saw the May proclamation as a stratagem to split the Whigs, also asserted that it was the product of fear engendered by Opposition solidarity 'in the divisions upon the Russian War'.[27] This suggests that the government was not as strong as Pitt would have liked it to be. His Commons majorities during the first four months of 1792 were respectable, if not impressive, but his response to Thurlow's malicious speech against the national debt reduction bill of 16 May was extreme: 'Mr. Pitt has this day stated the impossibility of his sitting any longer with the Lord Chancellor; it remains for my decision which of the two shall retire from my service.'[28] Having recently reunited his

Cabinet following Leeds's resignation, Pitt was determined to silence dissidents.

On 6 April Fitzwilliam had told Dundas that the conservative members of the Opposition would vote for any public order measures that might be contemplated.[29] On 30 April Dundas proposed that the conservative Whigs be invited to a Privy Council meeting to discuss the formation of county associations. 'I like this Idea very much' was Pitt's answer. He advocated staging a public dinner for 'all Members of Both Houses (which would probably be *all* the Peers and *four* fifths of the House of Commons) who concur in our Principles'. A formal union was not on the cards: 'it should be understood ('tho without any formal Association) that all who attend will act in Concert in their several Counties during the Summer to counteract these mischievous designs.'[30] It is not clear what these associations were supposed to have done over the summer of 1792; presumably they were to have monitored the connections between the Opposition Whigs and the popular political societies.

The latter were very much on the minds of the Portland Whigs. Pitt, using Auckland as an intermediary, approached this group on 1 May. Lord Loughborough replied, on behalf of his friends, with cautious interest: 'It seems difficult to find an adequate occasion for making such a declaration on any executive measures except during times of actual confusion.'[31] The Privy Council invitation was rejected in favour of a more general measure. Public opinion, thought the conservative Whigs, would be more responsive to a seemingly spontaneous display of confidence in the government. On 9 May Pitt informed Portland that he had the king's permission to confer on 'such measures as may on due consideration be thought necessary for checking any attempts dangerous to public order and tranquillity'.[32] The two men met on 10 May and Pitt presented Portland with a draft copy of the May proclamation. This Portland asked to be presented to Parliament. Sir Gilbert Elliot asserted that 'the union of all parties in opposing sedition and confusion' would make people think twice before 'they took a part in promoting the various schemes that are offered to them'. The government began to receive 'loyal' provincial addresses soon after the proclamation's appearance. Some of these had been organized by the ministry, and the conservative Whigs may have been responsible for others; during the May discussions 'several other measures were talked of as in contemplation'. By 15 June Grenville could write that 'our Addresses are going swimmingly'.[33]

Auckland, his duty to Pitt done, went back to the Hague, from whence he wrote to Keith not only that 'nineteen-twentieths of the nation is contented, anti-Gallican; and against the levelling or innovating ideas', but that 'our government does not feel any serious uneasiness'. The ministry was preparing for a potentially turbulent summer. Buckingham and Burges were afraid that the 1792 Bastille Day celebrations would be accompanied, as had been the case in 1791, by severe riots. *Conservative* rather than radical violence seems to have been the government's chief concern. In June 1792 Pitt finished the defence review prompted by the Birmingham riots:

County Meetings ...
List of Addresses
Arms at Birmingham
do. in London and other Places ...
Militia arms in other Counties
Strength of the Tower.[34]

The May proclamation served several purposes. It checked the growth of popular radicalism, discouraged the French and the FOP from stirring up trouble in the provinces, warned local authorities to be on their guard and reassured foreign powers that the British government was secure. No long-term radical threat to the Establishment was identified by a British government waiting for Austria and Prussia to crush the disordered levies of revolutionary France.[35] This complacence was not shared by the Portland Whigs, who, convinced that Europe was menaced by the awesome and apocalyptic destruction of the old order, began to search their souls on the admissibility of some formal union with the ministry.

Party Games

By the beginning of 1792 the Opposition was unhappily divided between the disciples of Burke and the followers of Fox. Many Whig MPs and peers, not yet prepared to abandon Fox to Sheridan, Grey and the radical Whigs, were nonetheless concerned about the formation of the FOP. The Duke of Portland, nominal head of the party, believed that Fox could be saved from his irresponsible friends. Other conservative Whigs like Loughborough, Sir Gilbert Elliot and Lord Malmesbury hoped that some alliance with the ministry was possible – perhaps even an admission to office. Opposition Whig hopes of ousting Pitt from power had been dashed in 1789 by the king's recovery; the unpopularity of the Prince of Wales during and after the Regency crisis led many of the Whigs to conclude that supporting the reversionary interest was no longer a route to power.[36]

When the split in Opposition ranks became public during the summer of 1791, the government began to solicit Burke's opinions on the state of affairs in Europe. Burke was delighted that ministers were taking an interest in the fate of the French Bourbons, in whose cause he was a tireless spokesman. He was, however, suspicious about this sudden show of ministerial goodwill. More than one attempt had been made to detach oratorical talent, of which the ministry was in short supply, from the Opposition or the independents over the 1780s.[37] This process was complicated by the Opposition Whig commitment to an ideology and code of party conduct. Contesting the power of Court and Cabal was a central plank of Whig unity and identity. Pitt had not yet been forgiven for upholding the prerogatives of the Crown in 1783. Without some recognition of party claims for recompense, no real meeting of minds could take place.

In May 1792 Pitt succeeded in removing yet another of the king's friends, Lord Chancellor Thurlow, from the Cabinet. Thurlow had owed his survival and occasional victory over Pitt to the personal protection of George III, but the Chancellor's malicious opposition to Pitt's 1792 budget was the last straw. On 15 May Pitt delivered his ultimatum to George III. Thurlow left office two days later. For a week London waited in suspense for the announcement of a successor. Pitt had some trouble filling the post, which was offered on 16 May to Lord Kenyon. When Kenyon refused, the Great Seal was put into commission. On 19 May Dundas told Loughborough, an old school-friend and Lord Chief Justice of the Common Pleas, that his claims to the Woolsack were under consideration.

On 9 June Loughborough advocated a formal coalition with the ministry at Burlington House. By 13 June he had persuaded Portland to discuss the matter with Pitt.[38] Opposition hopes were soon raised by the news that the Foreign Office could be given to Fox 'in a very few months'. So remarkable was this statement that Loughborough asked for clarification: '[Pitt] did not recollect that in all their Parliamentary altercations, a single word had dropped from any of them to prevent their acting together without any fair reproach being made of a disavowal of principles, an inconsistency of character.'[39] Barring the unfortunate affair of the 1785 Westminster Scrutiny, Pitt had never displayed any public hostility to Fox. Pitt, who was not a 'party man', had hoped throughout the 1780s that certain issues – economical reform, free trade, the reform of Parliament and the abolition of the slave trade – would transcend factional rivalries. It was not Pitt's vote that barred Fox from office.[40] The main obstacle was George III.

On 19 June Pitt assured Loughborough that Fox's conduct in 1783 and 1789 had been 'entirely obliterated from the *Royal Memory*'. The premier was not so sure about Fox's open support for the French Revolution: 'he had gone too far' and the king had tarred Fox with the brush of the FOP. George III could not, nevertheless, have prevented

Fox from sitting with the government in the Commons. Fox, when approached by Malmesbury, Loughborough and Elliot, said that he 'loved coalitions', but was 'a little hurt at the first approach not having been made to him'.[41] Admission to the ministry on equal terms was a vital issue for the survivors of 1783. The Whigs, particularly Portland and Fox, called for nothing less than Pitt's resignation. The Opposition blueprint for an alternative ministry placed Portland in the Treasury, Fox at the Foreign Office and Pitt at the Home Office. The government did not see the proposed alliance as a 'coalition' as defined by the Opposition Whigs, who believed that the simultaneous offer of two Cabinet posts represented an equal share of power. This was an unrealistic conclusion to have reached on the basis of the scanty information provided by Loughborough.[42]

Pitt and Dundas were not prepared to grant parity and, when Opposition insistence on this point became known, the talks were called off: 'the great difficulty We discussed so much at length when we last met at my house appears insurmountable. We have felt it impossible after various conversations to put it to ourselves in any practical vein.'[43] By 27 June the Portland Whigs had been told that the negotiations had been broken off because the Cabinet would not consent to the admission of Fox. There was 'no personal or political objection on the part of Pitt, and distinctly none from higher quarters [the king] because it had not been mooted there'. Fox's potential role in a Cabinet shuffle, although problematic in itself, was not the reason for the suspension of the all-party talks. The recognition of party equality was the issue at stake.[44]

Portland and Malmesbury were sceptical about the alleged Cabinet rejection of Fox and concluded that Pitt had ended the negotiations for 'personal and private reasons'. Pitt and Dundas did not want a coalition; they would rather see the establishment of closer ties between the Portland Whigs, amongst whom they would have liked to count Fox, and the ministry. Pitt and Dundas continued to cultivate friendly relations with the Opposition Whigs throughout July. The Garter was bestowed on Portland and the Marquisate of Rockingham was offered to Fitzwilliam. Heartened by these gestures, Portland and Fox decided to attempt the formation of a coalition on the basis of parity.[45] The Duke of Leeds, selected as a suitable neutral head for such a ministry, saw the king on 14 August. To his dismay, he discovered that George III 'had not heard anything on the subject for a long time'. When Pitt proposed to enlist the Portland Whigs in the production of the May proclamation and to show them other marks of government favour, George III had told Pitt that the 'Respectable Part of the Party' was not to have 'too much Power'.[46]

On 22 August a furious Pitt told Leeds to mind his own business.

Dundas, appalled, protested to Loughborough that their conferences had been misunderstood: 'The King's satisfaction in his present Government, and the vigour which the Government feels itself in the possession of, totally excluded all idea of *new arrangements*.'[47] Dundas stressed that he and Pitt welcomed Opposition fellow-travellers on an *ad hoc* basis: 'I have never from any communications I have had with Mr. Pitt on the subject been led to entertain any doubts of the King's willingness to add strength to His government by every honourable means that offered.' The gift of office did not constitute a formal acceptance of the Portland Whigs as a party. What they had seen as a half-share in office was not an invitation to share power. Pitt intended, at least for the moment, to keep the reins of government firmly in his own hands.

Radicalism Revived

Although the Portland Whigs remained well-disposed towards an alliance with the ministry, the two did not see eye to eye on several key issues: parliamentary reform, abolition of the slave trade, revolutionary France and British radicalism. When asked by Portland to reconsider these policies, Pitt replied that some thought would be given to them.[48] Nothing was done over the summer of 1792 and 1,341 loyal addresses in response to the May proclamation had reached Whitehall by the end of August. Many radical groups, intimidated by the strength of the loyalist response to the proclamation, cancelled their Bastille Day celebrations. 'We have nothing but peace and prosperity at home,' stated Grenville.[49]

Watchful complacency at home was echoed in British policy abroad. From May to November 1792 the ministry was inactive in Europe.[50] Prussia, the aggressive partner in the grand alliance, began to move troops towards the French frontier in June. The Austrians, far less enthusiastic about the war, hung back. On 25 July the Brunswick Manifesto, issued by the Commander-in-Chief of the allied army, threatened death to opponents of the Prussian advance and vicious reprisals against Paris if the French royal family was harmed. On 19 August the Duke of Brunswick's troops invaded France; on 23 August Longwy surrendered. On 1 September Verdun, the last fortress before Paris, fell to the allies. Grenville hoped that Britain and the United Provinces would be invited to attend the peace conference by which Austro-Prussian order would be imposed on France.[51]

By this time the French constitutional monarchy had collapsed. After the *journée* of 10 August, Louis XVI was stripped of his powers and, on 12 August, the royal family was moved to the Temple prison. The

Marquis de Chauvelin, the French ambassador, protested with horror to the British government, but then asked that his memo be returned. The Pitt ministry, faced with a seemingly complete collapse of executive authority in France and unwilling to antagonize the supporters of revolution and counter-revolution on the Continent, reiterated its neutrality, recalled its ambassador from Paris and released a proclamation denying asylum to French regicides. Pitt hoped that this statement would preserve Louis XVI's life until the Duke of Brunswick's army reached Paris. Shortly thereafter, British officials abroad were warned not to treat with French diplomats who were not accredited to the now defunct Court of Versailles. This suspension of relations was to be maintained until a new government was imposed upon France by the victorious allies. Pitt predicted that 'the last paroxysms of fear and rage will be dreadful'.[52]

In spite of the regicide proclamation, England was soon swamped by French refugees in flight from the September massacres. Dundas was afraid that the success of the Prussian army would redouble French efforts to woo the British public through emissaries of subversion: 'I should not like to see this Country ... overrun by the Banditti who have lately held in their hands the only power that exists at present in France.'[53] Subscription campaigns for émigré relief, led by Burke and Windham, were soon established – appeals to which the ministry grudgingly contributed in order to keep an eye on émigré numbers and movements. The government also took steps to prevent the distribution of seditious publications. Customs House officers were instructed to impound any offensive literature that they found in the baggage of cross-Channel travellers and, at the beginning of September, the Home Office moved against the sale of 'cheap editions of Mr. Payne's book'. Dundas summed up the government's policies: 'The foreign consists of a decided Neutrality and the domestick in watching all disaffection and making the most of our Prosperous Situation.'[54]

On 20 September the ministry reissued its regicide declaration at the request of its ally, the United Provinces, whose States General was concerned about the influence of French radical émigrés upon the revived Dutch Patriot Party. British attitudes towards the war in Europe, however, remained unchanged. When asked by the Duke of Brunswick for comment, Dundas responded carefully:

> It is impossible for me to say more than in general to express the hopes of His Majesty that the result of the present interference of the powers of Germany may be the re-establishment of such a government in France as would, on the one hand, protect other powers from a renewal of that spirit of restlessness and intrigue which has so often been fatal to the tranquillity of Europe; and, on the

other, secure to the Executive Government such a degree of energy and vigour as might enable it to extirpate those seeds of anarchy and misrule which had, so peculiarly of late, characterised the whole transactions of that distracted country.[55]

This was neither a condemnation of the French Revolution nor an endorsement of the Austro-Prussian military crusade. The British government, much like its neighbours, wished to see the establishment of a weak but stable government in France.

By mid-October this outcome to the revolution was looking increasingly unlikely. Most of the Prussians had left the western front at the end of September to participate in the second partition of Poland which had been prearranged with Russia, at which point the French began to recover. By 8 October they had beaten Brunswick's army at Valmy and liberated Verdun. British officials were astonished. When news of further French victories in Flanders, Nice and Savoy reached London, Pitt began to contemplate an emergence from isolation; the French retention of 'any other acquisition great or small might be argued to come within *un nouvel ordre des choses*'.[56] Despite this, the ministry refused all requests for diplomatic protests against prospective French attack coming from Sardinia and Switzerland. The war was also a cause for domestic concern. In October, when British radicals began to celebrate the news of French victories, frantic accounts of radical meetings, speeches and handbills poured into the Home Office. A rainy autumn induced many, both rich and poor, to expect a bad harvest and on 17 October the Board of Trade began to look into corn prices and supplies. By 31 October riots and strikes had been reported from the Midlands, East Anglia, the north-east and Scotland, in relation to which pleas for military assistance were received from Ipswich, Yarmouth, King's Lynn and South Shields.[57] Other cries of alarm were to be heard on the south coast of England, in a state of near hysteria about the *émigré* presence, and the City of London, apprehensive about the activities of metropolitan popular radicals. The government concluded that the nation was facing a public order crisis. Pitt and his colleagues were under compelling pressure to act.

The November Crisis

Worrisome as these overseas developments were, the restoration of public order at home was the ministry's first priority. While it has long been recognized that popular radicalism was not a revolutionary force in Britain during the early 1790s, the process by which Pitt came to conclude that the nation was facing the prospect of insurrection remains a subject of speculation. The thoughts of Grenville and Dundas are accessible and unambiguous, but Pitt's reactions to the events of late 1792 are far more obscure. Close as these men were by the end of 1791 – this triumvirate was to run the British war effort – it would be simplistic to assume that all of them came to the same conclusions for the same reasons.

There were three stages in the ministry's response to radicalism and riot. During the first phase, lasting from 8 to 14 November, Pitt concentrated on dealing with popular disturbances, identifying their causes and reassuring a worried public. The second stage, lasting from 14 to 24 November, involved the discussion of longer-term means by which to prevent the recurrence of riots. Here the support of the Portland Whigs was once more of crucial importance. France, though never entirely absent from the Cabinet's thoughts, did not take centre stage until 26 November, at which time the government's public order campaign entered its third stage and became subservient to its foreign policy.

Henry Dundas was easily the most frightened member of the Cabinet. On holiday in Perth, home to some particularly vocal Friends of the People, he had been horrified by the enthusiasm of Scottish radical support for the French cause. He demanded that Parliament be recalled as soon as possible.[58] Pitt, who as late as 26 October had not been particularly worried about public order, was now preparing a plan of action. On 8 November he and Grenville commissioned an inquiry into the causes of the autumn disturbances. Riot control measures were also considered. Some of these were conventional: the redeployment of troops to trouble spots and the adjustment of import duties on corn. Others were more novel: the introduction of legal deterrents to the production and distribution of seditious literature.[59] Bearing in mind the tone and contents of correspondence to the Home Office from provincial and metropolitan magistrates, it is not surprising to find that ministers held popular radicals responsible for the incidents of October.

Pitt, frustrated by the Home Office's impotence, wanted to prepare legislation that would suspend habeas corpus, make libel a felonious offence upon the second or subsequent conviction and clarify the law of sedition.[60] This legislative programme was designed to combat a danger couched in ideological terms. Grenville, while maintaining that the government could not remain idle, cautioned against too harsh an official crack-down. This, he felt, would only drive the radicals to violent extremes. On 14 November the two men began to receive answers to their enquiries. Having discovered that the celebrations of the Sheffield SCI could not 'in the most peacable times be called a riot', Pitt and Grenville concluded that provincial magistrates had panicked. The new legislation on sedition and treason was abandoned with relief. The proposed bills had posed a genuine dilemma to individuals for whom the rights and liberties of freeborn Englishmen, while prescriptively defined, were no myth. Pitt had tried to reconcile his legislation on sedition with 'the due liberty of the press'. To these reservations was added the realization that the enforcement of such legislation would impose heavy administrative and fiscal burdens upon the state.[61]

'The hands of government must be strengthened', declared Grenville, 'if the country is to be saved.' Pitt agreed, but believed that radical principles had not taken firm root in native soil. Abstract principles of redistributive justice, regardless of their origin, could not compete with a century of progressive affluence: 'Tho there has lately been a disposition to a great deal of Alarm, I believe the Bulk of the People here, and certainly the higher and middling classes, are still sensible of their Happiness and eager to preserve it.'[62] Reassuring though this discovery was, public order remained a problem. Pitt considered the repeal of taxes on salt, leather and candles; on 13 November an Order in Council prohibited the export of corn from the British Isles.[63] The official association of riot with social hardship marked the beginning of the government's practical response to the November crisis.

Pitt and Grenville prepared for further outbreaks of popular unrest. On 12–13 November principal members of the Cabinet were recalled to London and consulted about the redeployment of military forces throughout the country:

Means of bringing Artillery speedily to Act in cases of riot in London
Depots of Ammunition – & how secured
Advantage of having your Depots when you may have assistance from Ships of War.

So scarce had manpower been at the height of government alarm that, in the absence of troops, the Home Office had sent two naval sloops to assist hard-pressed magistrates in South Shields.[64] The Cabinet also contemplated the use of the county militia 'in cases of Riot'. The militia, denounced at regular intervals throughout the eighteenth century as a standing army in the making, had nevertheless become a source of extra troops for home defence. The militia could be called upon in two situations: native insurrection or the threat of invasion. If mobilized under the first pretext, militiamen could not serve outside their home counties.[65]

Calling out the county militia 'in such a manner as that there may always be some Part of it assembled in each part of the Country' presupposed that the regions in question were in a state of virtual and permanent insurrection. This was an impossible case to defend. Sending the militia across county boundaries 'in cases of Riots' would have been equally difficult to justify. By 21 November the Cabinet had not decided which route to pursue. Other measures had been settled upon. On 24 November magistrates were asked to 'make strict enquiry after any Persons distributing seditious Publications' and to indict the offenders at the next quarter sessions. Parliament was to be presented with addresses thanking the king and – by implication – his ministers for their 'attention to the peace and security of the Country'. Last but not least, the passage of an Alien Act would compel foreigners to register their presence in the kingdom and 'give security for good behaviour'.[66]

Anxious reports about an unsettled populace continued to reach the Home Office on a daily basis but most of these contained no direct references to radicals. Government enquiries had identified radical organizations and journals in several English towns, including Ipswich and Yarmouth, the scenes of colliers' strikes, but no direct connections could be traced between the radical societies and riots. The government case for punitive action was looking poor.[67] Pitt's programme of action was devised with two chief aims in mind: the reassurance of country gentlemen and the forging of closer links between the Home Office and the provinces. The prosecution instructions of 24 November had been accompanied by requests for comprehensive lists of country magistrates.[68]

Buckingham, amongst others, had complained to Grenville that 'your ministry are not *doing* enough', and Pitt also was concerned about the government's image.[69] Most alarmed were the conservative Whigs. Despite the disappointments of the summer, many of them believed that the time had come to bury the hatchet and give their votes to the administration. A back-bench revolt had been brewing in the Portland camp since October and, on 13 November, Burke and Windham went to Downing Street to lend their support to 'vigorous Measures at Home or abroad'.[70] As the two MPs could not speak for all their friends, Pitt and Grenville asked for a more detailed account of the dissidents and their motives. Unhappy as Burke was with this lukewarm reception, Pitt and Grenville were in fact anxious to offer the Great Seal to Loughborough. 'I am impatient to settle it, as if He accepts the sooner we have his compleat assistance in all legal Point both of Executive Government and with a view to Parliamentary Measures the better.'[71] Without expert legal counsel and a Chancellor to lead the House of Lords, the fate of the ministry's legislation on the militia and aliens was uncertain. George III, when presented with these arguments, gave his consent 'almost ... without reluctance'. Pitt was surprised when Loughborough refused the Woolsack on 22 November. The Scottish peer, however, did agree to advise the government in his capacity as a Privy Councillor and was taken into the Cabinet's confidence.[72]

Loughborough brought Pitt and Grenville more than professional advice. On 18 November he offered Pitt the prospective support of Devonshire, Egremont, Carlisle and Porchester. The premier asked after Fox and Grey, but Loughborough, like Windham, could not answer for the radical Whigs. By this time Pitt believed that the FOP had committed itself to the popular radical cause. On 7 November the London Friends, delighted by the success of the French army, reaffirmed their intention to promote reform in the next session of Parliament. A disgusted Pitt suggested to Dundas that prominent FOP members of the Opposition should be struck from the ranks of commissioned officers in the army, the list of King's Counsel and the county Commissions of the Peace. Neither Grey nor Fox was a target for Pitt's malice. The former had been horrified by the resolution of 7 November, while the ambivalence of the latter towards the FOP was well-known.[73] Although Pitt's schemes came to nought, they illustrate his conviction that the radical Whigs and their soapbox tactics were partly responsible for the revival of popular radicalism during the autumn of 1792. As Charles Long, Joint Under-Secretary at the Treasury, declared, the government would strike against those 'who should attempt to disturb the public peace or inflame the public mind'.[74]

Burges spoke for all when he denounced 'French cabals in this country'. The ministry nonetheless found it difficult to believe that the sponsorship of insurrection for its own sake was an official revolutionary objective.[75] France, despite its recent successes on the battlefield, was not strong enough to risk making more enemies. Consequently, domestic events did not affect the Cabinet's outlook on foreign affairs for much of November. As late as 7 November Grenville had declared that 'we will do nothing' in Europe. On 11 November the Dutch ambassador asked Pitt and Grenville for explicit assurances of British military and diplomatic support. On 13 November the ministry promised to defend the United Provinces against internal or external attack. Pitt described trenchant diplomacy as 'the best means of avoiding the Blow', but did not find war an attractive prospect. Grenville now asked British diplomats to solicit the views of Austria, Prussia, Russia, Spain and Portugal on the war. It was hoped that these overtures would elicit an allied request for a British-mediated armistice.[76]

Neither Pitt nor Grenville was anxious to negotiate with a state in which no *de jure* government had been established. At the same time Grenville admitted that Europe would recognize a French republic, should one 'hereafter be really and ultimately established'. The Pitt ministry would have preferred to restore the peace of Europe without French participation, which accounts for the British government's extreme reluctance to deal with any French diplomats over the winter of 1792-3. The ministry did not, however, plan to impose any political settlement upon France as a condition of the peace: 'the life of Louis XVI was not to be put in competition with the interests of this Kingdom.'[77] Neither Pitt nor Grenville could predict an outcome to the revolution for both were bewildered by the forces that it had unleashed. Further foreign intervention in France would, claimed Grenville, only prolong the existence of anarchy. Order could be restored only 'by the course of intestine struggles'. Pitt also thought it was best to leave France 'to arrange its internal affairs as it can'. Having appealed to the powers of Europe, the British lapsed once more into diplomatic silence, because it was 'impossible to decide on the course we ought to pursue'.[78]

Whilst reviewing Britain's internal defence arrangements, the government was acutely aware that troops might have to be sent to the United Provinces. Pitt prepared for war unhappily. When army recruiting orders went out on 17 November, he regretted so heavy an increase in government expenditure: 'It is indeed mortifying to be exposed to so many interruptions of a career the most promising that was ever offered to any Country.' On 17 February he had predicted fifteen years of peace and prosperity for Britain. These hopes were at an end, but Pitt felt that the costs of war could be minimized. Here lay the real attraction of his third militia project. Volunteer corps, first raised in 1778, paid their own way. Independent proposals of this nature had been submitted to the Home Office following the Birmingham riots; there was no shortage of willing recruits. By 24 November volunteers had been included in the government's mobilization plans.[79]

On 26 November the ministry learned that the Provisional Executive Council was insisting upon 'the *free* Navigation of the Scheldt', access to which lay in the hands of the Dutch.[80] By sending gunboats into the Scheldt estuary to shell Antwerp and defending their actions by vesting sovereignty over the river in natural law, not in the 1648 Treaty of Munster, the Executive Council was on course for confrontation with Britain and the United Provinces. This Grenville described as 'a concerted plan to drive us to extremities'. Pitt was confused: 'This can only proceed from a determination (at that time) to find some ground of quarrel with Holland.'[81] On 23 November Grenville had told Auckland that France would 'respect the rights of this Country and the Republic'. On 17 November Auckland and Grand Pensionary van der Spiegel had approached the French ambassador, Emmanuel de Maulde, who claimed to represent a peace-seeking General Dumourier, ex-Foreign Minister of France and commander of the revolutionary armies in the Netherlands, with a bribe of £100,000. Grenville and Auckland thought that the establishment of contact with Dumourier would facilitate the negotiation of a settlement on the military rights of the French in the Low Countries.[82] The Pitt ministry was not sure what to make of the contradictory messages from the French authorities. The arrival of fresh letters from Dundas put matters in a different light.

On 24 November Dundas demanded that the government send military reinforcements to Scotland.[83] The London response was swift and decisive: the volunteer corps bill was dropped, troops were dispatched northwards and the decision taken to embody the militia in selected English counties on the ancient pretext of insurrection. This took place in two stages: on 1 December Cumberland, Northumberland, Westmorland, the East and North Ridings of Yorkshire, Lincoln, Norfolk, Suffolk, Kent and Essex were ordered to call out their militia. On 5 December a second royal proclamation authorized militia embodiment on the south coast and in the rest of the Home Counties.[84]

This second proclamation had been produced in preparation for 'the increasing prospect of hostilities with France'. The motives behind the first proclamation, in which it was stated that 'the utmost industry is still employed by evil disposed persons within this Kingdom, acting with persons in foreign parts ... to destroy all order and government', are more difficult to explain.[85] Foreign Office documents published just before war was declared on France demand the repeal of the Scheldt decree and the more famous First Fraternal Decree. While few references to this decree of 19 November appear in the private papers of ministers, the French invitation to rebellion has been seen since 1918 as *the* event which prompted the British government to call out the militia.[86] Grenville, who wrote that 'almost undisguised attempts are made to foment insurrections here and in Holland', had maintained since early November that British radicals were biding their time until French troops set foot on Dutch soil. Little evidence was required to fan the flames of his fear. Dundas, who had dealt with radicals in the flesh, was convinced that a Scottish rising was in the making. Pitt remains the problematic figure. 'Suspension of Habeas Corpus & Power to take Security at least as to Foreigners' were under debate once more on 27 November, but Pitt remained concerned about the legal and constitutional propriety of such measures.[87] 'I *begin* to be persuaded', he wrote on 28 November, 'that the necessity will lead to measures on the whole best for the internal security of the country.' The proclamation on 1 December was explained to colleagues as a precautionary measure occasioned by 'the apparent necessity of sending in case of further riots a greater force to Scotland than we could at present spare'. Pitt admitted that the first militia proclamation might very well drive radicals to desperate measures, 'if any were in contemplation', but remained confident that the ministry would 'succeed in dissipating all the Mischiefs that are now around Us'. Dundas agreed.[88] The government strongly suspected that popular radicals were up to something sinister and, in the absence of hard evidence, the Home Office followed up every rumour of treason, sedition and conspiracy that came to its notice. It was in this atmosphere of tension that Lally Tolendal and Dubois de Longchamp received a hearing for their lurid account of the London insurrection.

The two royalists had presented the Home Office with details of a diabolical conspiracy, supposedly concocted by Birmingham radicals, metropolitan artisans and French *émigrés enragés*, to storm the Tower of London and the Bank of England as part of an armed rising sometime around 1 December. These two institutions were reinforced with troops, after which Grenville felt 'prepared for the worst'. Pitt took extensive notes from Longchamp's reports and pursued lines of enquiry that would lead to the apprehension of agents, specifically those attached to the French embassy in Portman Square.[89] The government was not taking any chances. Far-fetched though this may sound, the secret agents and their brief were real. Most of the junior French attachés had, as the ministry feared, been authorized by French Foreign Minister LeBrun to pursue 'revolutionary diplomacy'. By this was meant direct appeals to the British people, represented by the agents to their political masters as rebels only awaiting encouragement to rise in open revolt. This accounts in part for French refusals to compromise on the navigation of the Scheldt.[90]

On 12 December Longchamp signed a deposition attesting to the subversive activities of his fellow *émigrés* and their British conspirators. Here was the evidence that the Pitt ministry needed to proceed against sedition and treason. The details of the London insurrection were not, however, released to the general public or Parliament, although several versions of Longchamp's account were published by government newspapers. The Home Office was asked to furnish the ministry with an account of the autumn's events for use in the debates of the Lords and Commons but these were never used. The Cabinet was having doubts about the strength of its case. 'The calling out the Militia was so right and necessary that people will not be much inclined to cavil as to the application of the term *Insurrection*,' wrote Pitt, who still doubted 'whether we could, from our present materials, give as precise an answer as we should wish to cavils of this nature'.[91] Pitt and Grenville, apprehensive that they would lose Parliament's vote for the military and diplomatic succour of the United Provinces, concentrated upon the stimulation of a loyal public response.

Only two-thirds of the militia had been embodied; mobilizing the whole would have added greatly to the cost without increasing the impact of the measure.[92] The British government wished to keep down the costs of national security and, for this reason, turned to another source of free assistance, the Association for the Preservation of Liberty and Property against Levellers and Republicans (APLP). The APLP was founded by John Reeves, London police commissioner and ex-Chief Justice of Newfoundland, on 20 November. The organization came to the attention of ministers on 25 November: 'It has produced a great Impression which shews that there is a Spirit and Disposition to activity, which, if we give in the outset a right Direction, may be improved to very important Purposes.'[93] Suggested activities for loyalists included the distribution of 'useful writings', the collection of subscriptions for seditious libel prosecutions and the assistance of magistrates in cases of riot. Pitt, however, was no admirer of militant loyalism and did not envisage the long-term survival of the associations. Their most important contributions to the 'official' public order campaign were the petitions, prepared to conform to a model prescribed by Pitt and Grenville, sent to loyalist organizations in December 1792. These, signed by 'as many respectable Names as can be collected', were to be gathered from London 'and all the Counties and great Towns in England'. Dundas was asked to start a similar petition movement in Scotland.[94] The government's petition movement should not be seen as a Tory crusade, for the address produced by the Merchant Taylors' Hall and organized by Grenville on 5 December was not explicitly conservative in tone. So Whiggish was its declaration that it was capable of attracting moderate parliamentary reformers.[95] The ministry was interested in appealing to the broadest possible cross-section of British public opinion.

France was now seemingly implicated in an international conspiracy: at best to humiliate the British government; at worst to paralyse it. On 27 November Pitt had stated that trenchant diplomacy was the only means by which to avoid war.[96] Having acknowledged that the French government was conspiring to win the hearts and minds of the British public, the Pitt ministry had resolved to confront 'revolutionary diplomacy' with the solid face of British patriotism: 'It is clear that the French rely, in the present moment, on their intrigues in both Countries [Britain and Holland] and that they imagine they have brought us to a condition of inability to resist any demands which they may make.'[97] The more spontaneous any loyalism seemed to be, the stronger the government's international bargaining position would become. Copies of the APLP addresses were sent to Auckland, who was asked to bring the association movement to the attention of the Dutch government.[98] Parliament was legally obliged to meet within fourteen days of the issuing of the militia proclamation on 1 December. With a vote of confidence, the government felt secure enough to assert itself abroad.

Some ministers were more comfortable than others with the psychological brinkmanship of which the government's public order measures formed a part. Grenville declared on 5 December that the rising tide of loyalism would give the ministry 'enough energy in the country to assert its true situation in Europe'.[99] Pitt, who preferred conventional channels, was prepared to deal directly with the Executive Council. When an opportunity to do so offered itself at the end of November, he was swift to act.

Public Diplomacy

When news of the Scheldt decree of 16 November reached London, Pitt decided that the time had come to break silence with France. Chauvelin had been held at arm's length since the recall of Gower in August, for, to have acknowledged his status, would have constituted an informal recognition of the new French republic. On 28 November Grenville – probably prodded by Pitt and the Cabinet – invited Chauvelin to discuss the state of the war in Europe.[100] The meeting was not a success. The French army would not invade Holland, stated Chauvelin, who also defended the right of the republic to conduct war as it saw fit, upheld the 'natural law' by which the forcing of the Scheldt was justified and blamed the deterioration of Anglo-French relations on the coldness of the British government.

So fruitless a meeting was this that Grenville refused to see Chauvelin again. Charles Long was delegated instead by Pitt to go to Paris.[101] This was not the first time that Pitt had used personal envoys, but neither the king nor the rest of the Cabinet liked the proposed mission. When, on 29 November, the government learned that Hugues Maret, a new senior French Foreign Ministry official, was in London, Long's assignment was put on ice. Most of the government's information about the French diplomats came from Longchamp, the Pittite dissenter MP William Smith – a true 'friend of peace' – and that indefatigable busybody, William Augustus Miles. Officious and indiscreet though Miles was known to be, his friendship with French politicians had been useful to Pitt during the Nootka Sound affair. In early November Long was assigned to debrief Miles. When Scipion Mourgue, one of the juniors attached to the French embassy, arrived in London, it was Long who received him at Miles's house: 'Long later informed me that nothing could be done with Mourgue who, it appears, had insisted on the Rights of the Republic and on the inimitable Laws of Nature.'[102] This was essentially what Chauvelin had told Grenville. Miles claimed to have been told by Mourgue that the Convention would repeal the decrees of 16 and 19 November if Britain acknowledged the republic.

On 2 December Pitt saw Maret in Downing Street. Maret assured him that France had no intention of invading the United Provinces and that the Executive Council wished to establish cordial relations with the British and Dutch governments. Towards the end of the interview Pitt referred to 'the impression made here' by the decree of 19 November: 'that, while this was professed or attempted, and till we had full security on this point, no explanation could answer its purpose, and that such a conduct must be considered as an Act of Hostility to neutral Nations'.[103] According to Maret's record of the meeting, Pitt saw the repeal of the First Fraternal Decree as a mere technicality on the part of the Provisional Executive Council, instrumental though it had been made by the militia proclamation. In Pitt's account of the interview the Scheldt decree was the main priority. Maret stated that the decree of 19 November had been passed by the Convention 'in a moment of fermentation' and, while freely admitting that subversion was a French weapon employed against enemy nations, that it was not operative against neutrals.

Maret took his orders direct from LeBrun. Pitt, having found what appeared to be a trustworthy link to the French government, cancelled Long's mission. When Maret reported to the French Foreign Ministry, he warned LeBrun that Chauvelin was unofficially *persona non grata* in London and recommended that he, Maret, be given special powers to deal directly with the British government.[104] Chauvelin, who was furious that Maret had seen Pitt, appealed to LeBrun for confirmation of his senior status. On 14 December LeBrun's answer reached the French diplomats. Maret had lost the fight for LeBrun's favour. When the would-be special envoy saw Pitt that evening, he informed the Prime Minister that he had no powers to treat: 'Nothing more passed.'[105]

When Parliament met on 13 December, ministers 'carried all before them'. Chauvelin and Maret, alarmed by the success of the militia proclamations in rousing British hostility towards France, warned LeBrun that the people could no longer be relied upon to reject war.[106] From 14 December onwards Chauvelin presented Grenville with increasingly moderate stipulations of French rights *vis-à-vis* the conduct of war in the Netherlands. Even the most reasonable of these proved to be too much for the ministry to stomach, because, while offers to renounce the decree of 19 November were forthcoming, the Executive Council remained adamant on the issue of the Scheldt and the right of the French army to liberate the Netherlands.[107] The Pitt ministry insisted that the Dutch stand firm on the issue of maritime sovereignty. The new international doctrine of natural law was regarded in London as a fraudulent pretext for conquest and the Foreign Secretary refused to acknowledge the legitimacy of the theory, the diplomat or the state he represented.[108]

The British government did little to defuse the tensions of December 1792. When Grenville introduced the Alien Act in Parliament on 15 December, with the support of the Portland Whigs, the Executive

Council was appalled and furious. The Pitt ministry's contempt for the government and policies of revolutionary France was made public and explicit in the debates of the Lords and Commons. On 27 December Chauvelin demanded that he and his republic be accorded formal recognition by the British government. The response of 31 December was couched in uncompromising terms: 'England will never consent that France should arrogate the power of annulling at her pleasure – and under the pretence of a natural right of which she makes herself the only judge – the political system of Europe established by solemn treaties and ratified by all the Powers.' [109] The crux of the matter was the French military presence in the Low Countries. Following the decree of revolutionary warfare of 15 December, which imposed French rule upon conquered territories, Pitt and Grenville would have accepted nothing less than a complete and immediate French evacuation of the Netherlands.[110]

Confrontational as Anglo-French relations were in December 1792, the Pitt ministry was still willing to seek peace by other routes. On 19 December the Russian ambassador, Vorontsov, had sounded out Grenville on the subject of a counter-revolutionary alliance. As the British government did not support the restoration of the *ancien régime* Bourbon monarchy in France, the response that was sent to all the European courts on 28 December stipulated that the Pitt ministry did not care 'de se mêler de l'intérieur de la France, ou d'y établir par la force une forme quelconque de Gouvernement ou de Constitution'.[111] The rejection of the Russian proposal incorporated a British blueprint for an alternative mediation. Should France renounce her conquests, withdraw to her 1789 borders, repudiate policies of interference in the domestic affairs of other nations and abide by the conventions of European diplomacy, Britain and other willing states would recognize the republic, leave revolutionary politicians to their own devices and admit France to the community of nations. This was a peace package of startling moderation yet it effectively stated that peace could not be negotiated with France. An armistice could be imposed only by international consent.[112]

Such a settlement would have taken time to construct, had the other powers been amenable to doing so. By 1 February, when France declared war on Britain, no great interest had been displayed in the British mediation offer. January 1793 was a month of frustration and stalemate in which the Pitt ministry gradually resigned itself to war. The French government also came to the same conclusion. By 31 December neither side had left itself much room for manoeuvre. Having made no secret of their objectives – indeed, rarely had any diplomatic confrontation been conducted so openly – neither government could back down without losing face at home. On 13 January 1793 Pitt saw

Miles to receive a final peace offer from Maret and LeBrun. This suggests that Pitt was not happy with the stalemate in Anglo-French relations which had been produced by public diplomacy. He received Miles's letters, which offered Britain everything that its leaders had asked for, with 'good humour', but the Cabinet maintained that Miles had been the dupe of his French friends and advised Pitt to send him away.[113] Auckland was still trying to keep de Maulde and Dumourier in play on the other side of the Channel but, by 24 January, the British government felt that this negotiation was only buying time for the United Provinces to arm.[114] When the French declaration of war reached London on 9 February, no British minister was surprised.

Preparing for War

By 31 December 1792 the stage was set for war. Although the French and British governments had entrenched themselves behind barriers of propaganda, neither saw the war of 1793 as ideological in origin.[115] The French Revolutionary Wars were regarded in different ways by different ministers. By 1 December Grenville, the future Lord Chancellor Loughborough, Richmond and Chatham saw the war as a conflict in which the professions, weapons and strategy of France were inseparable from a policy of militant global revolution. According to such an analysis, the sponsorship of subversion in Britain was part of a grand scheme of revolutionary warfare. Pitt was less willing to ascribe such motives to the leaders of the republic and regarded French aggression as the product of misplaced over-confidence.

Bearing in mind that the emergence of popular radicalism had long been anticipated by Grenville, what remains surprising about the British government's domestic policy in 1792 is its moderation. At the end of 1792, as the prospect of disorder receded, punitive legislation became increasingly difficult to justify. The suspension of habeas corpus was mentioned in ministers' correspondence up to 16 December, but no bill was presented to Parliament. The Alien Act, aimed not at British radicals but at French spies, was the only new legislative public order instrument of late 1792. On 7 December provincial firms of solicitors were asked to undertake the presentments of seditious libels, but the Treasury solicitors proved reluctant to recommend prosecution or fund the cases.[116] As for the loyalists, neither Reeves nor the government exercised any real control over the APLP. The British state could do little to contain popular radicalism without additional sources of money and manpower. Loyalists and volunteers were recruited for practical – not intellectual – reasons at the end of 1792. Riot control and trenchant diplomacy were Pitt's main priorities. Patriotism and loyalism could be invoked to serve the cause of psychological brinkmanship, but this was not, for Pitt, primarily a war of ideas. The crises of 1792 set the British government firmly on a path of deterrence rather than repression.[117]

The British government, though flexible at home, was uncompromising towards France, if not towards other European states. Anglo-Dutch belligerence masked the simple fact that the bargaining position of the maritime powers was not strong; with French armies poised on the Dutch borders, compromise would have looked like the acknowledgement of a *fait accompli*. For revolutionary France, recognition of the republic was the issue at stake. British stubbornness on this point had little to do with any objections to the republic as a form of government, provided that guarantees of some description were forthcoming with regard to its stability and permanence. As these were not likely to materialize in the short term, the peace proposals of 28 December, had they been accepted, would have ensured the republic a *de jure* status in Europe. The Pitt ministry did not know whether Louis XVI would survive his trial and no formal recognition would have been accorded to the republic before the outcome of this was known.[118] Neither the British nor the Dutch could be sure that a treaty negotiated with the Provisional Executive Council would be binding upon the future leaders of France. By brokering a general peace-keeping treaty, the British government could free itself from sole responsibility for keeping the peace if France offended again.

Despite these uncertainties, which dogged Anglo-French relations throughout the autumn of 1792, the ministry decided on 13 November that it would go to war for the United Provinces if necessary. So important a region of strategic and commercial interest could not be allowed to fall under French control, regardless of the principles upon which a French government was founded.[119] In May Auckland had written that, if the French had 'overrun Brabant and Flanders, and menaced or disturbed this Country [the United Provinces] ... we must have interfered to stop their progress'.[120] The defence of a 'balance' in western Europe, if nowhere else, had been a key feature of British foreign policy for a century, and British ministers were aware that their conduct was under assessment not only by France, but by other powers. The Russian overture in December was the first real confidential communication that the British government had received since mid-1791 and, during January, the Pitt ministry also became the focus of Austrian and Prussian attention. As the diplomatic stalemate continued with no end in sight, the prospect of war looked increasingly attractive to a British government seeking readmission to the community of European nations from which it had been excluded in 1791. The First Coalition, in whose creation the Pitt ministry was to play a central role, represented the realization of that objective.

Notes

1. G. S. Veitch, *The Genesis of Parliamentary Reform* (1918), pp. 239–42; E. P. Thompson, *The Making of the English Working Class* (1968), p. 107; A. Goodwin, *The Friends of Liberty: The English Democratic Movement and the French Revolution* (1979), p. 249; D. G. Wright, *Popular Radicalism: The Working Class Experience* (1983), pp. 117–19.

2. W. T. Laprade, *England and the French Revolution, 1789–1797* (Baltimore, Md.: 1909), pp. 184–5; H. T. Dickinson, *British Radicalism and the French Revolution, 1789–1815* (Oxford: 1985), pp. 25–30; Dozier, *For King, Constitution and Country: The English Loyalists and the French Revolution* (Lexington, Ky.: 1983), pp. 117–19; T. P. Schofield, 'Conservative political thought in Britain in response to the French Revolution', *HJ* 29 (1986), pp. 601–2, E. Sparrow, 'The Alien Office, 1792–1802', *HJ* 33 (1990), p. 407.

3. J. Black, *British Foreign Policy in an Age of Revolutions, 1783–1793* (Cambridge: 1994), pp. 468–70; T. C. W. Blanning, *The Origins of the French Revolutionary Wars* (1986), p. 159; Holland Rose, *William Pitt and the Great War* (1911), pp. 57–108; P. Jupp, *Lord Grenville, 1759–1834* (Oxford: 1985), p. 149; M. Duffy, 'British diplomacy and the French wars 1789–1815', In H. T. Dickinson (ed.), *Britain and the French Revolution* (Oxford: 1989), pp. 130–1; T. Schofield, 'British politicians and French arms: the Anglo-French War of 1793–1795', *History* 78 (1993), pp. 183–210; J. Ehrman, *The Reluctant Transition* (1983), pp. 224–58.

4. G. Pendleton, 'The English pamphlet literature of the age of the French Revolution anatomized', *Eighteenth Century Life* 5 (1978), pp. 29–37; R. Hole, 'British counter-revolutionary popular propaganda in the 1790s', in C. Jones (ed.), *Britain and Revolutionary France: Conflict, Subversion and Propaganda* (Exeter: 1983), pp. 53–69.

5. J. Black, *A System of Ambition? British Foreign Policy 1660–1793* (Harlow: 1991), pp. 242–8; Blanning, *Origins of the French Revolutionary Wars*, pp. 133–4; Duffy, 'British diplomacy and the French wars', p. 130.

6. These perceptions were reinforced by the observations of British diplomats abroad: FO 64/24, 9, Morton Eden to Grenville, 28 January 1792.

7. FO 65/23, 7, Whitworth to Grenville, 10 February 1792, and 17, Grenville to Whitworth, 20 April 1792.

8. FO 37/17, 7, Grenville to H. Spencer, 27 March 1792; *Dropmore*, ii, Grenville to Auckland, 23 August 1791, p. 171, and 26 August 1791, p. 179.

9. R. H. Lord, *The Second Partition of Poland* (Cambridge, Mass.: 1915), pp. 238–61; Blanning, *Origins of the French Revolutionary Wars*, pp. 78–9, 114–17.

10. FO 64/24, 3, Grenville to Morton Eden, 27 March 1792.

11. The Prussian government had rejected a French alliance offer in January 1792.

12. FO 27/38, 6, Gower to Grenville, 9 March 1792; *Dropmore*, ii, J. Petrie to Grenville, 13 March 1792, pp. 253–61; G. Pallain, *La Mission de Talleyrand à Londres en 1792* (Paris: 1889), Foreign Ministry to Talleyrand and Chauvelin, 20 April 1792, pp. 219–42.

13. FO 27/38, Grenville to Gower, 9 March 1792; FO 37/37, 7, Grenville to H. Spencer, 27 March 1792.

14. Duffy, 'British diplomacy and the French wars', pp. 133–4 and 'British policy in the war against revolutionary France', in Jones, *Britain and Revolutionary France*, pp. 13–16.

15. BL Add MS 34441, Grenville to H. Spencer, 27 March 1793, fos 509–10; *Auckland Correspondence*, ii, Auckland to H. Spencer, 20 March 1792, pp. 347–8.

16. A. M. Wilberforce (ed.), *The Private Papers of William Wilberforce* (1897), S. Hoare to Wilberforce, 20 February 1792, pp. 89–90; PRO 30/8/161, Moore to Pitt, 10 June 1792, fo. 10; *Life of Wilberforce*, i, Diary, [February] 1792, p. 341.

17. *PR*, xxxi, 2 April 1792, pp. 255–77, 23 April 1792, pp. 350–3. Dundas did not oppose abolition *per se*: M. Fry, *The Dundas Despotism* (Edinburgh: 1992), pp. 199–201.

18. *PR*, xxxii, 27 April 1792, pp. 427–9, 1 May 1792, pp. 502–4; *Life of Wilberforce*, i, Wilberforce to W. Hey, 7 June 1792, p. 352.

19. *Life of Wilberforce*, i, Diary, [1792], p. 344; Diary, 5 October 1792, p. 369.

20. *PR*, xxxii, May proclamation text, 21 May 1792, pp. 130–2.

21. Dozier, *For King, Constitution and Country*, p. 21; O'Gorman, 'Pitt and the Tory reaction to the French Revolution', in Dickinson, *Britain and the French Revolution*, p. 26, and *The Whig Party and the French Revolution* (1967), pp. 84–6.

22. U1590 S5/C35/1, E. J. Eliot to Tomline, 4 May 1792.

23. *PR*, xxxiii, 30 April 1792, pp. 452–66; *PH*, xxix, text of FOP Petition, cols 1304–27.

24. L. G. Mitchell, *Charles James Fox and the Disintegration of the Whig Party 1782–1794* (Oxford: 1971), p. 173; *PR*, xxxiii, 25 May 1792, pp. 175–7; Scottish Record Office, Melville Castle Muniments, GD 51/1/17, Loughborough to Dundas, 24 April [1792].

25. *Dropmore*, ii, Grenville to Auckland, 29 July 1791, pp. 144–5; O. Browning (ed.), *The Despatches of Lord Gower, 1790–1792* (1885), Gower to Grenville, 19 January 1792, 147; HO 1/1, list of French and Irish agents, 23 May 1792; *Life and Letters*, ii, Sir Gilbert to Lady Elliot, 14 May 1792, pp. 23–4.

26. *Dropmore*, ii, Auckland to Grenville, 15 May 1792, pp. 268–9, and Grenville to Auckland, 19 June 1792, p. 281; *Auckland Correspondence*, ii, Bland Burges to Auckland, 29 May and 21 August 1792, pp. 410, 436; *LCG III*, i, Grenville to George III, 20 August 1792, p. 608.

27. Henry Edward, 3rd Baron Holland, *Memoirs of the Whig Party in my Time* (2 vols, 1852), ii, p. 17; E. A. Smith, *Lord Grey, 1764–1845* (Oxford: 1992), pp. 51–3.

28. [Philip], 5th Earl Stanhope, *Life of the Right Honourable Pitt* (4 vols, 1861–2), ii, George III to Dundas, 16 May 1792, p. 150.

29. Cited in H. Butterfield, 'Charles James Fox and the Whig opposition in 1792', *Cambridge Historical Journal* 3 (1949), pp. 296–302.

30. SRO GD 51/1/17/4, Memo, [April] 1792.

31. *Auckland Correspondence*, ii, Pitt to Auckland and Auckland to Lough-

borough, 1 May 1792, pp. 401–3; PRO 30/8/153, Loughborough to Auckland, 4 May 1792, fos 67–8.

32. J. Holland Rose *Pitt and Napoleon: Essays and Letters* (1912), Pitt to Portland, 9 May 1792, p. 249; PRO 30/8/168, Portland to Pitt, 9 May 1792, fo. 72.

33. *Ibid.*, Portland to Pitt, 13 May 1792, fo. 73; *Courts and Cabinets*, ii, Grenville to Buckingham, 15 May and 16 June 1792, pp. 207, 269; two drafts of the proclamation were rejected before it was finally released; *Life and Letters*, ii, Sir Gilbert to Lady Elliot, 24 May 1792, pp. 30–1; Auckland Correspondence, ii, Bland Burges to Auckland, 1 June 1792, p. 411; *Life and Letters*, ii, Sir Gilbert to Lady Elliot, 14 May 1792, pp. 23–4.

34. Keith Correspondence, ii, Auckland to Keith, 29 May 1792, pp. 518–20; Bod, Dep Bland Burges 48, Burges to Auckland, 29 May 1792, p. 513; *Dropmore*, ii, Buckingham to Grenville, 17 May 1792, pp. 270–1; PRO 30/8/198, Notebook 4, 10 June 1792, fos 103–4; HO 42/20, O. De Lancey to Dundas, 13 June 1792, fos 386–75.

35. FO 37/37, 1, Grenville to Auckland, 11 May 1792.

36. Malmesbury Diaries, ii, 10 June 1792, pp. 454–5.

37. Burke Correspondence, vi, Burke to R. Burke, 1 [September] 1791, pp. 396–7; Ehrman, *The Reluctant Transition*, pp. 178–9.

38. Fry, *The Dundas Despotism*, p. 186; Mitchell, *Charles James Fox*, p. 115; *Kenyon*, i, Pitt to Kenyon, 16 May 1792, pp. 535–6; Stanhope, *Life of Pitt*, ii, Pitt to Thurlow, 16 May 1792, and George III to Dundas, 16 May 1792, pp. 149–50; Burke Correspondence, vii, Burke to Loughborough, 13 June 1792, pp. 150–1; *Life and Letters*, ii, W. Elliot to G. Elliot, 11 June 1792, p. 41; Malmesbury Diaries, ii, 9 June 1792, pp. 453–4.

39. Malmesbury Diaries, ii, 15–17 June 1792, pp. 460–3.

40. *Life and Letters*, ii, W. Elliot to G. Elliot, 19 June 1792, pp. 43–4; Dundas and Grenville were unlikely to have objected either.

41. *LCG III*, ii, George III to Pitt, 1 May 1792, p. 591; *Life and Letters*, ii, W. Elliot to G. Elliot, 19 June 1792, p. 43; Malmesbury Diaries, ii, 16 June 1792, pp. 461–2.

42. *Ibid.*, 5 July 1792, p. 468.

43. SRO GD 51/1/17/5, Dundas to Loughborough, 22 June 1792.

44. Sheffield City Library, Wentworth Woodhouse Muniments, WWM F31–2, Portland to Fitzwilliam, 27 June 1792; Malmesbury Diaries, ii, Portland to Malmesbury, 27 June 1792, p. 467; *Life and Letters*, ii, William Elliot to Gilbert Elliot, 29 June 1792, pp. 45–52.

45. E. A. Smith, *Whig Principles and Party Politics: Earl Fitzwilliam and the Whig Party* (Manchester: 1975), pp. 143–4; O'Gorman, *The Whig Party and the French Revolution*, pp. 92–5; Ehrman, *The Reluctant Transition*, pp. 176–83; Malmesbury Diaries, ii, 3 July 1792, p. 468; Burke Correspondence, vii, Burke to R. Burke, 22 August 1792, pp. 179–80.

46. *Pol. Mem.*, 17–30 July, 14 August 1792, pp. 175–83, 188–9; BL Add MS 58906, Pitt to Grenville, 22 July 1792, fo. 126.

47. HA 119 T108/42, Pitt to Tomline, 22 July 1792; *LCG III*, i, Pitt to Grenville, 28 August 1792, p. 607; SRO GD 51/1/20/2, Dundas to Lough-

borough, 29 August 1792; CUL 6958/6, 114, George III to Pitt, 20 August 1792.

48. Malmesbury Diaries, ii, 15 June 1792, pp. 459–60.

49. Auckland Correspondence, ii, Bland Burges to Auckland, 31 July 1792, p. 423; *LCG III*, ii, Dundas to George III, 14 July 1792, p. 602; *Annual Register* (1792), pp. 158–61.

50. Auckland Correspondence, ii, Grenville to Auckland, 21 July 1792, p. 419.

51. *Dropmore*, ii, Grenville to Gower, 4 August 1792, p. 426.

52. FO 27/38, Chauvelin to Dundas (Grenville was on holiday), 16 August 1792; Grenville to Auckland, 4 August 1792, p. 426; Auckland Correspondence, ii, Auckland to Morton Eden, 25 August 1792, p. 437; *Dropmore*, ii, Pitt to Grenville, 17 and 18 August 1792, pp. 302–3; *LCG III*, ii, Dundas to George III, 17 August 1792, pp. 606–7; *Dropmore*, ii, Pitt to Grenville, 7 September 1792, p. 310.

53. HO 42/21, Dundas to T. Curry, 13 September 1792, fo. 533; *Dropmore*, ii, J. Mason to Burges, 12 September 1792, p. 318; SRO, Buccleuch Papers, GD 224/30/9/9(2)–(3), Dundas to Buccleuch, 19 September 1792; HO 1/1, List of Aliens, 20 September 1792; *LCG III*, ii, Dundas to George III, 22 September 1792, p. 616.

54. Dozier, *For King, Constitution and Country*, pp. 38–42; HO 42/21, Pitt to Dundas, 21 September 1792, fo. 579; Bod, Dep Bland Burges 48, 513, Bland Burges to George Monro, 29 May 1792; *Dropmore*, ii, Dundas to Grenville, 2 September 1792. Pitt seems to have prodded the Attorney-General to stage Paine's trial during the summer of 1792, but this did not take place until December 1792; PRO 30/8/198, Notebook 4, fo. 106.

55. *Dropmore*, ii, Dundas to Sir J. Murray, 12 September 1792, p. 313; Auckland Correspondence, ii, Auckland to Morton Eden, 8 September 1792, pp. 443–4; *Court and Cabinets*, ii, Grenville to Buckingham, 20 September 1792, p. 217.

56. Auckland Correspondence, Burges to Auckland, 9 October 1792, p. 454; *Dropmore*, ii, Pitt to Grenville, 16 October 1792, p. 322.

57. PRO BT 5/8, Minutes of the Board of Trade, 17 October 1792, fos 104–5; Auckland Correspondence, ii, Sheffield to Auckland, 3 October 1792, p. 448, and General Smith to Auckland, 9 October 1792, pp. 455–6.

58. HO 102/5, Dundas to Nepean, 14 October 1792, fos 364–5; Clements MS, Pitt to Dundas, 8 November 1792; K. Logue, *Popular Disturbances in Scotland* (Edinburgh, 1979), pp. 136–8; J. Brins, 'From reformers to Jacobins: The Scottish Association of the Friends of the People', in T. M. Devine (ed.), *Conflict and Stability in Scottish Society 1700–1850* (Edinburgh: 1990), pp. 36–7.

59. HO 42/22, Pitt to Lord Mayor of London, 26 October 1792, fo. 197; PRO 30/8/198, Notebook 4, 9 November 1792, fo. 109; Clements MS, Pitt to Dundas, 8 and 15 November 1792.

60. PRO 30/8/198, Notebook 4, 9–16 November 1792, fos 110–11. For further treatment of the government's domestic policies in 1792, see my 'Responses to revolution: the November Crisis of 1792', *Historical Research* 69 (1996), pp. 284–305.

61. Clements MS, Pitt to Dundas, 8 and 15 November 1792; *Court and*

Cabinets, ii, Grenville to Buckingham, 14 November 1792, pp. 226–7;
C. Emsley, 'Repression, terror and the rule of law in England during the
decade of the French Revolution', *EHR* 100 (1985), p. 806.

62. *Court and Cabinets*, ii, Grenville to Buckingham, 14 November 1792,
pp. 226–8; Clements MS, Pitt to Dundas, 15 November 1792.

63. *Court and Cabinets*, ii, Grenville to Buckingham, 7 November 1792, p. 224;
Clements MS, Pitt to Dundas, 15 and 17 November 1792.

64. PRO 30/8/198, Notebook 4, [12–18] November 1792, fo. 11; HO 42/22,
Nepean to R. Burdon, 5 November 1792, fo. 274; *Dropmore*, ii, Pitt to
Grenville, 11 November 1792, p. 328.

65. J. R. Western, *The English Militia in the Eighteenth Century: The Story of a
Political Issue, 1660–1802* (1965), p. 9; SRO GD 51/16/99, [18–24] November 1792.

66. Clements MS, Pitt to Dundas, 25 November 1792.

67. Stanhope, *Life of Pitt*, ii, Pitt to Dundas, 4 December 1792, pp. 176–7.

68. C. Emsley, 'The Home Office and its official sources of information and
investigation, 1791–1801', *EHR* 93 (1979), pp. 534–44.

69. *Dropmore*, ii, Buckingham to Grenville, 8 November 1792, p. 327;
Clements MS, Pitt to Dundas, 8 November 1792. The Portland Whigs
were very critical of government inertia: Malmesbury Diaries, ii, 11
December 1792, pp. 473–4; *Life and Letters*, ii, Sir Gilbert to Lady Elliot,
13 December 1792, pp. 79–80.

70. Burke Correspondence, vii, Burke to R. Burke, 18 November 1792, p. 291;
L. Melville (ed.), *The Windham Papers* (2 vols, 1913), i, Portland to Windham, 16 October 1792.

71. Clements MS, Pitt to Dundas, 17 November 1792; O'Gorman, *The Whig
Party and the French Revolution*, pp. 106–8; Smith, *Whig Principles and Party
Politics*, pp. 148–9; Mitchell, *Charles James Fox and the Disintegration of the
Whig Party*, pp. 127–9.

72. Clements MS, Pitt to Dundas, 24 November 1792; PRO 30/8/153,
Loughborough to Pitt, 24 November 1792, fos 69–70; Burke Correspondence, vii, Loughborough to Burke, 27 November 1792, p. 303; *LCG III*,
ii, Pitt to George III, 25 November 1792, p. 630; PRO 30/8/103, George
III to Pitt, 26 November 1792, fo. 462.

73. Smith, *Whig Principles and Party Politics*, p. 111; E. C. Black, *The Association*
(Cambridge, Mass.: 1963), p. 248.

74. *Dropmore*, ii, Pitt to Grenville, 18 November 1792, pp. 335–6; SRO GD 51/
16/99, [18–24] November 1792; *Pol. Mem.*, 23 November 1792, pp. 202–3;
Miles Correspondence, ii, Minute, 18 November 1792, pp. 352–3.

75. Bod, Dep Bland Burges 34, Burges to Grenville, 11 November 1792, fos
129–30.

76. Black, *British Foreign Policy ... 1783–1793*, pp. 411–12; *Courts and Cabinets*,
ii, Grenville to Buckingham, 7 November 1792, p. 223; *Dropmore*, ii, Pitt
to Grenville, 11 November 1792, p. 328; Rose Diaries, ii, Pitt to Stafford,
13 November 1792, p. 114; Clements MS, Pitt to Dundas, 15 November
1792.

77. Auckland Correspondence, ii, Grenville to Auckland, 6 November 1792,
pp. 464–7; Miles Correspondence, ii, 18 November 1792, p. 353.

78. Rose Diaries, ii, Pitt to Stafford, 13 November 1792, p. 114.
79. Clements MS, Pitt to Dundas, 17 November 1792; SRO GD 51/6/99; Clements MS, Pitt to Dundas, 24 November 1792; PRO 30/52/1, [24 November] 1792, fo. 61.
80. Clements MS, Melville Papers, 112, Pitt to Dundas, 26 November 1792.
81. Dropmore, ii, Grenville to Auckland, 26 November 1792, p. 344; Clements MS, Melville Papers, 112, Pitt to Dundas, 26 November 1792.
82. FO 37/41, 22, Grenville to Auckland, 23 November 1792; Dropmore, ii, Grenville to George III, 25 November 1792, p. 339; de Maulde, who made the first approach, saw the British and Dutch as sources of money to pay his debts: J. T. Murley, 'The background to the outbreak of the Anglo-French War of 1793', D.Phil. thesis (Oxford: 1959), pp. 221–36; Black, British Foreign Policy ... 1783–1793, p. 417.
83. HO 102/6, Dundas to Nepean, 24 November 1792, fos 48–53; PRO 30/8/157, Dundas to Pitt, 24 November 1792, fo. 142.
84. Court and Cabinets, ii, Grenville to Buckingham, 29 November 1792, p. 230; LCG III, ii, Grenville to George III, 30 November and 1 December 1792, pp. 632–3.
85. Court and Cabinets, ii, Grenville to Buckingham, 5 December 1792, p. 232; PR, xxxiv, Militia Proclamation Text, 1 December 1792, p. 30.
86. Veitch, The Genesis of Parliamentary Reform, pp. 234–5, and reproduced ever since.
87. Dropmore, ii, Grenville to Auckland, 9 November 1792, p. 329; Clements MS, Pitt to Dundas, 27 and 28 November 1792; PRO 30/8/198, Notebook 4, [26 November–1 December] 1792, fo. 112.
88. GLG, i, Pitt to Stafford, 1 December 1792, p. 61; PRO 30/8/157, Dundas to Pitt, 30 November 1792, fos 174–8; Clements MS, Pitt to Dundas, 28 November 1792; Court and Cabinets, ii, Grenville to Buckingham, 29 November 1792, pp. 230–1.
89. C. Emsley, 'The London Insurrection of December 1792: fact, fiction or fantasy?', JBS 17 (1978), pp. 66–86; LCG III, ii, Grenville to George III, 1 December 1792, p. 633; HO 42/23, Nepean to P. Salter, 1 December 1792, fo. 43; HO 1/1, Incendiaries now in England, 1 December 1792; PRO 30/8/198, Notebook 4, [29 November–7 December] 1792, fos 113–14; Court and Cabinets, ii, Grenville to Buckingham, 1 December 1792, p. 231.
90. Murley, 'Anglo-French War', pp. 120–2; Black, British Foreign Policy ... 1783–1793, p. 423.
91. HO 42/24, Hawkesbury to Nepean, 11 December 1792, fo. 277; Stanhope, Life of Pitt, ii, Pitt to Dundas, 4 December 1792, pp. 176–7; HO 1/1, Declaration of M. Longchamp, 12 December 1792.
92. Dropmore, ii, Buckingham to Grenville, [4] December 1792, p. 352.
93. For standard accounts, see Dozier, For King, Constitution and Country, pp. 57–9; A. Mitchell, 'The Association Movement of 1792–1793', HJ 4 (1961), pp. 179–90; Clements MS, Pitt to Dundas, 25 November 1792; Court and Cabinets, ii, Grenville to Buckingham, 25 November 1792, p. 229; Dropmore, ii, Grenville to Auckland, 26 November 1792, p. 341.

94. Clements MS, Pitt to Dundas, 25 November 1792; PRO 30/8/157, Dundas to Pitt, 30 November 1792, fos 174–7.

95. As claimed by Dozier, *For King, Constitution and Country*, p. 51. Grenville has always been identified as the minister most likely to have been involved with the Reevites. Not only was he the acting Home Secretary in Dundas's absence, but he and his brother Buckingham had been active in preparing a Buckinghamshire petition during the summer: *Court and Cabinets*, ii, p. 209; D. Ginter, 'The Loyalist Association Movement of 1792–1793 and British public opinion', *HJ* 9 (1966), pp. 182–3, draws attention to the moderate tone of the Merchant Taylors' loyal address. Tomline claimed that Pitt ought to have given the Reevites more support: *Life of Pitt*, ii, pp. 559–60.

96. Clements MS, Pitt to Dundas, 27 November 1792.

97. *Court and Cabinets*, ii, Grenville to Buckingham, 5 December 1792, p. 232; *Dropmore*, ii, Grenville to Auckland, 4 December 1792, pp. 351–2; Schofield, 'British politicians and French arms', p. 191.

98. FO 37/43, 21, Grenville to Auckland, 12 December 1792.

99. *Court and Cabinets*, ii, Grenville to Buckingham, 5 December 1792, p. 232.

100. FO 27/40, Minute of a conversation with Chauvelin, 29 November 1792, fos 169–72; BL Add MS 38192, Pitt to Hawkesbury, [28 November] 1792, fo. 91.

101. FO 27/40, Grenville to Long, November 1792, fos 298–9; Miles Correspondence, ii, 29 November 1792, p. 357; *LCG III*, i, Grenville to George III, 2 December 1792, p. 633; *Dropmore*, ii, George III to Grenville, 3 December 1792, p. 351.

102. Miles Correspondence, ii, Diary, 1 December 1792, pp. 362–3.

103. U1590 S5/09/14, draft of Maret meeting Memo; fuller version in BL Add MS 34446, fos 28–30. Maret also left a record of his interview with Pitt, for discussion of which see Murley, 'Anglo-French War', pp. 284–96; Miles Correspondence, ii, Diary, 23 December 1792, p. 368.

104. Murley, 'Anglo-French War', p. 268; Black, *British Foreign Policy . . . 1783–1793*, p. 424; Ehrman, *The Reluctant Transition*, pp. 233–4; *Dropmore*, ii, Grenville to George III, 3 December 1792, p. 351.

105. CUL 6958/6, 1088, Memo of second meeting with Maret, and 1185, Pitt to Chauvelin, 28 December 1792, 14 December 1792; Miles Correspondence, ii, Diary, 14 December 1792, pp. 388–9.

106. Murley, 'Anglo-French War', pp. 431–7; Black, *British Foreign Policy . . . 1783–1793*, pp. 426–8.

107. Ehrman, *The Reluctant Transition*, pp. 249–55; Black, *British Foreign Policy . . . 1783–1793*, pp. 428–54.

108. The correspondence was printed for the edification of Parliament: *PR*, xxxiv, pp. 342–71.

109. FO 27/40, Grenville to Chauvelin, 31 December 1792, fos 262–9.

110. News of the 15 December decree was received in London on 19 December.

111. FO 65/23, Grenville to Vorontsov, 19 December 1792, and 13, Grenville to Whitworth, 28 December 1792.

112. BL Add MS 58921, Grenville to Auckland, 29 December 1792, fo. 34;

BL Add MS 58857, Grenville to George III and the reply, 2 January 1793, fos 76–8; Black, *British Foreign Policy ... 1783–1793*, p. 434; Ehrman, *The Reluctant Transition*, pp. 240–1.

113. Spain was the only country to express any interest in the British peace proposals; Miles Correspondence, ii, Diary, 13 January 1793, pp. 42–4.

114. BL Add MS 58921, Grenville to Auckland, 24 January 1793, fo. 75; BL Add MS 34447, Burges to Auckland, 2 February 1793, fos 402–4; *Dropmore*, ii, Grenville to Auckland, 3 February 1793, p. 377.

115. M. Elliott, *Partners in Revolution: The United Irishmen and France* (New Haven, Conn.: 1982), p. 81.

116. C. Emsley, 'An aspect of Pitt's "Terror": prosecutions for sedition during the 1790s', *Social History* 6 (1981), pp. 161–2.

117. J. Derry, 'Governing temperament under Pitt and Liverpool', in J. Cannon (ed.), *The Whig Ascendancy: Colloquies on Hanoverian England* (1981), pp. 126–9.

118. Ehrman, *The Reluctant Transition, pp. 245–6.*

119. Blanning, Origins of the French Revolutionary Wars, p. 158; Black, *British Foreign Policy ... 1783–1793*, p. 466; Ehrman, *The Reluctant Transition*, p. 247; Holland Rose, *Great War*, pp. 98–101.

120. Keith Correspondence, ii, Auckland to Keith, 17 May 1792, p. 518.

Chapter 5

War without Conviction, January 1793– April 1794

When Britain went to war in 1793, none of its leaders believed that they were embarking on a lengthy conflict. War was a product of diplomatic stalemate; by the end of December 1792 the Cabinet was anticipating a probable outbreak of hostilities. The execution of Louis XVI on 21 January 1793 ended all hopes of a negotiated settlement, because Austria and Prussia remained committed, or so they said, to the French counter-revolution. This royalist zeal was not shared by the British government, which, despite its public and private denunciations of republican principles and policies, remained officially neutral towards developments in Paris for much of 1793. So different were the public and private faces of the Pitt ministry in early 1793 that its motives for participating in the Revolutionary Wars remain obscure.

An ideological definition of the war – fought primarily to repulse the threat posed by revolutionary principles to the political and social fabric of *ancien régime* Europe – would explain the arguments that the British government used to justify its involvement in the Revolutionary and Napoleonic Wars.[1] Such a definition does not, however, begin to address the Pitt ministry's interest in military theatres outside Europe nor its dealings with its continental allies throughout the 1790s, in which traditional eighteenth-century British diplomatic and strategic interests were of primary importance. To describe the war as purely conventional, a continuation of what has been called the 'Second Hundred Years War', would downplay the hatred and fear of revolutionary France on the part of ministers and diplomats. Ideology and pragmatism were not mutually exclusive and hostility to the revolution could play second fiddle to national interests defined in traditional terms.[2]

Earnestly though government spokesmen, journalists and pamphleteers used conservative arguments to condemn the personalities, policies and principles of revolutionary France, it was practical criteria – finances, manpower and organization – that were employed by ministers and officials to gauge the strengths and weaknesses of friends and foes. In no other individual could this logic be more clearly discerned than in Pitt, whose legendary optimism throughout the 1790s rested on a deep-seated misunderstanding of the enemy that he faced. The French republic as constituted in 1793, thought Pitt, could not resolve the social and political tensions that had torn France apart, let alone shoulder the fiscal and administrative burdens that it had inherited from the *ancien régime*. From January to April 1793 Pitt, anxious to maximize Britain's war returns, explored a variety of routes by which to strike at so vulnerable an enemy.

An Emerging Strategy

On 24 January 1793 13,000 Hanoverian mercenaries had been hired for the defence of the Dutch. Pitt and Grenville, despite having launched the peace project of 28 December, were taking no chances. By this time, however, it was unlikely that Britain's interest in the war would be confined to the United Provinces. On 4 January Grenville hoped that the British peace project would be accepted by Austria and Prussia because he strongly suspected that they 'had not as yet agreed on their own plan with any respect to any terms of pacification'.[3] He and Pitt were soon to learn otherwise. Eight days later Baron Jacobi and Count Stadion, the ambassadors of Prussia and Austria, called on Grenville not only to reiterate the commitment of their courts to the war, but to present the Foreign Secretary with indemnification terms.

Frederick William II proposed to take his post-war compensation in Poland, while Francis II had revived the long-sought Bavarian Exchange.[4] This news came as a surprise to a ministry that was expecting Austro-Prussian indemnification to come from western Europe. On 12 January Grenville, reported Stadion, described the second partition of Poland as 'screamingly unjust'. Although no minister in the Pitt Cabinet liked the Polish partition, more disturbing by far was the Bavarian Exchange, towards which British attitudes had long been clear: an independent Netherlands would sooner or later become a French Netherlands. Indemnification for the expenses of war, said Grenville to Jacobi and Stadion, could be taken 'only for conquests made upon France, and not from an invasion of the territory of another country'.[5] The Pitt ministry now had a strong motive for participating in the war. If it did not, Austria and Prussia were unlikely to conduct the 1793 campaign in terms of the interests of Britain or the United Provinces. 'I am inclined to believe', remarked Grenville after the meeting with Jacobi and Stadion, 'that nothing would be so advantageous to our Interests as the Re-establishment of the House of Austria' in the Netherlands.[6] Britain was moving towards an Austrian alliance.

With Austria and Prussia now intent on at least another campaign and with the safety of the United Provinces assured in the short term, the ministry could think of alternative uses for its 13,000 Hanoverians. Pitt and Grenville had decided on war by 20 January, when Grenville informed Auckland that the Hanoverian mercenaries 'might be employed elsewhere, supposing that by the circumstances of the war, His Majesty should be inclined to think the safety of the United Provinces should be otherwise secured'. Pitt told Loughborough that 'war was a *decided measure* ... that Russia was willing to go all lengths, that Spain was ready to join, and ... all the little powers waited our giving the signal'.[7] Pitt and Grenville were starting to think of offensive operations rather than defensive strategies. Flanders was emerging as one theatre of British operations; the West Indies was another.

When the news of Louis XVI's execution reached London on 23 January, Chauvelin was given his marching orders as stipulated under the Alien Act and, on 1 February, Pitt moved for an augmentation of the armed forces in the Commons. He demanded once more that France return to its 1789 borders and repeal the revolutionary decrees of late 1792. Pitt placed particular emphasis on these, stating that 'The liberty of France is the French army.'[8] This denounced the policies rather than the principles of the republic as engines of war, not revolution. By 4 February Grenville was resigned to war.

On 5 February, four days before the arrival of the French war declaration of 1 February, orders to open alliance talks had been sent to Morton Eden, the British ambassador in Berlin. By 8 February Grenville suspected that France had declared war on Britain and the United Provinces. Contentious though reparations were already becoming as a diplomatic issue, not a word about them appeared in any of the treaties that linked the members of what was to become the First Coalition. Heads of state were given the following terms of war:

> to consider no arrangement as satisfactory on the part of France which shall not include the abandonment of all Her Conquests and the renunciation of all Views of Interference on Her Part in the interior of other Countries, and of all Measures of Aggression or Hostility against them ... and also the renunciation of all Views and the disavowal of all Decrees, militating against the Internal Tranquillity, or against the existing rights of their Majesties, or of any Powers so admitted ...[9]

This did not commit the British government to a war of principle. If France agreed to peace within two months, having evacuated its conquests and abandoned unequivocally its expansionist policies, 'adding to them some stipulations for the personal security of Her Most Christian Majesty [Marie Antoinette] and Her Family', Britain would make peace with France – in the company, it was hoped, of Austria and Prussia.[10] This was a modification of the peace terms of 28 December.

On the subject of indemnification, the Pitt government was tight-lipped. Jacobi and Stadion had offered to ratify British gains overseas in return for recognition of their proposed eastern European arrangements. The European assumption that British compensation would be taken in the French colonies was accurate. The ministry believed that no real offence – or defence – could be mounted by the enemy overseas.[11] An eye had been kept on the French West Indies since 1789 and, by 1791, Pitt and Dundas had been approached by French planters in search of British protection against the reprisals of the Convention. The counter-revolutionary colonists were left, much to their chagrin, at arm's length until late December 1792, when Pitt, Dundas and Hawkesbury began to negotiate in earnest for the creation of a British protectorate in the Windward Islands.[12] On 19 February 1793 a settlement had been reached whereby British forces would hold St Domingo, the most lucrative of the French sugar isles, until peace had been secured, after which its fate would be decided by an allied peace conference. British plans for the West and East Indies were, however, to complicate Anglo-Spanish and Anglo-Dutch relations from 1793 to 1795.

The declaration of war against France by George III on 12 February 1793 brought an end to Britain's isolation in Europe. This process had started with the Russian mediation offer of 19 December. By the time Jacobi and Stadion visited Grenville in January, it was well under way. British ministers welcomed the opportunities presented by war diplomacy to resume old discussions or to continue them in a new setting. On 15 February Lord St Helens, British ambassador in Madrid, was directed to revive trade discussions which had been carried on in a desultory fashion since 1786. A month later similar proposals were received from Russia.[13] Although the Spanish government attempted to defer the conclusion of trade talks with Britain until the end of the war, the Nootka Sound dispute was finally resolved in 1794. The court of St Petersburg finally renewed its 1756 trade treaty with Britain in April 1793.[14]

The Pitt ministry also succeeded in securing allied acquiescence in British modes of warfare against France. Steps to protect merchant shipping were under consideration in January 1793; in March Spain agreed to joint Mediterranean blockade duty with the Royal Navy. Mindful of the 3,368 British merchant vessels lost to enemy privateers during the American War of Independence, the Admiralty published convoy schedules immediately following the outbreak of war.[15] Dutch ships were invited to join East Indian convoys and British naval protection was extended to Spanish vessels bound for the Caribbean. The most significant British coup was the consent of the Russian navy to police commercial shipping in the Baltic. Scandinavian neutrals had traditionally made rich profits from trading with warring European states. One of the worst offenders, in British eyes, had been Russia. When Catherine the Great proposed to man a Baltic patrol of ten ship-of-the-line and four frigates in March 1793, the British government was delighted.[16] George III remarked that Catherine's offer 'completely destroys the Russian system of an Armed Neutrality'.[17] The blockade of France was an important economic priority for Pitt, who believed that the enemy, plagued by financial crises since the early 1780s, could not survive the strains of war for long. He was to compile alternative French budgets for each year of the war, in which the *assignat*–sterling exchange rate, the prices of provisions and war materials, the returns – both real and presumed – of the French revenue, military expenditure and rates of inflation were religiously recorded.[18] His hopes of victory were based on such estimates. Pitt had great expectations for the British blockade. Not only was it expected to expedite the bankruptcy of the republic, but, as he said in the 1793 budget speech, 'commerce could flourish during war'. In March 1793 all friendly states were urged to suspend their trade with France.[19]

By this time, so expensive and extensive were British mobilization plans that a one-year war was no longer a feasible option. The defence of the United Provinces was the government's only real military obligation in 1793 but Pitt, having sent only 2,100 soldiers there in February, was now planning for a longer conflict. This was apparent in the instructions sent to British diplomats and military personnel. The Spanish government was urged to direct its attention to the province of Perpignan; Alsace-Lorraine was earmarked for the Rhineland members of the Holy Roman Empire and a redrawing of Dutch and Netherlandish boundaries was envisaged, the latter at the expense of the enemy. 'France must be greatly circumscribed', remarked George III, 'before we can talk any more of treating with that dangerous and faithless nation.'[20] The British vision of post-war Europe was taking shape, in which France would be stripped of its border provinces to create security zones on its eastern and south-western peripheries. This was the British answer to the French doctrine of natural frontiers.[21]

The most important project was the enlargement of the Austrian Netherlands. Vital to the reinforcement of Anglo-Dutch land and sea defences, it was not initially popular in Vienna. 'I mentioned the instance of a new Barrier', reported Morton Eden.[22] This, answered Austrian Foreign Minister Cobenzl, 'would be but a feeble defence' against France. Eden was ordered to persevere in his attempts to forge a long-term alliance between Britain and Austria. Pitt and Grenville were looking to the future and, having become disillusioned with the

Prussian wing of the Triple Alliance long before the outbreak of war, found the old system of union with Austria very attractive. The defence of the Netherlands was a long-standing common interest. At the end of February the Pitt ministry found another.

Dispatches from Vienna revealed that Frederick William was threatening to reduce his military contribution to the war unless Austria recognized the second Polish partition. The Merle Note of 15 October 1792 outlined Frederick William's intentions. After taking immediate possession of its new Polish lands, Prussia would henceforth play a secondary role in the French war. Frederick William was exasperated with his Austrian partner, Francis II, who in July 1792 had sent only 29,000 of a promised 110,000 troops to Flanders for military service.[23] The Prussian king had also been angered by Austria's post-war compensation demands, namely the Franconian Margraviates. The British government, though unwilling to take any action in eastern Europe, was equally opposed to Prussian expansion at the expense of Poland. Here lay further grounds for co-operation between London and Vienna.[24]

By 19 March the French were in retreat through the Netherlands and it was the turn of the allies to launch offensive operations. Having successfully defended the United Provinces, the British army could have gone home. Instead it was to be employed in 'embarrassing the retreat of the French Army'.[25] Military plans were drawn up at an allied war conference in Antwerp on 7 April: 'As many of the Troops as can with safety be spared from Holland, should be joined to this Country, and march to attack the French Frontier Towns ... as the taking of those Towns was looked upon by His Majesty's Servants, as a necessary means of establishing a permanent Peace with France.'[26] Auckland, who led the British military delegation, had received instructions to advocate this strategy because 'our military operations can be more easily adapted with those of the Austrians in Flanders than elsewhere'. On 8 April the Austrian high command decided to besiege a line of French border towns from Valenciennes to Lille. A delighted Auckland stressed 'the necessity of retaining those conquests, should they be made, for the future security of the Low Countries against France'.[27] Britain's commitment to this strategy took practical shape in the Dunkirk expedition planned for August 1793. In allied hands, the port was to link the line of captive border fortresses to the Channel. Dunkirk, to be given to Austria when peace was concluded in return for concessions to the Dutch in the Netherlands, made a useful entry point for allied troops and supplies, an ideal vantage point for the surveillance of enemy activity in the Channel and, not least, a means of rendering 'more palatable to this country the extensive co-operations which it may be necessary to adopt in the Low Countries'. So clear was Britain's interest in the Netherlands that, on 15 April, Morton Eden wrote that Austria was prepared to sign a defensive alliance with Britain, in the interests of which it was 'even ready to desist from the favourite project of exchanging the Austrian Netherlands for Bavaria'.[28]

No participant in the 1793 allied campaign believed that France was capable of resisting the combined armies of Europe. By March 1793 it was clear to the British that the French victories of 1792 were more attributable to divisions within the Austro-Prussian camp and the numerical superiority of the enemy's armies than to any skill or tactics displayed by the French. Pitt and Grenville remained concerned about the United Provinces until late March because the dual prospect of invasion and insurrection had reduced the Dutch government to a state of near hysteria: 'There is an extreme anxiety among our Friends here to have some ostensible show of the protection of England: They say it would be of essential Importance as to the Interior, which includes Amsterdam.'[29] Auckland had been passing on pleas of this nature since November 1792.

On 25 February 2,500 guardsmen were dispatched to the United Provinces. An additional 600 soldiers were sent a fortnight later. Pitt was not impressed by the slow pace of the Dutch mobilization.[30] Dutch panic was, in British eyes, what the Provisional Executive Council had hoped to induce in England through the pursuit of 'revolutionary diplomacy'. The Pitt ministry gave its ally what moral support it could, displaying a solicitous interest in the fortunes of the Patriots and their brethren which was returned by the Dutch, who had been concerned about the British reform movement since the May proclamation. European diplomacy was, in this respect, ideological during the 1790s, though it did not necessarily operate in Britain's interests.

In 1794 the government of the United Provinces, fearing that Pitt's power had been eroded by the anti-war propaganda of popular radicals, began to question Britain's commitment to the war. The other members of the First Coalition did not tend to ask embarrassing questions about the British reform movement, but this did not assuage the Pitt Cabinet's anxiety about its international image. Every proclamation, address of thanks and public order act of the 1790s was an act of diplomatic theatre. The militia proclamation and the Alien Act informed the powers of Europe that the British people would not rise in pursuit of liberty and that the British government was determined to defend the domestic and international status quo.

Public diplomacy of this description was little seen in the wrangling over national interest and status that marked the early months of the First Coalition. Here the intellectual dimension of the war was ignored. The 1793 continental campaign, unlike that of 1792, was not counter- or anti-revolutionary in conception. The allies were not going to Paris, the nerve centre of the enemy war effort, but to acquire indemnification on France's borders.[31] The imposition of an allied peace settlement on France had not been discussed at the Antwerp Conference, though the British government had been trying since November 1792 to persuade Austria and Spain to drop their insistence on the restoration of the Bourbon monarchy as a *sine qua non* of peace. This could only facilitate recognition of the republic against which the British government had so recently declared war on ideological grounds.

The post-war settlement of France was a matter of considerable interest to British politicians, who were anxious to know on what terms their government would make peace. On 12 February Pitt had told the Commons that Britain went to war 'to check the progress of a system, the principles of which, if not opposed, threaten the most fatal consequences to the tranquillity of this country, the security of its allies, the good order of every European government and the happiness of the whole human race!'[32] Pitt was in the unenviable position of having to construct working majorities in a Parliament that had not voted for a conventional war in Europe and the wider world.

Policy Defended

From 1793 to 1795 the ministry released a series of seemingly contradictory statements on the war with France. Throughout the 1793 session of Parliament the government was to maintain, occasionally in the same breath as an attack on the revolution's principles, that the existence of a republic across the Channel was no bar to peace. In January 1794 the ministry announced that the restoration of the monarchy in France was a British war objective. On 8 December 1795 Pitt declared that His Majesty's Government was prepared to receive overtures of peace from the Directory.[33]

Lords and Commoners were perplexed by their premier's extreme reluctance to commit himself on so crucial an issue as the future government of France. 'We cannot remain neuter', stated an exasperated Edmund Burke in September 1793.[34] Britain, according to Pitt, sought no more in war than it had in peace: namely the repeal of some offensive decrees, the evacuation of Nice, Savoy and the Netherlands. Was this 'indemnification for the past and security for the future'? This, the government's war platform during the 1790s, could be read in a conventional or ideological context. It was never clear whether the British government saw the policies of the republic as products of its principles. Burke and Fox were both suspicious. In the Commons debates on the British declaration of war Pitt had denounced French conquest as a perversion of liberty, but had drawn attention to the problems that his administration had faced over the past two months in dealing with a state which 'had not yet established any constitution of her own, that all, hitherto, was provisional and temporary'. The First Republic had not yet received the people's mandate to rule. The voice of the nation, 'as far as its wish could be collected, had expressed itself in favour of monarchy'. This suggested that Pitt favoured a Bourbon restoration but it could also mean that he would recognize a republican constitution ratified by the French electorate. The ministry's critics stood by for clarification.[35]

In April 1793 General Dumourier finally deserted his army and fled to Holland. The former French Foreign Minister was only one of several revolutionary notables to jump ship between the fall of the constitutional monarchy and the *journée* of 10 June 1793. A disillusioned Lafayette had defected the previous October. On 19 April Auckland had delivered an Anglo-Austrian memorial to the States General of the United Provinces demanding that political asylum be denied to ex-*conventionnels* and ex-members of the Provisional Executive Council. The memorial also demanded that all defectors on Dutch soil 'be delivered up to justice, that they might serve as a lesson to humanity'.[36] Sheridan attacked the memorial in the Commons on 25 April, claiming that its indirect call for the execution of French refugees on Dutch soil was inconsistent with Britain's war aims.

The Auckland Memorial was an embarrassment for Pitt, who had refrained from saying much about Louis XVI's death except to deplore it as an unfortunate event: 'It was not politic to enter into war for vengeance on account of crimes that were not committed in this country.' Pitt stressed that Britain had not gone to war for the memory of Louis XVI: 'The present war, he hoped, would restore the peace of France. The peace of France he believed would restore the peace of Europe.'[37] No British intervention in French politics, implied Pitt, would be involved in this process.

'Indemnification for the past and security for the future' was a slogan with several meanings. Indemnification could be interpreted as territorial compensation for the money and men involved in winning back the Netherlands, Nice and Savoy. Indemnification could also mean vengeance for what Grenville called 'the attack actually made upon us' – namely, French subversion in Britain and the United Provinces.[38] Security could also be seen in several lights: as the establishment of any government of a pacific disposition in Paris, the restoration of the Bourbon monarchy in some form, or the annihilation of France as a land and sea power. The Portland Whigs longed for an official declaration in favour of the Bourbon restoration, while the Foxites coined the term *bellum internecinum* to describe an ideological war of extermination possessing conventional features.

There were good reasons for Pitt to be vague about the government's intentions. The reports of the Antwerp Conference had reached London on 11 April, by which time ministerial disagreements about the deployment of Britain's armed forces had emerged. On 3 April Richmond, Master General of the Ordnance, had complained that valuable time was being lost by Cabinet indecision about Britain's military commitments. Eager to destroy 'this abominable French system,' he pressed Pitt for instructions: 'your ideas are quite clear that we must make expeditions to the coast of France and to the West Indies our *principal* object as soon as we are able'.[39] On 10 April Pitt explained his ideas to Richmond. 10,000 troops were to be sent to Flanders and a reserve of 15,000 recruited for 'Expeditions and other Services': 'To have a Corps of about 10,000 British to act in June, July or August upon the Coast of France, to send the same Force with reinforcements it might get from Gibraltar to the Mediterranean in August or September, & to detach from it in october a sufficient Corps for the West Indies for great operations there.'[40] Richmond gently pointed out that raising 20,000 British servicemen in less than six months was unrealistic. He drew attention to the probable poor quality of such raw recruits and noted that Pitt had made no arrangements for the replacement of dead, wounded and sick troops. Richmond's professional opinion was that Flanders and the French coast were the most appropriate theatres for British operations, whereupon Pitt replied that 'the Service in Flanders would not interfere with any of His Other Plans', which were 'what He really had in view'.

The ministry's interest in the West Indies dated from the 1780s, when it became apparent that, despite the triumph of British manufactures in continental markets, France was continuing to hold its own in trade, thanks to the export and re-export earnings derived from its Carribean colonies. Described by Michael Duffy as a 'precarious money box', the French islands, isolated in geographical and – after 1789 – social and intellectual terms from their homeland, were vulnerable to attack.[41] The attractions of the West Indies were great. Not only were the French islands suitable objects for one or two Caribbean expeditions, but their acquisition by Britain would deal a permanent blow to the commercial unity and military security of the French maritime empire. A successful West Indian campaign was also bound to be popular in Parliament and the country at large. Overseas victories were an effective and time-honoured way of popularizing a war, insofar as that was possible. Pitt may have been inspired by Chatham's policies of the 1750s though there is no evidence of any direct influence beyond the desire to strike at multiple targets simultaneously.[42] The influence of Dundas was not decisive.

Having said this, Pitt did not go to war for colonial conquest alone.

The ministry's emergence from isolation had been dictated by the danger in which the Low Countries had been placed by the intentions of France, Austria and Prussia. Britain was to make significant financial and military concessions to Austria over the next three years in order to maintain an influence over the fate of the Netherlands.[43] In 1793 Pitt was prepared to leave most of the European fighting to the land powers. Britain, with its small army, could not be expected to play a major part in the land war nor, in 1793, did there seem to be any necessity for it to do so. Pitt nevertheless earmarked half of Britain's army for Flanders and subsidized 22,000 mercenary troops in 1793. This was a significant commitment for a nation that wanted its voice to be heard at the peace table.

The defence of so heavy a continental commitment to Parliament remained problematic. Parliament had not voted to dismember France, to send expeditions to the West Indies or to thwart the Bavarian Exchange. The 'balance of power' was not, as the 1791 debates on the Russian armament had shown, a generally accepted geopolitical concept outside the Foreign Office nor did its recognition by some parties predispose them to conclude that Britain's role lay in redressing an imbalance. Here lay the utility of the Dunkirk expedition.[44]

> There exist in this country many strong prejudices against continental wars; and, with many, a strong prepossession against the strength of this country being directed in any other channel than that of naval operations. It is extremely necessary to meet these prejudices on as strong a ground as possible. The early capture of Dunkirk would operate most essentially in that point of view, and the expedition successfully conducted under the command of a prince of the blood, would give much éclat to the commencement of the war.[45]

The appointment of the Duke of York as Commander-in-Chief of the British army in Flanders was intended to appeal to British loyalists and royalists. He was placed under the direction of the Austrian command, where it was presumed that he would receive adequate supervision. York proved himself to be an able commander but, by the end of the 1793 campaign, Pitt was considering his replacement with a more experienced officer.[46]

Amphibious expeditions against France were equally difficult to justify. They had been mooted as early as December 1792. As the allied offensive took shape, Pitt, convinced that France was in no state to resist a multi-pronged offensive, felt that little effort would be required to strike crippling blows against military installations and commercial shipping centres. As Pitt had told Richmond in April, Le Havre, Brest, Marseilles and Toulon made good targets for such operations.[47]

Traditional though these schemes were – Captain William Bligh had carried out a crippling raid on Cherbourg in 1759 – their adoption during the 1790s was contentious because Poitou, Brittany and parts of Normandy were hotbeds of royalist counter-revolutionary resistance. In March the British government not only decided to hold Dunkirk in the name of George III, thereby remaining neutral to the revolution, but succeeded in establishing a tenuous link to the Vendée through the Channel Islands.[48] Even in its earliest communications, the Pitt ministry made offers of money and military supplies to the insurgents in the north-west. The British government was, however, reluctant to give direct aid to the royalists. On 15 March Whitworth was authorized to ask the Russian government whether it would field troops in Flanders or elsewhere: 'Attacking the vulnerable parts of the French Coast in the Channel or on the Ocean, so as to distract the attention of the Enemy, and to encourage any favourable dispositions which may show themselves in the Provinces.'[49] Because Catherine the Great was an ardent *ancien régime* monarchist giving shelter to the Comte d'Artois, the British hoped that their proposal would be greeted with interest. What they received was a Russian counter-project suggesting that the Pitt ministry fund an *émigré* army to be led by Artois.

British and Austrian diplomats strongly suspected that Russia's limited contribution to the First Coalition was driven not by any real interest in the war, but by a determination to meddle in the peace. Such apprehensions were confirmed by repeated Russian refusals to send troops to Flanders. Grenville responded to the subsidy request with a flat denial. Such an arrangement could never be explained to Parliament: 'The effect which such an engagement must produce on the public here must be that of the Government's endeavoring to do circuitously and by evasion that which if proper to be done at all, should be done as a direct and ostensible measure.'[50] Having categorically denied during the debates on the Auckland Memorial that Britain was at war to restore the Bourbon monarchy, Pitt could hardly ask Parliament to grant funds to *émigré* royalists.

The French rebels, useful and inexpensive though they were, could be regarded as nothing more than an auxiliary arm of the allied war effort. Britain, the United Provinces and Prussia were no friends to the royalist cause. All three had suffered too much at the hands of the French Bourbons in the past. Ever since the arch-conservative princes-in-exile had hoisted the standard of counter-revolution, British statesmen had surmised that restoration of the *ancien régime* would entail the reconstruction of the international dynastic confederacy that had made France the most powerful state in Europe before 1787. So insistent were the princes on the recovery of their hereditary rights and lands that no long-term benefits were likely to accrue to the foreign supporters of a restored monarchy. In May 1793 the Maréchal de Castries told Auckland that 'the combined armies should be satisfied in restoring order and the ancient monarchy to France and should not look to any indemnity for themselves'.[51] The princes were willing to cede the Isle de Bourbon and Isle de France to Britain, but baulked at the loss of the West Indies, French Flanders and Perpignan.

The reactionary tone of Bourbon royalism was best expressed in the declaration that Provence released following the death of Louis XVI on 23 January 1793. Provence announced that he would act as Regent for the young Louis XVII, held prisoner in Paris, and called for nothing less than the restoration of the *ancien régime* with minor cosmetic changes. So unpalatable a statement was this in diplomatic circles that only Russia and Spain recognized Provence's claims to the Regency. The other powers, including Austria and Britain, preferred to wait upon political developments in Paris.[52] By mid-summer it was apparent that these were to promise no respite from war and revolution.

By June 1793 the allied armies had retaken almost all the lands overrun by the French in 1792 and were pouring into Perpignan and Alsace-Lorraine. The National Convention, hard-pressed to defend the republic abroad, was faring no better against its enemies at home. Royalist counter-revolutionary forces were in virtual control of Poitou and south Brittany. Shortly before the fall of the Girondin ministry at the end of May LeBrun had made a final offer of peace to the United Provinces. This gratifying confirmation of French weakness encouraged the Pitt ministry to hold out for victory.[53] On 17 June, amidst the Convention's debates on the 1793 constitution, Fox brought a peace motion before the House of Commons. Under what conditions, he asked, would the government make peace with France?

Pitt once more denied that he sought to return the Bourbons to the French throne. To favour one form of government over another, he claimed, would be detrimental to Britain's quest for reparations and security. Whilst admitting that peace with republican France was 'full of difficulties', he outlined the conditions under which he was prepared to contemplate it:

> 1. That these principles should no longer predominate; or 2ndly. That those, who are now engaged in them should be taught that they are impracticable and convinced of their own want of power to carry them into execution; or 3rdly. That the issue of the present war will be such that by weakening their power of attack shall strengthen our power of resistance.[54]

This was neither Fox's *bellum internecinum* nor Burke's counter-revolution, but a statement of Pitt's thoughts on recent events in Paris.

News of the *journées* of 31 May and 10 June was fresh in London and Pitt observed that the power of the new regime rested on the whims of the Paris sections: 'The moment the mob of France becomes under a new leader, mature deliberations are reversed, the most solemn engagements retracted, our free will is entirely controlled by force.'

Pitt's attack on Parisian politics was no outright condemnation of republican ideals. He was criticizing the *journées* and the 1793 constitution in terms of their practical repercussions. The Constitution of the Year One, characterized by the strict separation of powers and the incorporation of direct democracy in legislative and administrative practice, did not give the central government the authority to maintain order at home, let alone guarantee 'a secure and lasting peace'. Pitt did not rule out the prospect of a stable republican settlement emerging in France. Paris, as he stated on 17 June, had made the revolution. Over the summer of 1793 the Convention continued to lose the goodwill of a nation; to royalist rebellion was added federalist revolt throughout France. By September 1793 the Pitt ministry was becoming impatient with the continued state of anarchy in France. More alarming were the widening rifts between the members of the First Coalition. The British government, which had been keeping its options open, began to move towards a more vigorous prosecution of the war.

New Horizons

As all available British troops were already committed to Flanders, the most direct route by which further blows could be struck against the republic during the summer of 1793 was the Vendée. Pitt had defended royalist aid as a legitimate military policy during the debate on Fox's peace motion on 17 June and, from the end of June to mid-July, coastal assault projects were once more under consideration by a Cabinet eager to capitalize upon royalist success in the north-west.[55] Here divisions in ideology and strategic thought became acrimonious.

Richmond, a staunch supporter of the counter-revolution, was eager to send aid to the Vendée. Dundas was anxious to appropriate the lion's share of British troops for service in the West Indies. 'I am of opinion that no service ought to be put in competition with the security of our Possessions.' Pitt agreed.[56] When Richmond protested, Dundas sent him a sharp reprimand:

> I could not assent to any such share of the force of the force of this Country on the Coast of France as would interfere with the objects which naturally present themselves in the West or East Indies. Success in those quarters I consider of infinite moment both in

humbling the power of France, and with a View to enlarging our National Wealth and Security.[57]

Global maritime supremacy was the chief goal of the war for Dundas, and his first West Indian expedition, due to sail in October, was given orders to execute a sweep of the French islands by April 1794. Dundas and Pitt were following the schedule laid down in April. 4,000 men were to be dispatched to Gibraltar for autumn service in the Mediterranean, after which they were to join the main British expeditionary force destined for the Caribbean.[58] A disappointed Richmond, whose influence with Pitt was rapidly waning, stopped attending Cabinet meetings in 1794. He was to be ousted from the Ordnance in 1795.

Disagreements in the Cabinet were minor in comparison to those within the First Coalition. The British government spent much of 1793 acting as a mediator in acrimonious Austro-Dutch quarrels about the renegotiation of the 1715 and 1718 Barrier Treaties. In August the Greffier Fagel arrived in London to obtain a secret British guarantee for Dutch claims to Lille, Liefenshock and Liège. Pitt, anticipating protests from the Austrians, agreed with reluctance to uphold the request, but only after making an unsuccessful attempt to buy off the Dutch in the East Indies. Negapatnam, over which Britain and the United Provinces had been haggling for a decade, was a major concession to have made to the Dutch. The ministry was prepared to make great sacrifices for the Austrians, 'to induce them to persist in the war instead of looking to other projects'.[59]

These projects referred to Poland and Bavaria. In April 1793 the new Imperial Chancellor, Baron Thugut, contended that Prussia could be kept active in the war only by withholding ratification of the Second Polish Partition until peace was made.[60] The British government, having come to the same conclusion, agreed not to divulge that the Anglo-Austrian alliance was based upon a fresh Austrian commitment to the Netherlands.[61] Renouncing the Bavarian Exchange had been a pragmatic decision; without the Netherlands in Austria's possession, it could not be exchanged for Bavaria. Francis, casting an uneasy eye at Frederick William, was now determined to prevent further Prussian inroads upon Poland. Indeed, Francis went so far as to say that Austria's indemnification would be taken in Poland if the Bavarian Exchange fell through. While committed to an enlarged Netherlands in theory, the Austrians displayed so obsessive an interest in Poland that the British thought that their ally might secretly revert to the Bavarian Exchange.[62]

Notwithstanding the all too apparent cracks in the coalition, in September the British began to ask their allies for their 1794 war plans. The ministry confessed to the Austrians that it wanted an end to the war within twelve months. 'The present prospects ... are such as to make it not unreasonable to hope that this duration might be sufficient for the ends we have in view.' Catherine was asked again to send troops to Flanders. Sceptical though Pitt and Grenville were about her response to their request, they felt that 'the Empress should be kept at least for the present as far committed as she is with respect to France'.[63] Prior to the dispatch of these queries, British military plans for the next campaign had been decided upon. As had been the case in 1793, these focused upon Austria and the Low Countries. The Pitt ministry, unimpressed by the military performance of Prussia, Spain and Italy in 1793, asked the Austrians to put pressure on their Italian friends. The British undertook to tackle Spain, though with no great enthusiasm. In June the Spanish government had declared no great interest in Perpignan and far too much interest in French St Domingo.

Pitt began to solicit military opinions on the 1794 campaign late in July 1793. The responses of Richmond and Dundas were predictable, but Sir James Murray, aide-de-camp to the Duke of York, came up with a bold and ambitious strategy. Murray recommended that two bodies of troops, each 30,000 strong, be detached from the allied armies in Flanders after the border fortresses had been secured. One of these would make an amphibious attack on Le Havre, capture it, and follow the River Seine to Paris. The second, headed for the same final destination, would move into central France from Landrecy or St Quentin: 'There seems little reason to apprehend the Progress of either of these Armies would be stopt by Superior Force.'[64] Were the British government to declare in favour of a Bourbon restoration, added Murray, French royalists were likely to emerge in force and join the allies. Murray's proposals were integrated with Pitt's amphibious assault schemes:

To be left on the frontier	30,000
To advance from Flanders towards Paris	50,000
To land at Havre and advance from thence to Paris	50,000
To attack Brest	50,000
To attack Toulon	50,000
	230,000 [65]

Most of these soldiers were to come from Austria and Prussia.

Time, money, lack of resources and allied disunity were pushing Pitt away from official neutrality to France. Late in the summer of 1793 the ministry finally established a link with Stofflet and Charette, the leaders of rebel forces in the Vendée. In the Châtillon letter of 18 August the royalist generals, who stated their force as being 10,000 strong, asked Britain for money, supplies and a Bourbon prince to lead them.[66] The Pitt ministry, while unwilling to commit itself in writing to the support of a Bourbon restoration, informed its Austrian ally on 7 September that an invasion of the French interior was necessary to compel the republic to surrender: 'any considerable progress of foreign troops may be joined to the internal distresses resulting from the present anarchy'. Grenville hoped that the post-war future of France would be settled by 'the reasoning and moderate part of that Nation after the experience they have had of the dangers of theoretical innovation'.[67]

On 13 September the British government learned that Toulon had surrendered to Admiral Lord Hood who, with Spanish assistance, had been on blockade duty in the Mediterranean since May. These tidings were all the more welcome when it was learned that Toulon's twenty-six ship-of-the-line, seventeen frigates and shore-based artillery fortifications were still intact. Pitt was amazed and delighted: 'this Blow is I think in every View the most important which could be struck towards the final success of the War'.[68] He noted that the capitulation was not ideal for the republican authorities of the city had delivered Toulon into Anglo-Spanish hands in the name of Louis XVI and 'the hereditary monarchy of France' as established by the Constituent Assembly of 1789.

It transpires that the governors of Toulon were in fact federalists depicting themselves as royalists to ensure lenient treatment from Hood. The British government, aware that Toulon was a city of divided loyalties, was unsure as to what was meant by 'the 1789 Constitution'.[69] During its two-year existence the Constituent Assembly had passed a bewildering array of reform statutes ratified by the 1791 constitution. The constitutional monarchy had been officially recognized by Britain and the United Provinces but all European statesmen knew that Louis XVI and his brothers-in-exile had been hostile to the 1791 settlement. The British government therefore announced that it would support the restoration of monarchy 'in some one of the forms by which that principle of government might be modified'. Pitt and Grenville began to discuss which parts of the 1791 constitution might be retained.

Grenville, who believed that the end of the *ancien régime* had been preordained by the inclusion of democratic principles in the 1791 constitution, nevertheless emerged as an advocate of that settlement. The Foreign Secretary, who was unwilling to alienate the residents of southern France and the *émigré* supporters of the French monarchy – divided into *pur* and *constitutionnel* camps – maintained that the ministry ought not to commit itself to any specific type of restoration.[70] Pitt, who disagreed, wanted the calendar of the revolution to be turned back to June 1789, allowing France to re-embark upon the quest for constitutional, fiscal, legal and administrative reform that had been derailed by civil strife and foreign war.

Pitt could be found demanding 'a more pointed recommendation of monarchy with proper limitations' in Grenville's draft of a royal proclamation to the citizens of France. In this document, published on 29 October, Grenville wanted to stipulate merely that the British government looked forward to the restoration of 'regular government'. For Pitt and Grenville, this meant a *de jure* government accepted by the people of France. Neither man objected to national self-determination *per se*, and Pitt remained willing to negotiate with any form of government that 'should be firmly established'. He remained privately convinced that monarchy 'was the only one from which we expect any good'. Pitt, who did not wish to give any encouragement to federalists, declared that the ministry 'could not go on secure grounds' if it collaborated with 'any groups that stop short of some declaration in favour of monarchy'. In the French version of the 29 October proclamation, 'gouvernement regulier' was changed to 'gouvernement héréditaire'.[71]

Pitt, together with Dundas, Lord Chancellor Loughborough and Sir Gilbert Elliot, had outlined an 'ideal' restoration in the official 'Instructions' that laid down the guidelines for the British occupation of Toulon. In August Elliot, one of the younger Portland Whigs, had become the would-be civilian commissioner of a captive Dunkirk. When York failed to take the Channel port at the end of the month, a defeat that dealt a severe blow to Britain's military prestige, Elliot agreed to go to Toulon instead. So severe was public criticism of the Dunkirk expedition that Pitt's eagerness 'to make a good use of Toulon' stemmed partially from a determination to restore the military and political credit of the British government at home and abroad.[72]

The restoration that was depicted in Elliot's private draft of his own Instructions, the contents of which were integrated into his official orders, represented a compromise between the wishes of the *ancien régime* royalists and their *constitutionnel* opponents. It called for the return of Louis XVII, the hereditary monarchy, the Estates General, the provincial estates and the *parlements*. Grievances were to be redressed by a process of consultation between the king and estates in 'a certain & Periodical meeting of the States-General in all time coming'. The estates were to hold the purse-strings of the state and to participate in the implementation of a constitutional reform programme, including 'the repeal of some specifick abuses in the *ancien régime* which are generally obnoxious' which had been listed as objects of royal attention in the *séance royale* of June 1789. As Elliot put it, the new French constitution would be 'santion'd by Antiquity, & recommended by recent reform of great abuses, & recent improvement on the side of Liberty'.[73]

The Pitt–Elliot restoration attempted not only to introduce France to 'the points of what we should call constitutional liberty', but to re-create the consensus that was thought to have existed in the French political nation before the revolution. The British commissioners were instructed to facilitate the rehabilitation of the provincial estates, the *parlements* and the Roman Catholic Church.[74] Similar instructions had been given to Elliot for the occupation of Dunkirk. As Dundas remarked: 'We must endeavour to be the Counterpart of the Convention of France, we must pay attention to the interests of the clergy and the other legitimate Orders of Society. We must restore a Magistracy founded on the antient System and consistent with the regular Exercise of Subordination and obedience to regular Laws.'[75] Grenville voiced strong objections to the convocation of the Estates General, the recall of the *parlements* and the revival of the *séance royale* reform agenda. These, he claimed, 'contained the very first seeds of dissention'. He thought that history stood to repeat itself if the Pitt–Elliot restoration was implemented and he asserted that the safest course of action for the ministry to follow was 'to collect opinions' on the restoration from the *émigrés*.[76]

Following the submission of these criticisms to Pitt, references to the Estates General disappeared from the Toulon commissioners' instructions. The recall of the provincial estates and *parlements* remained, as did the re-establishment of the Roman Catholic religion and the return of 'every species of Property that has been confiscated during the recent troubles'. Pitt's Toulon proclamation, released by Elliot on 20 November, merely confirmed the terms on which Hood had agreed to take possession of the port. This was quite deliberate for Elliot had been urged 'not to do violence to existing Prejudices' in the local community. The residents of Toulon were to be persuaded that government on a Bourbon model, as run by the allied occupation forces, was superior to all republican alternatives. Notwithstanding the extreme caution with which Elliot was ordered to act, Pitt was convinced that France was seething with closet royalists who only awaited external support to declare themselves. Elliot was ordered to investigate 'how far Troops can safely and usefully be formed from the Inhabitants and by what Means their aid may be rendered most effectual in the Prosecution of Military Operations'.[77]

The ministry also committed itself to the dispatch of money, supplies and troops to the Vendée. Lord Moira was appointed commander of a joint British–*émigré* expedition which, on 18 November, was given instructions to launch an attack on the Ile de Noirmoutiers off the coast of Poitou. Pitt would have preferred Moira to take St Malo or the Ile d'Yeu, but bowed to the wishes of the military professionals. After securing a base on Noirmoutiers, Moira was to meet mainland royalist forces and carry out an attack on Nantes. It was hoped that

Anglo-royalist forces would command the mouth of the Loire by the end of 1793, and Pitt described the Noirmoutiers expedition as 'the best chance which has yet appear'd of assisting, by a powerful Diversion, operations in every other Quarter, and giving the turn we want to the whole War'.[78]

By the end of November the British government was involved in four theatres of war: Flanders, the south of France, the Vendée and the West Indies. Finding manpower for all these commitments was difficult. The Austrians and Spaniards were asked to send troops to Toulon, together with Swiss and Hessian mercenaries for whom the ministry was prepared to pay. Faced with failure, Pitt denuded the West Indian expedition of eight regiments for service in Toulon and the Vendée. An appalled Dundas complained that British resources were overstretched. Continental operations, he asserted, were best confined to Flanders and the northern coast of France, 'and from these points to direct our operations to Paris'. Toulon and the Caribbean came third and fourth respectively on George III's list of military priorities. He preferred to see Britain's continental commitment restricted to Flanders, as British forces there were 'more easily supplied from hence and also, if enabled to move forward, more able to advance to Paris'.[79] The British government had adopted the Murray war plans of July.

Toulon was an unpopular theatre in government circles because it posed so many diplomatic problems. Hood's authority in the port was contested by the Spanish Admiral Gravina, who demanded a say in the disposal of the captive French Mediterranean fleet. To make matters worse, Gravina's masters in Madrid supported a pure restoration of the *ancien régime* and encouraged the Bourbon princes to place themselves at the head of the 'royalists' in Toulon. The Pitt ministry was horrified. So reactionary was the monarchism of Provence that his arrival in Toulon was not likely 'to conciliate the Minds of the Inhabitants'.[80] The Spanish were reminded that 'the people of Toulon' had declared for Louis XVII and the 1791 constitution. The princes and their followers, fearing – quite rightly – that the British government did not want 'to see them for the present at the head of a Royalist party, but would rather that the cause should, to a certain length, be carried on without them', lodged indignant complaints with the Portland Whigs.[81]

By November 1793 the armies of the Convention were scoring notable successes against the rebels. Lyons was retaken on 9 October and the royalists were meeting concerted republican resistance in the Vendée. Pitt, thinking that the presence of a Bourbon prince in southern France would rally the forces of counter-revolution, was softening towards the princes-in-exile. Toulon nonetheless remained an important possession for a government 'with an eye to War or Peace'. Its surrender had very much widened British military and strategic horizons. Grenville's proclamation of 29 October had included references to allied indemnification 'which may be required from France on the side of the Pays-Bas, and of Lorraine, or even Piedmont' to 'habituate [French] people early to the sound of such a proposition'.[82] Dismembering France was not to be so easy for, on 19 December 1793, Toulon fell to the republican armies.

The Prussian Subsidy

By the time Parliament met on 21 January 1794 Pitt had a lot of explaining to do. Dunkirk had not been taken, Moira's Noirmoutiers expedition had failed and Toulon was lost. To this litany of failures were added the expulsion of the Austrian army from Alsace and the threatened withdrawal of Prussia from the war. This last setback was the most serious in ministerial eyes, for the successful execution of the 1794 war plans depended upon the presence of a Prussian army in Flanders. Frederick William's commitment to the war had always been suspect. In September 1793 the British government was warned that the Prussian troops would be withdrawn from Flanders unless Frederick William received acknowledgement of his recent Polish acquisitions and an allied subsidy for the 1794 campaign. The British and Austrian governments rejected both demands and reminded the court of Berlin that, under the terms of the 1788 Anglo-Prussian alliance and the 1791 Austro-Prussian defence pact, it was obliged to field 52,000 troops for 'the common cause'.[83]

Throughout the autumn of 1793 Grenville claimed that the allies were better off without Prussia, but Pitt, who described Prussian aid as 'material for the next campaign', was willing to meet Frederick William half-way. He was prepared to supply bread and forage for the Prussian army of 52,000 owed to Austria and the Triple Alliance, but he also proposed that the First Coalition foot all bills for any additional Prussian troops. Incurring this expense, maintained Pitt, would produce 'a real and effective force at our disposal, in a quarter where it is essential to act with vigour, as part of the general plan for the next campaign'. British strategists, frustrated by the lack of co-operation displayed by allied generals in 1793, hoped to gain effective control of the Prussian army.[84]

In early November the Foreign Office received fresh dispatches from Berlin. In interviews with Pitt and Grenville, Jacobi declared that his royal master did not have the resources to honour his military obligations. The request for a subsidy was renewed. Grenville replied that, though Britain was unwilling to pay for the aid it was owed under treaty, were the Prussians to field an army of over 52,000 men for the 1794 Flanders campaign, the ministry would consider *'the means of facilitating to the King of Prussia any further co-operation which he might be disposed to employ in the present war'*.[85] No ratification of the Second Polish Partition was forthcoming from London. Having recently discovered that Frederick William's agents had been unable to raise a loan of 5 million florins in Amsterdam, Pitt and Grenville accepted that the Prussians were in financial trouble. These embarrassments were not, the British suspected, as severe as Jacobi had claimed. Lord Malmesbury, given the unenviable task of persuading the Prussians to comply with British demands, was told by Grenville that the Anglo-Prussian alliance would be broken off 'if the *alleged distress* of the King of Prussia's *treasury is wholly feigned'*. Pitt, reported Earl Spencer on 11 November, 'even went so far as to say he should not be surprised if they [the Prussians] were to withdraw entirely from the Confederacy'.[86]

When Malmesbury was sent to Berlin on 21 November, the Austrians were camped in Alsace, Moira was preparing to launch his attack on Noirmoutiers and Toulon was still in British hands. By 7 January Prussian military power had become 'almost indispensable with a View to the prosperous issue of the next Campaign'.[87] The Austrians and Dutch agreed with this verdict, but refused Britain's requests for contributions to a Prussian subsidy. Fagel told Malmesbury that funds for such an undertaking could only be raised through a loan from England. The Austrian government, dissatisfied since February 1793 by Britain's reluctance to confront Prussia, simply refused to contribute any money to the subsidy. Malmesbury, who noted that 'Poverty & goodwill are both undoubted facts in Berlin', put the matter succinctly: 'Can we or can we not do without the King of Prussia?' When the Prussian government demanded no less than £2m. for an army of 100,000 men, the Pitt ministry was stunned: 'We are under great difficulties from the enormity of the sum in question and the apparent improbability of procuring any considerable part of it otherwise than from the resources of this country.'[88] No subsidy meant no Prussians on the western front. This scenario, stated Pitt, was to be avoided at all costs: 'it must be considered a change of system which will reduce us to some second best system, which God knows must be deplorably bad'. On 28 January, with the 1794 budget due for presentation to Parliament within the week and an Austrian military delegation expected to arrive in London shortly thereafter, Grenville drafted fresh proposals for a subsidy for Malmesbury and Morton Eden.[89] The British government offered to put up £800,000 of the £2m. demanded by Prussia. The United Provinces, Austria and the empire were asked to come up with £400,000 each. Prussia was ordered to deposit £400,000 with the allies as security for the good behaviour of its army. According to Austrian estimates,

300,000 men would be needed for the successful prosecution of the 1794 campaign. Half this force was to secure and guard the border fortresses of the Low Countries, while the remainder was to strike at the French heartland.

From 14 to 16 February 1794 allied representatives, minus the Prussians, discussed the deployment of their forces in Flanders. 340,000 allied troops were to be spread out on an offensive line stretching from Basle to the Channel. An army of 95,000 Austrians was to spearhead the assault on France by seizing the border fortresses of Landrecies, Mauberge, Cambrai and Avesnes, after which 80,000 Austrian and 40,000 British troops would combine for the march to Paris.[90] The British government hoped that this would be launched during the summer of 1794 although General Mack and the Prince of Cobourg, Commanders-in-Chief of the Austrian army, argued that this was not feasible until 1795. An unspecified number of Prussians were placed in the rearguard and the Austrian military plans were accepted 'subject to the political considerations which it seemed right to insist on' – namely, Austrian and Dutch acquiescence in Grenville's new Prussian subsidy scheme.[91]

Neither the Dutch nor the Austrians were happy with the new Prussian subsidy. The United Provinces pleaded a lack of funds while Austria bluntly rejected the project and expressed doubts about the empire footing a bill of £400,000. Pitt, determined to devote as much strength as possible to the offensive wing of the Flanders army, decided that Britain and the United Provinces had to fund the Prussian army without imperial or Austrian assistance. He and Grenville had been preparing for this since January and, in mid-March, Malmesbury was sent another set of subsidy proposals: 'There is unquestionably no comparison between the mischief of hazarding the war, or even un-necessarily protracting its duration, and that of incurring a considerable increased Expence even beyond the amount of the Proposal with which you was first charged.'[92] The British government now proposed to supply bread and forage to the army of 30,000 men that Prussia was obliged to field under the terms of the 1788 Triple Alliance. A flat £1m. was offered for 50,000 troops. Dutch consent followed a British undertaking to lend the United Provinces the capital required.[93]

On 19 April 1794 the final subsidy treaty was signed in the Hague. The King of Prussia, having agreed to place 62,500 men at the disposal of the maritime powers, was to receive the following sums: £300,000 to prepare the troops for active service; £50,000 for each month of participation in the Flanders campaign; and a final payment of £100,000 after the army had gone home. Pitt and Grenville, who had originally insisted that the Prussian troops should fight with the armies of the maritime powers, withdrew this stipulation during the course of the subsidy negotiations. They ruled instead that Britain and the United Provinces must be free to dispose of any conquests made by the Prussian army in 1794. Any such acquisitions were to become allied assets for exchange, either amongst themselves or with the enemy at the peace table.[94] This had been the logic dictating the decision to besiege Dunkirk and to occupy Toulon. Britain was now seemingly in a position to dictate the territorial settlement of western Europe without incurring any losses in the wider world. Frustrating though the Prussian subsidy negotiations had been, the future still looked bright. Revolutionary France remained the unknown variable in the calculations of European statesmen and strategists. Much to the surprise of the allied contestants, the remarkable recovery of the republic in 1794 was to upset the British government's plans for a swift and final victory.

Responses to Revolutionary Government

From August 1793 to April 1794 the Pitt ministry had moved from a position of tolerance *vis-à-vis* the revolution to something resembling total war. Although this change of direction had been governed by conventional considerations of one kind or another – an acute scarcity of British manpower, the virulence of disputes amongst the members of the First Coalition, the emergence of widespread French resistance to the authority of the National Convention – British private and official attitudes to the enemy hardened perceptibly over the autumn of 1793.

Early in 1794 Pitt and Grenville listed their military and diplomatic priorities for presentation to Parliament. Although most of these had not changed since 1793 – '2. Acquisition of Places for Indemnity – Security. X3. Rendering the Effects of the War as little Grievous to ourselves as possible. X4. Intermediate means of annoying them' – ministerial war aims also included: '5th. Destroying the present system of France as desirable in itself and most likely to terminate the War.' As Malmesbury put it, the chief object of the European conflict had become 'the destruction of the atrocious system now prevalent in France'.[95]

From the mouth of Lord Mornington, one of Pitt's staunchest supporters, came a vitriolic denunciation of *gouvernement révolutionnaire* in the House of Commons on 21 January 1794. This set the tone of the ministry's public statements for the rest of the year. Most of the groundwork for what Sheridan described as a speech 'remarkable for its length in addition to its ability' had been laid by Pitt and Grenville: 'The Revolution of 31 May introduced an entirely new Government in France more atrocious than any of the former Systems and one which is more incompatible with the safety of other Countries.'[96] This was a retrospective remark on the part of Pitt, who had not expected the new 'Jacobin' regime to outlast the summer. He held much the same objections to the new French system as he had to its predecessor: its lack of *de jure* foundations – 10 October saw the shelving of the 1793 constitution and the declaration of *gouvernement révolutionnaire* – and its inability to command or inspire French public support, as demonstrated by the state of virtual civil war into which the Midi and the Vendée had been plunged following the *journée* of 31 May. By November 1793 Pitt recognized that the imposition of administrative and military control over the French *départements* was a sign of probable endurance, if not permanence: 'He seems in general to look upon the French as being at present in a situation less likely to dispose them to yield than they were some months ago, owing partly to the surrender of Lyons and partly to their successes in La Vendée, which he apprehends to be more decisive than they have ever been yet.'[97]

By January 1794 Pitt had realized that the law of *14 frimaire* marked the start of an institutionalized terror in France. Grenville and Mornington attacked the principles and policies of *gouvernement révolutionnaire*, but Pitt, who also saw the new regime as a genuine threat to liberty and property, reserved his abuse for the methods by which the revolutionary committees had found the resources for war:

Levée en masse
Requisition
Prehension
Armed People
Use of Capital of Country.[98]

Pitt was amazed and appalled by this expropriation of materials, money and manpower but his deprecatory attitudes towards revolutionary France underwent no change. They had in fact been reinforced. *Gouvernement révolutionnaire* was likely to be more unpopular than any previous political system, both inside and outside France. Pitt accepted that the centralization of executive authority had bought time for the republic, but at a cost that would hasten the downfall of the 'état de réquisition'.[99]

At the beginning of 1794 Pitt's belief in the possibility of an easy and swift victory was strong. Despite the setbacks of 1793, the British government was happy with its performance during the first campaign. Having joined the war at the eleventh hour, the ministry had succeeded in imposing some control over the conduct of the allied war effort and, as the paymaster of Europe, was seemingly in a good position to dictate the peace terms to France on the Continent and in the colonies within twelve months. Pitt took comfort not only from the relative ease with which the divided allies had driven back the armies of revolutionary France in 1793, but with the flourishing state of British trade, which worked towards minimizing the socio-economic impact of the war at home.[100]

Pitt's personal illusions concerning the strengths and weaknesses of France were to result in a persistent underestimation of enemy strength throughout the 1790s. While a pragmatic strategy seemed to enable the British to exploit any offensive opportunities that presented themselves in Europe, Pitt and his colleagues were so intent on prosecuting the war in conventional 'national' terms that they were slow to see its wider dimensions, particularly those that motivated its eastern European allies, or to understand the intellectual forces that drove its French opponents. Pitt's lack of insight went far beyond either inexperience in military logistics or an over-ambitious global strategy. In his exultation at the downfall of the *ancien régime*, he failed to recognize that the foundations upon which its power had been based – agriculture, manpower and industry – had survived the revolution largely intact. Richmond, when urging Pitt to a rapid and efficient deployment of British forces in April 1793, drew attention to the latent strength of France 'under all forms of Government ... That the moment is so critical and pressing, that if time is given, France, with her Resources, may recover.'[101]

Notes

1. R. Dozier, *For King, Constitution and Country* (Lexington, Ky.: 1983), pp. 117–18; Schofield argues that the war was ideological from 1793 to 1795: 'British politicians and French arms', *History* 78 (1993), pp. 192–3, 200.

2. J. Holland Rose, 'The struggle with revolutionary France' in A. W. Ward and G. P. Gooch (eds), *The Cambridge History of British Foreign Policy, 1783–1919* (3 vols, Cambridge: 1922), i, pp. 230–1; J. M. Sherwig, *Guineas and Gunpowder: British Foreign Aid in the Wars with France 1793–1815* (Cambridge, Mass.: 1969), pp. 2–3; T. C. W. Blanning, *The Origins of the French Revolutionary Wars* (1986), pp. 158–9; J. Ehrman, *The Reluctant Transition* (1985), pp. 247–8; M. Duffy, 'British policy in the war against revolutionary France', in C. Jones (ed.), *Britain and Revolutionary France* (Exeter: 1983), pp. 11–26, and 'British diplomacy and the French wars 1789–1815', *ibid.*, pp. 127–45. For the concept of the Second Hundred Years War, see J. Brewer, *The Sinews of Power: War, Money and the English State 1688–1783* (1989); J. Black, 'Anglo-French relations in the age of the French Revolution', *Francia* 15 (1987), pp. 431–3.

3. FO 29/1, 1, Grenville to Sir James Murray, 4 January 1793.

4. FO 64/27, 4, Grenville to Morton Eden, 12 January 1793.

5. R. H. Lord, *The Second Partition of Poland* (Cambridge, Mass.: 1915), p. 442; FO 37/44, 5, Grenville to Morton Eden, 5 February 1793.

6. M. Duffy, 'British war policy and the Austrian alliance', D.Phil. thesis

(Oxford: 1971), pp. 15–18; FO 37/44, 5, Grenville to Morton Eden, 12 January 1793; FO 37/43, 6, Grenville to Auckland, 13 January 1793; FO 7/32, Grenville's memo of a conference with Stadion, 5 February 1793; FO 29/1, 2, Grenville to Murray, 20 January 1793.

7. FO 37/43, 10, Grenville to Auckland, 20 January 1793; Malmesbury Diaries, ii, 20 January 1793, pp. 501–2.

8. *PR*, xxxiv, 1 February 1793, pp. 328–71.

9. Bod: MS Talbot b. 19, 3, Grenville to Fitzgerald, 8 February 1793, fo. 9; FO 64/27, 5, Grenville to Morton Eden, 5 February 1793.

10. FO 29/1, 3, Grenville to Murray, 6 February 1793; J. Knox Laughton (ed.), *The Barham papers, 1758–1813* (2 vols, 1902), ii, Middleton to Chatham, 6 October 1793, pp. 353–4.

11. There were only 12 French warships, including frigates, stationed in the French Antilles; only three French ships were in the East Indies: N. Hampson, *La Marine de l'an II: mobilisation de la flotte de l'océan, 1793–1794* (Paris: 1959), p. 252.

12. Duffy, 'The Austrian alliance', pp. 28–31; D. Geggus, *Slavery, War and Revolution: The British Occupation of St Domingue, 1793–1798* (Oxford: 1982), pp. 83–4; BL Add MS 38192, Pitt to Hawkesbury, 17 December 1792, fo. 93.

13. *Dropmore*, ii, Cabinet Minute, 25 January 1793, p. 373; FO 72/26, 4, Grenville to St Helens, 15 February 1793; FO 65/24, Grenville to Voronzov, 20 March 1793.

14. FO 72/26, 11, St. Helens to Grenville, 22 March 1793; FO 65/24, 18, Whitworth to Grenville, 5/14 March 1793. The 1766 treaty had expired in 1786, since when Pitt had been trying to get it renewed on terms favourable to Britain.

15. Brewer, *The Sinews of Power*, p. 198.

16. FO 72/26, 5, Grenville to St Helens, 12 March 1793; FO 65/24, Grenville to Voronzov, 26 March 1793. No British pressure was applied to secure the Russian ships: HO 32/3, 5, Dundas to Grenville, 23 April 1793.

17. *Dropmore*, ii, George III to Grenville, 19 March 1793, p. 385. The League of Armed Neutrality had been a contentious issue in Anglo-Baltic relations throughout the 1780s. See, for example, Dep Bland Burges 30, Auckland to Burges, 25 September 1790, fo. 61.

18. Pitt's notes on the French economy are scattered through PRO 30/8/333–5.

19. *PH*, xxx, 11 March 1793, col. 564; for the suspension of allied commercial relations with France, see FO 72/27, 9, St Helens to Grenville, 2 May 1793; FO 65/24, 21, Grenville to Whitworth, 28 March 1793; FO 7/33, 3, Morton Eden to Grenville, 9 March 1793; FO 37/44, 20, Auckland to Grenville, 6 February 1793; FO 64/27, 4, Grenville to Morton Eden, 26 January 1793.

20. Duffy, 'British policy in the war against revolutionary France', pp. 19–20; *Dropmore*, ii, George III to Grenville, 27 April 1793, p. 393.

21. A. Sorel, *L'Europe et la révolution française* (8 vols, Paris: 1893–1912), iii, pp. 144–52, 278–9; P. Sahlins, 'France's boundaries since the seventeenth century', *American Historical Review* 95 (1990), pp. 1423–51; P. Schroeder,

The Transformation of European Politics 1763–1848 (Oxford: 1994), pp. 115–17.

22. FO 7/33, 1, Morton Eden had just taken charge of the Vienna Embassy, 2 March 1793.

23. Duffy, 'The Austrian alliance', pp. 17–20; FO 7/32, 12, A. Straton to Grenville, 6 February 1793; J. H. Clapham, *The Origins of the War of 1792* (Cambridge: 1899), pp. 218–19.

24. Lord, *The Second Partition of Poland*, pp. 326–46, 363–7; Clapham, *The Causes of the War of 1792*, p. 220; FO 29/1, 1, Grenville to Beauchamp, 27 June 1793.

25. FO 37/46, 37, Grenville to Auckland, 19 March 1793; FO 29/1, Grenville to Murray, 19 March 1793; BL Add MS 58906, Pitt to Grenville, [7 April 1793], fos 164–5.

26. FO 7/33, 8, Morton Eden to Grenville, 27 March 1793.

27. Auckland Correspondence, iii, Grenville to Auckland, 1 April 1793, pp. 3–6; *Dropmore*, ii, Auckland to Grenville, 9 April 1793, pp. 12–13.

28. PRO 30/8/103, George III to Pitt, 29 March 1793, fos 488–90; Auckland Correspondence, iii, Dundas to Murray, 16 April 1793, pp. 24–5; FO 7/33, 15, Morton Eden to Grenville, 15 April 1793; M. Duffy, 'A particular service: the British government and the Dunkirk expedition of 1793', *EHR* 91 (1976), p. 532.

29. *Dropmore*, ii, Auckland to Grenville, 8 February 1793, p. 377.

30. *LCG III*, ii, Pitt to George III, 7 March 1793, p. 17.

31. Duffy, 'The Austrian alliance', pp. 18–19.

32. *PR*, xxxiv, p. 459.

33. *Ibid.*, 25 April 1793, pp. 301–6, and xxxvii, 21 January 1794, pp. 174–82; *PH*, xxxii, 9 December 1795, pp. 651–67.

34. Burke Correspondence, vii, Burke to Windham, 24 October 1793, pp. 460–1.

35. Dozier, *For King, Constitution and Country*, pp. 114–17.

36. *PH*, xxx, text of the Auckland Memorial, col. 705; Auckland Correspondence, iii, Rose to Auckland, 26 April 1793, p. 38.

37. *PR*, xxxv, 25 April 1793, pp. 301–6.

38. FO 7/34, 8, Grenville to Morton Eden, 7 September 1793.

39. J. Holland Rose, 'The Duke of Richmond and the conduct of the war in 1793', *EHR* 25 (1910), pp. 554–5; Ehrman, *The Reluctant Transition*, pp. 266–70; *Dropmore*, ii, Pitt to Grenville, 30 March 1793, p. 388; U1590 S01/14, Richmond to Pitt, 3 and 5 April 1793.

40. WO 30/81, 'Minute of Conversation with Mr. Pitt, Wednesday 10–11 April 1793'.

41. Duffy, *Soldiers, Sugar and Seapower* (Oxford: 1986), Chapter 1.

42. Brewer, *The Sinews of Power*, pp. 167–8; Duffy, *Soldiers, Sugar and Seapower*, pp. 23–4; Mackesy suggested that the war strategy of the First Coalition had been inspired by Chatham's success during the Seven Years War: *War without Victory: The Downfall of Pitt* (Oxford: 1984), p. 226. A. D. Harvey claimed that the government's war policy was made up on the spot; there is a lot to be said for this: *Collision of Empires: Britain in Three World Wars 1793–1945* (1992), pp. 13–15.

43. Sherwig, *Guineas and Gunpowder*, table of subsidy payments, pp. 365–8.

44. Ehrman, *The Reluctant Transition*, pp. 266–8; *Dropmore*, ii, Pitt to Grenville, 1 April 1793, pp. 388–9; Auckland had also suggested that Dunkirk
be held hostage against Belgian indemnification for Holland: FO 37/48,
'Most Secret', Auckland to Grenville, 9 April 1793.

45. Auckland Correspondence, ii, Dundas to Murray, 16 April 1793, pp. 24–5.

46. Duffy, 'A particular service', p. 532; L. Colley, 'The apotheosis of George
III: loyalty, royalty and the British nation', *P&P* 102 (1984), pp. 94–129.
See also Colley's *Britons: Forging the Nation 1707–1837* (1992), chapter 5.

47. FO 65/23, 13, Grenville to Whitworth, 29 December 1792; WO 30/81,
10–11 April 1793.

48. *Dropmore*, ii, Pitt to Grenville, 30 March 1793, p. 388; A. Cobban, 'The
beginning of the Channel Islands correspondence', in *Aspects of the French
Revolution* (1971) pp. 225–38.

49. WO 30/81, 10–11 April 1793; FO 65/24, Grenville to Vorontsov, 15
March 1793; J. Holland Rose, 'The struggle against revolutionary France',
in Ward and Gooch (eds), *The Cambridge History of British Foreign Policy*,
i, p. 156.

50. Auckland Correspondence, iii, W. Eliot to Auckland, 9 May 1793, p. 57;
FO 65/24, 35, Whitworth to Grenville, 18 April 1793.

51. Auckland Correspondence, ii, Auckland to Grenville, 18 May 1793,
pp. 62–3; M. Hutt, *Chouannerie and Counter Revolution: Puisaye, the Princes
and the British Government* (2 vols, Cambridge: 1983), pp. 109–10.

52. H. Mitchell, *The Underground War against Revolutionary France: The
Missions of William Wickham, 1794–1797* (Manchester: 1965), pp. 11–12;
Hutt, *Chouannerie and Counter Revolution*, pp. 111–12.

53. FO 29/1, 3, Grenville to Murray, 18 May 1793; FO 37/48, 51, Grenville
to Auckland, 21 May 1793.

54. *PR*, xxxv, 17 June 1793, p. 676; for the entire speech, see pp. 672–9; Pitt
was reasoning on much the same lines in January 1794: see PRO 30/8/335,
War and Peace Notes, fos 310–13.

55. *PR*, xxxv, p. 672.

56. U1590 So1/14, Richmond to Pitt, 5 April 1793; John Rylands University
Library of Manchester, Melville Papers, Eng MS 907, Dundas to Pitt, 29
June 1793; BL Add MS 58906, Pitt to Grenville, [June 1793], fos 182–3;
Duffy, *Soldiers, Sugar and Seapower*, pp. 23–4.

57. BL MS Bathurst Loan, 57/107, Dundas to Richmond, 8 July 1793.

58. BL Add MS 58915, Dundas to Grenville, 4–25 July 1793, fos 101–5;
Duffy, *Soldiers, Sugar and Seapower*, pp. 28–9; M. Fry, *The Dundas Despotism*
(Edinburgh: 1992), p. 191.

59. *Dropmore*, ii, Pitt to Grenville, 16 August 1793, pp. 415–16, and Grenville
to Auckland, 21 August 1793, pp. 416–17.

60. FO 7/34, 18, Morton Eden to Grenville, 24 April 1793.

61. Lord Yarmouth, however, let this slip at the Prussian HQ: Lord, *The
Second Partition of Poland*, p. 444.

62. FO 72/26, 'Private', St Helens to Grenville, 29 May 1793; FO 29/2, 6,
Yarmouth to Grenville, 17 September 1793.

63. FO 7/34, 8, Grenville to Morton Eden, 7 September 1793; FO 65/25,

15, Grenville to Whitworth, 17 September 1793. Spanish views respecting the West Indies were also solicited.

64. PRO 30/8/102, Pitt to Murray, 19 July 1793, fo. 214; PRO 30/8/162, Murray to Pitt, 7 June, 23 July 1793, fo. 179, fos 202–3.

65. PRO 30/8/195, troop estimates in Pitt's hand, [28 August 1793], fo. 49.

66. Hutt, *Chouannerie and Counter Revolution*, pp. 105–7; Cobban, 'The beginning of the Channel Islands correspondence', pp. 44–5; National Library of Scotland, Minto Papers, NLS 11159, Journal of Sir Gilbert Elliot, 12 September 1793.

67. FO 7/34, 8, Grenville to Morton Eden, 7 September 1793.

68. Rose Diaries, i, Pitt to Rose, 23 September 1793, pp. 129–30; CUL 6958/7, 1320, Pitt to Westmorland, 15 September 1793.

69. *Dropmore*, ii, Pitt to Grenville, 7 September 1793, p. 422; FO 7/34, 11, Grenville to Morton Eden, 27 September 1793; M. Crook, *Toulon in War and Revolution: From the Ancien Régime to the Restoration, 1750–1820* (Manchester: 1991), pp. 139–41.

70. PRO 30/8/140, Grenville to Pitt, 4 October 1793, fos 45–8; Holland Rose, 'The struggle against Revolutionary France', pp. 122, 152–5; R. Griffiths, *Le Centre perdu: Malouet et les 'monarchiens' dans la Révolution Française* (Grenoble: 1988); pp. 166–72; Hutt, *Chouannerie and Counter Revolution*, pp. 111–13.

71. *Dropmore*, ii, Pitt to Grenville, [27] September 1793, pp. 438–9; BL Add MS 58906, Pitt to Grenville, [10] October 1793, fos 216–19; texts of proclamations of 29 September and 20 November 1793 are to be found in *PH*, xxx, cols 1057–61.

72. Duffy, 'A particular service', pp. 551–2; P. Kelly, 'Strategy and counter revolution: the journal of Sir Gilbert Elliot, 1–21 September 1793', *EHR* 107 (1982), pp. 333–5; L. Melville (ed.), *The Windham Papers* (2 vols, 1913), i, Pitt to Windham, 13 October 1793, p. 160.

73. National Maritime Museum, Elliot Papers, ELL 108, 'Toulon', [September 1793]; NLS 11160, Elliot Journal II, 12–21 September 1793; PRO 30/8/334, fos 183–202, Toulon commissioners' Instructions. For further discussion of the government's Toulon policy, see my forthcoming 'The British government and the Bourbon restoration: the occupation of Toulon 1793', *HJ* (1997).

74. PRO 30/8/140, Grenville to Pitt, 4 October 1793, fos 45–8; PRO 30/8/334, fos 200–2.

75. NLS 11159, 9 September 1793.

76. J. Holland Rose, *Pitt and Napoleon: Essays and Letters* (1912), Grenville to Pitt, 4 October 1793, pp. 257–8.

77. PRO 30/8/334, Toulon commissioners' Instructions, fos 201–2.

78. Ehrman, *The Reluctant Transition*, pp. 321–5; BL Add MS 58906, Pitt to Grenville, [10–15] November 1793, fos 196–7; PRO 30/8/102, Pitt to Elgin, 16 November 1793, fo. 119, and Pitt to Moira, 25 November 1793, fos 204–5; *LCG III*, ii, Dundas to George III, 19 November 1793, pp. 125–6.

79. Elliot Papers, ELL 108, Dundas to Elliot, 28 December 1793; PRO 30/8/103, George III to Pitt, 17 November 1793, fo. 508; PRO 30/8/195, Royalist Aid Memo, 5 December 1793, fos 26–8.

80. Ehrman, *The Reluctant Transition*, pp. 315–20; FO 72/29, 28, Grenville to St Helens, 22 October 1793.

81. *Windham Papers*, i, Windham to Pitt, 16 December 1793, p. 190.

82. Elliot Papers, ELL 108, Dundas to Elliot, 28 December 1793; *Dropmore*, ii, Grenville to Buckingham, 29 September 1793, p. 429.

83. FO 29/2, 15 and 18, Grenville to Yarmouth, 7 and 26 September 1793.

84. *Dropmore*, ii, Pitt to Grenville, 2 October 1793, pp. 433–5; BL Add MS 58906, Pitt to Grenville, 10 October 1793, fos 216–19; FO 29/3, 22 and 25, Grenville to Yarmouth, 19 and 30 October 1793.

85. FO 64/28, Grenville's memo of a conference with Jacobi, 7 and 8 November 1793.

86. Malmesbury Diaries, iii, Grenville to Malmesbury, 20 November 1793, pp. 2–4; *Court and Cabinets*, ii, Grenville to Buckingham, 21 November 1793, p. 247; *Windham Papers*, i, Spencer to Windham, 11 November 1793, p. 179.

87. FO 7/36, 2, Grenville to Morton Eden, 7 January 1794.

88. Duffy, 'The Austrian alliance', pp. 39–44; FO 7/36, 1, Grenville to Morton Eden, 3 January 1794; *Dropmore*, ii, Malmesbury to Pitt, 9 January 1794, p. 494.

89. *Dropmore*, ii, Pitt to Grenville, 1 February 1794, p. 502; FO 64/31, 4, Grenville to Malmesbury, 28 January 1794; FO 7/36, 5, Grenville to Morton Eden, 4 February 1794.

90. Duffy, 'The Austrian alliance', p. 81; PRO 30/8/338, copy of Yarmouth to Dundas, 23 December 1793; Ehrman, *The Reluctant Transition*, p. 341.

91. WO 1/168, Yarmouth to Dundas, 2 February 1794; U1590 S502/4, Cornwallis to Pitt, 25 February 1794; *Dropmore*, ii, Grenville to George III, 16 February 1794, pp. 505–6.

92. FO 7/36, 7, Grenville to Morton Eden, 18 February 1794; FO 64/32, 9, Grenville to Malmesbury, 7 March 1794.

93. Grenville's dispatch crossed paths with a Prussian offer of 60,000 men for £800,000 and subsistence: FO 64/32, 10, Grenville to Malmesbury, 14 March 1794; *ibid.*, 22, Malmesbury to Grenville, 13 March 1794; Malmesbury Diaries, iii, Malmesbury to Grenville, 13 March 1794, pp. 77–82.

94. FO 64/33, 15, Grenville to Malmesbury, 14 April 1794; FO 37/52, 18, Grenville to H. Elliot, 14 March 1794.

95. BL Add MS 59065, [January 1794], fo. 4; FO 7/36, Malmesbury to Grenville, 27 December 1793.

96. PRO 30/8/335, fos 427–28, 'Further grounds for the necessity of the War against France which have arisen since the commencement of the War', January 1794; PRO 30/8/310, fos 410–13.

97. *Windham Papers*, i, Spencer to Windham, 11 November 1793, pp. 176–80.

98. PRO 30/8/335, fo. 428.

99. FO 29/3, 20, Yarmouth to Grenville: 'None ever overturned all Municipal Laws at one, abolished Public Worship, or fixed arbitrarily the Prices on all Produce and every Article of General Consumption.'

100. U1590 S501/19, Balance of Trade Figures, 1793–5; PRO 30/8/112, Pitt to Lady Chatham, 31 August 1793, fos 458–9.

101. U1590 S501/14, Richmond to Pitt, 3 April 1793.

Chapter 6

From Probation to Persecution, January 1793– June 1794

Although the crisis of November 1792 had awakened Pitt to the seditious nature of British popular radicalism, it did not bring about any
long-term emotional or intellectual conversion from Whig complacency
to Tory alarmism. Eager as the British government had been to invoke
and exploit exhibitions of public loyalism, the anti-Jacobin backlash was
not sustained at official and popular levels following the outbreak of
war, nor was the ministry's domestic policy consistent with its diplomatic conduct or platform *vis-à-vis* the war with France.

The Foxite Whigs were quick to spot this discrepancy between words
and action. Fox and his friends were convinced by the end of 1793 that
the government was playing upon conservative fears of the revolution
to conceal its pursuit of an aggressive war policy in Europe and the
colonies. Foxite suspicion was understandable. The repudiation of subversionary warfare by France had been demanded by the British
government as a precondition of peace, but, according to the public
statements issued by the ministry, the First Republic was marked only
for defeat, not annihilation. This suggested that revolutionary France
posed no intellectual or social threat to Britain.

Such an interpretation would explain the Pitt ministry's inactivity
on the domestic front throughout 1793. The only 'anti-Jacobin' legislation to be enacted that year was the Alien Act and the Traitorous
Correspondence Act. Neither struck directly at popular radicals. The
ministry's legal campaign against sedition lost much of its momentum
in 1793 and little was heard of a French fifth column apart from the
odd scaremongering article in the government's London newspapers.
The bogey of insurrection seemed to have vanished. While Pitt
admitted that the enemy had attempted to infiltrate and buy off the
radical wing of the British reform movement, he ultimately concluded
that so desperate a policy was a product of French weakness, not
strength. The republic, thought Pitt, had resorted to unorthodox modes
of assault because its conventional weaponry was unreliable. The continental events of January–June 1793 only confirmed this analysis, and
he saw nothing to fear from an enemy whose very survival was in doubt.

These were the attitudes that governed the ministry's treatment of popular radicalism in 1793.

The Varieties of Loyalism

Determined as the Pitt ministry had been to distance itself from the British intellectual debate on the French Revolution, it decided in 1792 that indefinite neutrality was no longer a viable option. The government's decision to side with the opponents of the revolution, lukewarm though its patronage of the 'Tory' cause was to be, had very much been a conscious one. Pitt's conduct was important to the long-term development of conservative theory and practice, but neither the response of Britain nor of its government to the French Revolution can be described in simple bipolar terms. Acceptance, rejection, ambivalence and apathy were expressed by reference to traditional and contemporary modes of discourse which were modified slowly by exposure to the revolution during the 1790s. Continuity rather than change remains the dominant feature of British political thought over the period from 1780 to 1820. The allegiance of the literate British public on the eve of the French Revolution, as Pitt knew all too well, could not be commanded easily.

British 'patriotism' could be, and often was, critical of the establishment. 'The Constitution', noted Lord Sheffield, 'is become the word, and it is as much a favourite as "Liberty, Property and No Excise" or any other word ever was.'[1] The Foxite Whigs were to accuse Pitt of Toryism throughout the 1790s: by persecuting popular radicals directly and indirectly he was attacking the civil liberties of the subject and increasing the powers of the state. Pitt not only insisted that he was no Tory but that 'he held, not the principles of some persons who had lately called themselves Whigs, but the principles of liberty settled at the Glorious Revolution'.[2] Pitt was no admirer of the Whig doctrine put forth in Burke's 1791 *Appeal from the Old to the New Whigs*. Burke had asserted that the true principles of Whiggism lay in the active defence of the constitution, as established by the conservative revolution of 1688, against the awesome assault on order which the French Revolution represented. According to Fox, this was Toryism. Burke's preservative Whiggism involved the adoption of repressive measures against dissenters, democrats and other social undesirables. In the pursuit of such policies, cardinal Whig causes – resistance to prerogative, authority and influence – went overboard.

Common to all conservative readings of the revolution was the contention that it possessed an irresistible emotional and intellectual appeal which, if unchecked, would work sedulously on the hearts and minds of the self-interested masses to undermine their respect for authority of all descriptions. This was the conservative interpretation of natural rights. Radicals contended that the universal dynamo of reason, operating upon a perfectible mankind, would usher in a new age of liberty. Were one to repudiate the 'spirit of the revolution' and the 'due process' from which it was inseparable in the minds of both supporters and opponents, one gained immunity from the fears that it could produce. Pitt, who found 'nothing to agree with' in any of Burke's writings, had successfully done so. 'Sentiment', he told the House of Commons when speaking of Louis XVI's death, 'was unavailing; but reason and reflection might be attended with the most beneficial effects.'[3] Pitt was afraid of riot, but not of revolution.

Pitt had been reluctant to experiment with executive and legislative remedies for Britain's public order ailments late in 1792. Inflammatory and 'mischievous' though radical principles might be, he was convinced by the time that Parliament met on 13 December that the country stood firm in support of an idealized Whig state. Pitt's loyalism was no Tory concept, old or new. William Paley, like most conservatives, was proud of Britain's prosperity but did not defend it or the constitution in explicitly polite and commercial terms.[4] On 17 February 1792, in the famous finance speech that predicted fifteen years of peace for Britain, Pitt not only paid tribute to the dead Adam Smith, but gave Parliament his vision of Britain's future:

> From the intercourse of commerce, it [Britain] will in some measure participate in the growth of other nations, in all the possible varieties of their situations. The rude wants of countries emerging from barbarism and the artificial and increasing demands of luxury and refinement, will equally open up new sources of treasure, and new fields of exertion, in every state of society, and in the remotest quarters of the globe. It is this principle which, I believe, according to the uniform result of history and experience, maintains, on the whole, despite the vicissitudes of fortune and the disasters of empires, a continued course of successive improvement in the general order of the world.

This optimism was not characteristic of Scottish philosophers, who always feared that *fortuna*'s wheel might overturn their hard-won civilization.[5] Pitt, no admirer of Gibbon's *Decline and Fall*, did not share that pessimism. This was one of the few speeches that Pitt corrected for publication, which suggests that he wanted it to be remembered as a statement of principle. It incorporated a defence of the constitution, that 'union of law and liberty', a guarantor of civilization and a regulator of socio-economic relations which 'affords to property its just security, produces the exertion of genius and labour, the extent and solidity of credit, the circulation and increase of capital, which forms and upholds the national character'. This it did by appealing to reason and self-interest, for each acted as an empowering and educating force, directing a society's endeavours into productive channels. Virtue, therefore, could be inculcated through self-interest.[6] Pitt was convinced that universal satisfaction in 'the blessings of our happy constitution' would prevent French doctrines from taking root in Britain. Having issued official warnings about the seditious activities of the popular radical clubs in 1792, the government decided that no further action was necessary. This was a policy of deterrence rather than direct persecution. The Archbishop of Canterbury rejoiced in the 'increased loyalty and zeal which pervades this country to such a degree, that wherever there is of a different sort in the kingdom, is silent and concealed'.[7]

By 16 December 1792 the alien bill and the traitorous correspondence bill were all that was left of Pitt's public order legislative programme. The Alien Office, a government department still shrouded in mystery, was established to monitor the movements of aliens in Britain.[8] Its surveillance activities predated the passage of the Alien Act by some six months for the ministry had been keeping an eye on French refugees since the beginning of 1792 and, from June onwards, called upon the London police offices set up under the Middlesex Justices Act to do the lion's share of the work. The Alien Office, which, according to Elizabeth Sparrow, created 'almost a mirror image of the much despised French system of secret police', did little more than issue visas to foreigners, intercept their mail and keep a discreet eye on their movements during the early years of the war. In 1795 the Alien Office extended its operations to Europe and, from 1797, it assumed a leading role in domestic counter-intelligence.[9]

During the parliamentary debates on the alien and traitorous correspondence bills, Burke's doctrine of conservative Whiggism was again pitted against Fox's defence of civil liberties. The conservative Whigs, who had been shown drafts of both bills, agreed to vote with the ministry, but when the alien bill came up for its second reading in the Lords on 31 December 1792, the Duke of Portland 'said nothing and looked embarrassed'.[10] Pitt and Dundas, anxious to strengthen the front and back benches, redoubled their efforts to lure Opposition MPs into the ranks of the ministry. This had nothing to do with the splitting of the Whig Party and everything to do with the increasing likelihood of war with France. On 19 January, with war decided upon, Grenville was hoping that a 'pretty large proportion' of the 'ci-devant Opposition' would join the ministry.

Loughborough finally took the Great Seal on 19 January 1793. Portland, who did not trust Pitt, was lukewarm about the appointment.

Many of the duke's followers contemplated a complete and formal end to opposition but their emotional ties to Portland were strong and his disapproval stopped them from giving *carte blanche* to the ministry.[11] Pressure on Portland to abandon Fox intensified throughout this period – to no avail: 'He has conceived that his present difference with Fox could be treated as a difference on a particular point, and be reconciled with a continuation of party principle.'[12] Britain's declaration of war on France finalized a tripartite division between Foxites, the unhappy followers of Portland, and a pro-government group of MPs led by Windham: 'Opposition, as lately called, seems suspended in a comical state,' remarked Lord Sheffield.[13] Most members of the third party regretted their breach with Portland but, as self-appointed representatives of British anti-Jacobinism, sought to keep the good opinion of the country by criticizing the ministry's policies.

Pitt and Dundas, who accepted that the public saw the conservative Whigs as defenders of the old order, hoped to reconcile Windham and his associates to the discrepancies in principle between themselves and the ministry. On 5 February 1793 Pitt hinted that government office was available for Malmesbury, Windham and Elliot. The latter two refused, after severe struggles with conscience and ego. Malmesbury agreed to rejoin the diplomatic corps for personal financial reasons, but Elliot suspected that employment was a trade-off for political quiescence: 'a comfortable apathy has taken the place of his former animation'.[14]

By 20 January Pitt was using the third party as a sounding-board for draft legislation. The conservative Whigs, though flattered and pleased by this mark of favour, were also critical of the government.[15] Windham and Burke believed that the enemies of France were engaged in a struggle for the survival of the old European order. Neither man could understand why Pitt was unwilling to declare either against the republic or for the restoration of the Bourbon monarchy. The government's obsession with the West Indies was no less confusing and equally objectionable: 'It is the vice of this Administration to be conducting great affairs with an eye to small concerns.'[16] 'Loyalism' at the high political level did not entail unquestioning support for Pitt's policies.

The schism in the Whig Party came to a head during the Commons debates on the traitorous correspondence bill in March 1793.[17] This legislation barred Britons from buying land or stock in France, trading with the enemy, or sending voluntary gifts across the Channel in support of the revolution. Thomas Hardy had organized a shipment of shoes to the French armies the previous autumn, while Dr William Maxwell of Birmingham had sent 5,000 daggers to France, one of which was brandished by Burke during the Commons debates on the Alien Act.

'The great object of the bill', stated Pitt, 'was to prevent any persons resident in this country from sending any articles to France which may be useful to our enemies.' [18] The Act discouraged Britons from forming, maintaining or pursuing any connections with the enemy, a message reinforced by the introduction of the infamous passport regulations that required British nationals to obtain visas to visit France. The traitorous correspondence bill was also a weapon of economic warfare which, by stopping the flow of hard currency across the Channel in support of the *assignat* would, it was hoped, precipitate the fiduciary collapse of France. The Foxite Whigs objected to the bill's association of commerce with treason, whereupon the trade sanctions were explained by Pitt as 'a humane warning to persons, to put them on their guard against acts which might bring upon them the penalties of high treason'.[19] This was not the language, nor were these the measures, of coercion.

The Commons debates on traitorous correspondence highlighted some of the jurisprudential problems faced by a government trying to clarify the law of treason. The original Statute of Treasons, 25 Edward III, listed four principal treasons: plotting or 'compassing' the death of the monarch; levying war against the king in his realm; adhering to the king's enemies; and forgery of the royal currency. Trade, claimed Pitt, fell under the third of these headings.[20] This was the construction of treason that the British government chose to stress throughout the 1790s. The Foxite barrister Thomas Erskine nevertheless questioned the importance of intent and commission in determining the guilt of suspects.[21] Government and Opposition speakers spent the decade defending supposedly 'pure' readings of the Statute of Treasons. Such debates revealed that there were no acceptable constitutional solutions for the public order problems facing Britain during the French Revolutionary Wars.

Pitt and his colleagues were reluctant to persecute radicals not because they might rise in pursuit of French liberty, but rather because the government was uncertain about the legal forms that new legislation on sedition and treason could take. This was under discussion by Grenville and Solicitor-General Sir John Scott as early as 18 October 1792. Any radical pamphlet that urged the people to take up arms was certainly seditious and, thought Grenville, '*ought* to be treason if to stir up rebellion were treason'.[22] While 25 Edward III established that rebellion against the Crown was indeed treason, seditious libel could not be so defined under any 'respectable' legislation. For Pitt and others who professed to defend the principles of the Glorious Revolution, little comfort could be derived from the statutes of the Tudors and Stuarts, which laid down only that treason was a particularly heinous offence. Government apologies for the introduction of repressive legislation were invariably conducted in post-1688 terms. The visa introduced by the traitorous correspondence bill was described by Pitt as 'novel from its mildness; for in the act of King William, passed by the most declared and best known friends of the Constitution, it was made infinitely more penal in a natural-born subject of the King to return from France to England without leave'.[23] Habeas corpus, as Henry Dundas was to tell the Commons in May 1794, had been suspended no less than nine times since 1688 on pretexts far more specious than any put forward by the Pitt ministry. It is doubtful whether this version of the Glorious Revolution was of much use in a Parliament that had been brought up on myths of 1688.[24]

Pitt, who concluded that the legal hazards of experimentation with central authority were greater than the potential threat of rebellion, did not take direct action against the radicals in 1793. Moreover, it is unlikely that Parliament would have supported such a policy. Despite the government's success in drumming up votes for the war, few MPs were committed supporters of the ministry. 'Indemnification for the past and security for the future' was a vessel large enough to carry alarmists, loyalists, patriots, pragmatists and some moderate reformers in an independent House of Commons. The radical societies were safe, provided that they did not stretch the bounds of official tolerance. This they were to do in 1794.

The Constituents of Deterrence

For a government supposedly obsessed by the potential overthrow of the British *ancien régime* on the part of revolutionary conspirators, the Pitt ministry did little to reinforce its military presence at home for much of 1793. On 5 May Pitt drew up troop dispositions for the British Isles: 'The regular Force to be retained in Great Britain, Guernsey and Jersey is about 5000 Rank and File.' Of these troops, 1,200 were earmarked for the Channel Islands, 2,000 for Westminster, 600 for the Tower of London, 600 for Newcastle and 600 for Scotland; 5,400 were allocated to foreign service in the first instance, with an estimated 10,600 in all to be sent overseas.[25] Having resolved to commit itself to the war in Europe, the Pitt ministry was required to find troops for its burgeoning military commitments. It was in this context that proposals for a volunteer militia came under official scrutiny once more.

Schemes for a volunteer militia had been circulating among the friends of the government since November 1792. At that time the rationale for militia embodiment, be it regular or voluntary, was 'cases of actual riot', but by February 1793 the volunteers were regarded by central and provincial authorities as auxiliary troops.[26] Offers to form artillery and infantry companies came from southern maritime counties fearful of invasion. On 18 February Pitt responded with interest to a scheme of Sir Francis Baring's to create volunteer artillery corps on the south coast: 'There will probably be no difficulty in mounting the Batteries, provided a sufficient number of the Inhabitants are willing to be trained to the use of the Guns, & I imagine fire locks may also be supplied, if a Volunteer Corps can be formed to act in cases of necessity under officers commissioned by the King.' Upon consultation, Richmond stated that guns could be provided for such an undertaking, but that artillerymen to instruct the locals were in short supply.[27] The limited resources of the British state induced its leaders to look in the direction of 'volunteers' to provide the manpower for those efforts that were directed towards unobjectionable ends. The ministry, conscious that loyalism was a potentially double-edged sword, gave it a shove in the right direction and then withdrew.[28] Pitt, Grenville and Dundas, grateful for the support they had received from loyalists during the winter of 1792–3, realized nonetheless that patriotic fervour could be ugly. The government allowed its loyal associations to die away in 1793. As part of a public relations campaign, they had served their purpose.

Those local loyalists anxious to move against the authors and distributors of seditious tracts did not receive much help from official quarters in 1793. The ministry disengaged itself from direct involvement in prosecutions against seditious writings and words. The Treasury solicitors, often uncertain about how to conduct such cases, insisted upon the receipt of definitive evidence before allowing a trial to proceed. The government expected such public dramas to drive home the message that political activism on French lines would not be tolerated. In practice, English juries, reluctant to convict, were unwilling to admit to the existence of sedition in publications which were critical of the Pitt ministry. Defamers of the king and constitution were not always so fortunate.[29] A policy of active persecution was more assiduously pursued in Scotland, where Robert Dundas staged a series of show trials which culminated in the sentencing of Thomas Muir and Thomas Fysshe Palmer to seven and fourteen years' transportation respectively. When the Pitt ministry upheld the sentences on 25 January 1794, it was enshrining the punishment of sedition by 'Banishment' in Scottish common law.[30]

The Home Office did little more than monitor the activities of London radicals throughout 1793 though some attempts were made to intimidate landlords into refusing them access to taverns and assembly rooms. As the Solicitor-General put it: 'there is still great industry exerting, at least in this seat of sin, to do and create mischief'.[31] Government spies had first been infiltrated into popular political

societies during the autumn of 1792, a step that was defended thus by
Dundas:

> I most certainly thought it my duty, as Secretary of State, & entrusted
> by my office with the preservation of the internal quiet of the
> Country, to have a constant lookout after the proceedings of the
> Societies, which I believed to be meditating mischief and sedition,
> & that therefore I always had, and always would take care to have
> persons amongst them to watch their plans & give me immediate
> information of every design they had in hand.[32]

Special constables were recruited for London parishes and the Lord
Mayor was asked to monitor signs of sedition and treason in the city.
Informers were employed up to 1820 because magistrates, those work-
horses of local government, could not act as an efficient police
force.[33] Provincial radicalism was not such an official priority. The
Home Office, though bombarded for the first six months of 1793 with
reports of radicals, riots and refugees, took no extraordinary action.
'Nothing', as Grenville wrote on 13 April, 'can be more satisfactory
than the state of affairs at home.'[34]

Pitt saved his attack upon popular radicalism for the Commons
debate on Grey's 1793 reform motion, in which he explicitly set out
to separate the moderate reformers from their radical colleagues.
Britons were warned that radicals were exploiting their interest in
reform for subversive ends: 'the fraud was too gross and palpable, it
was obvious from what quarter they came'. The radical societies were
identified as engines of French subversion: 'The French had disclosed
a system of procuring proselytes in every part of Europe, – a system
which they had particularly followed up with respect to this country.'
Popular radical organizations, therefore, did not represent any interests
or opinions but those of the enemy. Pitt also attacked what he saw as
the intellectual inconsistency of the Friends of the People. So anxious
were the Friends for public support, claimed Pitt, that they were
prepared to compromise or abandon their principles: 'I have learned
from their publications, that they not only proposed to guide the minds
of the people, but also to be guided by them, and that they resolved
to drop their views if they did not meet with a pretty general concur-
rence.'[35]

This was a harsh judgement to have passed on the FOP. Grey, having
become alarmed by the contemporary association of parliamentary
reform with French republicanism, had told the LCS and SCI in April
1793 that they would have to tone down their demands if they wanted
to remain affiliated to the FOP.[36] Grey was criticized for having allowed
his reform campaign to become dominated by extremists. Pitt declared

that he would rather abandon reform altogether than be associated with popular radicals and their principles. He nevertheless vowed that reform remained a fit subject for future debate. The reform of Parliament had not been abandoned, but deferred. 'When', Pitt was to ask in the debates on Grey's 1797 reform motion, 'has such a wish for moderate reform been expressed?'[37]

Moderate reformers were saddened by what they saw as Pitt's betrayal. At the beginning of 1793 Wyvill, more in sorrow than in anger, made a last attempt to get Pitt's permission to print the 'Head or Heads of a Bill or Bills for Amending the Representation'. Wilberforce, who acted as an intermediary, returned Wyvill's letter of entreaty 'with no answer', at which point Wilberforce confessed that he avoided discussing reform with Pitt: 'This whole subject is one on which I neither could nor can talk with Mr. Pitt without pain and perhaps mutual recrimination, therefore I avoid it.' Wilberforce, who continued to support moderate reform during the 1790s, declared in March 1793 that he, 'unlike Mr. Pitt', believed that moderate reformers ought to be brought 'to act cordially for the constitution and against the republicans'.[38] Here lies the answer to Pitt's conduct in the reform debates of the 1790s. He did not turn away from reform in principle, but from old tactics and allies.

In answering Grey, Pitt had claimed that his opposition to reform stemmed from apprehension that radical reformers 'aspired at something more than a radical reform' – namely, 'the introduction of those French principles which from their consequences I could not but regard with horror'.[39] He did not, however, believe that the events of the revolution were a natural product of its original principles. The triumph of democratic republicanism had not been an inexorable or inevitable process. On 30 May 1794, following the passage of the habeas corpus suspension bill, Pitt told the Commons that the existing government of France did not represent the true spirit of the revolution: 'The French Revolution might not, in the first instance, be so great an evil as it has since evinced itself to be. It might not have such pernicious effects as have since exposed themselves to our view.'[40] Pitt had not lost sight of the enlightened ideals which he deemed to have guided France's first steps towards reform. His study of republican politics was to be driven by a search for consensus and toleration throughout the 1790s.

In May 1793 Pitt, primarily interested in discrediting British radicals, denounced the petitions that they submitted to Parliament in support of Grey's motion. Throughout the spring of 1793 reformers from Nottingham, Sheffield and Manchester were to have their petitions rejected on the grounds that they were disrespectful to the House of Commons. In 1782 a young Pitt had declared that, 'if petitioning could ever be unconstitutional, it would be when addressed to the King against a tax bill'. By 1790 he had long since concluded that the social and intellectual background of a petition's supporters was more important than the number of signatures it could command and, in June 1792, Pitt told Loughborough that the submission of petitions set a bad precedent for the introduction of reform legislation.[41] Pitt's repudiation of reformers outside Parliament was to haunt him at Horne Tooke's trial for high treason in November 1794. Had he, Tooke asked, been present at a Thatched House Tavern reform meeting in 1782? Had he attended a reform meeting that included county deputies? Did he not sign a petition demanding parliamentary reform? Pitt took refuge in a faulty memory.[42]

Pitt was not the only person to object to the tone of the extraparliamentary reform petitions. Henry Duncombe told the House of Commons that he liked neither the objectives nor the language of his constituents from Sheffield; his fellow member for Yorkshire, Wilberforce, seconded Pitt's motion that the House reject the petition.[43] The radicals, disillusioned by Parliament's reception of Grey's motion and their petitions, resorted thereafter to other methods of agitation for reform. Pitt had anticipated that the decisive defeat of Grey's motion would kill off the reform movement outside Parliament, as had been the case in 1785. As he wrote to George III the day before the debate: 'The disposition of the house ... [will be] such as naturally might be expected.'[44] He was gratified by the Commons response: 'Compared to last November', Pitt wrote to Auckland, 'these are indeed prosperous days.'[45]

The government's claim to act as a leader of public opinion depended on its real and perceived political strength at any given time. When York's siege of Dunkirk ended in failure at the end of August 1793, critics called for the resignations of Chatham and Richmond. Spencer, amongst other Portland Whigs, was afraid that the administration would fall if the offending ministers were not dismissed. 'The Check before Dunkirk is certainly much to be regretted,' wrote Pitt, who hoped that the surrender of Toulon would cover any negative impression created by the failure of the expedition.[46] Hood's 'victory' at Toulon not only saved the government's military reputation at home and abroad, but helped to resolve official uncertainty about the direction of the next continental campaign. Dunkirk and Toulon nevertheless focused public attention on the strategy and aims of the war, an interest which intensified as the tides of war turned against the allies over the autumn of 1793. This shift in opinion was noted with unease by a ministry whose military and diplomatic initiatives – the opening of a new royalist front in the south of France; the forging of military links with the Vendée; the resolution of differences with members of the

First Coalition, most notably Prussia – had ended in failure by the end of 1793. When Pitt met Parliament in January 1794, he was by no means sure of how much support he could command.

Revolutionary France in British Domestic Policy

Peace with Girondin France had been unlikely because 'indemnification for the past and security for the future' were not liable to be guaranteed by so unstable a regime. A settlement with the *gouvernement révolution-naire* seemed even less likely following its draconian extension of state powers to commandeer men and materials for the war effort. The shift towards ideological war which was heralded by the capture of Toulon received a like-minded response from France – a call in the National Convention for an amphibious assault upon England.[47] Although Pitt and his colleagues did not believe that the republic had the resources to launch such an expedition, they conceded that the venture might be attempted. As Dundas put it: 'Madness is not to be despised.'[48]

'The language of the Convention looks like some serious attack might be expected here', wrote Grenville to Buckingham, 'serious at least as they attend it, but ridiculous I trust it will prove.'[49] Without naval superiority a full-scale invasion was inconceivable, but 'Buccaneering expeditions I take to be practicable. They will be unpleasant in their effect here.' The Cabinet, privately disposed to downplay the French invasion threat, did not want to face accusations of inattention to England's defences. The government, already scrambling to redeploy its military forces in response to changes in strategy as a result of the occupation of Toulon, was required to find additional troops with which to reinforce Britain's coasts. The detention of the West Indian expedition, against which Dundas protested, with Pitt's support, was discussed throughout the month of October:

> ... it [the West Indian expedition] is worth a few days delay to ascertain what turn things take in Flanders, & whether the French Project of Invasion is anything more than words, if it is, I am still for sending to the West Indies, but some additional exertions will then be necessary to male the country take care of its internal Defence.[50]

On 13 October the Duke of Richmond submitted a report on England's defences to Dundas. The two time-honoured landing-sites for a French invasion lay in Kent and Sussex, 'particularly at Brighton where the shore is good for that Purpose & the distance to London about sixty miles by seven different Turnpike Roads'.[51] Richmond, who advised

Dundas to station heavy concentrations of regular soldiers in both counties, also pointed out that such troop movements were likely to upset the residents of the south-east: 'It is a political consideration for you to determine how far such preparations as we have recommended may cause an Alarm in the Country.' Alarm, as the events of November 1792 had shown, could both support and criticize the ministry. Dundas, who thought the French army contemptuous, decided nonetheless to respect British concern: 'however idle the menaces of the National Convention might be, it would not become the king's ministers to be inattentive to them'.[52] In an ideal world, alarmism and loyalism would have been passive and obedient forces.

'I wish your Frenchmen at the bottom of the sea', complained Buckingham after fresh recruiting orders had gone out to England's southern garrisons. By mid-November the West Indian expedition had not yet sailed – indeed, it was in no state to do so.[53] The Grey–Jervis expedition, stopping at Gibraltar on the way to the Caribbean, was to carry much-needed reinforcements for Toulon. Grenville declared that any further delay in sailing would 'give an impression of Alarm which would operate against us as much as the troops [if kept back] could for us'. Confidence in the government at home and abroad would suffer if Britain's leaders were seen to display any fear of the French. Neither Rose nor the king, who *were* afraid of the enemy, wanted to 'sacrifice the *existence* of the Country to appearances!'[54] On 17 November the Cabinet decided to let the West Indian expedition go ahead.

Overseas indemnification had won the day against domestic security. Unobtrusive preparations were nevertheless made for a revival of what the government saw as French-sponsored radical unrest. New constables were appointed to the London police offices and the Alien Office was asked to double its surveillance of suspicious *émigrés*.[55] 'If [French] attempts to make an impression in the country seem likely to be successful,' thought Pitt, 'we [Parliament] certainly must meet at all events.' He was afraid that the Foxite Whigs and popular radicals would coalesce to exploit anti-war sentiment in the country at large and call for peace. The ministry's supporters were also anxious: 'What do you hear of the public temper respecting the war?', enquired Lord Mornington of Addington; 'I meet with much discontent and disappointment.'[56] The British Convention of late 1793 took place in Edinburgh against this backdrop of increasing official tension. National security involved the adoption of defence measures against internal and external enemies.

Pitt's concern about the unsettled state of opinion at Westminster was reflected in repeated attempts to secure the allegiance of the conservative Whigs. In June 1793 three posts were offered to the third party: the Home Office to Windham, the Lord-Lieutenancy of Ireland to Spencer and the governorship of Madras to Elliot. All three refused, questioning Pitt's motives for so generous a series of offers. In truth, Ireland and India were difficult to fill at the best of times, while Dundas had been complaining about his workload since April 1793. In November Addington briefly considered taking the Home Office. The Cabinet was feeling the strains of the war. In February 1794 Grenville asked to resign from the Foreign Office.[57]

Hope of office was dangled before the conservative Whigs once more in August 1793. On 3 September Windham decided that Pitt was sincere in his desire to form a coalition, but neither Portland nor his friends could bring themselves to express unconditional support for the ministry's war policies.[58] The events of the autumn only increased the conservative Whigs' confusion. Of Dunkirk, Burke said that 'The bad military plan has arisen from the false political principles.' The government's Toulon proclamations were no less contentious: 'It cannot be that we have taken up the wicked and frantick project of what is called the [French] Constitution.'[59] Equally alarming were the indemnity clauses in the proclamation of 29 September. These, thought the conservative Whigs, neither enhanced the purity of the Bourbon cause nor encouraged French royalists to flock to Britain's standard.

Reservations about the intellectual tone of official British royalism did not entirely overwhelm the conservative Whig delight that the war had become more overtly 'ideological'. Elliot, after all, became the civilian commissioner of Toulon. The conservative Whigs were, however, hesitant about joining the ministry without formal recognition of their policy and patronage demands. The new recruits were fearful of losing their party identity and wanted some guarantee of parity in terms of Cabinet seats. While the conservative Whigs were flattered to be offered important posts, many of these were far removed from London and not completely to the liking of individuals who wanted to remain at the centre of the decision-making process.

Ministerial attempts to lure the Portland Whigs into office from February to September 1793 did not represent genuine coalition offers. In Fitzwilliam's sceptical words, the object of the government was 'no more than catching a straggling bird'.[60] After the failure of the autumn discussions, Pitt continued to whet the appetite of the conservative Whigs. Over the autumn and winter of 1793 his desire to pick off individuals turned into a policy of all-out recruitment. The loss of Toulon and the failure of the Noirmoutiers expedition had been serious setbacks for the government and Pitt, anxious about his reception from Parliament in January 1794, was eager to suspend party differences. As matters stood at the end of 1793 the Foxites could be relied upon to heap coals of fire upon the 1793 campaign. As for the 'third party', 'There was some danger ... that the middle party might take the line of supporting the war but impeaching its conduct.'[61]

When Parliament met on 21 January 1794, the Foxite Whigs led the anticipated attack on the government's foreign and domestic policies. Faced with this imminent barrage of abuse, the Portland Whigs closed ranks and, at a meeting at Burlington House on 20 January, agreed to give their united support to the ministry. Portland had finally made up his mind to 'a full, firm, unequivocal support both of the War and its conductors'.[62] The government breathed a sigh of relief. Although the Portland Whigs were now in receipt of much official information, they remained employed in a consultative, rather than a policy-making, capacity and were yet to be admitted to the government's full confidence on military and diplomatic matters. Despite this, the Portland Whigs promised to back the Prussian subsidy: 'They trusted to the prudence of Government,' stated Loughborough, 'to make as good and secure a bargain as could be got, thinking that the consideration of expense was not to weigh against the magnitude of the object.' The Foxites were disgusted by the conduct of their ex-colleagues: 'Our old friends are many of them worse Tories than those they have joined,' wrote Fox.[63]

By January 1794 the government was convinced that the French invasion threat was real. This partially explains the ministry's public commitment to the annihilation of *gouvernement révolutionnaire*. When Pitt attacked the abolition of private property in France, the 'extinction of religion' and the excesses of the Reign of Terror, which were 'connected with the evident design of assimilating other Govts. to that System', he was stating categorically that no peace could be signed until the invasion of England was abandoned: 'This leads to the necessity of some augmentation of force, and possibly some of last year's plans will be reverted to.'[64] Information respecting the invasion came from several sources: Admiralty reports of French naval activity in the Channel ports; Home Office correspondence which suggested that a British radical rising would coincide with the French attack; diplomatic accounts from the United Provinces, from whence it had been reported that 'a Number of Troops would be embarked to raise an invasion in England, not so much with a view to gaining a solid Footing in the Kingdom as to terrifying the Inhabitants and diverting the attention of the Government'.[65] This was not reassuring to a Cabinet that took alarmism more seriously than radicalism. Reports about the unsettled state of the country came from three sources: the south coast, where fear of the *émigrés* was combined with general apprehensions of an attack from France; urban magistrates in the Midlands and north-west, who noted an increase in activity on the part of the popular political societies; and London spies and police officials, who reported on radical plans for a renewal of the parliamentary reform offensive in 1794.[66] Faced with three demands for troops – for police, home defence and foreign service – the government reviewed the public order schemes which had first been mooted in November 1792. The two projects chosen for implementation in 1794 were the establishment of a volunteer corps and the suspension of habeas corpus.

Defence of the realm was the ministry's first priority. Richmond's estimates of October 1793 had placed 14,000 infantry and 2,800 cavalry in the south of England. This was now thought to be inadequate. In late January the government reviewed its volunteer proposals; by 8 February 1794 Pitt, Grenville and Richmond had drawn up new defence plans which incorporated provisions for the creation and deployment of a volunteer militia.[67] The three men could predict where enemy landings were likely to take place but they could not ascertain whether the French would focus target on small seaside towns, major harbour installations or a combination of these. Pitt and Richmond concluded that 'Invasion in many Places at once with small Force in each' was most likely. Such a strategy would lessen the probability of interception and repulsion by the Channel fleet. It then became necessary to determine 'the Points where serious attempts will be made'.[68] The danger zone was finally narrowed down to a stretch of coast between Brighton and Southampton but 'places for local [volunteer] companies' were identified all over maritime England. Details of manpower and supplies for the 'sudden Levies' were yet to be decided, 'All the Terms to be settled and Printed'.

The creation of a 'militia cavalry to be raised by Volunteers' had been the most popular of the government's defence proposals in January.[69] Cavalry, the most mobile and versatile part of the armed forces, would be especially effective against an enemy whose transport problems ensured that it would be 'totally improvided with cavalry'. A volunteer cavalry was, however, so prohibitively expensive that relatively small numbers were likely to be raised. At this point, infantry units were added to the government's manpower estimates. Ministerial calculations revealed that, if every county added two volunteer companies to its regular militia reserves, an extra 6,000 men would be added to the national guard.[70] The government did not intend to get all its troops on the cheap. Regular forces were moved into the danger zones and, by the beginning of March, projected troop concentrations in the south, East Anglia and the West Country were little short of phenomenal:

> Eastern District
> 9,800 troops and 1,486 cavalry
> Southern District
> 23,000 troops and 6,872 cavalry
> Western District
> 6,000 troops and 1,062 cavalry.[71]

In February 1794 only 20,000 additional British troops had been earmarked for service in Flanders. As a statement of priorities, the figures speak for themselves.[72] As had been the case in 1793, Pitt and Dundas had vastly overestimated the number of battle-ready troops that they could raise at short notice for overseas service. This made the establishment of volunteer units increasingly important for home defence.

The details of the volunteer corps bill were finalized in early March. The creation of infantry, cavalry and artillery units would be encouraged 'in order to provide more completely for the safety of the Country against any attempts which may be made on the part of the ene-my'.[73] Volunteers could be raised as additions to the regular militia or as independent bodies. Infantry and artillery corps were recommended for coastal areas and particular emphasis was laid on the formation of independent cavalry corps, which could be used not only to repel invaders, but, unlike the other two categories of volunteers, could be called out of their counties 'in case of actual appearance of Invasion'. They were also available for riot control should they be summoned by 'the Lord Lieutenant or Sheriff of the County or in the adjacent Coun-ties', in which case they would be treated as regular troops and subject to the provisions of the Mutiny Acts. 'The only chance our enemies could have in case of an invasion', said Pitt, 'was by a co-operation with some internal disturbance.' Volunteer corps were as important an institution in 'large manufacturing towns and the interior of the country, as on the sea coast'.[74]

Although the chief appeal for volunteers was made to 'Gentlemen of weight and property', if only because this was the one social group both willing and able to fund and equip bodies of men, the volunteer corps were not established as a special police force to persecute radicals. The government was almost certain that a French invasion was in contemplation. On 22 March Lord Moira wrote that he was expecting an assault on the Isle of Wight.[75] Even Fox admitted that 'the enemy had not only professed their intention to make a descent, but had made extensive preparations for that object'. This did not stop the Foxites from attacking the volunteer corps bill as an illegal imposition upon the persons and pockets of Britons; they also condemned the test of loyalty that was implicit in the government's call to arms. Although Pitt hotly denied that the volunteer proposals imposed any unnatural obligations upon the nation at large, 'volunteering' would soon become associated in the public eye with 'loyalism' as defined in support of the Pitt ministry.[76]

Radicalism Contained

The British government was not entirely surprised to find popular radicals preparing to agitate for parliamentary reform again in 1794. The events of late 1792 had, in official circles, established the identity of radicals as a French fifth column. The British Convention of 1793 was only the first of several assemblies at which delegates openly defied the government and announced that they would combat official repression with unspecified measures of their own. Gatherings in London and the provinces during the months of January and February 1794 were followed by an open-air forum at Chalk Farm on 14 April, organised by the LCS, at which 2,000 people assembled to petition for reform and a dissolution of Parliament. Government spies continued to be active in the metropolitan radical societies, with many rising to positions of responsibility and leadership in the LCS. Their reports, which in 1793 had involved accounts of innocuous radical proceedings, now depicted a underworld of revolutionary subversion rife with discontented artisans and violent hotheads. As many of the informers were ex-solicitors, it was assumed at the Home Office that they knew their business. Some were *agents provocateurs*. Others, carried away by a sense of self-importance, embellished their reports with lurid and unrepresentative details of popular radical militarism; a few sought to extort overdue pay from a parsimonious government by telling the Home Office what they thought it wanted to hear. Biased as these reports may have been, it is unlikely that they were entirely fictitious. With access to such sources, it is not surprising that the British government came to some false conclusions.[77]

The government was aware by January 1794 that a British Convention was due to meet sometime that spring. 'Violence', reported one spy from the LCS, 'will be used very soon.'[78] Accounts of radical arms caches, secret drills on Hampstead Heath and plans for the mobilization of LCS divisions only alarmed already worried minds. Deterrence was about to be exchanged for persecution. On 9 April the London police authorities were notified that action would be taken against the radical clubs. John Reeves, acting in his police capacity, announced that metropolitan magistrates and constables 'expressed the greatest confidence that their respective Parishes would co-operate by adopting such measures as shall be proper to be planned'.[79] The police surveillance of radical groups was stepped up throughout the metropolis in preparation for a series of arrests.

Officials and ministers were clearly concerned. Radical plans for a British Convention sounded ominous when French naval vessels were reportedly collecting in the Channel ports. The Cabinet remained confident in the strength of the Royal Navy and the nation's loyalty, but felt obliged to forestall what it saw as a French plot to paralyse the British government. Pitt's proposal in May 1794 to suspend habeas corpus reflected a lack of knowledge about the specific plans of the London radicals and he stressed that the Act was to be in force for six months.[80] By 4 April the Cabinet had concluded that the radical clubs, directed from Paris, intended to stage an armed rising in support of a French landing on the south coast. Both projects were doomed to failure, but they would have exposed the government to widespread public censure, a scenario that radicals and other enemies of the ministry would have been eager to exploit.[81] Severe embarrassment would have followed, if not actual expulsion from office.

The British government cast a wide net in search of culprits to bring to book. No action was taken against the radicals until May because the Home Office did not have any evidence that would stand up in a court of law. The Pitt ministry, finding it difficult to identify any French agents responsible for organizing a radical rebellion at home, asked the Dutch authorities on 4 May to arrest any French refugees suspected of exchanging treasonable correspondence with England or their mother country, 'with a view to their being produced in Court, if necessary', at the trials of British radicals.[82] The Foreign Office had learned from the Hague embassy that the French invasion was not intended to inaugurate a British republic, but to discredit the Pitt ministry. By January 1794 this objective had unwittingly been achieved by British radicals, the French army and the Dutch Patriot Party. The Greffier and Grand Pensionary of Holland, alarmed by the strength of the British reform movement, began to voice concern about the power and stability of the ministry. Ambassador Hugh Elliott reported home thus in frustration: 'I entered at some length with them on the subject of the Disposition of the English Nation, but I was sorry to observe that the pains taken [by the Patriots in Holland] to propagate notions of the dangerous situation of the People's Minds had made but too much impression.' Grenville, anxious to remain on good terms with the Dutch during a British bid for contributions to the Prussian subsidy, told faint-hearted Dutch officials to consult the records of parliamentary debates for statements of confidence in the government.[83] This was a virtual admission not only that the ministry could not speak for public opinion outside Parliament, but that the popular radicals were giving the British government a bad name abroad. The British queries about traitorous correspondence to the United Provinces can be seen not only as a search for evidence of importance to national security, but as part of an international campaign to improve the image of Britain and its government in Europe. Jacobin conspiracy theories served many uses during the 1790s. The Prince and Princess of Orange were anxious to see the passage of the Habeas Corpus Suspension Act.[84]

It was not until 6 May that the ministry felt that it had enough information to move against the London radicals. The Home Office demand for reports from spies was to be the making of William Wickham, later to act as the British link to the counter-revolution in the south of France. During the spring of 1794 Wickham, then a humble police magistrate in Whitechapel, had been offered the services of one Edward Gosling, a recent recruit to the London Corresponding Society. Having been asked by Wickham on 16 April to discover whether the radicals 'were serious in their conversation and really intended to procure arms', Gosling's reports were full of violent LCS schemes.[85] Wickham compiled a report from these findings entitled *Substance of Several Informations of the Views and Proceedings of the Different Republican Meetings Known by the Name of Corresponding Societies – Particularly Those on the Eastern End of the Town and in the City*.[86] This document was sent to Evan Nepean at the Home Office and was well received in high places:

> I have communicated to Mr. Pitt and Mr. Dundas your letter of the 8th and the paper which accompanied it, and they very much desired me to know that they very much approve of your conduct. If the same degree of enquiry had been made by the rest of your Colleagues, we should have been much better acquainted with what has passed in these seditious assemblies than we are now.
>
> It is wished very much to know what proofs you have to produce in case it should become necessary to establish the several proceedings ... and whether these people, if they can be brot. forward to give evidence, are still pursuing their enquiries? I find no difficulty in making them a reasonable compensation, and will arrange that compensation with you when you return.[87]

Once the government was sure of its witnesses, it could move against the radicals. Lord Malmesbury, who had returned to London to discuss the details of the Prussian subsidy, found ministers 'so fully employed in their discoveries and examinations of sedition and treason that I had very short and few conversations with them'.[88]

On 12 May the papers of the LCS and the SCI were seized and the leaders of both organizations were taken into custody. A committee of the Privy Council, with government and Portland Whig representation, was appointed to examine witnesses and documents. From 12 to 14 May the committee was closeted with its witnesses for six hours a day. 'You will see the general purport and object of the business in the King's Message printed in the papers,' wrote Auckland, where it was announced that His Majesty's Servants had discovered a diabolical plot to set up 'a pretended Convention' for the purpose of introducing 'anarchy and chaos into the Country'.[89] So confident was Auckland of a successful outcome to the Privy Council enquiry that he summarized its report in advance: 'We shall be able to show that the Societies in question were well advanced and ripening to the introduction of the French horrors.'

This was not a foregone conclusion on 12 May. When the papers of the LCS and SCI were seized, the Home Office expected to find evidence of arms procurement and traitorous correspondence with provincial radical organizations and French agents. The Privy Council scrutiny of LCS papers only revealed that the radicals planned to gather *en masse* should anything resembling 'a national crisis' arise. The government was still convinced that a French attack was involved and, on 23 May, Pitt was finalizing arrangements for the removal of the *émigrés* from Winchester to Reading, Farnham and Stockbridge because 'he had taken an interest in the welfare of these persons'.[90] Pitt had not given much thought to French refugees since late 1792. Over the month of May the government widened its net of arrests to the provinces in an attempt to get to the bottom of the conspiracy. The 'General Convention' referred to by the LCS was to have been called if the ministry introduced any measures 'inimicable to the liberties of the people'.[91]

Some of these had long been known to the ministry: the landing of foreign troops on British soil (by which the radicals meant Hessians and Hanoverians); the passage of an anti-convention bill; the suspension of habeas corpus; the proclaiming of martial law; or 'preventing the People from meeting in Societies for Constl. Information'.[92] By suspending habeas corpus the government displayed its contempt for the public agenda of the popular radicals. The secret interests of the radicals were more worrying. On 13 May, by which date the Privy Council had completed its preliminary enquiries, a Secret Committee of the House of Commons was appointed to go over the same ground. The Commons committee, packed with nominees of the government and the Portland Whigs, was 'pretty unanimously chosen' by the ministry's supporters, who had been briefed by the Treasury before the ballot.[93] The Secret Committee report, based on the Privy Council findings, was laid before the Commons on 16 May, on which occasion Pitt moved for a suspension of habeas corpus.

The first report, read by Pitt, stated that the London radicals had been plotting to 'supercede the House of Commons in its representative quality and to assume to itself all the functions and powers of a national legislature'. This assumption of authority by the British Convention was to have been effected, claimed the Committee, by force: 'proposals have been received ... and measures have recently been taken, for providing arms to be distributed among the members of the societies'.[94]

Although the Pitt ministry believed that the General Convention was a pretext for a radical display of violence, lack of evidence forced the government to represent it as an end rather than a means. The Secret Committee fell back on radical sympathy for the revolution: 'The [London Corresponding] society have continued on various occasions to manifest their attachment to the cause of the French Revolution and have effected to follow, in their proceedings and in their language, the forms and even the phrases which are adopted in that country.' The evil designs of the radical societies, claimed the commitee, were attributable to 'the modern doctrine of the Rights of Man'. The government's case against the reformers could, on the other hand, be traced to more conventional origins.

When Pitt called for the suspension of habeas corpus on 16 May, he intended to try the radicals for high treason. The charge could be substantiated on two grounds: adhering to the king's enemies, namely the French; or the more dubious charge of levying war within the realm, which was supposedly represented by the projected assembly of a General Convention. Had the government been able to prove the first charge, it would have had a relatively straightforward case. The second was more complex and its association with radicalism dated back to the Irish volunteer conventions of the early 1780s. While it would be unwise to draw too many parallels between the Irish volunteers of the 1780s and the British reform movement of the 1790s, from an official perspective there were certain similarities between the two. Both demanded root and branch constitutional change, voiced contempt for existing institutions of political authority, had appealed with some success to public opinion and displayed alarming militant tendencies. Pitt had described the Irish conventions of 1782 and 1783, organized to discuss reform, as 'wild and unconstitutional efforts that strike at the root of all authority'. Pitt's comments on the projected 1784 Dublin Convention could have been applied to the British Convention a decade later:

> ... when the express purpose for which they are called is avowed to be ... to supercede both the form and substance of legal government by erecting a new representative body under the appearance of regular authority, I have no doubt that such an attempt is highly unwarrantable. By the same reasoning, the Congress (if it ever meets) will come under the same observation, if it assumes to itself the authoritative functions of a legal representative, and may thus require the interposition of executive government.[95]

No radical convention of the 1790s set out to supercede Parliament in any capacity but the staging of such assemblies could be seen as a

challenge to regular authority, especially if the attendance of regional delegates, the passage of resolutions and a propaganda war of
'proclamations' and 'addresses' was waged.[96] The Irish conventions had
been seen as potential anti-parliaments from 1780 to 1785 because it
was feared in London and Dublin that the Irish people would support
the volunteers' assumption of legislative powers and responsibilities.
No mass rising was anticipated a decade later. 'Even supposing the
executive government to have been guilty of every neglect of duty',
said Pitt, the radical conspiracy would have failed; 'however persuaded
he may have been of this fact, it was still right to prevent, by timely
interference, the misery which a small struggle might necessarily produce'.[97]

Most Lords and Commoners, with the exception of the Foxite
Whigs, agreed with Pitt. George III approved wholeheartedly of the
ministry's actions. With the backing of the king and the Portland
Whigs, Pitt anticipated no problems with the passage of the habeas
corpus suspension bill. Dundas predicted that it would pass all its
readings in two days.[98] He and Pitt reckoned without the belligerence
of the Foxite Whigs, who divided the House on the bill sixteen times.
The Lords, moreover, appointed their own Committee of Secrecy on
19 May and the bill did not receive royal assent until 26 May. The
government was now free to investigate the radicals to its heart's
content. What it was to discover over the summer of 1794 was
frustrating and inconclusive.

Towards a Coalition Ministry

Over the first five months of 1794 Pitt had successfully remodelled the
public image of his administration. By 1 June the British government
had seemingly become a crusading zealot for the old order at home
and abroad. This image was reinforced by the formation of a coalition
ministry with the Portland Whigs. On 6 May Malmesbury had written
that 'there is a chance of their all coming in'. On 4 May Dundas had
asked Windham to see him about 'the progress made by the seditious
clubs and the necessity of taking some steps to counteract them', but,
when the two met, he asked Windham to talk to the Duke of Portland
about a prospective coalition. On 12 May the Portland Whigs were
asked on 12 May to serve on the Commons Secret Committee. When
Pitt proposed to suspend habeas corpus on 16 May, the Portland Whigs
'unanimously and cordially concurred'.[99] It was Windham who made
the case for the ministry's move from probation to persecution in the
Commons:

By proclamations, by calling out the militia and by encouraging voluntary associations, &c., the government might have rationally concluded that enough had been done to crush this dangerous spirit. These means undoubtedly had a considerable effect, and had retarded that maturity at which seditious projects were lately arriving; but finding, notwithstanding all these checks, they were still making head with redoubled diligence, it was proper to meet them with means fully adequate to their suppression.[100]

In January 1794 Portland had been wary of union with the ministry. He had warned Windham that the conservative Whigs would forfeit the goodwill of the public if they joined a government whose policy objectives appeared to be contradictory. By 24 May, when Pitt visited Portland to discuss the prospect of coalition, the duke's attitudes had changed. Pitt, asserted Portland, now 'considered the expulsion of the Soul and Spirit of Jacobinism as a point of Union for us all'. The premier's wish and object, as reported to Fitzwilliam, was that this guiding principle 'might make us act as one Great Family'.[101]

The timing of such a political marriage could not be more ideal – or so thought the Portland Whigs at a meeting at Burlington House on 25 May: 'the public attention more than ever has been pointed to it and fitted to receive it'. Until the suspension of habeas corpus, the conservative Whigs had thought that the Pitt ministry was holding back on the introduction of repressive legislation. Burke, when consulted on the introduction of the Traitorous Correspondence Act, had been, 'as usual, for the strongest measures'.[102] While it would appear from the Commons debates of May 1794 that little separated Pitt in intellectual terms from the Portland Whigs, the government's campaign against sedition and treason was not conservative *per se*.

The formation of the volunteer corps can be seen not as the forging of a sword in the cause of social order, but as an attempt to neutralize a potential source of hostility to the government. The volunteers have been seen as a British people's army, a conscious attempt to call a nation to arms in defiant opposition to the French *levée en masse*. Pitt, however, explicitly repudiated the concept of an armed nation on 3 February 1794: 'from the present horrid system of force and compulsion' that was employed in France to raise armies, said he, *gouvernement révolutionnaire* had created 'a larger mass of armed men than they could have had by any other means; and to this mass of numbers they owed everything like success which they had obtained'. Pitt 'uncommonly fine on armed nation', noted an approving Wilberforce.[103]

Anxious as the Cabinet had been in late 1792, and was again in 1794, to stop the spread of sedition in England and Scotland, the ministry accepted in both cases that it had as much to fear from loyalists as from radicals. The former were far more numerous and influential than the latter. Auckland paid tribute to this on 15 May 1794: 'The country is in a proportion of ten to one, sound and loyal.'[104] Had any subversive radical schemes come to fruition, it was the frightened alarmism of the loyalists that would have weakened the British government in 1792 or 1794. The creation of a volunteer corps channelled that energy into activities that would not, or so it was thought at the time, threaten the government and constitution of the country.

The revolutionary diplomacy of 1792 had introduced the world to a new concept of nationhood, of which the 'people's armies' and the 'republic of virtue' were isolated components. By January 1793 the emotional power of these concepts had been recognized by the Pitt ministry in both positive and negative terms. Fear could be recruited and invoked in conscious or unconscious ways to praise or condemn British policies at home or abroad. In the case of Anglo-Dutch relations, by April 1794 the emotional and intellectual side-effects of the revolution were clearly weakening the 1788 alliance. The Pitt ministry found in 1792 that its image as a conservative regime at home strengthened its authority abroad; Britain's likely participation in the war as an ideological enemy of France had brought Austria and Prussia in search of alliances on 12 January 1793. In 1794 this image worked, in the short term, to reinforce the Anglo-Dutch alliance.

It was said by the Opposition Whigs on 30 June 1794 that Pitt was scaremongering to rouse support for his military policies, that he was deluding the public in the cause of an ostensibly ideological war. Although the British government was undeniably involved in opinion and self-image manipulation, all the supporting documentation, both official and private, confirmed that Pitt believed in the possibility of a radical rising led by a British Convention in concert with the enemy. The French North Atlantic fleet, decisively defeated by Lord Admiral Howe in the series of engagements known as 'The Glorious First of June', was a very real presence at Brest.[105] The London radicals, undaunted by Parliament's rejection of their reform petitions the previous year, were not only preparing for another attempt at reform, but were making preparations for organized action were habeas corpus to be suspended or foreign troops to land in Britain.[106] From an official perspective, such resolutions were, to say the least, suspicious. The government, believing that its tolerance in 1793 had been abused, was determined to make a stand by the spring of 1794, to state categorically that overt sympathy for the enemy was inadmissible in wartime.

Notes

1. Auckland Correspondence, iii, Sheffield to Auckland, 3 January 1793, pp. 480–1; H. Cunningham, 'The language of patriotism, 1750–1914',

History Workshop Journal 12 (1981), pp. 12–14; J. Dinwiddy, 'England', in Dinwiddy and O. Dann (eds), *Nationalism in the Age of the French Revolution* (1988), pp. 54–8;. J. Money, 'Freemasonry and the fabric of loyalism in Hanoverian England', in A. Birke and E. Hellmuth (eds), *The Transformation of Political Culture: England and Germany in the Eighteenth Century* (Oxford: 1990), pp. 243–7.

2. *PR*, xxxvi, 21 March 1793, p. 118.

3. Auckland Correspondence. iii, Pitt to Auckland, 8 November 1795, p. 320; *PR*, xxxiv, 1 February 1793, p. 386.

4. G. Claeys, 'The French Revolution debate and British political thought', *History of Political Thought* 11 (1990), pp. 59–62.

5. *PH*, xxix, 17 February 1792, cols 833–4.

6. Paley had said this of democracy in particular though he was no friend to 'unmixed governments': *The Principles of Moral and Political Philosophy* (2 vols, 10th edn, 1794), ii, Book VI, ch. vii; N. Phillipson, 'Adam Smith as civic moralist', in I. Hont and M. Ignatieff (eds), *Wealth and Virtue* (Cambridge: 1983), p. 181; J. Robertson, 'The Scottish Enlightenment at the limits of the civic tradition', *ibid.*, pp. 158–9, and 'The Scottish Enlightenment beyond the civic tradition: government and economic development in the *Wealth of Nations*', *History of Political Thought* 4 (1983), pp. 451–82.

7. Clements MS, Pitt to Dundas, 15 and 17 December 1792; Auckland Correspondence, ii, Moore to Auckland, 3 January 1793, p. 478.

8. R. Wells, *Insurrection: The British Experience, 1795–1803* (Gloucester: 1983), pp. 28–43; E. Sparrow, 'The Alien Office, 1792–1802', *HJ* 33 (1990), pp. 361–3.

9. Most of the surviving Alien Office documentation is concerned with the registration of foreigners: HO 1/1–HO 1/5; Alien Registers to be found in HO 5. J. Dinwiddy, 'The use of the Crown's powers of deportation under the Aliens Act, 1793–1826', *BIHR* 104 (1968), pp. 193–207; J. Ann Hone, *For the Cause of Truth: Radicalism in London 1796–1821* (Oxford: 1982), pp. 79–82; E. Sparrow, 'The Swiss and Swabian Agencies, 1795–1800', *HJ* 35 (1992), pp. 861–84.

10. Burke Correspondence, vii, Pitt to Burke, 22 December 1792, p. 324; *Dropmore*, ii, Pitt to Grenville, 31 December 1792, pp. 360–1.

11. Malmesbury Diaries, ii, 10 January 1793, p. 498; *Court and Cabinets*, ii, Grenville and Buckingham, 19 January 1793, pp. 236–7; L. Melville (ed.), *The Windham Papers* (2 vols, 1913), i, Tom Grenville to Windham, 10 February 1793, p. 111; *Life and Letters*, ii, Elliot to Malmesbury, 27 January 1793, pp. 108–9.

12. *Windham Papers*, i, Windham to J. C. Hippisley, 28 March 1793, p. 116.

13. Auckland Correspondence, iii, Sheffield to Auckland, 18 May 1793, p. 495.

14. *Life and Letters*, ii, Elliot to Malmesbury, 27 January 1793, pp. 118–19; Elliot to Lady Elliot, 5 and 16 February 1793, pp. 112, 115.

15. Malmesbury Diaries, iii, 20 January 1793, pp. 501–2; Burke Correspondence, vii, Pitt to Burke, 10 February 1793, p. 348.

16. *Ibid.*, Windham to Burke, 14 November 1793, p. 487.

17. F. O'Gorman, *The Whig Party and the French Revolution* (1967), p. 137.

18. Burke Correspondence, vii, Dundas to Burke, 27 December 1792, p. 328; *PR*, xxxv, 9 April 1793, pp. 185–6.

19. *PR*, xxxv, 21 March 1793, p. 111.

20. W. S. Holdsworth, *A History of English Law* (16 vols, 1966 edn), viii, pp. 307–18, 337–46; S. Pollock and F. W. Maitland, *A History of English Law* (2 vols, 1989 repr.), ii, p. 502; *PR*, xxxv, 8 April 1793, p. 183.

21. *PH*, xxx, 8 April 1793, col. 589.

22. BL Add MS 58906, Grenville to Pitt, 18 October 1792, fos 142–3. Pitt was at Walmer from 15 to 25 October 1792 and intermittently in London until 8 November.

23. H. Twiss, *The Life of Lord Chancellor Eldon* (1844), pp. 153–4; *PR*, xxxv, 21 March 1793, p. 112; P. Hamburger, 'The development of the law of seditious libel and the control of the press', *Stanford Law Review* 37 (1985), pp. 714–51, deals with early eighteenth-century libel cases.

24. *PR*, xxxviii, 17 May 1794, p. 295.

25. HO 42/25, Troop Dispositions, 5 June 1793, fos 506–7.

26. Scottish Records Office, Melville Castle Muniments, SRO GD 51/16/99; June 1793 estimates allocated 5,400 troops to foreign service, pending the raising of reinforcements, while 5,200 were reserved for home defence: HO 42/25, 5 June 1793, fos 506–7.

27. PRO 30/58/1, Pitt to Baring, 18 February 1793, fo. 62, and Richmond to Pitt, 18 February 1793, fo. 63.

28. CUL 6958/7, 1191, Reeves to Pitt, 8 January 1793; Dozier, *For King, Constitution and Country* (Lexington, Ky.: 1983), pp. 83–92.

29. C. Emsley, 'An aspect of Pitt's "Terror"', *Social History* 6 (1981), pp. 155–75; Lobban, 'From seditious libel to unlawful assembly', pp. 321–4.

30. HO 102/7, Dundas to R. Dundas, 4 January 1793, fo. 110. Muir and Palmer, prominent in the Edinburgh Convention of 1792, were sentenced on 31 August and 13 September 1793 respectively: PRO 30/8/198, 9 November 1792, fo. 110; F. K. Prochaska, 'English state trials in the 1790s', *JBS* 13 (1978), pp. 63–82.

31. Twiss, *Life of Lord Chancellor Eldon*, J. Scott to H. Scott, 11 January 1793, p. 217.

32. HO 42/21, Dundas to J. Noble (Mayor of Bristol), 12 September 1792, fos 508–11; West Yorkshire Record Office, Canning MS, 29 dii, Diary, 27–8 November 1794; Dozier, *For King, Constitution and Country*, pp. 35–7.

33. C. Emsley, 'The Home Office and its official sources of information and investigation 1791–1801', *EHR* 93 (1979), pp. 532–61; D. Eastwood, 'Amplifying the province of the legislature: the flow of information and the English state in the early nineteenth century', *Historical Research* 62 (1989), pp. 278–80; M. Thale, 'London Debating Societies of the 1790s', *HJ* 33 (1990), pp. 63–5.

34. HO 42/24, Dundas to Lord Mayor, 25 January 1793, fos 244–5; *Dropmore*, ii, Grenville to St Helens, 13 April 1793, p. 392.

35. *PR*, xxxvi, 7 May 1793, pp. 478–81.

36. Lt General Grey, *Some Account of the Life and Opinions of Charles, 2nd Earl Grey* (1861), p. 19.

37. *PH*, xxxiii, 26 May 1797, cols 673–4.

38. Wyvill Papers, iv, Wilberforce to Wyvill, pp. 41–4; York City Library, Wyvill MS, 7.2.82.10, Wilberforce to Wyvill, 30 July 1793; *Life of Wilberforce*, ii, Wilberforce to William Hey, [March 1793], pp. 8–9.

39. *PR*, xxxvi, 7 May 1793, p. 481.

40. *Ibid.*, xxxviii, 30 May 1794, p. 370.

41. Clements MS, Pitt to Sydney, [1782]; *Malmesbury Diaries*, ii, 17 June 1792, pp. 463–4.

42. T. B. and T. J. Howell (eds), *English State Trials*, xxv (1818), pp. 385–94.

43. *PH*, xxx, 21 February 1793, cols 460–1; 2 May 1793, cols 776–7.

44. *LCG III*, ii, Pitt to George III, 7 May 1793, p. 36; J. Dinwiddy, 'Conceptions of revolution in the English radicalism of the 1790s', in Birke and Hellmuth (eds), *The Transformation of Political Culture*, pp. 543–4.

45. Auckland Correspondence, iii, Pitt to Auckland, 15 May 1793, p. 62.

46. *Windham Papers*, i, Spencer to Windham, 18 September 1792, p. 154; Pitt to Windham, 13 October 1793, p. 160.

47. M. Elliot, *Partners in Revolution* (New Haven, Conn.: 1982), p. 35.

48. Dozier, *For King, Constitution and Country*, pp. 127–9; BL Add MS 58915, Dundas to Grenville, 7 October 1793, fo. 137.

49. *Court and Cabinets*, ii, Grenville to Buckingham, 11 October 1793, p. 245.

50. BL Add MS 58906, Pitt to Grenville, 11 October 1793, fo. 220.

51. HO 42/26, Richmond to Dundas, 13 October 1793, fos 723–5.

52. *Ibid.*, Dundas to Amherst, 14 October 1793, fos 750–1.

53. BL Add MS 58877, Buckingham to Grenville, 18 October 1793, fo. 32. Buckingham felt that too much attention was being paid to 'a silly Gasconade': Duffy, *Soldiers, Sugar and Seapower* (Oxford: 1986), pp. 45–52.

54. Auckland Correspondence, iii, Grenville to Auckland, 11 November 1793, and Rose to Auckland, [16] November 1793, pp. 139–41; *LCG III*, ii, George III to Dundas, 16 November 1793, p. 123; PRO 30/8/103, George III to Pitt, 17 November 1793, fos 508–10; Duffy, *Soldiers, Sugar and Seapower*, p. 54.

55. HO 42/27, Report on Sedition, [December 1794], fos 836–77.

56. DRO 152M 1793/OZ20, Mornington to Addington, 8 November 1793; DRO 152M 1793/OZ7, Pitt to Addington, 9 October 1793; U1590 S5/C/34, Tomline to Pitt, 10 October 1793.

57. Addington Life, i, Pitt to Addington, 14 November 1793, p. 108; PRO 30/58/1, Grenville to Pitt, 26 February 1794, fo. 91.

58. *Windham Papers*, i, Windham to Portland, 3 September 1793, pp. 147–9.

59. Burke Correspondence, vii, Burke to Windham, 24 October 1793, p. 460; Burke to Elliot, 22 September, 1793, p. 434.

60. WWM F31(a) 8, Fitzwilliam to Portland, September 1793.

61. Canning MS, 29 dii, Letter Journal, 25 January 1794, fo. 28.

62. Burke Correspondence, vii, Windham to Burke, 18 January 1794, p. 525; PRO 30/8/117, Burke to Pitt, 21 January 1794, fo. 80.

63. PRO 30/8/153, Loughborough to Pitt, March 1794, fos 81–2; Fox Mem., ii, Fox to Holland, 18 March 1794, p. 70; HO 42/28, R. H. Gibson to G. Aust, 27 January 1794, fo. 133.

64. PRO 30/8/335, [January 1794], fos 427–8; *Courts and Cabinets*, ii, Grenville to Buckingham, 30 January 1794, pp. 253–4.

65. The Admiralty, in fact, could find little evidence of intensive French preparation for a cross-Channel assault, but the French North Atlantic fleet at Brest was an ever present worry: J. Ehrman, *The Reluctant Transition* (1983), pp. 328–9; HO 42/28, Moira to Nepean, 22 March 1793, fo. 163; FO 37/50, 34, W. Elliot to Grenville, 27 November 1793.

66. HO 42/27 and HO 42/28.

67. BL Add MS 58065, Pitt–Grenville memo, January 1794, fo. 4; WO 1/60, Richmond to Dundas, 21, 24 and 25 January 1794; WO 30/81, 7, T. Hartrup to Richmond, 21 January 1794; J. E. Cookson, 'The English volunteer movement of the French wars 1793–1815: some contexts', *HJ* 32 (1989), p. 877.

68. PRO 30/8/245, Richmond to Pitt, Plan for Internal Defence, [8 February 1794], fo. 90; PRO 30/8/197, Pitt's notes on invasion, 10 February 1794, fos 130–2.

69. *Courts and Cabinets*, ii, Grenville to Buckingham, [1] February 1794, p. 255; PRO 30/8/242, Grenville's 'Plan for County Cavalry', fos 187–94, and Pitt's 'Cavalry Plan', fos 179–80.

70. HO 42/28, Buckingham to Grenville, 2 February 1794, fos 193–4, and Amherst to Dundas, 13 February 1794, fos 269–73; PRO 30/8/245, Richmond to Pitt, Plan for Internal Defence, [8 February 1794], fo. 90.

71. PRO 30/8/241, L. Morse to Rose, 10 March 1794, fo. 222.

72. PRO 30/8/242, Pitt's 'Memr. for Campaign', February [1794]. Some of these troops were awaiting transport to the Continent, but their concentration was nevertheless remarkable.

73. *PR*, xxxvii, 26 March 1794, Volunteer Corps Proposals, pp. 674–5.

74. PRO 30/8/244, Amherst to Pitt, 'Other bodies of Cavalry, Paper 4', 6 March 1794, fo. 184; *PR*, xxxvii, 3 February 1794, pp. 276–7; xxxviii, 1 April 1794, pp. 12–15.

75. HO 42/29, Moira to Nepean, 22 March 1794, fo. 163.

76. As claimed by Dozier, *For King, Constitution and Country*, pp. 140–5; J. R. Western, 'The volunteer movement as an anti-revolutionary force 1793–1801', *EHR* 71 (1956), pp. 603–13; R. Wells, *Wretched Faces: Famine in Wartime Britain 1763–1803* (Gloucester: 1988), p. 134; *PR*, xxxviii, 7 April 1794, Fox: pp. 36–42; Pitt: pp. 47–8; A. Gee, 'The British volunteer movement, 1793–1801', D.Phil. thesis (Oxford: 1990), p. 43; L. Colley, 'The reach of the state, the appeal of the nation: mass arming and political culture in the Napoleonic Wars', in L. Stone (ed.), *An Imperial State at War* (1994), pp. 165–84.

77. Emsley, 'The Home Office and its official sources of information and investigation', pp. 542–7; Hone, *For the Cause of Truth*, p. 59.

78. M. Thale (ed.), *Selections from the Papers of the London Corresponding Society* (Cambridge: 1983), 116, Lynam Report, 23 January 1794, p. 109.

79. SRO GD 51/1/242/1, Reeves to Dundas, 10 April 1794.

80. *PR*, xxxviii, 17 May 1794, pp. 318–24.

81. The Crown, in opening the case against Thomas Walker and friends, leaders of the Manchester Constitutional Society, at Lancaster County Court on 4 April 1794, read an indictment that accused the MCS of

conspiring to 'overthrow the government of this country' and 'aid and assist the French': *State Trials*, xxiii, 601, cols 1055–78.

82. FO 37/53, 1, Grenville to St Helens, 4 May 1794.

83. FO 37/51, 10, Hugh Elliot to Grenville, 28 January 1794, and 6, Grenville to Elliot, 31 January 1794.

84. FO 37/53, 9, St Helens to Grenville, 20 May 1794.

85. LCS Papers, p. 140, n. 115; cf. Gosling's 'Informations' to the accounts of LCS meetings submitted by other spies: LCS Papers, Part IV, 1794A.

86. TS 11/965/3510A: Wickham's paper was dated 6 May 1794; Sparrow, 'The Alien Office', pp. 364–7.

87. Hampshire Record Office, Wickham Papers, 38M 49D/6/6/1, Nepean to Wickham, 10 May 1794.

88. Malmesbury Diaries, iii, 6 May 1794, p. 96.

89. Auckland Correspondence, iii, Auckland to Henry Spencer, 13 May 1794, p. 212; *PR*, xxxviii, 12 May 1794, King's Message on Seditious Practices, p. 237.

90. HO 42/30, Col. de Lancey to Nepean, 23 May 1794, fos 239–40. Burke and Buckingham protested against the removal of the *émigrés* from Winchester: CUL 6958/8, 1440, Buckingham to Pitt, 26 May 1794.

91. LCS Papers, 113, LCS General Meeting, 20 January 1794, and 114, Address to the People of Great Britain and Ireland, p. 106.

92. *Ibid.*, 112, Report from George Lynam, LCS General Committee, 9 January 1794, p. 105.

93. Canning MS, 29 dii, Diary, 14 May 1794, fo. 78; BL Add MS 37844, Pitt to Windham, [5] May 1794, fo. 22. The Secret Committee members were Pitt, Windham, Dundas, Sir John Scott, Sir Archibald Macdonald, Welbore Ellis, Robert Dundas, the Earl of Mornington, Tom Grenville, Tom Steele, Pepper Arden, Robert Jenkinson, Henry Houghton, the Earl of Upper Ossory, Thomas Powys, [Lord] Mulgrave, Hawkins Browne, Anstruther, Thomas Stanley, Charles Townshend and Burke.

94. BL MS G15, Portland to Spencer, 17 May 1794; *PR*, xxxvii, 16 May 1794, pp. 246–53; *PH*, xxxi, First Report of the Committee of Secrecy, 16 May 1794, cols 477–8.

95. E. Ashbourne (ed.), *Pitt, Some Chapters of his Life and Times* (1898), Pitt to Thomas Orde, 25 September 1784, pp. 92–4.

96. T. M. Parsinnen, 'Association, convention and anti-Parliament in British radical politics, 1771–1848', *EHR* 88 (1973), pp. 504–33; Dinwiddy, 'Conceptions of revolution', pp. 544–5.

97. *PR*, xxxviii, 16 May 1794, p. 252.

98. *LCG III*, ii, Dundas to George III, Pitt to George III and George III to Pitt, 15, 17 and 18 May 1794, pp. 206–8.

99. *Malmesbury Diaries*, iii, 6 May 1794, p. 96; BL Add MS 37844, Pitt to Windham, [5 May] and 12 May 1794, fos 22, 26; Mrs Baring (ed.), *The Windham Diary* (1866), 1 May 1794 [composite entry for 1–17 May], p. 308; BL MS G15, Portland to Spencer, 17 May 1794.

100. *PR*, xxxviii, 17 May 1794, p. 305.

101. *Windham Papers*, i, Portland to Windham, 11 January 1794, pp. 199–208; BL Add MS 37844, Pitt to Windham, 12 May 1794, fo. 26; WWM

F31(6)13, Portland to Fitzwilliam, 25 May 1794; BL MS G15, Portland to Spencer, 25 May 1794.

102. BL MS G15, T. Grenville to Spencer, 26 May 1794; *Life and Letters*, ii, Elliot to Lady Elliot, [20] March 1793, pp. 127–8.

103. *PR*, xxxvii, 3 February 1794, pp. 276–7; *Life of Wilberforce*, ii, Diary, 3 February 1794, p. 43; D. Eastwood, 'Patriotism and the English state in the 1790s', in M. Philp (ed.), *The French Revolution and British Popular Politics* (Cambridge: 1991), pp. 158–60.

104. Auckland Correspondence, iii, Auckland to H. Spencer, 30 May 1794, p. 213.

105. Dozier, *For King, Constitution and Country*, p. 163.

106. LCS Papers, 156, Chalk Farm Resolutions, 14 April 1794, Res. vii, p. 133.

Chapter 7

The Winds of Misfortune, May 1794–December 1795

Pitt's poor opinion of the French army, first formed in 1792, had been confirmed by the events of the allied campaign in Europe in 1793. By the time he met Parliament on 21 January 1794, his attitudes towards revolutionary France as a military power had not changed despite the introduction of *gouvernement révolutionnaire*. The French successes of 1793 – the retaking of Toulon and the expulsion of the Austrian army from Alsace – Pitt saw as products of allied disunity rather than enemy strength. He had long since come to similar conclusions about the 1792 campaign.

The First Coalition was no more than a loose network of treaties joining several states against a common enemy. Bearing in mind the divisions amongst the coalition's would-be members throughout the first half of 1793, most notably over indemnification, it is unlikely that Pitt and Grenville wanted anything more binding. By August 1793, when the British government had emerged as the chief arbitrator in the quarrels between its allies, particularly Austria, Prussia and the United Provinces, its leaders thought that they could exercise some degree of leadership over the coalition. In this they were to be mistaken.

During the autumn and winter of 1793–4 the Pitt ministry moved to restore cohesion to the fast-disintegrating First Coalition, a process to which the British government contributed by casting its eyes to wider horizons. In February 1793 Pitt had primarily been interested in repulsing the French threat to the United Provinces and perhaps in making some West Indian colonial gains. By June he wanted to redraw the map of Europe. By November he was intent not only on using French mainland possessions as bargaining counters at the peace table, but on helping to shape the post-war political settlement of France. All these objectives exceeded the remit of the First Coalition as stipulated by treaty.

As Frederick William II was the first to point out upon removing his armies to Poland, by October 1793 all the military goals for which the coalition had gone to war had been reached.[1] The Low Countries had been liberated. The French had been driven back to their 1789 borders. The Prussians could go home. The only remaining war aim facing Britain and its allies at the end of 1793 was the French government's renunciation of 'revolutionary diplomacy'. The British government seized upon this to justify its continued involvement in the war. The ministry did not have much choice in the matter because Britain, the least objectionable of the republic's opponents in the eyes of the *conventionnels* for much of 1793, had become France's chief enemy after the surrender of Toulon. The British government was, in reponse, to advocate a war of principle at home and abroad throughout 1794. In so doing, a spurious conservative unity was imparted to Britain's foreign and domestic policies. This strategy was born, however, not of intellectual conviction, but of a misplaced confidence in total victory.

Total War

At the beginning of 1794 the government announced that it was now determined to pursue total war against revolutionary France. Despite the reverses of December 1793, which had put an end to Pitt's plans for the launch of amphibious assaults against the French coast, the ministry remained committed to the war plans that Murray had drawn up in August 1793. After securing the last of the border fortresses in Flanders, the allied armies were destined for Paris. The ministry began to prepare its supporters for victory in cautious stages. The first of these was represented by the debates on the address of thanks. From the ministry's gloss of the King's Speech, both Houses learned not only that Pitt 'would rather choose to persevere in the war, even amidst the worst disasters ... than to conclude a peace with the ruling powers of France', but that he continued to advocate the restoration of the Bourbon monarchy on the terms laid down at Toulon.[2]

By late spring, with the Prussian subsidy treaty all but signed, the government became more outspoken. On 7 April Pitt rose to announce that a bill for an *émigré* corps would be brought into the House of Commons. Given that persons inside and outside France were ready to rise 'in resistance to their present Governors', subsidizing the counter-revolution was sound military policy. According to Dundas, government spokesman for the bill, 'unless we overthrow the present system of France ... we could neither hope for peace or obtain security'.[3] The *émigré* army, he said, was to be led by Frenchmen who were distinguished by 'honour and military skill, but revered in their own country for the laurels with which they had adorned the Crown of France'. This was a polite fiction. Neither Pitt nor Dundas had been impressed by the military prowess of *émigré* royalists in exile. The royalist army, acting with British forces, was destined to lend the French people 'protection and support to bring them forward to crush the Convention'.

Many MPs were startled by so trenchant a statement of support for the *ancien régime*: 'It seemed to be avowed', wrote Fox, 'that the restoration of the old Government of France is now the object of the war.'[4] Portland, whose support for the bill had been solicited before its presentation to Parliament, was delighted with the legislation but felt that more could be done for the Bourbon cause: 'Sure I am that neither the capture of Martinico nor of all the French Possessions in the West Indies will have any effect here, or do one hundredth part of the service which the Common Cause would derive from the real French Army in the Vendée.'[5] The government had not finalized its preparations for war a moment too soon. The 1794 campaign, which ought to have started in March, had been held up by the Prussian subsidy negotiations and did not begin until 17 April. Contrary to all allied expectations, 1794 was the year of the republic's military recovery. When French forces began to advance upon the Austrian army in Flanders in May, the Prussian contribution to the allied campaign became a matter of some urgency. The Prussians had not yet taken up their positions and refused to do so until the required subsidy payments had been received in full. These were already a month behind schedule – for which Pitt was the chief culprit. His negligence was symptomatic of a general British over-confidence in the superiority of the allied armies. The Prussians, who had played a supporting role in the successful campaign of 1793, were expected to do so once more in 1794, and 120,000 British, imperial and Dutch troops were already in the field. The early defeats of the allies were therefore seen as temporary setbacks in London and the military situation on the Continent was not perceived to be crucial until mid-June.[6]

In mid-May Malmesbury and Lord Cornwallis were sent to Prussian headquarters to discuss the deployment of the subsidized army. Marshal Mollendorff, its commander, refused to move without commands from his sovereign, who was now in Poland.[7] By the end of June the Prussians had not yet joined the armies in the west. The allied military situation was deteriorating fast for Charleroi had been taken on 25 June and Jourdan's victory on the 26th took the French into the Austrian Netherlands. Pitt, frustrated and dismayed by the Austrian defeats and the non-appearance of the Prussians, began to play with alternative strategies with which to resume the offensive. With characteristic optimism, he wrote to Auckland that 'the Tide may soon be turned', but he admitted that all his schemes relied upon the support of the Prussian force, without whom 'we are reduced to a wretched defensive'.[8] Assuming that the Austrians regrouped and the Prussians came to the rescue, the allied forces, which were expected to number 200,000 by the beginning of August, could either be devoted to the original attack on the border fortresses or split between defensive positions in the Netherlands and an expedition to the Vendée. Pitt outlined four possible strategies for the offensive redeployment of the allied army; the Netherlands was so important to Britain that three of these involved 'driving the Enemy out of Flanders'.[9] Pitt, however, was beginning to wonder whether it was too late in the campaign season for this commitment to make any significant impact on the enemy.

Pitt's growing interest in the Vendée was a reflection of his frustration with the continental war. Throughout the summer of 1794 he could not decide whether to attempt a partial or full recovery of the Low Countries immediately or to leave their reconquest until 1795. Two of his June schemes involved the embarkation of 50,000 or 100,000 allied troops for the Vendée. The political problems involved in the support of French royalism were seemingly forgotten. Swift victory had been a primary attraction of British participation in the European war and for Pitt, intent on 'pursuing the war offensively', the royalists not only seemed more amenable to control than Britain's German allies, but had the added advantage of ready-made reinforcements in the French interior.

Pressure for commitment to the Vendée also came from the Portland Whigs following their union with the ministry. Rose, who thought that the government ought to cut its losses in the Low Countries, feared that Windham would 'induce Mr Pitt, or strengthen him in his determination, to pursue the war in Flanders or on the Northern Frontier offensively'.[10] The French army decided the matter for the ministry. With the enemy advancing through the Netherlands, the allied armies began to look to their rearguard: 'The defence of the Rhine is now become a subject of the highest importance.'[11] The Pitt ministry demanded action from its allies but reports from the battlefield did not suggest that help would materialize. Cornwallis, now stationed with the British army in the Low Countries, wrote in disparaging terms about the levels of leadership and morale in the Austrian army.[12] The British government, which had long been dissatisfied with the lack of initiative from the Austrian high command, began to petition the court of Vienna for a change of generals or the installation of Cornwallis as commander-in-chief of the allied armies.

The defence of the Netherlands now depended upon the arrival of the Prussian army. In mid-July Pitt was still expecting Prussia to fulfil its military commitments and was willing to subsidize an additional 30,000 Prussian soldiers after 'the present force is completed to its stipulated amount'.[13] Effective Austrian aid was to be obtained by an immediate negotiation for 100,000 troops, to be provided 'if possible in this campaign, and, at all events, before the next'. It was also hoped that a long-term Anglo-Austrian alliance would finally be signed.[14] Pitt had not forgotten the royalists and was considering taking 'steps to assist the levies of French troops, as well as on the recognition of the French King and the regent, as soon as any footing shall be gained in the interior of France'.[15] This necessitated a formal agreement with the Bourbons, and arrangements were in train to bring Artois and the Castries to England for the co-ordination of Anglo-*émigré* operations. On 15 July the Cabinet resolved to place its faith in Austria and the invitation were rescinded.

Two recent recruits to the ministry, Lord Spencer and Thomas Grenville, were appointed to convey its demands to Vienna. Both were Portland Whigs; when Tom Grenville joined the ministry, a long-standing rift in his family was healed. The Foreign Secretary, delighted that Tom was entering the government's service, wrote that 'a little more exertion and energy' was '*the only* thing wanting to ensure success'.[16] The two special envoys left London on 19 July with orders to insist on an Austrian counter-attack in the Netherlands. Spencer and Tom Grenville were also authorized to transfer the Prussian subsidy to Austria if the latter government undertook to replace the delinquent Prussians and resume the offensive in Flanders. This carrot was not to be offered to the Austrians unless they refused to act otherwise. On 23 July Portland reassured Malmesbury that he and Pitt would not discontinue the subsidy payments to Prussia 'as long even as any *negative* good could be derived from our apparent connection'.[17] Pichegru, who took Antwerp on the 27 July, did not appear to be intimidated by the potential appearance of the Prussian army.

The transfer of the Prussian subsidy was one of the first subjects that the Austrian government brought up, declaring itself helpless in the Netherlands without financial aid from Britain. In May 1794 an Austrian state loan of £3m. had been floated on the London money market. By July only £300,000 had been subscribed. When the Austrian agent in London, the Vicomte de Sandrouin, had sounded Pitt out about the prospect of a British guarantee for the loan, the premier had not been dismissive. Were the Austrians immediately to reinforce their Flanders contingent and to field an army of 160,000 in 1795, the ministry, said Pitt, might underwrite £1m. of the 1794 loan and guarantee a further £2m. in 1795.[18] Spencer and Tom Grenville had been entrusted with revised military plans to retake the Low Countries as soon as possible. No subsidy was available for Austria but other financial arrangements were not out of the question.[19] The Austrians were not proposing to abandon the Netherlands altogether, but, with forces split between Poland and the Low Countries, it was felt in Vienna that the resumption of the offensive against France could wait until 1796. On 12 July the Austrian government, alarmed by the speed of the French advance and disgruntled by the Pitt ministry's failure to send an additional 20,000 British troops to the Continent, had sent Count Mercy d'Argenteau to London in search of British financial and military support.

The count, already in poor health, was delayed for a fortnight by adverse winds in the Channel and died four days after reaching London, but not before telling Pitt and Grenville that his government was unable to maintain any significant military presence on the western front unless the subsidy was transferred to Austria and the May 1794 loan was guaranteed. Mercy's loss was a severe blow. Unlike Starhemberg, the Austrian ambassador, Mercy had been a strong Anglophile and was therefore a more flexible negotiator.[20] Pitt and Grenville, while staggered by the scale of the Austrian demands, had not been entirely unprepared for them. On 5 August St Helens, now at the Hague, had been instructed to sound out the government of the United Provinces on a prospective Anglo-Dutch guarantee for the Austrian loan: 'we should willingly lend ourselves to any measure that seemed really advantageous as a means of saving part of the whole'.[21] Although Cabinet opinions were divided on the wisdom of financial aid for Austria, Pitt decided to authorize cash advances of £100,000 a month to keep the imperial army on the Meuse.[22] When the loan arrangements were finalized, the advances would be deducted from the total. The British government was faced with an unpalatable truth. Were it to lose the goodwill of Austria, Britain would be left to fight alone against revolutionary France.

The Pitt ministry never understood the Polish problem. For the British government, the partitions represented a squalid struggle to enlarge the territories of Prussia, Russia and Austria. Pitt and Grenville never accepted the Austro-Prussian contention that the French Revolution had destabilized eastern European politics and that Poland was therefore as important a battleground as Flanders.[23] In British eyes, Austria had to make a final and irrevocable choice between the east and west. In July 1794 the ministry called for a reaffirmation of Habsburg commitment to the Low Countries. When the Austrian government claimed not only all the barrier fortresses in the Pays Bas, but also some true French lands, the Pitt Cabinet began to fear that its ally was counting on post-war compensation at the expense of British conquests in the West Indies.[24] Never before had the Austrians expressed so strong an interest in western Europe; viewed in the light of Chancellor Thugut's proposal to place the war in the west on hold for a year, the new claims suggested that Britain was expected, as had been often the case during the eighteenth century, to ransom the Netherlands at the peace. The Pitt ministry's ratification of the Austrian demands 'in order to include the possibility of retaining some parts of the Frontier of France, but which are not actually in the Low Countries', was conditional upon the receipt of reciprocal guarantees for British acquisitions 'not actually on the Continent of Europe'.[25]

The Austrian government was offered a British guarantee for a loan of £3m. in return for the immediate dispatch of 60,000 troops to the western front and the supply of an additional 160,000 men in 1795. If these terms were not accepted, Pitt wanted to 'employ £200,000 in getting Troops where we can'.[26] With these soldiers, Antwerp might be retaken, which would 'at least check the operations of the Enemy, damp their spirits and raise those of our Army'. Pitt was clutching at straws. On 12 September the ministry discovered that its proposals of 29 August had been rejected. On the 13th it received the news that Condé and Valenciennes had fallen to the French. The government, appalled by the loss of the last major border fortresses, finally decided to abort its 1794 war plans. Pitt and Grenville, now thinking defensively, felt that 'Part at least of the Low Countries' could be saved.[27] 80,000 to 100,000 Austrians, acting with British and mercenary forces, were now considered adequate for this purpose. Their objects were straightforward: 'recovering the Netherlands and of preserving them during the next Campaign, and even of placing ourselves in a Situation to seize any favourable opportunity, which the Course of Events may produce for attacking such Part of the Barrier as may be thought most vulnerable.'[28] The offer of a loan was renewed on 14 September.

The Pitt ministry did not intend to rely exclusively on the Austrian army in 1795. Arrangements were in train to send arms and supplies to the Vendée during the winter of 1794–5. An amphibious assault on the Brittany coast was planned for the spring, 'when it may be attempted with a very considerable force'.[29] This was to coincide with the launch of the allied offensive in Flanders: 'In this way, we shall be able to push that, whichever it may be ... at the time most likely to succeed.' In late September Pitt's vote swung briefly towards an autumn expedition to the Vendée. The Comte de Puisaye, a charismatic and resourceful veteran of the *chouan* war, was brought to the ministry's attention at a time when British faith in Austria was at an all-time low. Pitt was so determined to rescue something from the wreck of the 1794 campaign that he wanted Spencer and Tom Grenville to be recalled from Vienna unless the 14 September proposals received unconditional acceptance: 'We must look to more limited exertions on the side of Flanders and turn our principal exertions to the French coast.'[30]

Pitt's excited enthusiasm for an autumn expedition to the Vendée did not last long. Within twenty-four hours he had accepted the War Secretary's admonitions that little was known about the strength and situation of the Vendée. Though still interested in the project, Pitt was persuaded to be content with supplying the royalists over the winter.[31] Puisaye was by no means forgotten. His local expertise was to be invaluable in planning the Quiberon expedition in 1795. His brief moment of favour in September 1794 was, however, indicative of the wild mood swings to which Pitt was subject when gripped by intense anxiety and frustration. Under such conditions he succumbed to attacks of panic and self-doubt: 'I distrust extremely my own thoughts on military subjects,' he confessed to Windham.[32]

While the Austrians studied the British proposals of 14 September, the allied military situation continued to worsen. By 2 October the French armies were on the banks of the Rhine. St Helens tried to bolster the resolve of a Dutch government fast losing heart for the war, while, on 10 October, the Pitt ministry had resumed the *ad hoc* subsidy payments to German mercenary troops now fighting for the security of the empire. The Prussian subsidy was finally abandoned on 23 October. The Cabinet had been disgusted by what was perceived as Dutch cowardice since August: 'I cannot pretend to tell whether Holland will or will not escape being completely overrun,' wrote Dundas at the end of October; 'If they are, it is certainly their own fault.'[33] The British government was so dismissive of the Dutch defence that requests for the transfer of the Prussian subsidy to the United Provinces were curtly refused.

By 18 November Pitt, Grenville and Dundas were analysing the impact of a Dutch surrender on the war in Europe and the colonies.[34] Dundas drew up a *précis* of revised military objectives for 1795 in which three main areas of concern were identified: Britain itself, the colonies and Europe. The loss of the Netherlands and the United Provinces left France free to attack Britain's coastal defences, native shipping and trade routes to Europe. Pitt proposed the destruction of the Dutch fleet in harbour, much as the French Mediterranean fleet had been scuppered at Toulon.[35] Britain's home defences did not pose so serious a problem. Home-based units had been strengthened during the first half of 1794 and reorganization, not augmentation, was the priority.

Dundas advocated the recall of the British army from the Continent for the reinforcement of the West and East Indies. He was intent on preserving Dutch possessions which might otherwise fall into the hands of France, and anxious to reinforce the British presence in the Caribbean, an operation long overdue. In four months the Grey–Jervis West Indian expedition, which had left England in December 1793, had taken Martinique, St Lucia, and Guadeloupe. A bridgehead had also been established on St Domingo, but the army, decimated by disease during the summer of 1794, had been forced to abandon it. By the end of July much of Guadeloupe had been lost and the British position on the remaining islands was decidedly shaky.[36] When news of the West

Indian losses reached London in mid-August, all spare British troops were being thrown into Flanders. After impassioned pleading with his colleagues and the service chiefs, Dundas hastily scraped together 8,200 men for the West Indies, of whom only 6,400 reached the islands in dribs and drabs over the winter of 1794-5. For Dundas, the real war lay not in Europe, but in the colonies, and he stressed the importance of colonial indemnification to a Cabinet torn between numerous drains on finite resources: 'I should consider His Majesty's Servants as unfaithful to the interests of their Country if they did not advise His Majesty to make immediate adequate Provision for the Security of our West Indian Possessions in preference to every existing Service.'[37] Dundas had intended to send an additional 10,000 men to the Caribbean at the end of 1794 but the state of affairs on the Continent made this impossible. Pitt voted for the reinforcement of the West Indies once it became clear that the Low Countries could not be saved. Attracted to the path of least resistance, he looked for success where he thought it could be obtained most swiftly. Orders for the recall of the British army from the Continent were sent out on 20 November. The German mercenaries in British pay were attached to the Austrian army in 1795.

Late in October the ministry received the Austrian answer to the financial aid package proposed on 14 September.[38] Spencer and Tom Grenville followed shortly thereafter. A £6m. loan was asked of the British government – £3m. to cover the military expenditures of 1794 and another £3m. to meet the estimated expenses of 1795. In return, Austria proposed to place an army of 200,000 men on the Rhine. The size of the loan staggered a Cabinet nevertheless impressed by the number of troops on offer. By November there was no longer any question about the need for Austrian troops to pursue the war in 1795:

> The Army to remain there to consist of the German troops in British pay, joined to a corps of Austrians under an Imperial General; and on the Rhine the Army of the Empire strengthened by a force of Imperialists, to effect which Great Britain must either grant Austria a subsidy or grant such a loan as may be necessary to enable her to keep both corps in the field.[39]

Revised British war plans were sent to Vienna on 26 November.[40] Aware that the allies would be hard-pressed to prevent the United Provinces from falling into the clutches of France, let alone stage another attack on the Netherlands, Pitt and Grenville had envisaged the Austrian army harassing the French borders while launching its offensive in Alsace and the Franche Comté. The Austrian army was to be spread along a front that stretched from the Channel to Switzerland. The loan was preferable to a subsidy for the guarantor was responsible only for the interest. This was far less onerous a financial burden in the short term. Grenville sought to reduce the price of the troops but the British government had agreed to the scheme in principle.[41] Provided that the Austrians accepted Pitt's financial terms, all that remained to be done was explain the allied losses of 1794 to Parliament and persuade it to authorize a £6m. loan for Austria.

War and Peace

Pitt, though faced with the unenviable task of defending the government's war policy in Parliament, was not anticipating any trouble from the back benches. Canning reported him to be 'stout and undismayed'.[42] The formation of the coalition ministry in July 1794 had neutralized the most dangerous opposition group in Parliament and Pitt prepared to justify the continuation of the war in 1795 by recourse to the arguments that had been used throughout 1794. Ideological warfare had not, however, produced any results. With the Prussian alliance in tatters, the French in occupation of the Netherlands, the British army evacuated from Europe and the Dutch preparing to make peace, Wilberforce, who had always deplored Britain's involvement in the war, rose on 30 December to move a peace amendment to the address of thanks: 'There appears to be humanely speaking no possibility of a limited monarchy being established in France ... I am inclined to believe it might be our best plan to declare our willingness to make peace on equitable terms.'[43] Wilberforce hoped that his friendship with Pitt would survive so open a defection and, though the peace amendment wounded Pitt deeply, the two men agreed to disagree in May 1795, after which their relations were restored to some, if not all, of their former intimacy.[44]

Wilberforce's amendment was symptomatic of a wider process of soul-searching about the wisdom of the government's war policies. Dissent spread rapidly through the ranks of the independent MPs during the winter of 1794–5. Towards the end of January it took the form of complaints about the competence of the Portland Whigs. As Solicitor-General Sir John Mitford wrote to Pitt: 'they say they have seen you looking about for support and resting on broken reeds'.[45] So worrisome was the palpable discontent on the government benches that the Treasury issued an unofficial statement to clarify the ministry's position before the debates on the Grey–Bedford peace motions of 27 January:

> ... it is not the *form* of Government there [France], but its *power* & *will* to afford *Security* to other Countries that we consider as

indispensable, that about Monarchy or Republicanism, or Revolutionary Committees, or this or that set of Men or set of principles, we
have no care or consideration – *further* than they go to promise or
make improbable the secure maintenance of Peace, if on other
grounds Peace should be desireable.[46]

During the Commons debate on Grey's motion Pitt claimed that the
existing French government was still too unstable to give Britain any
guarantees for 'a secure and lasting peace', but that the exhaustion of
the enemy would provide this blessing within a year.[47] The British
retreat from ideological warfare had begun. The Cabinet, sensitive to
anti-war sentiment, was to become increasingly anxious about the mood
of the House throughout 1795.

The defection of Wilberforce and the 'friends of peace' had come
at a particularly bad time for the ministry. The trenchant tone of the
King's Speech, in which the government reiterated its commitment to
ideological war, can be attributed to the ministry's anxiety to improve
its image in Europe, particularly in the United Provinces, where British
influence was fading fast. British exhortations to make a determined
military stand against France, to reject enemy offers of an armistice
and to insist on a neutral status following the peace, were all ignored.
As had been the case during the winter of 1792–3, the British government saw itself as an important source of Dutch morale, in the
maintenance of which large Commons majorities were regarded by Pitt
as vital. The Treasury had been instructed to ensure 'as full an attendance as possible' at the Commons debate on the address of thanks,
where he intended to 'renew in the strongest manner' his assurances
of support to the United Provinces.

By 15 November 1794 the Cabinet had resigned itself to the Franco-
Dutch peace.[48] The reinforcement of the First Coalition was now a
crucial priority and, on 6 February, Whitworth was instructed to ask
the Russian government for a naval squadron in the North Sea. The
existing Russian Baltic patrol was regarded as far from effective, but,
with the Dutch fleet all but in French hands, the ministry felt obliged
to seek help.[49] Alliance overtures had been received from St Petersburg
throughout 1793. They had been treated with caution because Russia
was unwilling to send troops to Flanders and insisted on large subsidies
for any soldiers that it might send to the west. This option was
considered briefly in January 1794, at which time the ministry was looking for replacements for the defaulting Prussians. A British offer of
£500,000 for an army of 12,000 men whetted the appetite of the
Russians, who not only demanded £1m. for their armed services, but
strove to incorporate a British commitment to the defence of the
Russian empire in the proposed subsidy treaty.[50] Russia was not an ideal

partner because its motives for participation in the war were more blatantly self-interested – that is to say, had less to do with France – than those of any other European power. The British government, resenting the recognition of the second Polish partition that was implicit in the proposed terms of the alliance and appalled by the prospect of involvement in Russia's disputes with its neighbours, retorted that its consent was conditional upon a Russian undertaking to help defend the British empire.[51] Throughout the summer of 1794 the Pitt ministry remained interested in subsidized Russian troops but by September the greater part of the Russian army was once more in rebellious Poland.[52]

The third partition in 1795, which followed the Polish rising of 1794, resulted, amongst other things, in the reduction of Austria's participation in the western war. On 6 December Morton Eden had sent a revised loan project to London. For £4m. the Austrian government proposed to keep 120,000 soldiers on the Rhine and an additional 40,000 in Italy.[53] Grenville, though relieved that the price of the Austrian troops had come down was, with Pitt, anxious to acquire as large an army as possible. The conditions of the British loan were revised. By December 1794 the Austrian army had received £40,000 for the hitherto unsuccessful defence of the United Provinces. If this money was reimbursed, the Pitt ministry proposed to lend Austria the full £6m. in return for the supply of 240,000 men. Were the Austrians to keep the advances, the British government would raise £4.5m. for an army of 200,000.[54]

The reduced number of Austrian soldiers now on offer made it unlikely that the Netherlands and the United Provinces would be liberated in 1795. Pitt, for whom these objects were of crucial importance, proposed at a Cabinet meeting on 18 February that Prussia be approached for troops once more. Grenville voiced immediate objections: Prussia was rumoured to be treating for peace with France; Frederick William II had demanded payment of the 1794 subsidy in full before dealing with Britain again; the mending of Anglo-Prussian fences would place Grenville's triple alliance scheme with Austria and Russia at risk.[55] Pitt, whose distrust of Prussia was as great as Grenville's, nevertheless claimed that the renewal of the subsidy would at least prevent Prussia from joining forces with France.

This was the least likely course of action for a monarch with troops tied down in Poland. The consideration that it was given by Pitt reflects not only the depths to which Prussia had sunk in British eyes, but also his inability to see the repercussions of the third partition for east–central European politics. Grenville argued that an alliance with Russia would check any proposed alliance between Prussia and France. The issue was brought to a head at a Cabinet meeting on 1 March, at which Grenville was outvoted by a majority of one.[56] The Foreign Secretary, upset that Pitt had seen the Prussian ambassador behind his back to discuss the revival of the subsidy, proposed to resign the following day.[57] He was persuaded to delay his departure until the end of the 1795 parliamentary session.

Pitt's determination to pursue the Prussian subsidy had been strengthened by the receipt of dispatches from Vienna on 20 February. The Austrians were protesting at the 7.5% rate of interest set by Pitt, who had wanted to make the loan attractive to investors, and announced that an Austrian Treasury analyst would be sent to London to wrangle over the details.[58] The loan arrangements were presented to Parliament as part of the 1795 budget on 28 February and, despite murmurs of discontent, both were approved without a hitch. Pitt committed the ministry to a 6% return for the Austrian loan and undertook to make up the remaining 1.5% in interest if the loan treaty fell through.[59]

Pitt was also concerned about the impact of a Prussian peace upon imperial unity. On 14 November 1794 the Cabinet had voiced strong objections to a joint mediation offer from neutral Denmark and Sweden on behalf of France and the Holy Roman Empire. Correspondence from Vienna suggested that Prussia was encouraging other members of the empire to sue for peace.[60] The premier was reminded about the impact of a Franco-Prussian peace on the unity of the empire by George III, who, apparently ignorant of the dispute between the Prime Minister and the Foreign Secretary, sent Pitt some information that he had received from Hanover regarding the fears of its Regency Council on this subject.[61] The king, concerned for the security of his electorate yet doubtful that Parliament would vote for another Prussian subsidy, suggested that Prussia should receive military supplies from Britain for the duration of the war and eventual financial compensation from a free United Provinces once peace was made.[62] Pitt's attempts to use this information to raise support for the subsidy amongst his colleagues were dashed by definitive news that Prussia was negotiating with France. The Cabinet voted for the Triple Alliance on 9 March.[63]

On the same day Grenville wrote to St Petersburg with a subsidy offer for Russian troops. An army of 55,000 men, for which Britain would pay £500,000, was sought for service on the Rhine or on the coasts of France.[64] Whitworth was urged to wind up the alliance talks of 1794 and, remembering the acrimonious exchange of dispatches on the subject of imperial defence guarantees, was reminded to keep the subsidy treaty separate from the alliance. Grenville was prepared to recognize the partitions of Poland in order to secure the alliance, but beyond this he was wary. The amended treaty, complete with carefully worded mutual defence stipulations, reached London late in May. It was signed without delay.

The ministry was forced to reconsider the Prussian subsidy question again upon discovering, on 28 March, that the Austrians were still unhappy about the interest terms of the loan. In contrast, reports from Berlin claimed that Frederick William II's hatred of revolutionary France was as strong as ever. George III, afraid for Hanover, came down strongly in favour of the subsidy: 'There is no Force sufficient without the Prussians, to prevent the French seizing every Port on the North Sea.'[65] The Cabinet reversed its decision on 8 April with Grenville as the sole dissenter. When he refused to sign the outgoing Berlin dispatches, Pitt drafted the subsidy offer, which went out under Dundas's signature. On 16 April it was learned that Prussia had signed a peace convention with France at Basle.

George III and Pitt were appalled though the premier still thought that victory was within allied sights: 'At all Events, the Loss of our Ally is, I am in hopes, more than compensated by the Embarrassing weakness and distraction of the Enemy, which I am persuaded will in a short Time much more than Verify all the Expectations we had formed on that Subject.'[66] Grenville was now frantic to see the Austrian loan ratified and, in a private letter to Morton Eden on 17 April, he urged the latter to make the Austrian government see the necessity of 'acting soon, and (at all Hazards) acting offensively'.[67] Confronted with repeated delay, the British government had run out of constructive ideas about the conduct of the land war: 'We cannot pretend to form a Judgement here, such as will enable us to express a decided Preference, in favour of Operations against one Part of the Frontier, rather than another.' Faced by the growing cost of the war, hostile opinion inside and outside Parliament and intense dissatisfaction with Britain's allies, the government turned to royalism as a means of expediting the Thermidorean reaction in France. The Pitt ministry was now eager to fan the flames of Russian anti-Jacobinism and the Austrians were prodded to take a more open-minded attitude towards the Bourbon restoration.[68] Having lost all other avenues of direct British action against the enemy, the government, to the delight of the Portland Whigs, prepared to give the French counter-revolution some serious attention.

Supporting the Counter-Revolution

After the British army had been evacuated from Europe, royalist strongholds in France became increasingly attractive as bases from which blows could be struck against the republic. British connections to the Vendée were now well-established via the Channel Islands, the Comité de Londres and the Portland Whigs. At the end of 1794 an additional link was established to south-east France through neutral Switzerland.

Émigré appeals for British money to support the counter-revolution had been coming from Switzerland since late 1793. These had been treated with caution by a ministry anxious not to associate itself too openly with the royalist cause. In mid-October 1794 Jean Joseph Mounier and Jacques Mallet du Pan, constitutional monarchists known to the British government, had sent Lord Robert Fitzgerald, the British ambassador in Zurich, particulars of a peace proposal purporting to come from two royalist deputies in the National Convention. The two *émigrés*, claiming to act as go-betweens, asserted that the *conventionnels* represented a larger body of monarchist sentiment in the Thermidorean Convention and were willing to stage a *coup d'état* if amnesties were given to those implicated in the murder of Louis XVI. William Wickham, last seen at the Alien Office, was sent under diplomatic cover to Berne on 16 October 1794 to liaise with Mounier and Mallet du Pan.[69]

The royalist conspiracy proved to be an elaborate hoax but Wickham's mission was not in vain, for the *émigrés* put him in touch with the White Terror in the Franche Comté. By March 1795 he could report that the insurgents in the south-east, already persecuting 'Jacobins' at home, wanted only financial assistance and professional military aid to rise in open revolt.[70] By 18 December the British government was committed to 'an attack on the Coasts of France and that, if possible, in co-operation with the Royalists in the North Western Provinces of that Kingdom'. Succour for Wickham's friends was not going to materialize, however, until the Austrian loan was finalized. The moment that this took place, immediate pressure was applied to the court of Vienna for an Austrian military presence on the borders of south-east France.[71] Wickham had submitted such promising accounts of the White Terror in the south that Pitt was besotted with the prospect of revolt. £10,000 was sent to the Prince of Condé, whose *émigré* regiment, nominally attached to the Austrian army, was to join the projected attack on Alsace and the Franche Comté. Pitt and Dundas began to organize in earnest for a Vendée expedition at the end of May. After consultation with Puisaye and other royalist representatives, it was decided to land the *émigré* corps and supplies in Brittany, in preparation for simultaneous risings in the Vendée and south-east.[72] On 12 June Grenville wrote to Morton Eden to demand that the Austrian army use Condé's forces to divert the attention of the Convention from the Vendée by attacking Alsace and the Franche Comté at the beginning of July.[73] Windham, not surprisingly, was ecstatic, and Pitt shared the Secretary at War's optimism, if not his love of the royalists: 'If our Austrian Allies can be brought to second these attempts by any vigor in their Operations on the Frontier, I really think the prospect of decisive success will once again be very favourable.'[74]

The Quiberon expedition sailed on 17 June. Early reports from the Vendée were cautious, but encouraging. Commander Warren wrote to

Spencer at the Admiralty that the *chouans* were 'numerous and zealous, yet like all irregulars, they are uncertain for any distant expedition'.[75] On 10 July Grenville sent a tart message to Vienna; unless the Austrian army made an attack on French forces in the east, the Vendée would be exposed to the full wrath of the Convention's armies. Demands for the replacement of Clerfayt, commander-in-chief of the Austrian forces, soon followed.[76] 'It is vain to lament how backward every preparation still appears to be on the part of the Austrians,' remarked Pitt, who did not want to put Wickham's White Terrorists in danger needlessly.[77] Puisaye's royalists were routed on 20 July.

On 22 July the British government learned that Spain had made peace with France.[78] Unconfirmed reports of armistice negotiations had been reaching London since January but the event still took the ministry by surprise. Pitt and Dundas turned their attentions to the defence of the West Indies, threatened by the rumour that Spanish St Domingo had been ceded to France. 'Our plan must be changed', wrote Pitt, 'and the only great part [of our military strategy] must be the West Indies where I think enough may be gained to counterbalance the French successes in Europe.'[79] When asked for his opinion on the feasibility of another assault on the French coast, Moira, commander of the British *émigré* corps, stated that such a venture was pointless without a strong mainland base.[80] Reinforcements for the Vendée were cut to 4,000 men, who were ordered instead to seize one of the offshore islands, either Noirmoutiers or the Île d'Yeu: 'there is the greatest reason to hope that if we establish some other point of communication, our disappointment may soon be repaired.'[81]

Dundas was delighted that the Cabinet had decided to relieve the West Indies. British fortunes in the Caribbean were at a low ebb; disease had decimated the original 1793–4 expedition, which Dundas had not been able to reinforce according to plan. The West Indian contingent for 1795 sailed in February, having been delayed for two months by bad weather and the lack of a suitably large naval escort to protect the troop transports and large fleet of merchant vessels that had gathered in the Channel ports to avail themselves of the Admiralty's protection as advertised in its convoy schedules. Dundas, determined to preserve the Dutch East Indian colonies from French conquest, had reduced the size of the Caribbean relief force in January, and admitted in consequence that no major West Indian offensive could be attempted in 1795.[82]

British setbacks in the Caribbean were due not to superior French opposition, but to yellow fever and slave revolt. Since 1793 French commanders had been offering slaves their freedom in return for fighting; in February 1795 the Convention abolished slavery. Toussaint l'Ouverture, leader of the black republicans in Guadeloupe, had issued summons to insurrection to all neighbouring islands. Not only was the British conquest and occupation of enemy territory very much complicated by slave resistance, but British planters on neighbouring islands were afraid for the safety of their estates. Dundas was anxious that troops be sent to the British islands most at risk, 'to the amount that may be necessary for their internal and external security'.[83] The possession of Guadeloupe, he claimed, was essential to 'extirpate disaffection in its seat'. Success in the West Indies alone, he told Pitt, would enable the ministry to 'dictate the terms of peace'. The Cabinet, dismayed by the Franco-Spanish peace, agreed on 14 August.[84] The 1796 expedition, scheduled to sail in September, was to retake Guadeloupe and consolidate the British position on the Leeward Islands.

In April Dundas had decided to resolve the manpower crisis in the West Indies by authorizing the formation of negro levies.[85] The Cabinet had considered emancipation as a reward for voluntary military service but, bowing to pressure from colonists fearful of the effect on their plantations, voted against the measure. The British government, suspecting that emancipation had been adopted by the enemy to compensate the French forces in the Caribbean for reinforcements that could not be spared from Europe, did not foresee the negative impact of its decision on the morale of British troops in the West Indies. Pitt is not likely to have voted for emancipation. He had conceded the theoretical 'equality' of slaves in 1789 and had voted for abolition throughout the 1790s but he did not feel that freedom was a viable option. Pitt had objected to the treatment of slaves on humanitarian grounds, but not to the institution of slavery itself.

Despite Pitt and Wilberforce's best efforts to end the trade, as expressed in a Commons debate of 26 February, there was little relief in sight for British plantation labourers. The plight of the French, whose lot Pitt had described in the House of Commons as little better than slavery, seemed equally grim.[86] No major offensive on the western front materialized until the end of 1795, for the Austrian government, determined to extricate itself from its eastern European commitments, had told its commanders to remain on the defensive.[87] British diplomats in Vienna, with the Bourbon armies and in Switzerland strove to persuade the Austrians to come to the aid of a fast-collapsing Vendée revolt. Wickham found the Austrian generals unwilling either to explain their military plans or to allow Condé's regiment to see action: 'They have never been serious in their Intentions of attacking the French upon the Rhine ... and they never meant to commit their great army at all.'[88]

Unsatisfactory as the Austrians were as allies, the Bourbons did not improve upon acquaintance. Artois had not been enthusiastic about leading guerrillas in the Vendée. Provence remained set against any hint of reform in the *ancien régime* monarchy. Following the death of the young Louis XVII on 8 June, Lord Macartney, recently returned from an unsuccessful embassy to the Emperor of China, had been appointed special plenipotentiary to Provence's 'court'. Macartney's job was not an easy one. Notwithstanding his best efforts to convince the future Louis XVIII that a public commitment to tolerance and reform was an essential precondition of a successful restoration, the Declaration of Verona, released by Provence on 24 June, was so haughty in tone that it was described by Buckingham with some sarcasm as 'not so good as Lord Clarendon's from Breda'.[89] Conspicuously absent from the Verona Declaration was any grant of an amnesty to regicides. The constitution of the *ancien régime* was regarded by Provence as 'the wisdom of ages, the perfection of reason, etc. and as the only kind of government suitable to the French nation'.[90] The Pitt ministry, committed in public and private to endorse the establishment of any political system that would reconcile dissident social elements in the old and new regimes, was fast becoming exasperated with Bourbon intransigence. Over the autumn of 1795 Pitt gave serious consideration to the terms on which he could make peace with the Directory.

Towards a Peace Settlement

At the end of August the ministry began to review its options. Unsuccessful though the allied campaign of 1795 had been, the exhaustion of revolutionary France appeared to be real. Britain's relations with Austria nonetheless took a turn for the worse after the failure of the Quiberon expedition. Despite Morton Eden's incessant complaints about the inactivity of the imperial army on the Rhine, no new offensive was launched over the summer of 1795, nor did the Austrians permit the Bourbons to try their luck on the battlefield alone. British strategists were surprised to find that the Austrian army's reluctance to fund and equip Condé's regiment was founded upon fears that military support for the Bourbon 'conquest' of French towns might be seen as recognition of Provence's right to ascend the French throne with his domains intact. The Austrian government wanted to hold the Franche Comté and Alsace as hostages for the return of the Netherlands. The Pitt ministry tried to reassure its ally that neither the 'summoning of places in the name of the French King' nor the 'holding out to the Country the general object of the restoration of Royalty' affected Austria's claims to French indemnification when peace was made.[91]

The British government believed that the military inertia of Austria stemmed from its 'Timidity and Uncertainty' about the empire's attitude to the war.[92] In April Morton Eden had gloomily predicted that the

Imperial Diet, disillusioned by Austrian inaction and in particular by the Franco-Prussian peace, would vote for peace in August.[93] Several states – led, not surprisingly, by the Rhineland – declared themselves neutral over the summer of 1795. Most damaging of these withdrawals for the Pitt ministry was that of Hanover. When the Cabinet voted on 7 September to stop funding the Hanoverian mercenaries who had been in British pay since 1793, George III was 'much hurt and very sore'.[94] This Dundas thought paradoxical: 'he forgets that Hanover is already within his own approbation in a state of Neutrality, and if the Emperor is *driven*, it is his Hanoverian and not his English Ministry who are the *drivers*.' The Austrians saw little difference between the two.

Dundas saw Hanover's disappearance from the war as an opportunity to call upon Russia for extra troops. 15,000–20,000 Russians, he stated, would enable Britain to retake the United Provinces 'in place of treating about it when Peace comes'. The ministry's subsidy offer in March had been rejected because Catherine had been preoccupied with the consolidation of Russian power in her new Polish lands. An offer of troops from St Petersburg in June had been dismissed by Grenville on cost grounds.[95] By September, however, the Pitt ministry was contemplating the prospect of war with Spain, reputedly on the verge of signing a defensive alliance with France. Franco-Spanish naval co-operation, particularly in colonial theatres, was so alarming a scenario that the British were now doubly determined to shift some of the burden for the policing of European waters onto Russia. On 19 September Grenville sent a naval subsidy offer to Whitworth.[96]

On 20 September the Cabinet met to discuss the war, a meeting precipitated by the imminent arrival of a French envoy, Louis Monneron, whose visit was ostensibly inspired by a sudden French desire to exchange prisoners of war. Dundas suggested that Monneron, employed in the Paris banking-house of Jacques Perregaux, was coming to England to speculate in the funds. Pitt thought that Monneron was coming to test the waters for peace. Auckland, who still possessed contacts in Paris, was asked to sound out Perregaux about Monneron's mission and received a favourable, if cautious, answer:

> He knows either nothing more than appears relative to M. Monneron's Mission, or he thinks it proper to say nothing. I suspect however from his general language respecting the necessity of making peace at the expense (if we require it) of great Sacrifices on the part of the republic, & also from the pains taken by Perregaux to give a good opinion of Monneron, that the Mission means more than appears.[97]

The timing of the visit was significant, for, when the Cabinet learned of it, France had just had a referendum to ratify the 1795 constitution. Pitt, watching the Directory take shape over the summer, had concluded that the new government would be forced to sue for peace by a war-weary nation.

The Convention, aware of its own unpopularity in the country, had been uneasy since the Paris *journée* of 1–2 prairial (20–1 May), the popular rising that had capped a series of nationwide protests against central authority. On 21 August the Convention passed the infamous 'Law of Two Thirds', which dictated that the new Council of Five Hundred, the 'Lower House' of the Directory, be packed by deputies who had sat in the old Convention. Constitutional royalists and moderate republicans were horrified. Satisfied on the whole with the constitution of the Year III – characterized by a bicameral legislature, strict separation of powers, high property franchise and declaration of rights and duties – the constitutional monarchists had planned to seize power legally through the election of their deputies to the two directorial assemblies. Once possessed of a majority there, they would replace the supreme executive power, the five directors, with Louis XVIII.[98] The Law of Two Thirds scuppered this conspiracy, details of which were transmitted to the Foreign Office through the Agence de Paris, the shady counter-revolutionary spy organization run by the Comte d'Antraigues with which Francis Drake, the British resident in Verona, had made contact in the autumn of 1794.

In 1956 Harvey Mitchell drew attention to the twenty-eight 'Dropmore Bulletins' that the Historical Manuscripts Commission had published in its selection of Grenville's papers. This is a fragment of a much larger collection of agency correspondence which reached not only the British government, but also its counterparts in Spain, Austria and Russia. The agency dispatches were d'Antraigues's compilations of third-rate spy reports, based largely on Paris coffee-house gossip and French newspaper clippings.[99] It is unlikely that Grenville and Pitt swallowed all of d'Antraigues's so-called intelligence, although their interest in the Mounier–Mallet du Pan overture of October 1794 is attributable to its corroboration of information that had come from Drake and d'Antraigues. From the agency the British government learned of the very real royalist–*modéré* republican plans for the 1795 referendum and, following its demise, the new strategy, which involved the instruction of France's primary assemblies to accept the 1795 constitution but not the Law of Two Thirds. Both were sent to referendum on 6 September. Pitt was impressed by the tactics and plans of the constitutional monarchists:

It may be doubted whether more ought to be desired in the first instance, than prevailing upon the primary assemblies to negative the proceedings required under the new Constitution; and whether it may not be best (if the plan succeeds) to defer any direct attempt for Royalty till the Convention have felt the embarrassment of the disappointment of their present project.[100]

The Paris sections, the majority of which had come under *modéré* control by the end of 1794, followed orders on 6 September, which, as Pitt remarked, was 'certainly a very fortunate event'.[101] Although d'Antraigues made grandiose claims for the influence wielded by the agency, even he could not claim to speak for all of France. Grenville thought that it would be very advantageous if Wickham's friends in the south elected as directorial deputies 'those royalists who have already introduced themselves into the Municipal Offices'.[102] The electoral ratification of both the 1795 constitution and the Law of Two Thirds was announced, by slim majorities, on 23 September, but on 20 September, with referendum returns still coming in, Pitt could say of Monneron's mission: 'There can be little doubt that he means some overture on the subject of peace.'

The Cabinet debated two main issues on 20 September: the likelihood of Austria's continued participation in the war; and the merits of the official plans for the 1796 campaign, the 'last' before peace would be made with France. The ministry decided to raise the issue of peace with the Austrians, 'to prevent the Emperor being alarmed into a separate peace, or at least being deserted by most of the princes of the Empire'.[103] Should no peace offer be forthcoming, Britain, Austria and those imperial states that chose to remain in the war would keep fighting. If the empire deserted its Holy Roman head *en masse*, the Austrian operations based in north Italy 'might be very considerable and at least sufficient to make a powerful Diversion' from royalist activities elsewhere.[104] The third – and least attractive – scenario depicted Britain and Russia, minus Austria, 'engaging in the war either on the side of Poland or of Hanover'. Pitt did not want to continue the war without at least one land ally. He sought, nevertheless, to keep his options open:

To secure the active co-operation of the Emperor
To prevent the Peace of the Empire taking place before ours, or a separate peace for the States on the Rhine
To encourage as much as possible the Exertions of the Royalists without committing ourselves to the Continuance of the War
To secure the Perseverance of Sardinia and Naples
To keep the Baltic Powers, Prussia & Spain quiet
To secure Russia.

So convinced was he that France would sue for peace that he was unsure whether to respond 'till we have had the benefit of our successes in the West Indies'.[105] If, after the 1796 Caribbean expedition had sailed, the Directory offered Britain 'all the sacrifices we should require', the continuation of hostilities in the colonies would obstruct the peace talks. The Cabinet also had to assess whether the Austrian government's jealousy of British colonial gains might lose the ministry the 'co-operation of Austria, at least on the Rhine', should the 1796 continental campaign be launched before France surrendered.

On 23 September Grenville wrote to Vienna. The Austrians were warned that no British money would be forthcoming in 1796 unless the grand army stirred its stumps before the end of the year. The Austrians were demanding another British guarantee for a loan of £3m.; Pitt was prepared to meet this, but not without proof of Austria's commitment to the vigorous prosecution of the war. The British government was nonetheless preparing for peace and, on 9 October, sent Francis James Jackson to Vienna to discuss peace terms.[106] A rerun of the war plans for 1795 was proposed for 1796 – the invasion of Alsace and the Franche Comté in support of royalist resistance to republican government and the reconquest of Savoy. The French Revolution was, as Grenville wrote to Morton Eden on 23 September, no longer to be feared:

> Much has already been done, by the Resistance which the Powers of Europe have opposed to the Progress of Jacobin Principles. Great as the Successes of the French Armies have been on the Continent of Europe, the Distresses and Difficulties which the Exertions for the Purpose have produced, have much diminished the Malignity of the System itself. Instead of a Nation universally armed acting either in the Influence of Terror or Enthusiasm in Support of the Principles of Anarchy, and anxious to extend them over every Part of Europe, we see a People languid and exhausted, weary of the Miseries they have suffered, openly renouncing all the Maxims which have produced their Revolution, and wishing only for Repose under any System of Government which may hold out to them personal Security and Protection of Property.

This was a lot to read into the ratification of the 1795 constitution and ignored both the creation of the Batavian Republic, established by the Treaty of the Hague, and the annexation of the Netherlands, formally implemented on 10 October. More important was Grenville's belief that the economic and military collapse that he and Pitt had been anticipating since 1793 had finally come to pass. Pitt, recalled Wilberforce, 'could not believe that it would be possible for the French to find money and resources sufficient for their expenditure, both of money and men'. This conviction underpinned the British government's frustration with its ally. Had Austria, wailed Grenville, exerted itself in 1795, 'the increasing distress & difficulties of the French would before now have compelled them to accept of almost any Terms of Peace which the Allies might have been disposed to offer'. The ideology of the revolution posed no international threat without the will and means to implement it: 'Nothing is wanting but some appearance of Vigor and Concert, to ensure both for them and us, a safe and creditable Issue of the Contest.' [107] This had been the British government's stand on events in France since 1793 and was presented to the nation in *Some Remarks on the Apparent Circumstances of the War*, the pamphlet written by Auckland to prepare British minds for the public declaration on 8 December that the ministry was ready to make peace with France. Auckland's *Remarks* were a literal paraphrase of Grenville's dispatch to Morton Eden on 23 September.

Pitt had to confront a Parliament whose support for the war was by no means guaranteed. 'Our Session here was the most unpleasant I ever remember,' reminisced Mornington in July; 'more ill temper of all sorts floating in the House of Commons & less cordiality & union amongst those who used to have one Common principle of action.' [108] Pitt's uneasiness about the temper of Parliament evinced itself in queries to friends and colleagues throughout the summer. At the end of September Chatham wrote that the mood of the Commons 'must very much determine the measures to be pursued'.[109]

Although the Law of Two Thirds had been ratified and the royalist *journée* of 13 *vendémiaire* (5 October) ended in failure, the British government remained convinced that France would sue for peace. Pitt, noted Wilberforce, 'could almost calculate the time at which their resources would be exhausted'. Monneron arrived on 6 October and departed on the 19th without communicating any special messages from the Convention.[110] No peace overture was going to come from France before the Directory was established. In mid-October the Bourbons were told that Britain would do no more than fund and equip the royalists in 1796. Windham protested in vain. On 10 November a Russian request for the recognition of Louis XVIII as King of France was refused, on which date Grenville wrote to Whitworth that the 1795 constitution, 'altho' liable to many objections, is unquestionably less dangerous in its principles than the former revolutionary Government that preceded it'.[111] This in itself was not enough to make His Majesty's Government treat for peace. If the directors were 'men of moderate principles, really desirous of restoring Peace to their country as the only mode of terminating its distractions and calamities', negotiation was possible.

The Austrians, finally freed from Poland, were quite prepared to turn to France, and the British peace proposals met with firm refusals. Jourdan's attempt to invade Germany was repulsed in September and Pichegru was defeated at Mannheim on 19 October. On 11 November 'Govt. received the account of the Austrians having driven the French back across the Rhine'.[112] By the end of the month the Palatinate had been retaken. A swift victory now looked possible. After consolidating its political position at home, the British government decided to take the initiative abroad. On 22 December Grenville wrote to Vienna and St Petersburg. The Russian government's subsidy project of 1794 was resurrected; Britain, declared Grenville, was now prepared to pay '£1m Sterling for 55,000 men' to serve in the Rhineland. Austria was congratulated on the recent victories of its army and exhorted to follow them up. Grenville tried to incite eastern competition for British gold. The Russians were told that the fate of the Austrian loan for 1796 was doubtful and the Austrians were given lavish details of the proposed Russian subsidy.[113] Grenville notified Eden that Britain would initiate peace negotiations in 1796 if no overtures were received from France. The British government was not so sure that its French counterpart would come begging for peace: 'the Nomination both to the Directory and to the Ministry, seem to make it much less likely than it had before appeared, that the present Government of France will apply themselves with good faith, to the Restoration of Peace.'[114]

By 'men of moderate principles', Grenville had meant constitutional monarchists. The new directorial 'Cabinet' was, nevertheless, staffed with moderates. Aubert-Dubayt (War) and Truguet (Navy) had been imprisoned under the Great Terror, as had Foreign Minister Delacroix. Faipoult (Finance) had lain low during Robespierre's reign. Benézech (Interior) and Douai (Justice) were gifted administrators of *modéré* principles. The five directors were more objectionable. All of them had served on either the Committee of Public Safety or the Committee of General Security: Carnot, the 'organizer of victory', and Barras, responsible with his friend Bonaparte for putting down the 13 *vendémiaire* rising, were particularly offensive from a British perspective.

The Austrians learned that the peace terms to be demanded by Britain were an amnesty for *émigrés*, colonial compensation for Britain, the restoration of an enlarged Netherlands to Austria and the cession of Liège to a free United Provinces. Such an overture was likely to have ended in failure, but, having made the effort, Pitt argued in January 1796, Parliament would unite behind the ministry in support of the war. On 8 December Pitt told the Commons that Britain was ready to negotiate for peace. Parliament had been prepared for the statement by the King's Speech, in which it was declared that the miseries of France had swung its citizens in favour of peace. Fox was gratified and

Wilberforce was overjoyed. George III was not, and later described the declaration as a measure 'well calculated to stave off any evil impression which Opposition might create in the over tender friends of Government in the House of Commons'. Pitt, however, did not wish to be forced to sue for peace by Parliament. In such a case, 'all hopes of good Terms would be at an end'.[115] Indemnification was the major issue: 'The issue of the war (though far from equal to all that might at some periods have been hoped) still would be honorable and probably advantageous.'

Towards the end of January 1796 Pitt outlined several possible outcomes to peace talks. The first posited a return to the strict *status quo ante bellum* – in which case, all British conquests would be returned to France. This was not an ideal scenario for Britain or Austria. Other options allowed France to demilitarize the United Provinces and keep all or part of the Netherlands – in which case Britain would give back selected Caribbean islands. Should France remain in possession of Luxembourg and the Netherlands, 'the Palatinate to the Elector on his ceding Bavaria to Austria', a settlement for which British consent could be bought at the cost of St Domingo or the Leeward Islands: 'If it goes to the Extent of their keeping all their Conquests (except Savoy) We must keep everything in the West Indies that We have obtained, or give back Guadeloupe only they ceding all the rest.'[116] In short, the more Britain acquired in the West Indies, the better its status would be at the peace table: 'No idea of peace before another campaign,' Wilberforce noted after an interview with Pitt on 27 December 1795.[117] None of these settlements was ideal, but they do indicate that Pitt was making a real effort to consider a secure and lasting peace. His plans were flawed from the outset by long-standing illusions about the strength and intentions of the enemy.

Policy Reviewed

By 1792 Pitt was convinced that France had been removed from the ranks of the great powers by its own revolution. As a verdict on European diplomacy from 1787 to 1791, this was accurate but, as a judgement on France as a military power, it was misguided. In dismissing France as a fiscal and military state, Pitt had not made allowance for the natural resources on which the power of the *ancien régime* had been based. Throughout the 1790s the ministry was to concentrate on short-term strategies for success, underestimate the strength of the enemy and give insufficient attention to the priorities of Britain's allies.

By June 1793, with the republican armies in disarray and Pitt's predictions of French collapse seemingly half-confirmed, the British government was determined to cripple its age-old enemy on the Continent and in the colonies. Having imposed some control over the first allied campaign of 1793, the Pitt ministry assumed that the former objective was shared by its allies. The possibility that Austria and Prussia might be in favour of a strong France to counterbalance England never crossed the Cabinet's collective mind. The British government, knowing that its Austrian and Prussian counterparts shared a coalition-wide contempt for republican France as a military power, could only see the departures of Frederick William II and Francis II for Poland as manifestations of petty jealousy and self-aggrandizement. The long-term diplomatic and strategic implications of the French Revolution in eastern Europe were of little importance to British strategists. By the end of 1795 the Pitt ministry, having launched two grand campaigns that began to fail before they were really underway, realized that Britain's control over its allies was an illusion. Membership of the First Coalition had been a sobering experience and in December 1794 Grenville told the Russians that Britain was not anxious to participate in another European war.

From October 1794 Pitt saw the West Indies as an escape route. He never enjoyed war, for too much of it was unpredictable and unknown. He viewed peace in January 1796 with mingled relief and regret. The longing with which Pitt sought an end to an inconclusive, expensive and frustrating conflict was tempered by a hankering after lost opportunities. The acquisition of colonial bargaining counters to be exchanged at the peace table was a time-honoured British strategy, and Pitt's commitment to the maintenance of a 'balance of power' in Europe was strong enough for him to sacrifice everything in the West and East Indies. Britain's commitment to continental warfare had been impressive, though Pitt had not often seen the First Republic as his worst enemy. In 1793 Britain was at war with the French army, not, as Pitt tried to make clear in the ministry's public statements, the French government, whatever that might become. By 1794 Britain was at war with both, a development that had arisen from ministerial frustration with allied disunity and enemy anarchy. The former was always more worrying to Pitt than the latter, and, by January 1796, he was so disillusioned with Austria that he was not working too assiduously to achieve a status quo peace. A United Provinces free from the French army was the one compulsory stipulation. Everything else, including the Netherlands, was negotiable, though Pitt would have preferred to keep at least part of this in Austrian hands.

War, according to Pitt's schedule of revolution, would only weaken an already feeble France, which he did not see as having been the aggressor up to 1794. In 1792 France had gone to war in defence of its revolution. Throughout 1793 the republic was fighting for survival at home and abroad. The French victories of 1794 were pyrrhic, for they only hastened the downfall of *gouvernement révolutionnaire*. *Thermidor* did not come as a surprise to the British government, which was so convinced that France had been devastated by war and revolution that in 1796, when Lord Malmesbury was sent to open peace talks with the Directory, he wrote home from Paris that the spirit of a nation had been crushed by the revolution.[118] The Malmesbury mission was an eye-opener in other respects. From 1793 onwards Pitt expected France to come to the peace table as a supplicant seeking recognition and acceptance from the rest of Europe. When Malmesbury discovered at Lisle not only that the 'one and indivisible republic' was a genuine entity in the minds of the directors, but that their concept of diplomacy was radically different from that of the old European powers, Pitt finally began to realize that the maxims of traditional foreign policy were inapplicable to the nation that France had become.

Notes

1. *Dropmore*, ii, Bland Burges to Grenville, 30 September 1793, p. 430.
2. *PR*, xxxvii, 21 January 1794, pp. 174–82.
3. *PH*, xxxi, 17 April 1794, cols 414–18.
4. Fox Mem., ii, Fox to Holland, 25 April 1794, p. 71.
5. Burke Correspondence,vii, Pitt to Burke, 11 April [1794], p. 537; J. Holland Rose, *Pitt and Napoleon: Essays and Letters* (1912), Pitt to Portland, 8 April 1794, p. 249; L. Melville (ed.), *The Windham Papers* (2 vols, 1913), ii, Portland to Windham, 16 April 1794, pp. 212–13.
6. Outgoing dispatches reveal dismay, but not panic at the end of May: FO 64/29, 6, Grenville (composed jointly with Pitt) to Rose, 30 May 1794; *Dropmore*, ii, Grenville to Malmesbury, 5 June 1794, p. 566; U1590 S5 03/13, Malmesbury to Pitt, 2 June 1794.
7. FO 64/34, 41, Malmesbury to Grenville, 11 June 1794.
8. Auckland Correspondence, iii, Pitt to Auckland, 30 June 1794, p. 218; *Dropmore*, ii, Pitt to Grenville, 29 June 1794, p. 592.
9. PRO 30/8/195, 'Flemish Campaign', 29 June 1794, fo. 35.
10. NMM ELL 121, Dundas to Elliot, 11 July 1794; Rose Diaries, i, Rose to Pretyman, 14 July 1794, pp. 193–5.
11. M. Duffy, 'British war policy and the Austrian alliance, 1793–1801', D.Phil. thesis (Oxford: 1971), pp. 94–100; FO 64/34, 25, Grenville to Malmesbury, 1 July 1794.
12. U1590 S5 02/4, Cornwallis to Pitt, 2 July 1794.
13. PRO 30/8/195, 'Austria and the War', [July 1794], fos 18–25.
14. BL Add MS 58906, Pitt to Grenville, [1–4] July 1794, fo. 52; the acquisition of additional Austrian troops had been under consideration since early July.
15. PRO 30/8/195, 'Austria and the War', fos 18–19; *Dropmore*, ii, Minute of Mr. Pitt in Reference to Military Operations against France, 15 July 1794, pp. 599–600.

16. *Court and Cabinets*, ii, Grenville to Buckingham, 19 July 1794, pp. 258–9.

17. FO 64/34, 26, Grenville to Malmesbury, 19 August 1794; Malmesbury Diaries, iii, Portland to Malmesbury, 23 July 1794, p. 124.

18. PRO 30/8/195, 'Note of a Conversation with the Vicomte de Sandrouin on the Austrian Loan', 25 July 1794, fos 42–7; U1590 S5 09/29, 'July 10, 1794', budget notes incorporating a £3m. loan for Austria.

19. FO 7/38, 1, Grenville to Spencer and T. Grenville, 19 July 1794.

20. For the conference with Starhemberg, see FO 7/38, 4, Grenville to Spencer and T. Grenville, 20 August 1794.

21. Duffy, 'The Austrian alliance', p. 120; *Dropmore*, ii, Grenville to St Helens, 5 August 1794, p. 610; C. Ross (ed.), *The Correspondence of Charles, 1st Marquis Cornwallis* (3 vols, 1859), ii, Pitt to Cornwallis, 24 August 1794, p. 258; FO 7/38, 5, Grenville to Spencer and T. Grenville, 29 August 1794.

22. The first instalment was issued on 30 August: BL MS G15, Pitt to Spencer, August 1794. Pitt felt that the prospect of Austrian succour 'fully justifies every pecuniary sacrifice that is necessary': *Court and Cabinets*, ii, Grenville to T. Grenville, 29 August 1794, pp. 275–6.

23. T. Blanning, 'The French Revolution and Europe', in C. Lucas (ed.), *Rewriting the French Revolution* (Oxford: 1991), pp. 189–90; P. Schroeder, *The Transformation of European Politics* (Oxford: 1994), pp. 144–7.

24. FO 7/38, 3, Spencer and T. Grenville to Grenville, 12 August 1794; *Court and Cabinets*, ii, T. Grenville to Grenville, 1 September 1794, pp. 288–9.

25. FO 7/38, 5, Grenville to Spencer and T. Grenville, 29 August 1794.

26. *Windham Papers*, ii, Pitt to Windham, 10 September 1794, pp. 231–3.

27. FO 7/38, 7, Grenville to Spencer and T. Grenville, 14 September 1794; *Dropmore*, ii, Grenville to George III, 13 September 1794, p. 629.

28. M. Hutt, *Chouannerie and Counter Revolution* (2 vols, Cambridge: 1983), pp. 128–31; BL Add MS 37844, Pitt to Windham, 19 September 1794, fos 52–3: 'The first Question that occurs is whether it is yet possible to form any effectual Concert with the Austrian Army, which will be adhered to and acted upon for the rest of this Campaign; and whether upon that supposition a joint Movement may be made in order to dislodge the Enemy before they can succeed in making themselves Masters of any of the Fortresses'; *Court and Cabinets*, ii, Grenville to T. Grenville, 15 September 1794, pp. 301–2.

29. *Court and Cabinets*, ii, Grenville to T. Grenville, 15 September 1794, p. 301.

30. P. Stanhope, *Life of the Right Hon. William Pitt* (3 vols, 1861–2), ii, Pitt to Camden, 24 September 1794, pp. 259–60; BL Add MS 37884, Pitt to Windham, 25 September 1794, fo. 68. On 25 September Grenville threatened to break off the 1793 Anglo-Austrian alliance unless the Austrian army moved to defend the United Provinces.

31. PRO 30/8/157, Dundas to Pitt, 24 September 1794, fos 168–72; BL Add MS 37844, Pitt to Windham, 25 September 1794, fos 70–4.

32. *Windham Papers*, ii, Pitt to Windham, 21 September. 1794, p. 246.

33. *Dropmore*, ii, Grenville to St Helens, 7 August 1794, pp. 612–13; NMM ELL 121, Dundas to Elliot, 21 October 1794. British attempts were made

to solicit individual subsidized contributions from the German states, but such efforts were fruitless.

34. *Dropmore*, ii, Cabinet Minute, 18 November 1794, p. 646. Grenville dreaded the French occupation of Holland: FO 37/54, 56, Grenville to St Helens, 21 November 1794.

35. Clements MSS, Dundas Papers, Pitt to Dundas, 11 October 1794.

36. M. Duffy, *Soldiers, Sugar and Seapower* (Oxford: 1986), pp. 89–115.

37. BL Add MS 58915, Dundas to Grenville, 16 November 1794, fo. 177.

38. FO 7/38, 8 and 9, Spencer to Grenville, 22 September and 1 October 1794; *Dropmore*, ii, T. Grenville to Grenville, 1 October 1794, p. 636.

39. *Dropmore*, ii, George III to Grenville, 1 December 1794, pp. 648–9.

40. FO 7/39, 1, Grenville to Morton Eden, 26 November 1794.

41. FO 7/37, Grenville memo of conference with Starhemberg, 11 November 1794; J. Ehrman, *The Reluctant Transition* (1983), pp. 519–20.

42. Canning MS, 29 dii, Diary, [25 December] 1794.

43. *Life of Wilberforce*, ii, Wilberforce to Bankes, December 1794, p. 67; *PR*, xl, 30 December 1794, Wilberforce: pp. 27–37, Pitt: 45–56.

44. U1590 S5 04/11, Wilberforce to E. Eliot, [22 December 1794].

45. PRO 30/8/170, Mitford to Pitt, 25 January 1795, fos 158–61.

46. *Dropmore*, iii, Grenville to Pitt, 21 January 1795, p. 11; Canning MS, 29 dii, 24 January 1795.

47. *PR*, xl, 25 January 1795, pp. 323–9.

48. *Dropmore*, ii, Cabinet Minute, 15 November 1794, p. 646; Canning MS, 29 dii, Diary, 25 December 1795, fo. 88; Rose Diaries, i, Pitt to Rose, 26 December 1794, p. 192; *LCG III*, ii, George III to Pitt, 14 January 1795, p. 294.

49. FO 65/27, 17, Grenville to Whitworth, 5 August 1794.

50. For the subsidy offer, see FO 65/26, 5, Grenville to Whitworth, 17 January 1794.

51. FO 65/27, 16, Grenville to Whitworth, 5 August 1794; BL Add MS 58906, Pitt to Grenville, [1–4 August] 1794, fo. 58.

52. FO 65/28, 49, Whitworth to Grenville, 19 September 1794.

53. FO 7/39, 1, Morton Eden to Grenville, 6 December 1794. In the original bid, 200,000 men were requested for Flanders and an additional 60,000 to serve in Italy. Thugut's amended offer placed 160,000 on the Flanders front and 40,000 in Italy: Duffy, 'The Austrian alliance', pp. 146–50.

54. FO 7/40, 6, Grenville to Morton Eden, 13 January 1795.

55. *Dropmore*, iii, Pitt to Grenville, 20 February 1795, p. 10; FO 7/40, 10, Grenville to Morton Eden, 13 January 1795.

56. CUL 6958/9, 1661, Cabinet Minute by Pitt, 1 March 1795: Dundas, Windham, Portland, Loughborough and Cornwallis sided with Pitt; Chatham Hawkesbury, Mansfield and Spencer supported Grenville.

57. *Dropmore*, iii, Pitt to Grenville, 28 February 1795, p. 25; BL Add MS 58906, Pitt to Grenville, [2] March 1795, fos 67–8; PRO 30/8/339, Grenville's memo on the Prussian Alliance, [March] 1795, fos 203–12.

58. The 7.5% rate was deceptive, for, due to the operation of compound interest, the Austrian government would pay proportionately less as the stock was redeemed: Duffy, 'The Austrian alliance', p. 149, n. 1.

59. *PH*, xxxi, debate on the Budget, 28 February 1795, cols 1313–14; see Duffy, 'The Austrian alliance', p. 150, n. 1, for interest calculations on the Austrian loan.

60. FO 7/37, Cabinet Minute, 14 November 1794. Eden recorded Austrian suspicions of Prussian interference: FO 7/39, 7, Morton Eden to Grenville, 22 December 1794; Grenville was not blind to this point and held that Russia would keep Prussian malice against Austria in check: FO 65/29, 4, Grenville to Whitworth, 9 March 1795.

61. *LCG III*, ii, George III to Pitt, 2 March 1795, p. 309.

62. CUL 6958/9, 1665, note by Pitt, 2 March 1795; *Dropmore*, iii, Pitt to Grenville, 3 March 1795, p. 31.

63. Mrs Henry Baring (ed.), *The Diary of the Right Hon. William Windham 1784–1810* (1866), 10 March 1795, p. 435.

64. FO 65/29, 4, Grenville to Whitworth, 9 March 1795.

65. *LCG III*, ii, Cabinet Minute, 8 April 1795, pp. 330–1; FO 64/37, 7, H. Spencer to Grenville, 23 February 1795; PRO 30/8/104, George III to Pitt, 29 March 1795, fo. 13.

66. *Dropmore*, iii, Grenville to George III, 8 April 1794, p. 30, and reply; *LCG III*, ii, pp. 321–3. I have largely followed Duffy's account of the dispute: 'Pitt, Grenville and the control of British foreign policy in the 1790s', in J. Black (ed.), *Knights Errant and True Englishmen* (Edinburgh: 1989), pp. 159–62; KAO U840 C1 90A/1, Pitt to Camden, April 1795; PRO 30/8/112, Pitt to Lady Chatham, 20 April 1795, fos 464–5.

67. FO 7/41, Grenville to Morton Eden, 17 April 1795.

68. *Ibid.*, 14, Grenville to Morton Eden, 13 February 1795.

69. *Dropmore*, ii, Grenville to George III, 5 October 1794, pp. 637–8; HRO 38M 49/1/16,1, Grenville to Wickham, 15 October 1794; HRO 38M 49/1/15,1, Grenville to Wickham, 10 December 1794.

70. H. Mitchell, *The Underground War against Revolutionary France* (Manchester: 1965), pp. 41–6; G. Lewis, 'Political brigandage and popular disaffection in the south of France 1795–1804', in C. Lucas (ed.), *Beyond the Terror: Essays in French Regional and Social History 1794–1815* (Cambridge: 1983), pp. 199–201; E. Sparrow, 'The Alien Office, 1792–1802', *HJ* 33 (1990), pp. 367–70; HRO 38M 49/1/20, 67, Wickham to Grenville, 22 May 1795.

71. FO 7/41, 34, Grenville to Morton Eden, 15 May 1795, and 'Secret', Morton Eden to J. Trevor, 11 May 1795.

72. Wickham Papers, i, Grenville to Wickham, 8 June 1795, pp. 75–78.

73. FO 7/41, 38, Grenville to Morton Eden, 18 June 1795.

74. U840 C1 23/4, Pitt to Camden, 28 June 1795.

75. J. Corbett (ed.), *The Private Papers of George, Second Earl Spencer, 1794–1801* (2 vols, 1913), i, Warren to Spencer, 8 July 1795, p. 81.

76. FO 7/41, 40, Grenville to Morton Eden, 10 July 1795, for demands for Austrian movement. For replacement of Clerfayt (the first of several dispatches), see FO 7/42, Grenville to Morton Eden, 22 July 1795.

77. *Dropmore*, iii, Pitt to Grenville, 24 July [1795], p. 604.

78. Rumours of a Spanish peace start in FO 72/35, 63, F. J. Jackson to Grenville, 10 December 1794; FO 72/36, 10, F. J. Jackson to Grenville, 20 March 1795.

79. Stanhope, *Life of Pitt*, ii, Pitt to Chatham, 8 August 1795, p. 349.
80. CUL 6958/9, 1784, Moira to Pitt, 30 July 1795. It was proposed that Moira be sent to St Domingo: Holland-Rose, *Pitt and Napoleon*, Pitt to Portland, 6 August 1795, p. 253.
81. Stanhope, *Life of Pitt*, ii, Pitt to Chatham, 8 August 1795, p. 349.
82. Duffy, *Soldiers, Sugar and Seapower*, pp. 151–2.
83. Rylands MS 907, Dundas to Pitt, 30 June 1795, fo. 8; Dundas to Pitt, 5 July 1795, fo. 9.
84. BL Add MS 59306, Cabinet Minute, 14 August 1795; *LCG III*, ii, Dundas to George III, 15 August 1795, pp. 380–1.
85. HO 30/1, Dundas to Williamson, 17 April 1795, fos 9–10. Local commanders had been warned to exercise 'the greatest caution and circumspection' in selecting both officers and men. See Ehrman, *The Reluctant Transition*, pp. 359–61 and 564–66.
86. *PH*, xxxi, debate on the abolition of the slave trade, 26 February 1795, cols 1342–3.
87. Wickham Papers, i, Grenville to Wickham, 24 July 1795, pp. 125–6.
88. *Ibid.*, Wickham to Grenville, 8 August 1795, pp. 142–9; Grenville to Wickham, 12 August 1795, pp. 152–3.
89. *Dropmore*, iii, Buckingham to Grenville, 21 August 1795, pp. 103–4.
90. Wickham Papers, i, Macartney to Wickham, 15 October 1795, pp. 181–2.
91. FO 7/42, 63, Grenville to Morton Eden, 19 September 1795.
92. Wickham Papers, i, Grenville to Wickham, 8 September 1795, p. 156.
93. FO 7/41, 48, Morton Eden to Grenville, 23 April 1795.
94. PRO 30/8/104, George III to Dundas, 9 September 1795, fo. 46; BL MS G15, Dundas to Spencer, 10 September 1795; *LCG III*, ii, Dundas to George III, 8 September 1795, p. 400.
95. FO 65/30, 12, Grenville to Whitworth, 23 June 1795; BL Add MS 58915, Dundas to Grenville, 28 August 1795, fos 196–7.
96. FO 65/31, 24, Grenville to Whitworth, 19 September 1795. The Baltic patrol was not much respected, for the Russian navy did not intercept all neutral shipping; Foreign Office memos were repeatedly sent to Whitworth and to Voronzov, with little effect: FO 65/30, 22, Grenville to Whitworth, 10 September 1795; BL Add MS 58915, Dundas to Grenville, 17 August 1795, fos 189–90.
97. PRO 30/8/110, Auckland to Pitt, 17 September 1795, fos 269–71.
98. J. Godechot, *The Counter Revolution* (English edn, 1972), pp. 260–1.
99. H. Mitchell, 'Francis Drake and the Comte d'Antraigues: a study of the Dropmore Bulletins 1793–1796', *BIHR* 29 (1956), pp. 123–44.
100. Sparrow, 'The Alien Office', pp. 369–71; *Dropmore*, iii, Pitt to Grenville, 29 August 1795, p. 129; HRO 39M 49/1/67, 2, extract from J. d'André to Wickham, [September] 1795.
101. Rose Diaries, i, Pitt to Rose, 11 September 1795, p. 202.
102. Wickham Papers, i, Grenville to Wickham, 8 September 1795, pp. 156–8.
103. Holland Rose, *Pitt and Napoleon*, Pitt to Portland, 20 September 1795, p. 254.
104. PRO 30/8/197, 'Thoughts on the War', 19 September [1795], fos 3–5.

105. Holland Rose, *Pitt and Napoleon*, Pitt to Portland, 20 September 1795, p. 254.
106. FO 7/42, 64, Grenville to Morton Eden, 23 September 1795; FO 7/43, 66, Grenville to Morton Eden, 9 October 1795; *Dropmore*, iii, Grenville to Morton Eden, 10 October 1795, p. 137.
107. *Life of Wilberforce*, ii, Diary, [June] 1795, pp. 91–2; FO 65/32, 68, Grenville to Whitworth, 10 October 1795; BL MS G15, Pitt to Spencer, 31 October 1795; PRO 30/8/195, 'Expenses of France since the Revolution [1795]', fos 57–8; Schofield, 'British politicians and French arms', *History* 78 (1993), pp. 197–8.
108. U840 C1 21/1, Mornington to Camden, 22 July 1795.
109. PRO 30/8/122, Chatham to Pitt, 25 September 1795, fos 125–6.
110. *Life of Wilberforce*, ii, Diary, [June] 1795; Stanhope, *Life of Pitt*, ii, Pitt to Addington, 4 October 1795, p. 328; HO 1/3, 53–78, on Monneron's mission; DRO 152M 1795/OZ 16, Hatsell to Addington, 9 October 1795.
111. FO 65/32, 69, Grenville to Whitworth, 10 November 1795.
112. C. Abbot (ed.), *The Diary and Correspondence of Charles Abbot, Lord Colchester* (3 vols, 1861), i, Diary, 11 November 1795, p. 6.
113. FO 65/32, 71, Grenville to Whitworth, 22 December 1795; FO 7/43, 73, Grenville to Morton Eden, 22 December 1795.
114. FO 7/43, 68, Grenville to Morton Eden, 17 November 1795.
115. Holland Rose, *Pitt and Napoleon*, George III to Pitt, 27 January 1796, pp. 237–8; Stanhope, *Life of Pitt*, ii, Pitt to George III, 29 January 1796, p. xxx.
116. U1590 S5 09/27, January [1796], peace with France; *Dropmore*, iii, Pitt to Grenville, 31 January 1796, p. 166.
117. *Life of Wilberforce*, ii, Diary, 27 December 1795, p. 136.
118. Malmesbury Diaries, iii, Malmesbury to Grenville, 24 October 1796, pp. 270–2.

Chapter 8

Radicalism Suppressed, July 1794– December 1795

Pitt went into the summer of 1794 determined to get to the bottom of an international Jacobin conspiracy to subvert the British government, if not its constitution. The ministry was so convinced that a radical rising was in contemplation that in May 1794 the Home Office and Treasury solicitors embarked on a witch-hunt for the British conspirators and their French paymasters. By so doing, the government completed the last stages of its public metamorphosis from aloof spectator of the revolution to zealous defender of the conservative status quo. This transformation was, as the Portland Whigs discovered in the realms of foreign and military policy, no more than skin-deep. Portland, Burke and Windham were appalled by their colleagues' readiness to make peace with republican France at the end of 1795.

At home, Pitt appeared to be set on a policy of intolerance and repression. In the state trials of November 1794 the government had been intent on hanging the leaders of the metropolitan radical societies and, after it had failed to do so, introduced the infamous 'Two Acts of 1795' which redefined treason in accordance with a constitutional doctrine that placed Crown, Cabinet and Commons above criticism. Calls for the removal of the king's 'evil counsellors' could never have been made again had the legislation been placed on the statute book permanently. The Seditious Meetings Act was, however, enacted for three years in the first instance, while the Treasonable Practices Act was to expire at the end of the Parliament following George III's death. Nobody expected the king to survive much beyond the end of the century that had produced him. Both acts were produced in response to a specific public order crisis at the end of 1795 in which dearth and discontent had created a mass audience seemingly ripe for exploitation by disaffected popular radicals.

The British government found its ideas challenged in 1795 not by the French Revolution, but by the hardships of the French war. When, in the face of two deficient harvests, the British constitution was no longer seen as producing the polite and commercial prosperity in which Pitt had gloried for a decade, the Cabinet was forced to consider whether it could exercise its authority in the redistribution of food. The ministry's response to scarcity in 1795 was hesitant because the government's limited powers to control supply and demand were matched – in the case of some ministers, exceeded – by its reluctance to do so. The official disputes over the wisdom and legality of intervention in the provisions market formed part of a greater debate about the maintenance of a proper balance between liberty and control.[1] By the end of 1795, with a starving and riotous populace on its hands, the Pitt ministry resorted once more to appeals rather than injunctions to maximize the available supply of provisions. By introducing limited and short-term expedients to deal with the food crisis, it was only to defer the problem of scarcity until the next crisis.

Order and Disorder

When the Duke of Portland agreed in principle to join forces with Pitt at the end of May 1794, the government's political position was deceptively strong. The ministry had succeeded in acquiring more than respectable majorities for the passage of the Habeas Corpus Suspension Act but its military and diplomatic policies of 1794 were fast disintegrating and Pitt was anxious to strengthen his forces at home. The 'war of principle' required a shot in the arm. The Portland Whigs were the first to acknowledge that their pretensions to moral superiority – namely, the conduct of an ideological war – involved the acceptance of responsibility for its setbacks and failures: 'The accession of a great mass of reputation taken out of a state of perilous neutrality, and brought to the decided support of the Crown, and an actual responsibility of measures rendered questionable by very great misfortunes, were the advantages which Mr. Pitt derived from the coalition.'[2] The truth was that the Portland Whigs were needed as much as they were wanted. This explains Pitt's generosity in the distribution of loaves and fishes. The Portland Whigs took no less than six posts in a thirteen-member Cabinet. Pitt's supporters were amazed; many expressed 'mortification and unease' that they had been passed over for promotion. Doubts were voiced about the competence of the Portland Whigs: 'The only considerable talents gained are Windham's,' remarked Rose.[3] Pitt's personal friends were also bewildered. As Wilberforce put it: 'Pitt need not have let them in (I will not say take them in) ... in such full force. I must confess all this is not very pleasant to me.'[4]

The distribution of posts to the Portland Whigs confirms that they had not been admitted on equal terms. Several Cabinet shuffles were to take place before the new recruits were satisfactorily settled but the chief command posts remained in trusted hands. Mansfield, as Lord

President of the Council, possessed no real responsibilities; Spencer, a landsman at the Admiralty, was putty in the hands of his naval advisers; Fitzwilliam insisted upon appointment to Ireland; Portland took the Home Office; and Windham, as Secretary at War, was directly responsible to Pitt, Dundas and Grenville. Pitt wanted the conservative Whigs to share the burden of running the war but their power to influence it was strictly limited.

A decade of Opposition animosity towards Pitt did not disappear overnight. A month passed before the Portland Whigs agreed to take office. By 10 June they had no reservations about Pitt's stand against sedition and treason, but they were still suspicious about the government's war policy. Portland insisted upon receiving an explicit declaration in favour of a monarchical restoration in France before consenting to join the ministry: 'The Basis and *sine qua non* condition must be the Re-establishment of Order and Good Government in France ... in other words, the Restoration of the French Monarchy, and Restitution of Property, or, at least a Government of which Property forms the basis.'[5] Pitt endorsed these objectives in theory but baulked at the recognition of Provence as Regent, which had also been demanded by Portland.[6] The Portland Whigs had no other stipulations to make except to call for reform in the government of Ireland, an issue which will not be dealt with here.

Pitt had to exercise all his tact in dealing with the new recruits. During the coalition negotiations Portland had expressed an interest in taking on the War Department. Pitt was horrified: 'I feel it impossible to venture the experiment of leaving the War Dept. in the Duke's hands,' he wrote. So close were Pitt and Dundas that the former described every act of the latter as 'being as *much* mine as *his*'. If, claimed Pitt, 'all the details of the war ... were to be settled by communication with a person both new to me and *to others*, I am sure the business could not go on for a week.'[7] Pitt was unwilling to introduce an inexperienced minister to so important and sensitive a department, whose relations with the armed services were already acrimonious.[8] He was also uneasy about the potential manifestation of Portland's anti-Jacobinism in British military policy. As diplomacy was dictated to some extent by strategic considerations, Pitt asked Grenville to leave the Foreign Office. Grenville may have been praying for such a release because he offered to resign in October 1794.[9] As his loss would have been a severe blow to the ministry, Pitt looked for another solution. Determined to keep Dundas at all costs, he decided to revive the third Secretary of State's office that had existed before the passage of Burke's Establishment Act of 1782.[10] Portland initially wanted to keep the colonies within his portfolio, but, when told that the conduct of the war in the West Indies would be jeopardized by so awkward a division of responsibilities, he agreed to be content with the management of law and order. He refused the Foreign Office and Grenville remained at his post.[11] At this point Dundas, afraid that the division of office represented a demotion in status within the new Cabinet, threatened to resign. Pitt pleaded with him to reconsider. 'I shall give up all hope of carrying on the Business with comfort and be really completely heartbroken if you adhere to your Resolution.' A mollified Dundas agreed to become the Secretary of State for War and the Colonies.[12]

Portland's acceptance of the Home Office was providential, if not premeditated, for the government could not have found more zealous an advocate of a crack-down on radicalism. Portland's influence at the Home Office was not really felt until the end of August, by which time the government had finished its investigation of the London radical clubs. The second report of the Commons Secret Committee, published on 6 June, presented the nation with further particulars of the radical plot to overthrow the government of Britain. This, like the first report, was based largely on official presuppositions rather than hard evidence and drew attention to the purchase and distribution of arms in London and the north. The only traitor to be caught during the summer of 1794 was Robert Watt, whose scheme to storm Edinburgh Castle was the product of a deranged mind. News of this plot was greeted with derision by the Foxites, who refused to believe that 'eighteen pike-heads, ten battle axes and twenty blades unfinished' amounted to a national conspiracy.[13] The Home Office, ignoring such criticisms, believed that its spies had successfully infiltrated the 'Military Institutions' supposed to exist in the LCS. In places, the Secret Committee's account drew upon reports from informers pertaining to the covert manufacture and distribution of arms and uniforms. Even the reorganization of LCS membership registration procedures, which had started to take place during the spring of 1794, were interpreted in a paramilitary context.[14]

The ministry's study of Home Office reports from spies suggested that the so-called armed rising had been successfully nipped in the bud. The distribution of arms and equipment had barely begun. The date on which the rebellion was to have started could not be ascertained by the Privy Council or the Commons Secret Committee.[15] Here again, informers had supplied the details. At the end of January the ministry had been warned that 'in Scotland they would soon break out'; in mid-February it was notified that 'it would not happen to day, nor tomorrow, but, in all probability in *Six Months*'.[16] In justification of the ministry's actions, the Secret Committee dwelt at length on the history of London-based connections with provincial radicals: 'It appears that this business of Jacobinism was connected with all the seditious clubs in Scotland and Ireland. It was taken at the right time and is no longer dangerous.'[17] Although the Home Office had not discovered any documents linking the British radicals to French agents, the Secret Committee equated a community of spirit with a confederacy of purpose. The Privy Council had been enlightened thus by a report from a spy: 'There was a communication & a Correspondence between some of the Members of the French National Convention, & the leading Members of the Conventions in England, Scotland and Ireland.'[18] The Secret Committee could not elaborate on the evils of correspondence that it did not possess, but government spies, who continued to operate within the metropolitan radical organizations, notified the Home Office that some LCS papers had escaped seizure. Pitt, confident that these would soon be tracked down, concluded that the committee had exposed 'a detestable conspiracy against our happy constitution'.[19]

The Cabinet, still convinced that British radicals had intended to rise as a diversionary exercise in aid of a French invasion, spent the rest of the summer in search of evidence that would connect the reformers with France. Unfortunately for English radicals, the French government had sent an agent to the United Irishmen. William Jackson, who had been under surveillance since passing through London on his way to Dublin in April 1794, did not receive a warm welcome from the Irish radicals, who thought that he was a member of the SCI or, worse, an English government *agent provocateur*. Jackson, not the most discreet of agents, was arrested in August after his correspondence to France had been intercepted. The London authorities, who were not particularly interested in Jackson's Irish activities, devoted their attention instead to his French and English connections – in so doing, making enquiries as far afield as Holland. The Castle was disgusted by English attitudes to Irish security.[20]

Although the Privy Council enquiry had confirmed that British popular radicals were neither numerous nor influential, a watchful eye was kept on the London reformers. At the end of May the Duke of Richmond complained that army units could not be detached for foreign service 'without essentially weakening our Home Defence'.[21] Volunteers, like their more professional military counterparts, needed time to reach the approved standards of training without which it was unwise to send regular troops abroad. Howe's 'glorious' victory over Villeneuve on 4 June 1794 was presented as the decisive battle that had freed England from the threat of invasion. Dubious an argument though this was, by 22 June a semaphore station network was in place between London and Penzance. The Cabinet was not entirely convinced that the suspension of habeas corpus had subdued the radical spirit. The LCS continued defiantly to restate its goals in the face of government persecution throughout the summer of 1794 and alarmed reports continued to come in to the Home Office from London and provincial magistrates. On 14 June news was received of radical military drills on the outskirts of London. A week later Pitt learned that the incarcerated LCS leaders were still transmitting instructions to their followers from the Tower of London.[22] Official alarm was to be aroused once more at the end of August, when London became the scene of widespread riots.

The resentment that sparked off the Crimp House riots stemmed from two sources: the London militia bill of 1794 and the press gangs. The new ballot regulations that had been contained in the bill enabled those selected for the militia to avoid service by funding a substitute, an expensive business. This was an escape clause that struck the people of London as unjust and popular rejection of the bill, combined with hatred for the varieties of impressment – an old wartime grievance – resulted in the display of violence against the 'crimps', the civilian agents who recruited and traded in militia substitutes.[23] Between 15 and 23 August London was the scene of attempts to demolish the crimps' recruiting-houses. The rapid spread of the disturbances was ascribed by alarmists to the ill will of popular radicals; Auckland and Loughborough advocated a swift recourse to the army, but Portland, supported by Dundas and Lord Amherst, was determined not to call upon professional military assistance until the situation became critical. Portland, ignoring pleas for troops from the Lord Mayor and metropolitan magistrates, acted with restraint. After order had been restored in London the new Home Secretary was praised by his predecessor: 'I feel it unfair to the Duke of Portland, to wish him in any other Situation than where he now is, for I believe he is universally acknowledged to be one of the best Magistrates that exists in the metropolis.'[24] Backbench MPs might complain about Portland's lack of experience but the Home Secretary had won the respect of his colleagues. Portland and Dundas were to work amicably together for the next seven years.

The Home and War Secretaries had proceeded with caution because they did not want to antagonize the rioters or play into the hands of the radicals, who were widely believed to be involved in the disturbances. Popular hatred of the army was great, and the appearance of troops had been known on many occasions in the eighteenth century to exacerbate a riot. Six county regiments had been moved to the environs of London in readiness for orders from the War Office but Portland, having been warned by local JPs that an unnecessary show of force would encourage the radicals to play upon the anger of the mob, left the soldiers in peace:

It would be very desireable that Mobs of this description should be dispersed without Military Interference for should the Soldier and the Mob come to blows, it is to be feared that Mischief would soon extend itself, especially if there are evil disposed Persons ready to make use of the prejudices and passions of the Common People to serve their own Purposes.[25]

Radical pamphlets and handbills had been picked up by JPs on the streets of riot-ridden parishes. While it is highly unlikely that these had been produced by the LCS, an oft-professed enemy of violence, magistrates were quick to declare that the violence of the mob had been incited 'by the leaders of the Seditious Societies, whose views extend very far beyond the Recruiting Houses'. Patrick Colquhoun, one of the Worship Street police magistrates, wanted ballad singers and hawkers to be detained and questioned, for 'it is believed they they are made use of for the purpose of circulating Inflammatory and Seditious Writings'.[26] The radical societies, claimed Colquhoun, were attempting to redirect the rage of the mob from the crimps to the magistrates. This, he argued, was 'the most direct means of introducing that Anarchy and Confusion which they wish to establish'. Two men were later charged and sentenced for distributing handbills during the Crimp House riots, but neither they, nor the twenty-three individuals committed for trial as a result of their participation in the riots, were identified as members of the LCS.[27]

Portland had not been able to put down the Crimp House riots without assistance. The creation of special constables for troubled London parishes had long been an emergency measure by which the ranks of the metropolitan police could be swelled. What was unusual about Portland's recourse to this expedient in August 1794 was the Home Office call for 'volunteer' special constables. The Crimp House riots occurred at a particularly bad time from the perspective of law and order. Many of the regular magistrates were on holiday and, therefore, absent from London.[28] At the suggestion of William Devaynez, one of Reeves's police office subordinates, Portland sent out a circular letter on 20 August advising all magistrates in riotous parts of the metropolis to call upon the assistance of the 'voluntary associations'.

Some – though not all – of these parochial bodies had been formed as early as November 1792 and cannot be dissociated from the public order crisis of that year. The voluntary organizations to which Devaynez referred are unlikely to have been the 'loyal' associations launched by Pitt, Grenville and Dundas in December 1792. Not much discrimination had been exercised as to the social and political background of the government's 'loyalists'; these were not the people to be entrusted with special police duties. The metropolitan associations correspond more closely to what Pitt had described in November 1792 as 'armed bodies'; these were creations of the London police magistrates. Other 'armed associations' had been formed following the passage of the Volunteer Corps Act and were to be resorted to once more during the Crimp House riots.[29]

The government's response to the anti-crimp riots of 1795 suggests that they were seen first and foremost as a general protest against the war. Portland, on whom the discovery of the radical handbills and the arrest of Jackson had made no small impression, emerged from the Crimp House riots determined to tighten up on the surveillance of radicals throughout Britain. In future popular disturbances in which a radical presence was suspected he was to commend those who took swift and decisive action.

> I very much approve of your exertions in dispersing the Rioters, and I trust that the speedy Trial and punishment of such of those who have been secured, as shall be found the most guilty, will act as a salutary example to all Persons who are unfortunately misled by the Instigations of Individuals who evidently aim at the destruction of all order and Government.[30]

At the beginning of September Portland asked William Wickham to take over the management of the Alien Office. He was instructed to ensure that the department was 'well informed of the descriptions and abodes of all foreigners'. This was a surprising step for Portland, a champion of the *émigré* cause, to have taken, but, as he put it: 'I shall not think I have fulfilled my duty to the public as I ought until I am confident & indeed fully assured that nothing has been left undone on my part which can affect our domestic security.'[31]

The government was determined to leave no stone unturned in its search for information that would shed light on the secret plans of the radicals. Throughout the summer of 1794 the coalition ministry had feared that a resurgence of radical activism would expose the inadequacies of its summer enquiries. By 1 September no evidence had been unearthed to either prove or disprove the official hypothesis that English radicals had been in collusion with the enemy over the water. The frustration and uncertainty of the ministry was to remain unresolved during the autumn of 1794.

The State Trials of 1794

The British government faced the last months of 1794 very much on the defensive. After the Crimp House riots, many Cabinet members were prepared to believe the worst of the Pop Gun plot, a far-fetched scheme by which George III was to have been murdered by a poisoned dart delivered by an air gun.[32] On 27 September the Home Office took two members of the LCS into custody following the receipt of reports from informers alerting the authorities to the existence of this pathetic conspiracy. The culprits were hauled before the Privy Council on 28 September, but, as Portland regretfully told the king, the evidence was so inconclusive that the government decided not to proceed with any prosecutions: 'The actors in it are all members of the London Corresponding Society, the name and character of which is but all too well known to your Majesty.' It was clear to the Cabinet that the popular radicals were still prepared to resort to desperate schemes. 'We must not', wrote Grenville, 'count upon the continuance of a state of domestic tranquillity which has already lasted so long beyond the period usually allotted in the course of human events.'[33]

Having been denied at least one conviction, the Pitt ministry became all the more determined to indict the leaders of the LCS and SCI for high treason. Poor though the prosecution case was, the government was also under considerable pressure to make an example of its suspects. The Portland Whigs insisted upon indictments for treason, as did some of the government's back-bench supporters, the majority of whom were prepared to uphold convictions for this offence. Pitt and Grenville were advocates of the eighteenth-century legal doctrine that severe punishment prevented crime. Neither man had ever been disposed to pardon convicted men. Grenville, as Home Secretary, had never asked George III for the free pardon of a capital convict, while Pitt once said of a 1789 case in which two convicts walked free: 'Lenity shown on this occasion can give no Foundation of Hope to those who might offend in future and will therefore in no degree interfere with the Great Grid of Punishment.'[34] For Pitt, the penal code was an instrument of social control designed to frighten off would-be offenders. The social significance of the 'bloody code' has been questioned in recent years, but there can be no doubt that the legal system of the 1790s was manipulated for the protection of property, that the death penalty was seen as a deterrent, and that trials for sedition and treason were regarded by both plaintiff and defendant as a display of élite power. Juries, however, displayed more independence of mind than one would expect, even when they were rigged.[35]

In the weeks leading up to the state trials, the government was confident that it would carry its prosecutions: 'The Spirit of Faction,' wrote Dundas, 'or I should say Sedition and Treason at home, seems both in England and Scotland to be compleatly subdued, and being so, I trust we shall be able to keep it so.'[36] When the Attorney-General, Sir John Scott, opened the case for the prosecution against Thomas Hardy on 28 October, he declared that the LCS had 'compassed' the death of the king by its schemes to stage an armed rising, call a 'General

Convention' of radical delegates and usurp the legislative powers of Parliament. This doctrine of constructive treason was not accepted by Hardy's jury, who decided in only three hours that the 1352 Statute of Treasons was framed for the protection of the king's person, not that of Pitt's government. Hardy's acquittal was followed in quick succession by that of John Horne Tooke. Having half-heartedly embarked on the trial of John Thelwall, the ministry dropped all charges against the remaining prisoners when he also was acquitted on 5 December.[37]

The government's supporters were alarmed by the acquittals and none of the legal officers involved in the trials escaped censure. Canning was disgusted by the conduct of the Chief Justice and the judge while Addington vented his disappointment on the hapless Attorney-General: 'It seems to me that sufficient strength was not laid by the Counsel for the Prosecution on the establish'd Principle that an attempt to subvert the Government is an overt act of compassing the King's death.'[38]

Unfortunately for the Pitt ministry, British legislation on treason, be it Plantagenet, Tudor, Stuart or Hanoverian, was constituted to protect executive authority as vested in the king and his family. Scott's failure to send Hardy to the gallows did not ruin his political or legal career. He left a confused account of his actions in an 'Anecdote Book' after he became Lord Chancellor, careful perusal of which reveals only that he thought he could win his case.[39] Although Scott admitted that convictions would have been easier to secure had the radicals been prosecuted for sedition, he defended the treason charges on the grounds that he 'did not wish to let down the character of the offence'.[40] This meant that the government was determined to uphold its case for the suspension of habeas corpus in May. Scott claimed that the Privy Council, not least its lawyers, had urged him to charge the radical leaders with high treason. His fellow law officers were no less dismayed by Hardy's acquittal: 'I have received a letter', remarked Addington, 'from the Solicitor General expressive of Chagrin & Surprize.'

The government case against the radical clubs, based as it was on circumstantial evidence, was easily overturned by Thomas Erskine, the Foxite counsel for the defence. The radicals, particularly Hardy and Horne Tooke, won the sympathy of the court by conducting themselves with the dignity of martyrs. Hardy's acquittal 'occasion'd a great deal of surprize and uneasiness' in government circles. By attempting to register its interpretation of high treason in the court of the King's Bench, the ministry had bound itself to respect the verdict that established a precedent at common law. When it became evident that Horne Tooke would be acquitted, the government had no choice but to abandon the state trials or suffer the establishment of not one, but several rulings at common law contradicting its doctrine of treason.[41] The ministry realized that it was obliged to play by the rules of its own jurisprudential game: 'It is of more consequence to maintain the Credit of a mild and unprejudic'd Administration than even to convict a Jacobin.'[42]

Pitt did not seem dismayed by the failure of the state trials. Canning found him 'open, free, ready to answer questions without reserve'.[43] The government had undeniably been humiliated by its failure to convict the radicals but the Cabinet could comfort itself with the fact that the suspension of habeas corpus and the state trials had dealt a severe blow to the radical cause. Windham was not the only man to describe the LCS leaders as 'acquitted felons', and the membership registers of the LCS bore testimony to the bad odour in which radical societies were held by the general public from May 1794 to June 1795. The state trials had finally established that radical agitation for reform would not be tolerated by the ministry while Britain remained at war with revolutionary France. Scott defended his eight-hour summation of the evidence at Hardy's trial with the claim that duty obliged him to lay all the government evidence before the public in order to expose the activities of the radicals. Pitt also said in retrospect that: 'When that immense mass of matter was laid open, and the real designs of these societies developed, it served to open the eyes of the unwary, to check the incautious, and to deter the timid.'[44] As an exercise in intimidation, the state trials were a success.

By the time that Hardy's case came up for trial, the government was convinced that popular radicalism was on the decline. Not only were the reform societies much less vocal than they had been since the beginning of the war, but *gouvernement révolutionnaire* was at an end in France. Robespierre had been executed on 28 July and the Reign of Terror had been dismantled over the autumn of 1794. The leaders of Thermidor had begun to move against popular politics in France. The submission of collective petitions to the National Convention had been banned on 16 October, along with the practice of reciprocal affiliation amongst French political clubs. On 13 November the Jacobin Club in Paris was closed. By 28 November Auckland could write: 'I even believe that the spirit of Jacobinism is losing ground in France.'[45] Pitt had long expected the material collapse of the republic to be accompanied by the intellectual bankruptcy of the revolution. It was in this spirit of confidence that he prepared to meet Parliament in December 1794.

Starvation and Suffering

By January 1795 the government was concerned about morale both inside and outside Parliament. The Crimp House riots had been seen as an expression of anti-war protest and a bad harvest in 1794 promised that 1795 would be a turbulent year. Food riots were an unpleasant fact of eighteenth-century life and Pitt, aware that British grain yields had been falling since the late 1780s, had been keeping an eye on the situation since 1789. At the end of 1792, faced with widespread evasion of the 1791 Corn Law, popular disturbances of uncertain origin, and corn-factor testimonials that overseas supplies of grain were non-existent, the government bought up the corn stocks on foreign ships standing in English ports and confiscated cereal cargoes bound for France.[46] Throughout 1793 foreign wheat had entered Britain at the lowest rate of duty. The sale of neutral cargoes and the purchase of foreign corn in 1794 had supplemented a crop that was high in quality but low in quantity. According to Claude Scott, the government's corn agent, if the ministry had not kept an eye upon the domestic supply of grain, there would have been 'great distress'.[47]

Scott advised the government to look first to America and the Baltic for additional corn. The European harvest had been so poor that he doubted much could be spared for export. British diplomats were nevertheless instructed to look for supplies in Prussia, Austria and Spain.[48] The ministry, unwilling to frighten the public by publicizing the extent of the corn shortage, remained mute but active. Two bills – one extending the duty-free importation of provisions, the other prohibiting the export of food from Scotland – were pushed through Parliament at the end of 1794. Corn-factors, distillers and farmers were called before the Board of Trade and the Privy Council to give evidence on supply and demand. The Lord Mayor, amongst others, suggested that distillers and hair-powder manufacturers cut down upon their use of grain. This recommendation was endorsed by the Board of Agriculture, which commissioned an investigation of the scarcity.[49]

By the beginning of March the Board of Trade, having conducted an enquiry into famine relief, had considered and rejected proposals to introduce agricultural subsidies for the domestic production of alternative foodstuffs. In February the government had learned that no succour would be forthcoming from America or the Baltic. Reluctant to antagonize vested interests in the provisions trade or to experiment with the extension of executive power to the market-place, the ministry decided to rely on its existing policies until the next harvest. From January 1795 onwards the Home Office began to receive accounts of provincial food riots. Popular radicals were not prominent in these disturbances, but magistrates reported with apprehension that local troops were sympathizing with the poor and participating in attacks upon shopkeepers. County authorities were instructed to extol the virtues of thrift and charity.

The production of mixed and inferior grain breads had been suggested to the Privy Council at the beginning of 1795 but the government, conscious of the socio-economic status of 'fine wheaten' in the working man's diet and the body of eighteenth-century dietary theory that upheld the superior nutritional value of white bread, was reluctant to regulate the diet of Britons. When asked by the Board of Trade whether the statutory introduction of coarse-grade wheaten flour would increase existing supplies of 'nutritive Corn', no less an authority than Arthur Young replied that this was a false economy: 'He had talked with Labouring people, and their Accounts had been uniform, that they could not support themselves on anything so cheap and so well as the finest bread.'[50]

The government, faced with a real shortage of grain and several theoretical solutions by which to alleviate it, was soon divided over which course to adopt. Portland, a staunch opponent of price subsidies and importation, had no objections to lowering the price of bread by adulterating its quality. Hawkesbury, the President of the Board of Trade, shrank from involvement in so contentious a debate:

> ... it is the Opinion of very intelligent Men, that more nutriment is derived from a smaller Quantity of the finer sort of Bread, than would be derived from a smaller Quantity of the Coarser Sort. Whatever may be the Truth of this Proposition, it would not be wise for Government to interfere on so uncertain a Point.[51]

Hawkesbury, hoping that the 1795 harvest would answer the ministry's prayers, told Portland not to encourage the coarse-bread advocates. The only path of action was to encourage 'the Importation of Wheat from Foreign Countries'.

Pitt, who called himself a disciple of Adam Smith, was no friend to artificial price regulation. He had authorized the official purchase of neutral cargoes but was not prepared to endorse the direct and sustained intervention of the government in the provisions market. This is not to say that Pitt was insensitive to the sufferings of the poor. On 6 May the Berkshire magistrates devised the famous Speenhamland resolutions which regulated the levels of outdoor relief in proportion to the price of bread and the number of a claimant's dependents.[52] A sliding scale of relief payments in relation to the price of bread was to figure prominently in Pitt's 1796 bill for bettering the condition of the poor. While he did not oppose schemes to lower the price of bread in the short term by charitable subscriptions, he warned Tomline that such projects would only succeed if they encouraged the poor to practise self-discipline:

> I do not recollect accurately enough the usual price of bread to judge of the reduced Rates proposed in the [County] Resolutions; but I hope you will recollect if they are fixed too low, tho' they will give temporary Relief and satisfaction, they will ultimately encrease the Mischief by preventing the Poor from narrowing their Consumption, which they ought to do in some degree, tho' certainly not in the same Proportion as those who can afford to substitute other Articles.[53]

As was so often the case during the 1790s, the Pitt ministry did not adopt coercive measures when moral pressure would suffice. Not only could an appeal for the voluntary reduction of wheat and flour consumption be defended as a 'wise precaution' rather than a 'necessity', but such tactics justified a continued state of official inertia. Many provincial requests for grain, some verging on the desperate, were refused by the government throughout the spring of 1795. At the beginning of July an Order in Council advocated the national manufacture of standard wheaten bread.[54]

The deliberations of the Privy Council Corn Committee were interrupted by acrimonious debates with the City of London. As London was the largest single market for corn, it had received a disproportionately large share of the government's scanty supplies. Metropolitan authorities nevertheless resisted every proposal to standardize the price or quality of bread. At the beginning of July the ministry's patience ran out and Londoners were told to join the nation in the practice of food substitution.[55]

The government, having restored habeas corpus in June 1795, was not expecting any trouble from the radicals: 'As for the feelings of the Country,' wrote Dundas, 'they are infinitely better than one could expect considering the price of provisions.' The LCS had, however, been recovering in strength and numbers since the spring of 1795 and, on 29 June, staged a 'Meeting in St. George's Fields of Parlimentary reformers calling out "War and Want" or "Peace and Plenty"'.[56] Attendance estimates range from 50,000 to 100,000.[57] The ministry, which still paid spies to report on the activities of the London radicals, received advance notice of the demonstration and an alarmed Portland made extensive preparations for the eruption of violence, calling upon the police magistrates, the Lord Mayor's office, the War Office and troops stationed in central London. So orderly was the St George's Fields demonstration that these precautions were unnecessary. The government could conclude that the radicals had learned their lessons.

Although there were enough riots in 1795 to suggest some degree of radical involvement to an apprehensive Cabinet, the popular disturbances of the summer were not attributed to any sinister external agency. Even Pitt, the object of personal attack in July, believed that the demonstrations were products of war weariness and social hardship. Anti-crimp riots, which had occurred sporadically since the beginning of the year, took place once more on 11 July, amidst a week of severe food-related demonstrations. On 13 July a window at No. 10 Downing Street was broken by an angry crowd shouting: 'No war, No Pitt, Cheap Bread.' To Pitt, this was not the attack of a revolutionary populace: 'I take shame in not reflecting how much a Mob is magnified by Report; but that which visited my Window with a single pebble was really so young and little versed in its Business that it hardly merited the Notice of a Newspaper.' [58] James Bland Burges was more frightened by the mob that occupied Downing Street for two days: 'it was found necessary to have a guard of constables stationed at our end of it to prevent the mob from coming any further.' As Portland and his Chief Secretary, John King, were both absent in the country, Pitt had been obliged to deal with the situation in person. Burges was outraged: 'The only people who have stood forward are Pitt, Nepean and myself. I have taken a great deal of trouble to little purpose. So has Nepean ... What has passed has merely served to do mischief by encouraging the mob and by exposing the soldiers to derision.' [59] Soldiers summoned to the scene of a riot often stood by doing nothing and were insulted by the mob. This was one of the reasons why the army hated riot duty. Pitt had called in troops, but was not using them. Burges, required to read the Riot Act to an angry crowd, was upset. His fears that the riot would escalate were groundless, however, for the Downing Street disturbances died down as swiftly as they had begun and Pitt left London on 17 July convinced that 'the disposition to disturbance which has appeared in some parts of the Town was over, at least for the present'. The Home Office, magistrates and army had been instructed to 'prevent any serious Mischief', should popular violence recur. [60]

'Busy all day writing letters about scarcity,' wrote Wilberforce on 9 July. 'This now much dreaded.' [61] The Home Office and Privy Council continued to counsel moderation in the use of flour and the distribution of alternative foodstuffs:

Their Lordships [of the Privy Council] wish to recommend that public Subscriptions should in part be applied to provide and encourage the Use of some sort of food, which may be a substitute for Wheat, rather than so far as to cheapen the price of bread, as to occasion thereby the immediate Consumption of too great a Quantity of Flour, which may produce in the subsequent weeks a greater want of it, and a more pressing distress. [62]

Meat and vegetables were suggested as appropriate substitutes. Neither was cheap. Despite the government's best efforts to buy wheat abroad and distribute it in controlled amounts, the national grain shortage worsened over the summer. On 30 July the Privy Council was warned that the British harvest in 1795 would be poor. During August and September arrangements were made to victual the navy from the cargoes of captured French ships and to open Irish ports for the export of corn to mainland Britain.[63] The harvest returns of the autumn confirmed the ministry's worst fears. On 1 October the Privy Council renewed its pledge to reduce consumption of grain and flour in its own households. By mid-October Hawkesbury and the interventionists had won the battle of economic doctrine against Portland and the free-traders. Import bounties were introduced at the beginning of 1796. Other relief measures were in contemplation; these Pitt intended to lay before Parliament.[64] Scarcity was easily the most pressing issue on his mind as he prepared for the opening of the 1796 session. The events of 29 October were to redirect the ministry's attention to popular radicalism.

The Two Acts of 1795

When the LCS held its open-air meeting at Copenhagen House on 26 October, Portland responded by calling out the police magistrates of two London bureaux, the City guard and two volunteer units of militia. This was a relatively minor display of force and suggests that violence was not anticipated.[65] On 29 October the king's coach was attacked by an outraged mob as it bore George III to the state opening of Parliament. The government response was swift and savage. On 6 November Grenville introduced the treasonable and seditious practices bill in the House of Lords. On 10 November Pitt brought the seditious meetings bill before the Commons. The speed with which both bills were presented to Parliament suggests that they had existed in draft form for some time.

This accusation cannot be substantiated from documentary evidence, but the Two Acts represent more than a knee-jerk reaction to mob violence. The Treasonable and Seditious Practices Act embodied the doctrine of constructive treason which had been developing in government circles since the end of 1792 and closed all avenues of radical access to the high political world. Pitt had maintained throughout his career that reformers could not appeal to Parliament unless they observed the established rules of 'polite' conduct. Popular radicals, by adopting what was regarded as a confrontational strategy, had forfeited the right to a hearing. The attempted coercion of one or both Houses of Parliament was to be explicitly forbidden by the Treasonable and Seditious Practices Act. When asked by the Foxites whether the government intended to outlaw petitions altogether, Pitt replied that, when the practice of petitioning was abused, careful distinctions needed to be made between 'true' and 'false' petitions:

> He then proceeded to remark, that those men were not, in his opinion, the best friends either to the Constitution or to the lower ranks of the people, who endeavour to habituate them to petitioning; who encourage those to frequent deliberations on public affairs, who, of all men, by education and habits of life, and means of information, were the least capable of exercising a sound judgement on such subjects, and who are most likely to be improved upon by others.[66]

Improving subjects were the stock in trade of Hannah More's *Cheap Repository Tracts*, for which Pitt expressed a great admiration.[67] *In memoriam* for the events of 1794, treasonable offences were newly defined to incorporate the direct or indirect intimidation of the monarch. The ministry had finally succeeded in establishing the definition of constructive treason that it had failed to lay down in the state trials. The penalty for such offences, in accordance with precedent, was death. The punishments for authors and publishers of seditious libels were more recent in conception and can be dated to November 1792. Individuals found guilty of composing or distributing material – spoken or written – inciting persons to hatred or contempt of the king, government or constitution were subject, upon the second or subsequent conviction, to heavy fines or transportation.

The ministry did not want to redefine its statutory powers and a note of apology can be detected in Pitt's attempts to justify the Two Acts. The treasonable and seditious practices bill, derived from Elizabeth's Second Treason Act of 1571, went 'to guard against all ambiguous and doubtful interpretation' of 25 Edward III. It also made the pains and penalties for the commission of treason clear to the public. This was deterrence legislation. When the House was in Committee following the second reading of the bill, Sir William Young moved that no time limit be placed on its enactment. Pitt opposed this on the grounds that the legislation had been prepared for a specific emergency and could be renewed if necessary.[68] Treason was not redefined on a permanent basis. The seditious meetings bill, based on Charles II's Act against Tumultuous Petitioning of 1661, was not, stated Pitt, 'an abrogation of the right of petitioning' laid down in the 1689 Bill of Rights.

The government was afraid not of the reform movement, but of the mob violence that it had seemingly unleashed. For much of 1795 the ministry had thought that radicalism was a waning force. When the Privy Council learned from bystanders that radical handbills had been distributed at the scene of the attack on the king's coach, the Cabinet changed its mind. Witnesses at the Copenhagen House demonstration of 26 October were examined by the Privy Council, following which a royal proclamation on 4 November condemned both handbills and mass meetings: 'A great number of persons were collected in fields, in the neighbourhood of the metropolis ... and that divers and inflammatory discourses were delivered to the persons so collected; and divers proceedings were had, tending to create groundless jealousy and discontent, and to endanger the public peace.'[69] On the same day London magistrates were instructed to break up large gatherings and to apprehend the distributors of seditious literature: 'Papers are dispersed against property. Prints of guillotining the King and others.'[70] Although the meeting on 26 October had been quiet and orderly, specific features of the LCS platform appeared to herald a new era of militant radicalism. The LCS had not only reaffirmed its commitment to democratic parliamentary reform, but, declaring that it had lost all faith in the Pitt ministry, proceeded to abuse the government's policies – the prosecution of an unjust war and the failure of the ministry to provide relief to a starving nation. By playing on the all too real grievances of its audience, the radicals were creating a potentially explosive situation. The only hope for Britain, asserted the LCS, lay in the exertions of its common people. 'IF EVER THE BRITISH NATION SHOULD LOUDLY DEMAND STRONG AND DECISIVE MEASURES, WE BOLDLY ANSWER – "WE HAVE LIVES!" AND ARE READY TO DEVOTE THEM, EITHER SEPARATELY OR COLLECTIVELY, FOR THE SALVATION OF OUR COUNTRY.'[71] The Seditious Meetings Act dealt with the soap-box tactics of the LCS. Not only did it require meetings of more than fifty people to be licensed by a JP, but it conferred the authority of the 1715 Riot Act upon magistrates carrying out their duties. These regulations were aimed at the mass meetings of the LCS and 'lectures and discourses on political subjects, where money was received, and where sedition was the source of livelihood of certain persons'.[72] When the bill was under debate in the Commons, the Home Office moved to counteract the 'radical poison' by distributing loyalist handbills of its own composition. Colquhoun proudly claimed to have broken up a disorderly assembly with his tracts.[73]

Rebels, then, were only dangerous in large organized numbers: 'Much will depend', counselled Auckland, 'on the doing enough and the doing it well, without doing too much.' Great care went into the drafting of the Seditious Meetings Act, which may not, in the first instance, have included the infamous license restrictions on *all* meetings. Wilberforce 'went to Pitt to look over the Sedition Bill' on

11 November and 'altered it much for the better by enlarging'. Pitt and Portland remained apprehensive that violent protest would accompany the passage of the Seditious Meetings Act: 'I see that he expects a civil broil,' observed Wilberforce.[74] Heavy concentrations of troops were moved into London in readiness for riots:

> The Town will be envisioned with a Force sufficient, it is presumed ... to keep in awe, or to disperse any Mob, however numerous, that may be assembled on Monday next or on any other Day, until the Bill now under the discussion of Parliament for the prevention of such disorderly assemblies of the Common People, has been passed.[75]

So uneasy were government consciences about the legality of the Two Acts that strenuous efforts were made to legitimize the measures with a display of loyal extraparliamentary support. Soon after the contents of the proposed bills had been made public, the House of Commons started to receive petitions of protest from a nation horrified by the severity of the legislation.[76] 'I am anxious', wrote Grenville, 'that our support should be as great as the opinion is I believe general to the necessity of these measures.'[77] John Reeves stood forth once more as the orchestrator of a loyal response: on 7 November he inserted an advertisment in the *True Briton* calling upon the public to sign a loyal address in support of the Two Acts.[78]

Reeves was anxious to offer Pitt his 'help out of doors to obtain co-operation & consent, in my prior way', but received no response. Independent loyalism was the last thing that the government wanted in a crisis.[79] Friends of the ministry were, however, active further afield. Buckingham not only composed loyal petitions at the dictation of Grenville, but would have rewritten the county address of thanks had he not 'sent that which was settled to several persons'.[80] Useful though Reeves had been in many capacities since 1792, Pitt shed no tears when he was impeached by the House of Commons for the publication of a Tory libel. In *Thoughts on the English Government* (1793) Reeves had stated that the king could rule without Parliament, thereby implying that all authority in the realm was grounded upon divine right and passive obedience. By dredging up this pamphlet and declaring it disrespectful to the House of Commons, the Foxites were trying to redress the balance in the war of 'seditious' libel prosecutions.[81] Reeves, appealing for Pitt's vote, was appalled that the House should 'catch at words and phraseology' when 'such inundations of seditious publications pass unnoticed'.[82] Pitt told the Commons on 23 November that the Foxites had taken a passage out of context, but this was the best that he could do for Reeves. Burke, on the other hand, thought Reeves's doctrine no libel, 'neither more nor less than the law of the land'.

The Reeves impeachment was part of the Foxite attack on the Two Acts, and it was in the Commons on 17 November that an account of Pitt's revolution settlement finally emerged: 'What indeed was the Bill of Rights but a measure taken by our ancestors on account of their finding themselves in new circumstances?' 1688, said Pitt, had witnessed a conservative revolution, because the constitution of the realm had not been changed although opportunities to do so had existed. The events of 1688–9, which Pitt regarded as forming part of a wider revolution settlement that was completed in 1714, laid down that Parliament was the highest authority in the land: 'the revolution itself conspired to shew that it was to Parliament, or to the people in Parliament, and not to the people outside Parliament, that the right of framing alterations to the Constitution always devolved.' Pitt's de-nunciation of Reeves's divine right doctrine was preordained by principle.[83]

The Directory was not held responsible for the events of late Oct-ober, and Pitt explicitly stated during the November debates that the enemy could offer no intellectual inspiration or practical assistance to British radicals. France had been reduced by the war to 'a state so wretched that even the French themselves complained of the tyranny under which they laboured'. Habeas corpus had therefore been rein-stated in the belief that 'the delusion would cease'.[84] The government was alarmed to find that the LCS was still acting as a partisan of the republic, insisting at Copenhagen House that the Directory was capable of maintaining peaceful relations with Britain. The Pitt ministry could only conclude that native radicals had received secret instructions, possessed a standing mandate for sedition, or, most disturbingly, were acting as independent agents. Radical actions were governed either by the hope of creating what 'mischief' they could or by the desire to coerce the ministry into signing a premature armistice. The British government wanted neither to come to the peace table as a supplicant nor to lose face with its remaining allies. The ministry, protecting itself against the politics of riot, included within its new definition of treason any attempt to intimidate the king into changing his counsels or policies: 'My head would be off in a fortnight were I to resign', stated Pitt.[85]

Unwilling though Pitt was to become the victim of coercion, he could not ignore the distress of a starving and volatile populace. On 2 November he placed several famine relief proposals before Parliament. Industrial sanctions on the use of grain were to be extended to brewers and starch-makers. Food substitution projects were also in contemp-lation. The introduction of mixed-grain breads had received the Board of Agriculture's seal of approval: 'From repeated experiments,' Pitt told the House, 'he was enabled to state that mixed bread ... might be as wholesome, and as palatable as any we had been accustomed to eat.'[86] In the third report of the Commons Select Committee appointed to consider the price of corn the nation was informed that good bread could be made 'with no greater Proportion than 3/5 or 2/3 of Wheaten Flour'. Both Lords and Commons pledged themselves to consume nothing but mixed bread.[87] The government was hoping to set an edifying example, but changing the dietary habits of a nation proved to be beyond the powers of the Pitt ministry.

Pitt's thoughts were also turning to agriculture and the poor law:

6th. Relieving the labouring Poor from the Presure of the high Price while it lasts. Additional allowance over & above the usual Wages, in a given Proportion to the excess of the Price of different Articles of Grain beyond a certain Amount, to be raised in each Parish by a Rate on the Occupiers of Land (Q. Arable) & Encreased Allowance in proportion to the Number of Children.

7. Means of encouraging Supply of Grain for the Future.

Q. Genl. Enclosure Bill (substitute for Tithes)[88]

In 1796 Sir John Sinclair's wastelands bill and Pitt's bill for bettering the condition of the poor were presented to Parliament.

The Board of Agriculture, created in 1793, produced its first national agricultural survey in 1795. Sinclair, the board's president, had throughout the year been advocating general enclosure and, by September 1795, was claiming that the cultivation of waste and common lands would make Britain agriculturally self-sufficient.[89] Pitt's interest in enclosure was new but coincided with the revival of an older project, the commutation of tithes. This had first been mooted in 1786 and, in 1791, Pitt had proposed to replace greater and lesser tithes with a corn rent, an annual levy equal to a fixed proportion of the grain harvest. Prospective corn-rent yields depended upon the market price of grain in any given year. With grain of all descriptions in short supply at the end of 1795, Pitt preferred to opt for general enclosure.

As Ehrman points out, Pitt did not give Sinclair's wastelands bill much support in the Commons and it was lost at the committee stage in March 1796. Tithes, as it happened, were a major stumbling-block to the progress of legislation. This was normal with enclosure bills, which proposed to abolish tithe collection rights on property destined for enclosure. Lay and clerical improprietors were normally compensated for their loss of these rights with land. In 1796 lay improprietors had complained about Sinclair's compensation arrangements and the bill was widely thought to have been poorly drafted. Pitt agreed with these criticisms though he was not hostile to Sinclair's bill. The young Charles Abbot, having tried in vain to solve the legal problems arising from the draft legislation, recorded Pitt's consoling words when the bill failed: 'I had done more for Sir John Sinclair than anyone had.' Abbot was soon at work on Pitt's bill for bettering the condition of the poor.[90]

On 8 December 1795 the Foxite MP Samuel Whitbread begged leave of the Commons to bring in a bill for regulating the wages of labourers in husbandry. Pitt opposed this on the grounds that the proposed measure would enable magistrates to set minimum wages, a practice that Pitt felt would artificially inflate the price of food. Wages and prices, he stated, were best left to 'find their own level'.[91] As Roger Wells and Ehrman have noted, Pitt's attachment to *laissez-faire* was not apparent in the food policies of the later 1790s. Pitt, in fact, was criticized by Grenville in 1800 for having abandoned free-market principles. During the 1780s, recalled the Foreign Secretary, 'we had in truth formed our opinions on the subject together, and I was not more convinced than you were of the soundness of Adam Smith's principles of political economy till Lord Liverpool lured you away from our arms into the mazes of the old system'.[92] Grenville, like many twentieth-century economists, equated political economy with *laissez-faire*. The same cannot be said of Pitt, whose admiration for Smith's work stemmed as much from its theories of history as from its economic doctrines. In November 1800 Pitt introduced a package of scarcity relief measures, following the appalling harvest of 1800, with a statement of principles seemingly inspired by a classic passage from Smith's *Theory of Moral Sentiments* (1790 edn):

> ... it is unsafe in the attempt, it is unworthy of a statesman in the design to abandon the system which practice has explained and experience has confirmed, for the advantages of a crude, untried theory. It is no less unsafe, no less unworthy of the active politician, to adhere to any general theory, however just its general principles, which excludes from its views those particular details, those unexpected situations, which must render the scheme of the philosophic politician inapplicable to the general circumstances of human affairs.[93]

Smith had written in the *Theory of Moral Sentiments* that the 'man of spirit' – the good legislator – would work in harmony with 'the great orders and societies, into which the state is divided'. The 'man of system', enamoured of pet theories, would attempt to embody these in law without regard for vested interests and public opinion. Although Smith's science of a legislator contained no provision for unforeseen disasters like the food shortages of the 1790s, his 'wisdom of Solon' entailed the adoption of 'the very best laws the people would bear'.[94] For Pitt, these involved limited intervention in the provisions trade to maximize existing supplies of grain. He had considered, but ultimately

rejected, the introduction of statutory penalties for forestalling, regrat-
ing and engrossing, those variants upon price speculation in the
provisions of trade. Any attempt to prosecute these offences, he said,
would 'bring us back to something worse than the system that prevailed
500 years ago'. Such measures were not appropriate for 'the new
interests and demands of another state of society'.[95]

Pitt's solution to *das Adam Smith Problem*, the reconciliation of moral
sentiments with market principles, had involved the creation of a wage-
price index to govern relief payments to able-bodied claimants in the
unsuccessful 1796 bill for bettering the condition of the poor.[96] In June
1795 Pitt voted for a suspension of the laws of settlement that determined the eligibility of the poor for relief. By 31 December he had
devised a system of outdoor relief by which income supplements were
to be calculated according to relative regional differences between corn
prices and average wages. Sliding scales for poor relief were to be set
by each parish.[97] Pitt's income supplements, like those of the Speenhamland magistrates, were to be calibrated according to the size of a
claimant's family. The other features of the bill for bettering the
condition of the poor – old age pensions, parish employment, cow
money and a youth training scheme – were worked out over the winter
of 1795–6. Pitt, though disillusioned by the defeat of the bill for
bettering the condition of the poor in 1797, did not lose interest in a
cost-of-living index. In 1799 it was to appear again in a draft bill for
the commutation of tithes.[98]

By 1799 Pitt had eschewed the corn rent in favour of a plan for
converting tithe rights to cash via an enclosure-type valuation schedule.
The proceeds were to be vested in the Consolidated Fund.[99] The tithe
redemption scheme was presented, amongst other things, as '*an Aid to
Public Credit*'. The money raised from commutation, once invested in
a special church consolidated fund, was expected to grow in value
through a judicious policy of dividend reinvestment, generating an
increasing revenue that would more than compensate lay and clerical
impropriators for their loss of tithe. Pitt hoped that the Church divi-
dends would be put to good use – 'the *further Augmentation of Small
Livings* or perhaps even of *New Endowments*'. Such income rises were
to be determined by reference to a consumer–price index:

> In order to ascertain from Time to Time the Actual Encrease, A
> Commission might be appointed to consist of the Archbishop, the
> Lord Chancellor, and a certain Number of Bishops and Privy Coun-
> cillors, who should select those Articles of Grain, Meat, &c. according
> to which the Price of Living may most properly be computed, and
> from a Table of such Articles (according to the Proportional Quan-
> tities of each which may be supposed to enter into the Ordinary

Computation of a Family) stating the respective Prices of each Article on the Average of such a Number of Years preceding as may be thought most expedient.[100]

The poor law reform bill was withdrawn from Parliament in February 1797, after meeting overwhelmingly negative criticism during the Christmas recess. The commutation bill was killed by the Episcopal Bench before it saw the light of day.[101] The events of 1795 inaugurated a new phase of fiscal and administrative reform in the Younger Pitt's career. In the budget for that year he had begun to shift the sources of government revenue from indirect to direct taxation with the introduction of the tax on collateral successions, the predecessor of modern death duties.[102] His interest in general enclosure, poor law reform and tithe redemption indicated that he was giving some thought to the foundations of the agricultural economy on which so much of England's wealth was based. The three reform bills that have been outlined here were devised to promote agricultural growth and efficiency, to reform the structures and practices of local government and to maximize national resources for the war effort. Pitt's response was characteristically thorough and, in conceptual terms and goals, akin to the legislative approach of the 1780s. The economic and social pressures that were impelling him towards reform in the later 1790s were, however, the products of a lengthy war with revolutionary France whose hardships had taken, and were to take him again, by surprise.

A Premeditated Policy?

While it would be easy to say that Pitt's programme of November 1792, complete with its new sentences for sedition, the volunteer corps and habeas corpus suspension, set the stage for the official response to radicalism during the 1790s, such an analysis would downplay the ministerial soul-searching that preceded the introduction of each extraordinary public order measure of the 1790s. Responsible government, as conceived by Pitt, was always devoted to the preservation of a constitution in which the common good, as interpreted under wartime conditions, was not to compromise the liberties of the individual in the long run. Even the Two Acts, passed during what was perceived as a state of national crisis, contained safeguards to protect 'the rights of the freeborn Englishman'. For the Younger Pitt during the 1790s, 'liberty' was a relative absence of constraint.

The crisis of 1792 is important not so much for the agenda of repression that it gave Pitt, but for the response patterns that it laid down. In 1792 and 1795, confronted by what looked like widespread social disorder in the making, Pitt devised extraordinary legislative solutions for temporary problems which, on later reflection, were later modified or abandoned. Under extreme pressure, what was perhaps a hereditary tendency to manic depression manifested itself.

In 1821 the ever faithful Tomline claimed that Pitt's foreign and domestic policy possessed an intellectual unity that dated from 1789. As one of Pitt's confidants on the subject of 'plots and treasons', he was in a good position to deliver a verdict: 'Mr. Pitt, though he saw the evil at a distance, and anxiously watched its gradual approach, was yet aware, that time must be given for its coming so near, as to be visible to every common beholder, before it would be wise, or rather practicable, to oppose its further progress.'[103] This echoes a speech that Pitt made in 1800, in which he claimed that Britain was menaced by 'a danger, the greatest that ever threatened the world' – a retrospective judgement on the past seven years of war. Its citation by Tomline in the aftermath of the 'Six Acts' and the trial of Queen Caroline is interesting, as is the analysis of the speech given by the bishop.[104] Pitt, claimed Tomline, had seen 'the real designs of the seditious societies' in 1792, but, despite this foresight, had been dragged unwillingly into war and repression:

> He perceived the formidable co-operation of internal and external enemies; but the former could not be effectively resisted, except by open war, nor the latter, without coercive acts of the legislature: and he was persuaded that neither of these expedients, exclusive to his own earnest wish not to have recourse to them, would be approved, till their necessity was obvious and uncontestable.

Making allowances for Tomline's claim that Pitt was omniscient, what emerges from this assessment is the fact that popular radicals were not as worrisome as the voices of Parliament or public opinion. Pitt was not afraid of the democratic reformers all the time. By 1799 he had acquired a copy of the Abbé Barruel's *Mémoires pour servir à l'histoire du Jacobinisme*, according to which Freemasons, Jews, *philosophes* and other supposed social misfits were responsible for the birth of a sinister international conspiracy to subvert the old order. This kind of reasoning would not have impressed Pitt, who needed something resembling evidence to believe in Jacobin plots; the Home Office went searching for this in 1792 and 1794. By 1795 the structures and practices of subversion were assumed to be established and, up to 1800, Commons Secret Committees were continuing to claim that the evil design 'to overturn the laws, constitution and government ... in concert with a foreign enemy ... has never been abandoned'.[105]

Pitt's experience with reform had not been a happy one. By 1792 he was all too familiar with the obstacles that MPs encountered in their search for unity in purpose and action from the extraparliamentary lobby. The remarkable outward cohesion of the parliamentary reform movement during the 1790s could only be put down to an external agency. The British public did not, thought Pitt, behave under normal conditions with such determination and consistency. Radical unity could only be a product of French aid. Pitt always saw that assistance as practical rather than intellectual. In 1821 Tomline had identified the two principal revolutionary objectives of 1792: the extension of France's dominions by conquest; and the subversion, 'through the joint action of intrigue and fear', of every established government in Europe. Inertia-producing fear came not from British radicals, but from conservatives, which led Pitt to place a conventional interpretation upon French motives for subversion. An alarmist lobby was potentially capable of keeping the British government neutral in 1792. From 1793 onwards it could have forced Britain to pull out of the war. Subversion, as the British government knew from its dealings with the Vendée and Franche Comté, was warfare on the cheap. It could be resorted to in confidence, as the First Fraternal Decree of 19 November 1792 had demonstrated; in desperation, as was seemingly the case from October 1793 to May 1794; or in a spirit of opportunism, as French intrigue in America, the United Provinces and the Austrian Netherlands had suggested from 1776 to 1791. The readiness and ability of France to help the rebels of Europe depended not on the principles of its government, but on its fiscal and military strength at crucial periods in the war.

According to the Foxite Whigs and their historians, who strongly suspected that Pitt was afraid neither of revolutionary France nor of the British reform movement, the premier manipulated the fears of the British public to drum up support for what, from 1793 to 1796, was a war of conquest and, from 1797 onwards, was an unsuccessful war. The British government always believed in the existence of the various radical conspiracies that it thought it had uncovered during the 1790s. Pitt was scaremongering in describing their potential social effects. By 1798, at which time the United Societies did want to overthrow the constitution, Pitt was aware that Mancunian offshoots of the United Irishmen had sworn their followers to 'establish here a Republican Government', but he never thought that such plans stood any chance of success without French military help.[106]

The predominant frustration for the Foxites between 1793 and 1795 was the multifaceted nature of Pitt's war platform. 'Indemnification for the past and security for the future' contained something for every MP in the independent House of Commons. The government could stress whatever aspect of its policy was most appropriate to the actual state of Britain's military, diplomatic and socio-economic fortunes at home and abroad – be it colonial conquest, the maintenance of a 'balance of power' in western Europe, the restoration of the Bourbon monarchy or the social evils of anarchy. All had their moments in the sun.

It would be ahistorical to credit Pitt with a foresight that he did not possess but there is no doubt that 'indemnification for the past and security for the future' covered every foreign and domestic contingency of the 1790s. The beauty of the platform lay in its flexibility, an important attribute for a British government trying to keep its options open in February 1793. The public face of the ministry also reflected the reality of a Parliament gripped by alarmism at the end of 1792, but in which no wholesale conversion to conservatism had taken place. The living Pitt could not and did not rely exclusively upon a conservative intellectual platform in a Parliament that, in the despairing words of Burke following the debates in 1790 on the repeal of the Test and Corporation Acts, 'will not hear of an abstract idea'.[107] By 1806 the ambivalent features of the British government's public persona were to confuse the dead Pitt's would-be followers in the search for the 'true' principles of their saint.

Notes

1. W. Stern, 'The bread crisis in Britain 1795–1796', *Economica*, New Series 31 (1964) pp. 168–87; R. Wells, *Wretched Faces: Famine in Wartime Britain 1763–1803* (Gloucester: 1988), pp. 230–1.
2. Auckland Correspondence, iii, Auckland to H. Spencer, 10 July 1794, p. 220; L. Melville (ed.), *The Windham Papers* (2 vols, 1913), i, Burke to Windham, 16 October 1794, p. 263.
3. *Rose Diaries*, i , Rose to Tomline, 14 July 1794, pp. 193–4; *Addington Life*, i, Lord Mornington to Henry Addington, 27 July 1794, p. 122.
4. Canning MS, 29 dii, Diary, 7 July 1794, fos 116–17; R. I. and S. Wilberforce (eds), *The Correspondence of William Wilberforce* (2 vols, 1840), i, Wilberforce to Lord Muncaster, 9 July 1794, p. 103.
5. WWM F31(b)13, F31–15–1, Portland to Fitzwilliam, 14 June 1794.
6. WWM F31–19, Portland to Fitzwilliam, 19 June 1794.
7. CUL 6958/8, 1451, Pitt to Portland, 5 July 1794; *Dropmore*, ii, Pitt to Grenville, 9 July 1794, p. 595.
8. Relations between Dundas and Richmond were particularly acrimonious, so much so that Richmond had stopped attending Cabinet meetings. Richmond, who was asked to resign his Cabinet seat in July 1794, was virtually dismissed from the Ordnance in January 1795, after disagreements with the new First Lord of the Admiralty, Lord Spencer. 'I see that yr. resuming a seat in the Cabinet must prove unpleasant and embarrassing to Public Business,' wrote Pitt: CUL 6958/9, 1622, Pitt to Richmond, 26 January 1795. See also U1590 S5 03/14, Richmond to Pitt, 15 December 1794.
9. CUL 6958/8, 1513, Grenville to Pitt, 13 October 1794.
10. After the 1782 Act, military and colonial affairs were included in the

Home Secretary's portfolio: R. R. Nelson, *The Home Office, 1782–1801* (Durham, NC: 1969), p. 20; M. Fry, *The Dundas Despotism* (Edinburgh: 1992), pp. 187–8.

11. *Dropmore*, ii, Pitt to Grenville, 7 July 1794, p. 597.

12. For Dundas's comments on the separation of offices, see CUL 6958/8, 1454, Dundas to Pitt, 9 July 1794. For Pitt's pleas, see SRO GD 51/1/24/2, Pitt to Dundas, 9 July 1794. For details of the coalition negotiations, see J. Ehrman, *The Reluctant Transition* (1983), pp. 411–13; HO 30/1, Division of Responsibility Memo, 24 July 1794, fos 1–2.

13. *PH*, xxxi, Second Report of the Committee of Secrecy, 6 June 1794, cols 693–8; debate on the second report, col. 920; supporters of the government thought that the LCS was a party to the Watt conspiracy: Auckland Correspondence, iii, Morton Eden to Auckland, 8 September 1794, p. 240.

14. LCS Papers, 154, report from Spy Taylor, LCS Division 29, 8 April 1794, p. 132; compilation of Gosling's 'Informations,' April–May 1794, scattered throughout LCS Papers, 1794A and B.

15. *PH*, xxxi, Second Report of the Committee of Secrecy, col. 705.

16. LCS Papers, Report from Spy Lynam, LCS General Meeting, 20 January 1794, p. 107, and report from Groves, 13 February 1794, p. 113.

17. Auckland Correspondence, iii, Auckland to Lord H. Spencer, 30 May 1794, p. 213.

18. LCS Papers, Groves report, 13 February 1794, p. 113.

19. *PH*, xxxi, debate on the second report, 6 June 1794, col. 916.

20. FO 37/52, 9 and 10, St Helens to Grenville, 20 and 23 May 1794; M. Elliott, *Partners in Revolution* (New Haven, Conn.: 1982), pp. 63–7.

21. U1590 S5 03/14, Richmond to Pitt, 28 May 1794.

22. HO 42/31, Lord Hardwicke to the Home Office, 14 June 1794, fo. 123, and T. Clements to the Home Office, 22 June 1794, fo. 244; BL Add MS 58877, fo. 59, Buckingham to Grenville, 30 June 1794.

23. J. Stevenson, 'Disturbances and public order in London, 1790–1821', D.Phil. thesis (Oxford: 1973), pp. 48–51.

24. Auckland Correspondence, iii, Auckland to Loughborough, 22 August 1794, p. 233; Nelson, *The Home Office*, p. vii; Stevenson, 'Disturbances and public order in London', pp. 59–60; BL Add MS 58915, Dundas to Grenville, 24 August [1794], fo. 192.

25. HO 42/33, W. Devaynez to E. Nepean, 20 August 1794, fo. 114.

26. *Ibid.*, P. Colquhoun to Portland, and Colquhoun to all magistrates, 21, 22 August 1794, fos 160, 234.

27. Stevenson, 'Disturbances and public order in London', pp. 304–7.

28. HO 42/33, W. Devaynez to J. King, and W. Blanning and A. Lonham to Nepean, 20, 21 August 1794, fos 107, 113.

29. PRO 30/8/198, Notebook 4, 'Novr. 9' [1792], fo. 109. Some 'associations for preserving public order' were referred to in an internal Home Office report written at the beginning of 1793. This had been meant for public issue and the question of government involvement in the formation of the armed associations was left unresolved: HO 42/24, An Enquiry into the Causes for Public Measures, by Thomas Palmer, 21 January 1794, fos 190–226; PRO 30/8/164, W. Ogilvie to Pitt, 14 March 1794, fos 41–3;

HO 42/33, Colquhoun to Portland, 21 August 1794, fo. 160: 'it is my duty to inform your Grace that the Armed Associations which are forming in this quarter of the Metropolis cannot be ready to act for a considerable length of time, so that from them we cannot be expected to derive any aid'.

30. HO 43/16, Portland to Birmingham magistrates, 25 January 1795, cited in Nelson, *The Home Office*, p. 106.

31. HO 1/2, Wickham to T. Broderick, 5 September 1794; HRO 39M 49/1/40/1-8, Portland to Wickham, 8 September 1794.

32. LCS Papers, Thale account of the Pop Gun plot, pp. 220-3.

33. *LCG III*, ii, Portland to George III, George III to Portland, and Portland to George III, 29, 30 September, 10 October 1794, pp. 247-8; *Court and Cabinets*, ii, Grenville to Buckingham, 27 September 1794, p. 305.

34. Nelson, *The Home Office*, p. 97; Clements MSS, Pitt Papers, Pitt to Sydney, 8 March [1789].

35. D. Hay, 'Property, authority and the criminal law', in Hay *et al.* (eds), *Albion's Fatal Tree: Crime and Society in Eighteenth Century England* (1963), and D. Hay and F. Snyder (eds), *Policing and Prosecution in Britain 1750–1850* (1989); P. King, 'Decision makers and decision making in the English criminal law', *HJ* 27 (1984), pp. 25-58.

36. NMM ELL 121, Dundas to Elliot, 21 October 1794.

37. H. Twiss, *The Public and Private Life of Lord Chancellor Eldon* (1844), pp. 241-3; W. S. Holdsworth, *A History of English Law* (16 vols, 1966 edn), viii, pp. 317-19.

38. Canning MS, 29 dii, fo. 116, Diary, 20 November 1794; DRO 152M C1794/OZ 46, Henry Addington to Hiley Addington, 9 November 1794.

39. F. K. Prochaska, 'English state trials in the 1790s', *JBS* 13 (1978), pp. 67-8.

40. Twiss, *Life of Lord Chancellor Eldon*, Anecdote Book, pp. 282-4.

41. DRO 152M C1794/OZ 43, Addington to Hiley Addington, 11 November 1794; Auckland Correspondence, iii, Baron Hotham to Auckland, 15 November 1794, pp. 286-7; T. A. Green, *Verdict according to Conscience: Perspectives on the English Criminal Trial Jury* (Chicago: 1985), p. 353.

42. DRO 152M C1794/OZ 43, Addington to Hiley Addington, 11 November 1794.

43. Canning MS, 29 dii, Letter Journal, 22 November 1794, fo. 113.

44. Twiss, *Life of Lord Chancellor Eldon*, Anecdote Book, p. 183; *PR*, xliii, 19 November 1795, p. 187.

45. Auckland Correspondence, iii, Auckland to Pitt, 28 November 1794, pp. 271-2; *Court and Cabinets*, ii, Grenville to T. Grenville, 26 August 1794, p. 272.

46. BT 5/8, fos 155-6, Minutes of the Board of Trade, 22 November 1792; PRO 30/8/176, memo by Claude Scott, 'Corn purchases in 1792', fo. 68.

47. BT 5/8, Minutes, 16 May 1793, fo. 220; PRO 30/8/176, 'Account of the Sums of Money paid by Government for Corn purchased by Claude Scott in the following years; and also of the Money paid thro him for Neutral Cargoes', fo. 60; Scott to Pitt, 13 December 1794, fos 61-2.

48. Stern, 'The bread crisis of 1795-1796', pp. 176-8.

49. Wells, *Wretched Faces*, pp. 185-6; HO 42/35, Lord Mayor to Privy

Council, 6 January 1795, fos 16–18; PRO 30/8/176, Sinclair to Pitt, 5 January 1795, fo. 122.

50. BT 5/9, Minutes of the Board of Trade, 2 February 1795, fo. 191.

51. HO 42/36, Hawkesbury to Portland, 19 May 1795, fo. 386; Sheila Lambert (ed.), *Sessional Papers of the House of Commons* (Wilmington, Del.: 1975), 99, Corn Committee Minutes, 6 February 1795.

52. M. D. Neuman, 'A suggestion regarding the origins of the Speenhamland Plan', *EHR* 84 (1969), pp. 317–22.

53. HA 119 T108/42, 219, Pitt to Tomline, 29 June 1795.

54. The Privy Council remained committed to this policy until 1 October.

55. *Commons Sessional Papers*, 99, 4556, 'Minutes of the Evidence Taken before the Corn Committee', 27 April 1795, pp. 29–30; 2 July 1795, pp. 37–44; Wells, *Wretched Faces*, pp. 188–9, 203–4.

56. KAO U840 601/1, Dundas to Camden, 1 June 1795; *Life of Wilberforce*, ii, Diary, 9 July [1795], p. 94.

57. LCS Papers, p. 252, n. 29.

58. PRO 30/8/112, Pitt to Lady Chatham, 18 July 1795, fos 468–9.

59. J. Hutton (ed.), *Selections from the Life and Correspondence of James Bland Burges* (1885), Bland Burges to Ann Burges, 14, 15 July 1795, p. 287; T. Hayter, *The Army and the Crowd in Mid-Georgian England* (1978), p. 28.

60. PRO 30/8/12, Pitt to Lady Chatham, 18 July 1795, fos 468–9.

61. *Life of Wilberforce*, ii, Diary, 9 July 1795, p. 94.

62. HO 42/35, Home Office to Mayor of Exeter, 15 July 1795, fo. 183.

63. *Commons Sessional Papers*, 99, Corn Committee Minutes, 2 July 1795, p. 410.

64. Wells, *Wretched Faces*, pp. 190–2; *PR*, xliii, 30 October 1795, pp. 57–8.

65. HO 65/1; in comparison to the St George's Field demonstration of 9 July.

66. *PR*, xliii, 17 November 1795, p. 243.

67. More Memoirs, ii, H. More to P. More, [May] 1796, p. 475.

68. *PR*, xliii, 17 November 1795, p. 245; 10 December 1795, pp. 718–19; 30 November 1795, p. 471.

69. *PH*, xxxii, text of Royal Proclamation against Seditious Meetings, 4 November 1795, cols 243–4.

70. *Life of Wilberforce*, ii, Diary, 18 November 1795, p. 112.

71. LCS Papers, 'Proceedings of a General Meeting of the London Corresponding Society, Held on Monday, 26th October, 1795; in a field adjacent to Copenhagen House, in the Country of Middlesex', pp. 315–17.

72. *PR*, xliii, 9 November 1795, pp. 112–15; M. Thale, 'The London Debating Societies of the 1790s', *HJ* 33 (1990), pp. 70–2.

73. PRO 30/8/123, P. Colquhoun to Pitt, 23 November 1795, fo. 199.

74. PRO 30/8/110, Auckland to Pitt, 8 November 1795, fo. 55; *Life of Wilberforce*, ii, Diary, 11 and 16 November 1795, p. 114.

75. HO 42/35, Pitt–Portland memo, 14 November 1795. Three troops of the 1st Dragoon Guards were in Hackney, while four troops of the Cornish Fencible Cavalry were stationed in Hampstead, Highgate and Barnet. The Lancashire militia were covering Greenwich, Lewisham and Eltham. The 10th Light Dragoons were in Hounslow; the 15th Light Dragoons were

to be found in Croydon, and the East Kent militia in Bow and Stratford; *LCG III*, ii, Portland to George III, 12 November 1795, pp. 419–20; Malmesbury Diaries, iii, Malmesbury to the Duke of York, 7 December 1795, pp. 255–6.

76. Fox Mem., iii, Fox to Fitzpatrick, 9 November 1795, p. 127: 'We talk of measures without doors'; Fox to Holland, 24 December 1795, p. 127.

77. U1590 S5 02/12, Grenville to Tomline, 13 November 1795; BL Add MS 58934, Grenville to Portland, 13 November 1795.

78. PRO 30/8/170, Reeves to Pitt, 7 November 1795, fo. 255.

79. Dozier, *For King, Constitution and Country* (Lexington, KY.: 1983), pp. 170–1.

80. *Dropmore*, ii, Buckingham to Grenville, 8, 12 and 19 November 1795, pp. 144–7.

81. J. A. W. Gunn, *Beyond Liberty and Property: The Process of Self Recognition in Eighteenth Century Political Thought* (Kingston, Ont.: 1983), p. 180.

82. PRO 30/8/170, Reeves to Pitt, 18 November 1795, fos 265–6; *PR*, xliii, 23 November 1795, pp. 308–9.

83. Burke Correspondence, viii, Burke to Windham, Burke to Dundas, [25] November, 6 December 1795, pp. 346–7, 353–4; *PR*, xliii, 17 and 26 November 1795, pp. 240–2, 642–4; A. V. Beedell, 'John Reeves' prosecution for seditious libel 1795–6,' *HJ* 36 (1993), pp. 815–18, 823.

84. Auckland Correspondence, iii, Auckland to Burke, 28 October 1795, p. 317; *PR*, xliii, 9 and 16 December 1795, pp. 187, 666.

85. LCS Papers, p. 314; *Life of Wilberforce*, ii, Diary, 11 November 1795, p. 114.

86. PRO 30/8/291, Draft Notes, [November 1795], fos 38–9; *PR*, xxxviii, 2 November 1795, pp. 66–8. Wells has claimed that mixed-grain bread originated with Auckland, but such proposals had already come before the Privy Council in 1795: *Wretched Faces*, pp. 210–11.

87. *LCG III*, ii, Portland to George III, 2 October 1795, pp. 407–8; *Commons Sessional Papers*, 99, 4563, Third Report, 9 December 1795, pp. 229–30; Stern, 'The Bread Crisis of 1795–1796', pp. 180–6.

88. PRO 30/8/197, Corn Memo, [November] 1795, fos 1–2; KAO U1590 S5 010/6, 'Parliamentary Considerations', [endorsed November 1795 but possibly 1800]; PRO 30/8/196, Corn Trade Bill, fos 33–5.

89. PRO 30/8/176, Sinclair to Pitt, 5 September 1795, fos 134–5; *Commons Sessional Papers*, 99, 4582, First Report from Waste Lands Committee, 23 December 1795, pp. 258–63.

90. Ehrman, *The Reluctant Transition*, pp. 468–9; E. J. Evans, *The Contentious Tithe: The Tithe Problem in English Agriculture, 1750–1850* (Leicester: 1976), pp. 8–12, 16–36; Abbot, *Diary*, ii, 2 April 1796, pp. 49–50.

91. J. R. Poynter, *Society and Pauperism* (1969), pp. 55–7; D. Eastwood, *Governing Rural England: Tradition and Transformation in Local Government 1780–1840* (Oxford: 1994), pp. 117–19; *PR*, xliii, 8 December 1795, p. 689.

92. For modern criticisms of Pitt, see Wells, *Wretched Faces*, p. 88, and Ehrman, *The Consuming Struggle*, pp. 282, 290–2; Stanhope, *Life of Pitt*, iii, Grenville to Pitt, 18 October 1800, p. 371.

93. *PR*, xiii (3rd series), 11 November 1800, pp. 47–8. Smith, as Donald Winch

has pointed out, was not always read by an eighteenth-century audience as a *laissez-faire* economist: see Winch, *Riches and Poverty: An Intellectual History of Political Economy in Britain, 1750–1834* (Cambridge: 1996), pp. 20–1.

94. A. Smith, *The Theory of Moral Sentiments*, ed. D. D. Raphael and A. L. Macfie (Oxford: 1976), Part VI, Section II, ch. ii, pp. 233–4.

95. PRO 30/8/196, Corn Trade Bill, [November 1800], fos 33–5; *PR*, xiii (3rd series), 11 November 1800, p. 47.

96. '*Das Adam Smith Problem*' was the term used by German intellectual historians at the turn of this century to describe a key problem in Smith studies, the seemingly contradictory messages to be found in the *Theory of Moral Sentiments* (1759) and the *Wealth of Nations* (1776). One asserted that active benevolence towards the poor was a duty of the rich, while the other stated that the unfettered operation of a free market in corn would bring long-term prosperity to all social groups. See Winch, 'Science and the legislator: Adam Smith and after', *Economic Journal* 93 (1983), pp. 501–20, and 'Adam Smith: Scottish moral philosopher as political economist', *HJ* 35 (1992), pp. 91–113.

97. For this, Pitt needed statistical information and he was starting to collect it: Rose Diaries, ii, Pitt to Stafford, 6 November 1795, p. 204; PRO 30/8/119, J. Call to Pitt, 21 December 1795, fo. 80.

98. PRO 30/8/197, Food Memo, [December] 1795, fos 134–5; PRO 30/8/307, Heads of a Bill for the Better Relief and Employment of the Poor and Poor Relief Calculations (w. m. 1794–late 1795/6), fos 11–23, 135–5. All commentators were negative to the bill.

99. J. Holland Rose, *William Pitt and the Great War* (1911), pp. 331–3; Ehrman, *The Consuming Struggle*, pp. 106–8.

100. PRO 30/8/310, draft Commutation Bill, [w. m. 1796–late 1798], fos 74–5, 86.

101. Evans, *The Contentious Tithe*, p. 80.

102. PRO 30/8/278, Collateral Successions, [w. m. 1795], fos 217–19; CUL 6958/9, 1838, 1858, 1865, Auckland to Pitt, 20 October, 11 and 24 November 1795.

103. HA 119 T108/45, Tomline to Mrs Tomline, 14 October 1794; G. P. Tomline, *Memoirs of the Life of the Right Hon. William Pitt* (2 vols, 1821), ii, pp. 616–18.

104. PH, xxxiv, cols 1442–3.

105. *Report from the Committee of Secrecy of the House of Commons Relative to the Proceedings of Different Persons and Societies in Great Britain and Ireland Engaged in a Treasonable Conspiracy* (1799), cited in M. Elliot, 'French subversion in Britain in the French Revolution', in C. Jones (ed.), *Britain and Revolutionary France* (Exeter: 1983), p. 40.

106. *Dropmore*, iv, Pitt to Grenville, 7 April 1798, pp. 166–7.

107. Burke Correspondence, vii, Burke to J. Noble, 14 March 1790, pp. 101–2.

Conclusion:
Illusion and Delusion in
British Politics and Policy

When all is said and done, the adoption of a conservative public agenda
by the British government in the 1790s demonstrates that William Pitt
and his colleagues had some sympathy for the social, intellectual and
political principles of an emerging Toryism. However, it is dangerous
to conclude that the British government subscribed wholeheartedly to
a conservative creed. There are too many inconsistencies in both official
and private documents to stamp the Pitt ministry with a Tory seal of
approval. Both the words and actions of Pitt during the first half of the
1790s represent a departure from a strictly intellectual or, for that
matter, conventional response to the French Revolution.

Pitt accepted neither the construction nor the conclusions of the
conservative case against the revolution. He was not, however, the sole
contributor to the policy or propaganda of the British government
during the 1790s; to this can be attributed many of its contradictory
features. From 1791 onwards the Duke of Richmond, Lord Grenville,
Henry Dundas and Lord Chatham were all staunch opponents of the
French Revolution. Richmond was the first, in April 1793, to call for
Britain to support the counter-revolution. Grenville and Chatham,
admirers of Burke from afar, shared Pitt's dismissive opinion of revolutionary France as a military and diplomatic power. So too did Dundas,
whose fear of the revolution was practical rather than intellectual
and whose obsession with the colonial war reflected this outlook.[1] From
1794 onwards the Portland Whigs became the chief advocates of ideological warfare and the Bourbon restoration. These differing opinions
about the character and aims of the war produced inevitable tensions
within the Pitt ministry. In August 1793 Richmond and Dundas clashed
over the deployment of British troops overseas. Portland protested with
horror at the Cabinet's decision in September 1795 to release an official
peace statement, while Windham complained to Pitt, Grenville and
Dundas about the ministry's half-hearted support of the French royalists
throughout the 1790s.[2] Grenville, who thought that Europe was the

'real' battlefield of the war', was to oppose Malmesbury's peace missions to France in 1796 and 1797. This mix of what were often incompatible priorities was, on the whole, reflected in the ministry's official and public policy.

The conduct of His Majesty's Government was not inconsistent with the views of its royal head. George III, who had welcomed the war in 1793 and sought to combat the revolution in all its forms, was, nonetheless, a realist. The last thing that the king wanted at the end of 1795 was peace with France but he accepted Pitt's claim that some statement on the subject was necessary to keep the confidence of the House of Commons.[3] The monarch seems to have lost some of his vigour after the porphyria attack of 1788–9. To boot, he lost his last personal contact in the Cabinet when Thurlow was dismissed in May 1792, by which time the king's hostility to Fox had been strengthened by the Regency crisis of 1788–9 and the Opposition leader's partisan support for Russia and France. Dundas and Grenville, very much Pitt's followers if not his creatures, had also established close working relations with the premier and had been promoted to senior Cabinet rank. Following the declaration of war in 1793, George III's influence on government policy became less evident, if only because it was impossible for him to keep track of business in all government departments. By the beginning of 1794 Grenville and Dundas were already complaining about their workloads, and the two Secretaries of State, in partnership with Pitt, were carefully controlling the flow of information to the king, who, though entitled to see all incoming military and diplomatic correspondence, invariably received it with supporting memoranda, proposals and Cabinet minutes which he seldom questioned and never vetoed.[4] George III could be troublesome over the details of a military or diplomatic initiative, but he rarely questioned, let alone obstructed, the government's major policies.[5]

For all its internal disagreements, the Pitt ministry was a remarkably cohesive unit when it came to dealing with the king. George III tended to be neutral in Cabinet disputes; judging from his conduct during the Prussian subsidy question in 1795, he was largely unaware of their existence. Pitt and his colleagues stifled or resolved the vast majority of their differences before going into the Closet. Hawkesbury, the last of the old 'king's friends', was isolated in the ministry after 1792 and, as President of the Board of Trade, did not have the right of access to the Closet. Moreover, Hawkesbury did not think that his duty to the Crown involved the telling of tales about his colleagues; nor, for that matter, did Portland and his followers, who in many respects were intellectually closer to George III than to Pitt. Whatever paths the conservative Whigs had wandered down since parting from Fox, support of the royal prerogative was not one of them.

Pitt, confident that the Cabinet would not contradict him, could – and did – oppose the wishes of his sovereign. George III would have preferred to see Britain's military operations restricted to Flanders, the government as a more committed and active supporter of the Bourbon restoration, and a rigorous official crackdown on popular radicalism. When habeas corpus was suspended in May 1794, George III remarked that 'there cannot be an impartial man who, when the papers are brought to light, will not see that if Government has erred, it has been in not stepping forward earlier'.[6] Pitt, aware nevertheless that his monarch could not be pushed too far, avoided confrontation on personal issues to ensure acceptance of general policies. When the Duke of York was made Commander-in-Chief of the British army in Flanders, nobody in the ministry thought that he would have to exercise much independent leadership. By the autumn of 1793 Pitt was considering York's replacement by Cornwallis, but he did not demand the royal duke's removal until the British army was recalled from Europe in the autumn of 1794. George III was very hurt.[7]

The king shared his government's official neutrality towards the French Revolution until the end of 1792. Like Grenville, George may have seen neutrality as part of a British intellectual *cordon sanitaire*. Pitt did not. When he finally spoke out against the revolution on 30 April 1792 the decision of Parliament, as he saw it, had already been taken. Four-fifths of the Commons and all of the Lords would, as Pitt wrote to Auckland, support a general denunciation of the British reform movement.[8] General apprehension about the activities of reform clubs did not, however, translate into rabid anti-Jacobin conviction. The Foxites' insistence that, in issuing the May Proclamation, Pitt was trying to do no more than split the Whig Party is interesting, because it suggests that the only major counter-revolutionary group in Parliament to which Pitt could have appealed was the conservative Whigs.[9]

Was the British government leading or following public opinion inside and outside Parliament from 1792 to 1795? The debates of Lords and Commoners on the May proclamation proved that Pitt's analysis was correct – that Parliament was sympathetic neither to the principles of the revolution nor to their dissemination in Britain. The extent of its concern about France, its revolution and the native reform movement was unclear. In appealing to this constituency of voters, Pitt was responding to an independent shift in opinion at Westminster. The loose governing consensus on which Pitt's power had always been based had already showed signs of moving to the right, but in May 1792 its concern was recruited to the ministry's service for specific purposes. The voice of Parliament not only gave official weight to a condemnation of FOP and Foxite activities, but it also authorized what the Opposition called a 'loyalty test'. Pitt wanted to know what the

country at large thought about radical publications and reform organizations.

The loyal addresses that the ministry received over the summer of
1792 more than satisfied Pitt's curiosity. In 1983 Robert Dozier claimed
that, by 1792, the literate British public had already become familiar
with the issues of – and debate on – the French Revolution through
the metropolitan and provincial press. Dozier's work has been much
criticized but his study of south-eastern newspapers, limited as it is,
indicates that educated people in the Home Counties would not have
been ignorant of French events by or in 1792.[10] This knowledge
predisposed some of them to respond positively to the loyal address
initiative of the 'county associations' formed by the friends of the
government, but the extent to which their beliefs were shaped by the
May proclamation is unknown. At this stage, the uses to which 'loyal'
concern about the French Revolution might be put were not defined
at official levels. Grenville thought that county addresses endorsing 'the
sentiments of *Parliament*' might be useful in future debates, but no
participation in the French war was anticipated during the summer of
1792.[11]

By 8 November 1792 the State Papers Domestic bore testimony to
the growth of British anxiety about the native radical presence. Conservatism had received an accession of strength through alarmism. For
a week this predisposed Pitt to make the government's domestic policy
overtly Tory. By 28 November, when the Cabinet agreed to embody
the English militia and recall Parliament, the ministry had made a
conscious decision to answer the revolutionary diplomacy of France in
the same vein. Its own decree of 13 November had committed the
British government to a defence of the United Provinces. The militia
proclamation of 1 December inaugurated an Anglo-French war not of
ideas, but of images – of unity versus disunity, and confidence versus
fear. The actual call-out of the militia was regarded as a precautionary
measure by a premier convinced that 'we shall soon succeed in dissipating the mischiefs around us'. Parliament, that source of loyal
addresses and votes of confidence, was a legitimating instrument of
incalculable value, provided that it could be persuaded to accept a
conservative account of war and revolution; Pitt was having doubts
about this on 4 December.[12] He was less worried about public opinion
following the emergence of the Reevites. There can be no doubt that
Europe was facing an international crisis at the end of 1792 and
that, were France to declare war on the United Provinces, it was better
to get Parliament's support for Britain's participation in that war at the
outset rather than ask for it after the event. At the same time, the brinkmanship exercises of 1787, 1790 and 1791 had shown that the
government possessed much more freedom of diplomatic and military

action when Parliament was in recess than when it was sitting. By recalling Lords and Commoners, Pitt was committing himself in public to whatever case he chose to present to them.

The intellectual inspiration for this conduct came primarily from Burke and his friends, the one group anxious for the adoption of vigorous measures. The war of principle was little more than an intellectual and rhetorical device in December 1792 because it bore no resemblance to the actual conduct of war and diplomacy or, for that matter, to the maintenance of public order. While it justified resistance to French arrogance and aggression, it did not necessarily justify war.[13] Pitt tried to persuade Parliament that French principles and policies were inextricably linked throughout December 1792 and January 1793. He went no further, because he was afraid that Parliament might not agree that Britain was a guardian of the old European order. In April 1791 the Commons had rejected Pitt's personification of Britain as the defender of Poland, Turkey and 'the scale of Europe'. On 20 January 1793, with war decided upon, Dundas and George III were analysing the Commons divisions on the Ochakow debates: 'Portland 30, Fox 44, Doubtful 30', noted the king. The French solved this problem by declaring war first.[14]

In 1793 'indemnification for the past and security for the future' represented a synthesis of all the major opinions in Parliament except that of the Foxite Whigs. Pitt was reluctant to rely exclusively on the war of ideas because it was a potential vote-loser. The Foxites and Portland Whigs were oddities in the House of Commons that had been returned by the general election of 1790. Neither Pitt nor many of his contemporaries saw the French Revolution as the 'greatest' – to quote Fox – or worst – to paraphrase Burke – event 'that ever happened in the world'.[15] Pitt was by no means the only 'independent Whig' to undergo a 'reluctant transition' during the 1790s. The majority of MPs voting with the ministry up to 1795 were slow to re-examine their morals and principles in the light of the revolutionary experience, let alone to apply this reconstructed thought to an evaluation of the government's policies at home and abroad. When the ministry embarked wholeheartedly on 'total war' in 1794, a development that did not stem from a conversion to the canons of counter-revolutionary conservatism, but from the need to justify a war effort whose diplomatic and military parameters had changed drastically since 1793, Wilberforce, Fox and other MPs were confused. When the Portland Whigs appeared on the Treasury benches in 1794, howls of complaint could be heard from Pitt's followers, who did not accept that Burke's defence and defenders of the old order, described by Solicitor-General Mitford as 'broken reeds', were worthy of Cabinet office.[16] By the beginning of 1795 the war of principle, baulked of legitimizing victories, had become a political liability. Total war could have continued to be useful to Pitt if he had been prepared to explain his government's failures by reference to the universal evils that the revolution had unleashed upon the world, but Pitt was not, at this stage, prepared to do this. From January 1795 onwards he was preparing a path of retreat. When the war of principle was dropped in May, nobody was surprised.[17]

Government propaganda outside Parliament served three purposes during the 1790s: the rebuttal of Opposition and radical attacks in the metropolitan and provincial press; the explanation of the ministry's foreign and domestic policies to the nation; the maintenance of 'the spirit of the public' or 'spirit of the country' at appropriate levels. The government did not take much interest in a conservative press prior to the winter of 1792. When the *Sun*, soon to become one of the ministry's chief London newspapers, was set up in August 1792, its directors, Bland Burges and Long, found it difficult to get government advertisements for the paper, bad news for an organ of the press in any day or age. Grenville did not like the partisan tone of the *Sun*, so much so that Long, as Pitt's guest at Walmer Castle, passed on Grenville's criticism of the newspaper's blatant pro-government bias to his partner. For Burges, writing half the articles under pseudonyms, objectivity meant lip service to Sheridan as a 'great wit' and Fox 'as a party leader'.[18]

By December 1792 the *Sun* and the *True Briton* had become vehicles of official Toryism to rouse the nation in support of the government.[19] There was a party-political dimension to this. The ever helpful Miles had told Long not only that Brissot's *Le Patriot français* was carrying accurate advance reports of Fox's Commons motions, but that James Perry, editor of the Opposition *Morning Chronicle*, was a regular dinner guest in Portman Square. By January 1793 this paper was seen by government supporters as an organ of sedition. Canning told his family, then subscribing to the *Chronicle*, to take the *True Briton*, the '*antidote* with the poison'.[20] By 1797, when the Solicitor-General moved to police the press, the ministry had long since concluded that Opposition and radical papers were collaborating with the enemy. Lord Auckland wrote that the *Morning Chronicle* and the *Courier* had been specific targets of the new legislation: 'there was reason to believe [they] were employed not only to promote the Principles of Jacobinism; but to give to the Parisians such Impressions [of England] as the Directory might wish to dictate; & also (which was still worse) to convey intelligence.'[21] For the origins of these suspicions one must look to the activities of Vorontsov during the Ochakow crisis of 1791. Liberal and radical journalists, particularly those known to support the Opposition Whigs, did not fare well during the 1790s.

As Britain's military position *vis-à-vis* France deteriorated from 1794 onwards, the Tory press became increasingly important as a defender of the government's failures. In many respects the conservative press was preaching to the half-converted here. The *Morning Chronicle, Courier, True Briton* and *Sun* were nonetheless produced for the higher and middling ranks of British society. Canning, for one, found the bombastic tone of the *Sun* 'vile', and his dissatisfaction with the metropolitan conservative press partially explains the appearance of the *Anti-Jacobin* in 1797, to which Pitt contributed two articles on finance. His specimen of Arab poetry is likely to be genuine; Beilby Porteus, Bishop of London, wrote to Hannah More on 16 January 1797 that Pitt was 'quite in raptures' with Arab riddles 'and can say most of them by heart'.[22]

Pitt was prepared to explain some of the realities behind diplomacy to the élite of the country. This was not the sort of information to be released to social groups whose political rights were not clearly defined. For the general reader, the war of principle made a convenient authorized guide to the events and policies of the 1790s, both in Britain and the wider world. The educated public, like its representatives, got a subtle mix of conventional and ideological motives for war.[23] On 17 November 1792 Pitt identified what he saw as the natural constituency of 'loyalists', 'the higher and middling classes'. It was primarily for the latter group that Pitt's stable of hack writers, people like John Bowles and William Playfair plied their trade.[24] The dividing line between loyal supporters and loyal opposers was, nevertheless, thin, and the government did not want to embody, let alone empower, an opinion group that might very well turn against it. The modes of loyalist response to the official recruitment drives of the 1790s were always as carefully defined – and, in some cases, prescribed – as possible.[25]

Historians have tended to explain the British government's interest in loyalists and volunteers in terms of a campaign to bolster the forces of conservative repression. Loyalism was not, however, a monolithic creed, nor was it seen by the ministry as such. It could be useful to a decentralized government and was so described by Grenville in July 1791, before either radicalism or war became affairs of state. An official investigation of the Portsmouth dockyards had been sparked off by rumours that French spies had been sent to fire British ships. These accounts had given rise to a public alarm 'which was not discouraged as this is one of the cases where security arises out of a general apprehension of danger'.[26] Spies and saboteurs were a recurrent worry for any government in *ancien régime* Europe and 'loyalism' could serve conventional defence purposes. In October 1793, however, Dundas decided to reinforce the south coast against an invasion threat that the government did not take very seriously because criticism from the British élite was a greater threat than the French people's army: 'too much alarm is as bad in its effects as too much supineness'.[27] The Pitt ministry was intent on preventing alarmists from trying to control or manipulate official policy. The 'loyalists' might well lose confidence in Pitt because he wasn't *'doing* enough'. The government was never quite sure of the Portland Whigs' allegiance until they joined the ministry in July 1794.[28] Ideological conviction would keep conservatives loyal unless there was a credible alternative creed for them to adhere to. The ministry, fearful that one would emerge, treated the élite with respect and the middling sort with great caution.

'As to Jacobinism, strictly speaking, by which I mean the love of insurrection for the purpose of reducing all mankind to equality,' wrote Auckland to Pitt on 28 November 1794, 'I do not think that it exists in the country, except in the lowest and most ignorant classes, and perhaps among some individuals of a better description.'[29] 'Jacobin' is one of the great vexatious terms of the 1790s, as much so in Britain as in France. Some used it indiscriminately from 1789 onwards to describe all persons, principles and policies of left-wing tendencies. The British government, with the help of the *émigrés*, sorted out all the French political groups of the revolution. Pitt shared Eden's definition of the term 'Jacobin', but did not spend the 1790s or any other decade of his life in perpetual fear of the lower orders. When the Foxites described the seditious meetings bill as an instrument of class warfare, Pitt was amazed. In denying the charge, he asked whether it was necessary 'for the high and low to meet separately and present their several petitions, or might it not rather be said, that each rank would find some advocate in the other, and that the interests of all would be blended?'[30] Parliamentary representation, he claimed, encompassed all ranks of men, 'not excepting the lowest'. This statement would not have been out of place in the Parliament of 1785: 'When any civil society was far advanced, a clear line of separation between actual and virtual representation could not subsist.'

Here was a seemingly Tory vision of utopia – the organic community defined. 'Did I ever tell you,' wrote Hannah More to her sister Mary in May 1796, 'of the satisfaction Pitt expressed one day about our tracts? He said he had just heard that 40,000 had been sent to America and that he had not met with anything in a long time that pleased him more, than that such reading was gaining ground in the country.'[31] At the end of 1792 More had made her name as a defender of the British constitution in *Village Politics*, a 'useful writing' very popular with the APLP. By 1796 More had left loyalist political commentary behind for moral and religious instruction.[32] It was to these 'other subjects' that Pitt had indirectly referred as fit for mass study on 17 November 1795. Before concluding that Pitt was an evangelical of secret and devout fervour, a statement that distressed Wilberforce greatly during the 1800s, it must be recalled that Pitt was by no means unusual in regarding religion as an instrument of social control. This concept was integral to any defence of the Test and Corporation Acts on the grounds of expediency and emerged in 1793 as a key feature of British plans for the occupation of Dunkirk and Toulon. In June 1795, when Pitt was telling the Bishop of Lincoln to preach charity to the rich and self-help to the poor, tracts like More's *The Riot; or Half a Loaf is better than no Bread*, which came out in August, served the purposes of polity and society. In December 1795 she referred to the formation of 'two highly respectable committees, Members of Parliament etc.', in the City and Westminster 'for the regular circulation of our Repository Tracts'. This bore a suspicious resemblance to the events of late 1792 and, while it is likely that government associations were active in the distribution of loyalist tracts in 1795, there is little evidence of direct and sustained official sponsorship for the production of popular conservative propaganda.[33] What Cabinet ministers did in their spare time is another story. Grenville, Mitford and Windham were all active in county 'loyalist' groups. Pitt was not, nor did he spare much thought for the common people until famine threatened to overwhelm the land.

There can be no doubt that Pitt preferred conservative concepts of social harmony to theoretical natural rights models. He nevertheless admired – and, to a certain extent, shared – the radicals' faith in man as a rational animal. Social inequality saved man from his worst instincts, but the existence of original sin, one of the few innate entities in Pitt's universe, did not presuppose that the masses lacked intellectual faculties fit for improvement or that enlightenment was inappropriate to their station. Man was not irredeemable. In February 1795 Pitt was still defending a vision of Africa and its inhabitants that few MPs had shared, almost all of whom now associated that vision with the cult of equality that the French Revolution had produced. The human right to life and personal liberty was universal and Pitt did not exclude the pursuit of happiness from the exercise of the mind. Instruction in one's duties predated, but did not necessarily preclude, some kind of education in rights:

> Mr Pitt used to say that Tom Paine was quite in the right; but then he wd. add, 'What am I to do? If this country is overrun with all these men full of vice and folly, I cannot exterminate them. It would be very well, to be sure, if everybody had sense enough to act as they ought; but, as things are, if I were to encourage Tom Paine's opinions, we should have a bloody revolution; and, after all, matters would return pretty much as they were.'[34]

This was a tongue-in-cheek criticism not only of Paine's belief in the perfectibility of man, but also of Burke's theory of revolutions. Pitt, who felt that nothing about the revolution was inevitable, disliked other aspects of Burke's conservatism that had been taken up by other authors: intolerance, fear, and an exccessive, often irrational, veneration for the past. Unlike many conservative pamphlets, the *Cheap Repository Tracts* promoted a positive and often critical vision of British society without reliance upon xenophobia, materialism and bigotry.[35] Pitt, no friend to intolerance, relied on this material and the values that it promoted to keep the nation loyal. He was also prepared to appeal to age-old anti-French prejudice, because it militated against the emergence of any republican democrats in the British Isles.

From his Cambridge days onwards Pitt had stated that doctrines of resistance were 'of dangerous tendency'.[36] He also thought that these ideas did not produce disorder without intermediary agents. It is necessary to distinguish here between actual and potential subversion, because official perceptions of both depended upon wartime economic, social, diplomatic and military conditions rather than upon the fortunes of popular radicalism. Radical reform was to be resisted because it represented a synthesis of French and British political thought couched in terms that would appeal to a public with enough political awareness to understand the basic message of reform, if not its subversive undertones and ulterior motives. So specific were these that Pitt saw the radical siege as a temporary product of the war. Radicals were promoting 'a pretended parliamentary reform'. For Pitt, 'not fond of the applause of a mob', the readiness of the Foxite Whigs to encourage the popular radicals made them reprehensible. In October 1794 Dundas found 'The Spirit of Faction' indistinguishable from 'sedition and treason'.[37]

Actual or suspected collaboration with the enemy over the water was needed before the government took action. The passage of the Two Acts at the end of 1795 is an exception to this rule, but Pitt's panic on this occasion was extreme and very much a reaction to the state of national emergency that had been produced by two consecutive bad harvests. The ministry relied less upon official instruments of persecution than upon semi- and unofficial agents of deterrence. The British government's treatment of its critics was not as harsh as has been supposed, if only because the state did not, as Pitt and Grenville acknowledged in November 1792, possess the resources to police dissidents with any rigour: 'Our laws suppose magistrates and Grand Juries to do their duty, and if they do it not, I have little faith in its being done by a Government such as the Constitution has made ours.'[38] Equally important in the slow development of the ministry's anti-Jacobin domestic policy was the unwillingness of its leaders to redefine their powers and responsibilities. Reconstructing the public order infrastructure of the state was neither feasible nor desirable, and this was reflected in the arguments that Pitt used. In 1793 he sought to base the Traitorous Correspondence Act on 25 Edward III and, more strongly, on legislation that had been passed in 'the best of ages', the years between 1688 and 1714. In 1794 Pitt wanted to establish his doctrine of constructive treason at common – not statute – law. The particularism of English common law made the court of the King's Bench an appropriate register of jurisprudential solutions to public order problems which were peculiar to a time and place.[39] The 'absolute' legitimacy that Parliament could confer upon the government's interpretation of the law on treason ill fitted it for such a purpose. When Pitt was faced with what looked like actual insurrection at the end of 1795, he was forced to grasp the nettle – and here it is significant that his respect for the constitutional proprieties still prevailed. The Two Acts, like the government's other repressive measures of the 1790s, were temporary and partial in conception and execution.

In 1891 Lord Rosebery found it inconceivable that Pitt alone could have been untouched by the French Revolution. While nobody, including this author, would say that Pitt did not undergo some metamorphosis during the 1790s, be it ever so reluctant, the fact remains that no deep sea changes took place in his political and social thought. Ehrman is right in claiming that the direction of Pitt's policies was determined by circumstance rather than will.[40] It remains difficult to separate the private man from the minister, for Pitt, in coming to terms with war and revolution, was guided as much by the constraints of office as by personal inclination. Certain paths were marked out by precedent or official practice; the very structures of the British state shaped the government's response to the foreign and domestic challenges of the 1790s. Any assessment of Pitt's career in whole or in part rests upon a definition of his art of the possible. Here the personal convictions that underpinned thought and action were of paramount importance. From these he derived the personal strength and good cheer which his friends, colleagues and followers found truly amazing: '*I cannot allow myself to doubt*' was Pitt's solution.[41]

Pitt's convictions were often illusions. The Foxites were not in the pay of the French. The radicals did not, from 1792 to 1795, represent a fifth column. The First Republic would not crumble in the face of that ever elusive final allied campaign. France was not swarming with closet constitutional royalists. When proved frightfully wrong by events, Pitt's world began to crumble at the edges. He was arguably at his most creative during such crises – if this is an appropriate description for either the programme of repression devised by the government in late 1792 or the strategy of social and economic reform produced at the end of 1795. Pitt's resolution in the face of repeated disasters, praised by colleagues and supporters, was a testament to the triumph of his convictions. This was seen by Fox as self-delusion: 'The foolish sanguinity of ministers is beyond belief.' By 1795 there was nobody in the Cabinet who was much inclined to contradict Pitt's version of the facts. Richmond, who had tried to do so in 1793, was dismissed in 1795, the year in which Dundas could be found apologizing profusely for speaking and writing 'what perhaps for the moment you would rather be excused from hearing and reading'. By the 1800s Hester Stanhope was describing the inner circle of Pitt's friends and confidants as 'sycophants'.[42]

What Professor Blanning has called the 'Coppelia effect' governed Britain's military policy for the first two years of the war. When Britain embarked on hostilities against France in February 1793, the threat of French arms and ideas was much less important than the future of the armed conflict in the Low Countries. If Pitt's conduct during the diplomatic crises of 1787 and 1790 is representative of a British response to the prospect of war with France, then an Admiralty overcome with paranoia for the security of trade routes to – and outposts in – the colonies would have wasted no time in sending immediate reinforcements to the East and West Indies. So low had France sunk in British eyes that arms and money went to the Flanders theatre first in an attempt to patch up relations with Austria and Prussia.[43]

By June 1793 Pitt was hoping to cripple France on the Continent and in the colonies. The scenario of haughty Gaul's prostration was so enticing that the British government was planning for nothing less than complete victory. This, thought Pitt, was a matter of one or two sustained campaigns. In 1793 the government had anticipated an end to the war in two years, which predisposed it to be lenient to the republic in the first instance. From 1793 to early 1795 the ministry knew little of what was taking place in France. Here the Pitt ministry was a victim of its own convictions and poor sources of information about the French interior. The Foreign Office received the major Paris newspapers until the end of 1792, but, following the outbreak of war, it received only the *Moniteur* on a regular basis and that came via Switzerland.[44] In the absence of other sources, it is possible that the British government believed some of the disinformation – one cannot call it intelligence – coming from the Agence de Paris, but the information that the Pitt ministry received from Paris through the press and the *émigrés* only confirmed its presuppositions about the parlous state of France's government, resources, army and finances.

From 1787 to 1789 Pitt had regarded the revolution as an aristocratic challenge to royal authority. From 1789 to 1791 events in France took on the character of a constitutional reform movement intent on weakening the Crown. Events up to 1792 represented Pitt's 'true' revolution, and from March 1792 onwards he and Grenville suspected that, unless the combined armies got to Paris first, war would radicalize the revolution and probably overthrow the 1791 constitutional monarchy. Both believed nonetheless that France would fight in its defence. By the end of October 1792 they accepted that this battle had been won. A month later British perceptions of French war aims began to change; for this the decrees of 16 and 19 November 1792 were responsible.

While Grenville was now convinced that the war had become ideological, Pitt did not entirely agree. Success on the battlefields of Flanders had raised the sights of the French, who, as Chauvelin told Grenville on 29 November 1792, wanted formal recognition of the First Republic and its recent conquests. Participation in the war depended, for the Pitt ministry, upon the fate of France's hostages – Nice, Savoy and the Austrian Netherlands. French refusals to compromise on the Scheldt strongly suggested that the republic hoped to keep them without having to fight Britain and the United Provinces, an extension of the war which it was trying to avert through the sponsorship of sedition in both countries. Pitt always saw the revolution militant in all its forms not only as the revolution betrayed, but as a means rather than an end. Neutrality to the revolution and formal recognition of the republic from the rest of Europe were, in Pitt's eyes, the key objectives of France in 1792. As Grenville's dispatches of 28 December made apparent, Britain would grant these if France relinquished its gains. Revolutionary diplomacy did not, however, create an atmosphere of especial mistrust in 1792. After the breakdown of executive authority in France, the British government could never be sure who or what the French diplomats were representing.[45]

In February 1793 the Pitt ministry was still prepared to recognize the republic and, despite telling Parliament that Britain was going to war to save the world from evil, the government was trying to reconcile the European powers to its existence. By September 1793 this policy had been abandoned; no permanent system of government had been established in France, nor was there much prospect of one emerging in the near future. At this point, when Toulon delivered itself into British hands in the name of the Bourbons, an imposed settlement began to look like a viable option.

Pitt, much attracted to a constitutional monarchy in theory, nonetheless believed that France would not reinstate the Bourbons unless they accepted that the social, economic, legal and political grievances that had been raised by the Estates General in 1789 were, in the words of Sir Gilbert Elliot, 'generally obnoxious' and in need of redress.[46] Pitt and Grenville, aware that such a settlement would be difficult to construct because France had no experience of limited monarchy, were constantly frustrated by the failure of the French royalists to come up with something resembling the beloved British constitution, not to mention the refusals of Provence, the would-be Louis XVIII, to contemplate serious reform of any description.[47]

Notwithstanding his personal preference for constitutional monarchy, Pitt realized that the republicans might reach an acceptable consensus before the royalists. In some respects, this was more desirable, not only because he found the *ancien régime* distasteful, but because a France stripped of its old dynastic connections would be isolated in Europe. From November 1792 Pitt prepared to admit the new France to the international diplomatic community, provided that its government was stable and it deferred to the code of conventions observed by other states. Peace was made probable, wrote Pitt in January 1796, by the establishment of any French government 'which shall appear to possess sufficient Stability, Authority, Good Faith & Pacific Disposition to make such a Treaty a reasonable Ground of Security'.[48] Stability and authority were not to be found in direct popular sovereignty. In June 1793 Pitt told the architects of the 1793 constitution that their ideas were 'impracticable' and that they did not possess the power to carry them into execution. Here was some respect for the mission of the Constitutional Committee, if no confidence in its success.

Before the government of France was declared 'revolutionary until the peace', Pitt did acknowledge the existence of some integrity in the republic. On the whole, however, he saw the politics and policies of France from August 1792 to October 1795 as a series of factional power struggles between desperate self-seeking demagogues. He found the dictatorship of the revolutionary committees appalling and inexcusable. This was the one French system to which Pitt would give no quarter, and in December 1799 he wrote to Canning: 'we should never think of peace with a *Revolutionary Jacobin* Government'.[49] Were another 'Reign of Terror' to be established in France, Pitt would fight 'to any Period to which Dr Laurence himself could look forward'. French Laurence, Regius Professor of Civil Law at Oxford and Burke's anointed successor, was not normally Pitt's favourite author.

Republican government could take several forms and it was here that Pitt saw the stability and authority that would give peace to Europe. After the coup of 18–19 *brumaire* (9–10 November 1799) that finished off the Directory, Pitt gave some thought to peace with the emerging Consulate. Although he was no fan of Napoleon, a man driven by 'Military Passion – necessity of Distinguishing himself – Revenge', Pitt stated that the establishment of a 'mixed and moderate Plan of Government' in France, 'on the model of the American or any other', would make it impossible for Britain to object to peace: 'no man can pretend that there would be any Thing in the Form or ostensible Principles of such a Government which would make Treaty with it unsafe.' Pitt, like French *émigrés constitutionnels*, was always more interested in the structures of governments than in their principles, because he did not see the French Revolution as a social revolution. When Pitt told the Commons on 8 December 1795 that the constitution of the Year Three was more likely to be permanent than its predecessors, this was no mere rhetoric. His interest in the royalist coup of 13 *vendémiaire* (5 October 1795) proved that he saw the Directory as a stable and acceptable system. For the next four years the British were to devote their subversionary activities in France not to the Directory's destruction, but to its strengthening through the election of royalists to its bicameral legislature.[50]

Stability and security, for Pitt, lay in the ordering of relationships between individuals, corporate groups and institutional authorities. In the process of doing so, constitutions created 'artificial distinctions (I am not afraid to use the term)' which laid down guidelines for a society's conduct and, by virtue of this, a framework of civil and political liberty which 'set in motion all the springs which actuate the great mass of the community through all its various descriptions'.[51] This Pitt had said of the British constitution in 1792. This doctrine originated with Montesquieu and Jean Delolme, but Pitt was prepared to apply it to all systems of government, whose direct and indirect powers to constrain human action were so great that the theoretical foundations on which citizenship were based became, for practical purposes, almost meaningless. Government existed to secure 'the tranquillity and welfare both of individuals and the public', goals that could be interpreted in national contexts, but which ultimately comprised 'the only true foundation and only rational object of all political societies'.

Liberty involved the maintenance of a balance between the presence and absence of such constraints. The rights that a constitution conferred upon a people were not inherited from the wisdom of ages, nor were the institutions through which social, political and economic intercourse took place. Rights were derived from utility, not history. One would not, nevertheless, expect to find Pitt embracing radical reform. A government's free character came not from the suffrage that could return representatives to Commons, Congress or Convention, but from the success of any given constitution in maintaining the balance between freedom and constraint which allowed liberty to exist. This the British system already did 'beyond the frame of any government that has ever existed'.[52]

Pitt emerges from the 1790s as a maverick sum of conventional parts. Defining him as a 'liberal Tory' is possible, but contentious, for his defence of things as they were was only partial. Placement as a 'conservative Whig' is equally difficult, bearing in mind what Pitt thought about Burke and his friends. What, then, were Pitt's perceptions of the best of times and the worst of times? In assessing the impact of the French Revolution on the ideas and policies of William Pitt, one finds no overwhelmingly negative response. He did not fear and oppose the revolution consistently from 1787 to 1795; he regarded it, on the whole, in objective and dispassionate terms. In drawing up a final balance sheet of Pitt's thoughts on war and revolution, what strikes the observer is the eternal optimism with which he faced the future. Pitt never stopped hoping that the revolution would bring some good to France, Britain and the rest of the world.

Notes

1. P. Jupp, *Lord Grenville 1759–1834* (Oxford: 1985), p. 145; PRO 30/8/335, 'Appraisal of the French Army', [1793], fos 185–7; BL Add MS 37884, Pitt to Windham, 25 September 1794, fos 70–4.

2. *Dropmore*, iii, Portland to Grenville, 21 September 1795, pp. 135–6; PRO 30/8/168, Portland to Pitt, 28 September 1795, fos 97–8; J. Holland Rose, *Pitt and Napoleon: Essays and Letters* (1912), Windham to Pitt, Pitt to Windham, 16 and 18 October 1795, pp. 278–9.

3. [Philip], 5th Earl Stanhope, *Life of the Right Hon. William Pitt* (4 vols, 1861–2), ii, George III to Pitt, 13 November 1795, pp. xxviii–xxix; *Dropmore*, iii, George III to Grenville, 27 October 1795, p. 143.

4. SRO GD 224/30/9/10(3), Dundas to Buccleuch, 23 August 1793; PRO 30/58/1, Grenville to Pitt, 26 February 1794, fo. 91.

5. D. G. Barnes, *George III and William Pitt* (Stanford, Calif.: 1939), pp. 269–301; M. Duffy, 'Pitt, Grenville and the conduct of British foreign policy in the 1790s', in J. Black (ed.), *Knights Errant and True Englishmen* (Edinburgh: 1989), pp. 171–2.

6. *LCG III*, ii, 1069, George III to Pitt, 17 May 1794.

7. Holland Rose, *Pitt and Napoleon*, Pitt to Grenville, 23 November 1794, pp. 231–3.

8. Auckland Correspondence, ii, Pitt to Auckland, 1 May 1792, pp. 401–2.

9. Henry Edward, 3rd Baron Holland, *Memoirs of the Whig Party in my Time* (2 vols, 1852) ii, p. 14.

10. Dozier, *For King, Constitution and Country* (Lexington, KY.: 1983), pp. 15–20.

11. *Court and Cabinets*, ii, Grenville to Buckingham, 21 June 1792, pp. 211–12.

12. Clements MS, Pitt to Dundas, 28 November 1792; Stanhope, *Life of Pitt*, Pitt to Dundas, 4 December 1792, pp. 176–7.

13. J. Black, *British Foreign Policy in an Age of Revolutions, 1783–1793* (Cambridge: 1994), p. 159; T. C. W. Blanning, *The Origins of the French Revolutionary Wars* (1986), p. 362; J. M. Walsh, *Edmund Burke and International Relations* (Basingstoke: 1995), pp. 92, 122.

14. *LCG III*, ii, Dundas to George III, 20 January 1793, pp. 645–6.

15. Fox Mem., ii, Fox to R. Fitzpatrick, 30 July 1789, p. 361.

16. PRO 30/8/170, Mitford to Pitt, 25 January 1795, fo. 158.

17. *Life of Wilberforce*, ii, Diary, 2 May 1795, p. 86.

18. L. Werkmeister, *The London Daily Press 1782–1792* (Lincoln: 1963), pp. 368–71, and *A Newspaper History of England* (Lincoln: 1967), p. 103;

Bod, Dep Bland Burges 45, Long to Burges, 16 October 1792, fos 86–7; Dep Bland Burges 46, Bland Burges to Long, 15, 17 October 1792, fos 150–1, 156.

19. BL Add MS 16919, J. Heriot [*True Briton* editor] to J. Moore, 29 November 1792, fo. 111; BL Add MS 16924, J. Walter to Reeves, 7 January 1793, fo. 51; A. Aspinall, *Politics and the Press 1780–1850* (1973 edn), pp. 78–83, p. 203; J. J. Sack, *From Jacobite to Conservative* (Cambridge: 1993), pp. 12–14.

20. Miles Correspondence, ii, Miles to Long, 24 September 1792, pp. 333–4, minute of 15–16 December 1792, pp. 390–1; J. T. Murley, 'The background to the outbreak of the Anglo-French War of 1793', D. Phil thesis (Oxford: 1959), p. 350; p. 350; Black, *British Foreign Policy ... 1783–1793*, pp. 426, 429; Canning MS, 29 dii, 22 January 1794, fo. 26.

21. Aspinall, *Politics and the Press*, pp. 38–9; Christie, 'James Perry of the *Morning Chronicle* 1756–1821', in *Myth and Reality in Late Eighteenth Century British Politics and other Papers* (1970) p. 347; HRO 38M 49/1/1, 19, Auckland to Wickham, 24 December 1798; Ehrman, *The Consuming Struggle*, pp. 112–14.

22. A. V. Beedell, 'John Reeves' prosecution for seditious libel 1795–6,' *HJ* 36 (1993), p. 821; Canning MS, 29 dii, 21 January 1794, fo. 25; More Memoirs, iii, Porteus to More, 16 January 1797, pp. 3–4; Ehrman, *The Consuming Struggle*, pp. 110–14.

23. T. Schofield, 'British politicians and French arms', *History* 78 (1993), pp. 195–6; E. Vincent, '"The real grounds of the present war": John Bowles and the French Revolutionary Wars, 1792–1802', *History* 78 (1993), pp. 378–98.

24. Clements MS, Pitt to Dundas, 17 and 25 November 1792; Sack, *From Jacobite to Conservative*, pp. 17–25.

25. H. Cunningham, 'The language of patriotism 1750–1914', *History Workshop Journal* 12 (1981), pp. 8–14; L. Colley, 'Whose nation? class and national consciousness in eighteenth-century Britain', *P&P* 113 (1986), pp. 108–9; H. T. Dickinson, 'Popular conservatism and militant loyalism 1789–1815', in *Britain and the French Revolution, 1789–1815* (1989), pp. 122–4.

26. J. Dinwiddy, 'England', in Dinwiddy and O. Dann (eds), *Nationalism in the Age of the French Revolution* (1983), pp. 53–70; J. E. Cookson, 'The English volunteer movement of the French Wars', *HJ* 32 (1989), pp. 868–90; J. Money, 'Freemasonry and the fabric of loyalism in Hanoverian England', in A. Birke and E. Hellmuth (eds), *The Transformation of Political Culture* (Oxford: 1990), pp. 235–71.

27. BL Add MS 58919, Grenville to Auckland, 22 July 1791, fos 124–6; HO 42/26, Dundas to Amhert, 14 October 1793, fos 750–1.

28. *Dropmore*, ii, Buckingham to Grenville, 8 November 1792, pp. 327–8.

29. Auckland Correspondence, iii, Auckland to Pitt, 28 November 1794, p. 271.

30. *PR*, xliii, 17 November 1795, pp. 241–2.

31. More Memoirs, ii, Hannah to Patty More, [May] 1796, p. 475.

32. R. Hole, *Pulpits, Politics and Public Order in England 1760–1832* (Cambridge: 1989) pp. 132, 138–40.

33. More Memoirs, ii, Hannah to Patty More, [December] 1795, pp. 430–1; J. R. Poynter, *Society and Pauperism* (1969), pp. xvii–xviii; Aspinall, *Politics and the Press*, pp. 152–4.

34. [G. Meryon], *The Memoirs of the Lady Hester Stanhope* (3 vols, 1845), ii, p. 22.

35. R. Hole, 'British counter-revolutionary popular propaganda in the 1790s', in C. Jones (ed.), *Britain and Revolutionary France* (Exeter: 1983), pp. 56–7, and *Pulpits, Politics and Public Order*, pp. 132, 138–40. Hume and Paley had advocated an appeal to prejudice to control public opinion: J. W. Burrow, *Whigs and Liberals* (Oxford: 1988), pp. 54–5.

36. Tomline, *Life of the Rt. Hon. William Pitt* (2 vols, 1828 edn), i, p. 9.

37. *PR*, xxxvi, p. 480; *Memoirs of the Lady Hester Stanhope*, ii, p. 73; NMM ELL 121, Dundas to Elliot, 21 October 1794.

38. *Court and Cabinets*, ii, Grenville to Buckingham, 14 November 1792, p. 227.

39. M. Lobban, 'Blackstone and the science of law', *HJ* 30 (1987), pp. 313–15; D. Liberman, *The Province of Legislation Determined: Legal Theory in Eighteenth Century Britain* (Cambridge: 1989), pp. 71–2; C. Emsley, 'An aspect of Pitt's "Terror"', *Social History* 6 (1981), p. 175.

40. J. Ehrman, *The Reluctant Transition* (1983), pp. ix–x.

41. *Ibid.*, p. 543; E. Ashbourne (ed.), *Pitt: Some Chapters of his Life and Times* (1898), Pitt to Rutland, 8 August 1785, pp. 111–12.

42. Fox Mem., iii, Fox to Holland, 14 June 1795, pp. 109–10; U1590 S5 06/22, Dundas to Pitt, 28 September 1795; *Memoirs of the Lady Hester Stanhope*, ii, pp. 60–1.

43. T. C. W. Blanning, *The Origins of the French Revolutionary Wars* (1986), pp. 208–9; the West Indies got some troops, but not many: M. Duffy, *Britain and the French Revolution: Soldiers, Sugar and Seapower* (Oxford: 1986), pp. 28–30.

44. HRO MS 39M 49/1/27, 5, 'Private', Grenville to Wickham, 20 February 1795.

45. Black, *British Foreign Policy ... 1783–1793*, pp. 461–4.

46. NMM ELL 108, Toulon, September 1793.

47. *Dropmore*, iii, Grenville to Jay, 11 May 1795, pp. 69–70.

48. *PR*, xxxviii, 30 May 1794, pp. 373–4; U1590 S5 09/27, 'Notes on Peace with France', [January 1796].

49. Canning MS, 30, Pitt to Canning, 3 December 1799.

50. *Ibid.*, PRO 30/8/197, 'Peace Notes', [December 1799], fos 317–19; Mitchell, *The Underground War against Revolutionary France*, p. 33; Hutt, *Chouannerie and Counter Revolution* (2 vols, Cambridge: 1983), i, pp. 113–14; E. Sparrow, 'The Swiss and Swabian Agencies, 1795–1800', *HJ* 35 (1992), pp. 861–84; Ehrman, *The Consuming Struggle*, pp. 332–6.

51. *PR*, xliii, 9 December 1795, p. 666; *PH*, xxviii, 17 February 1792, col. 836.

52. *Ibid.*

Primary Source Bibliography

Manuscripts

Bodleian Library, Department of Western Manuscripts, Oxford
Bland Burges Papers: Dep Bland Burges 30–51
Talbot of Malahide Papers: MS b. 19

British Library, Department of Manuscripts
Abolition Committee Minute Books (Slave Trade): Add MS 21254–8
Auckland Papers: Add MS 34420–56
Dropmore Papers: Add MS 58877, Add MS 59065, Add MS 58906–9, Add
  MS 58914–5, Add MS 58934
Leeds Papers: Egerton MS 3498–3504, Add MS 28059–66
Liverpool Papers: Add MS 38192
Melville Papers: MS Bathurst Loan 57/107
Reeve Papers: MS 16919–31
Rose Papers: Add MS 42722
Spencer Papers: MS G15
Windham Papers: Add MS 37844

Cambridge University Library, West Road, Cambridge
Pitt Papers: CUL 6958, Political Papers, 1788–95, Boxes 3–9

Devon Records Office, Castle Street, Exeter
Sidmouth Papers: 152M OZ/1787–95, 152M OM/1793–5

Hampshire Records Office, County Hall, Winchester
Wickham Papers: 38M 49/1/15, 38M 49/1/26–7, 38M 49/1/40, 38M 49/6/6

John Rylands University Library, Deansgate, Manchester
Melville Papers: Eng MS 926/670–93
Pitt Papers: Eng MS 907

Centre for Kentish Studies, County Hall, Maidstone
Pratt Papers: KAO 840, c. 3, c. 106, c. 121–3, c. 235, c. 254, c. 267, c. 269,
  KAO 1968, 0142A, 0153, 190A
Sackville Papers: KAO U269
Stanhope Papers: KAO U1590 S5 01/1, S5 01/4–5, S5 01/10, S5 02/4, S5
  02/12, S5 02/15, S5 03/2–3, S5 03/8, S5 03/13–14, S5 04/9, S5 04/11,
  S5 05/1, S5 05/5, S5 06/22–3, S5 06/30, S5 07, S5 09–12,
  S5 Z4, S5 Z94, S5 C series
  S 60

National Library of Scotland, Edinburgh

Minto Papers: NLS 11130, 11139, 11159–60

National Maritime Museum, Greenwich

Barham Papers: MID 1/1-MID 1/2
Elliot Papers: ELL 105–8, 121–2

Pembroke College, Cambridge

29.1.35.1–15: Tomline's notes and drafts for the *Life of Pitt*
LCI 83: miscellaneous Pitt correspondence

Public Record Office, Ruskin Avenue, Kew

Army in Germany: FO 29/1–7
Board of Trade: BT 5/7–9
Chatham Papers: PRO 30/8/11–12, PRO 30/8/101–94, PRO 30/8/195–8,
    PRO 30/8/240–5, PRO 30/8/273, PRO 30/8/310, PRO 30/8/332–5, PRO
    30/8/338–45
Dacres Adams Papers, now in the ownership of G. A. F. E. Adams, Woodford
    Lodge, Near Kettering, Northamptonshire: PRO 30/58/1, PRO 30/8/7,
    PRO 30/8/8
Foreign Office: Austria, FO 7/10–43, FO 97/58–60; France, FO 27/16–44,
    FO 95/99–100; Holland, FO 37/21–57, FO 97/248; Prussia, FO 64/7–39,
    FO 22/10, FO 95/1, FO 97/323–4; Russia, FO 65/15–32, FO 95/8, FO
    97/341–2; Spain FO 72/9–39, FO 97/375; Army in Germany, FO 29/1–7
Home Office: HO 1/1–HO 1/3, HO 30/1, HO 32/1–5, HO 42/14–37, HO
    102/5–7
Stafford Papers, PRO 30/29/384
War Office: WO 1/60, WO 30/58, WO 30/81

Scottish Records Office, West Register House, Edinburgh

Melville Castle Muniments: GD 51/1/16–17, GD 51/1/20, GD 51/1/24–5,
    GD 51/1/234, GD 51/1/237, GD 51/1/242, GD 51/1/246, GD 51/16
Buccleuch Papers: GD 224/30–1

Sheffield Central Library

Wentworth Woodhouse Muniments: WWM F5, F30-F31

William L. Clements Library, University of Michigan at Ann Arbor

Pitt Papers: no foliation
Melville Papers: items 105–14

Suffolk Record Office, County Hall, Ipswich

Pretyman Papers: HA 119 T108/39–42, HA 119 T108/44–5, HA 119 Acc
    562

West Yorkshire Record Office, Sheepscar, Leeds

Harewood Estate Papers: Canning MS 29c, 29d, 29 dii, 30

Parliamentary Speeches

Cobbett, W. (ed.), *The Parliamentary History of England, from the Earliest Period to the Year 1803*, vols 21–35 (1806–15).

Debrett, J. (ed.), *The Parliamentary Register: or History, Debates and Proceedings of Both Houses of Parliament* (45 vols, 1780–96), 1st series.

Hathaway, W. S. (ed.), *The Speeches of the Right Honourable William Pitt in the House of Commons* (4 vols, 1806).

Published Primary Sources

All published in London unless otherwise stated.

Annual Register, 1780–95.

Anson, W. R. (ed.), *Autobiography and Political Correspondence of Augustus Henry, Third Duke of Grafton* (1898).

Ashbourne, E. (ed.), *Pitt, Some Chapters of his Life and Times* (1898).

Aspinall, A. (ed.), *The Later Correspondence of George III*, vols i–ii (1963–6).

Bath and Wells, Bishop of (ed.), *The Journal and Correspondence of William, Lord Auckland*, vols i–iii (1861).

Baring, Mrs Henry (ed.), *The Diary of the Right Hon. William Windham, 1784–1810* (1866).

Belsham, W., *Memoirs of the Reign of George III ... to 1793* (1795).

Bickley, Francis (ed.), *The Diaries of Sylvester Douglas, Lord Glenbervie*, vol. i (1928).

Browning, O. (ed.), *The Political Memoranda of Francis, 5th Duke of Leeds* (1884).
—— *Despatches from Paris, 1784–1789* (2 vols, 1909–10).
—— *The Despatches of Lord Gower, 1790–1792* (1885).

Buckingham and Chandos, Duke of (ed.), *Memoirs of the Courts and Cabinets of George III*, vols i–iii (1853–5).

Clarkson, T., *A History of the Rise, Progress and Accomplishment of the Abolition of the Slave Trade* (2 vols, 1808).

Cobban, A. and Smith, R. A. (eds), *The Correspondence of Edmund Burke*, vols v–viii (1967–9).

Corbett, J. (ed.), *The Private Papers of George, 2nd Earl Spencer, 1794–1801*, vol. i (1913).

Flood, W., *Memoirs of the Life and Correspondence of the Rt. Hon. Henry Flood, MP* (1838).

Granville, Castalia (ed.), *Lord Granville Leveson Gower, Private Correspondence 1781–1821*, vol. i (1916).

Green, T. H. and Grose, T. (eds), *The Philosophical Works of David Hume* (4 vols, 1885–6).

Grey, Lt Col., *Some Account of the Life and Opinions of Charles, 2nd Earl Grey* (1861).

Harcourt, L. V. (ed.), *The Diaries and Correspondence of the Rt. Hon. George Rose* (2 vols, 1860).

Historical Manuscripts Commission, 13th Report, Part VII, *The Manuscripts of J. B. Fortescue Preserved at Dropmore*, vol. i (1892).
—— 14th Report, Part I, *The Manuscripts of the Duke of Rutland Preserved at Belvoir Castle*, vol. iii (1894).

—— 14th Report, Part V, *The Manuscripts of J. B. Fortescue Preserved at Dropmore*, vols ii–iii (1894–9).

—— 14th Report, Part VI, *The Manuscripts of Lord Kenyon Preserved at Gredington* (1894).

Holland Rose, J., *Pitt and Napoleon: Essays and Letters* (1912).

Howell, T. B. and T. J., *English State Trials*, vols xxiii–xxv, 35 & 36 Geo. III (1818).

Hutton, J. (ed.), *Selections from the Correspondence of Sir James Bland Burges, Bart.* (1885).

Knox-Laughton, J. (ed.), *The Letters and Papers of Charles, Lord Barham, 1758–1813* (2 vols, 1909).

Malmesbury, 3rd Earl of (ed.), *Diaries and Correspondence of James Harris, Earl of Malmesbury*, vols i–iii (1845).

Melville, L. (ed.), *The Windham Papers* (2 vols, 1913).

Meryon, G., *The Memoirs of Lady Hester Stanhope, as Related by Herself in Conversation with her Physician* (3 vols, 1845).

Minto, Countess of (ed.), *Life and Letters of Gilbert Elliot, First Earl Minto from 1751–1806*, vols i–ii (1874).

Montesquieu, C. Secondat de, *The Spirit of the Laws*, ed. Cohler, A., Miller, B., and Stone, H. (Cambridge: 1989).

Miles, C. P. (ed.), *The Correspondence of William Augustus Miles on the French Revolution, 1789–1817*, vols i–ii (1890).

Paley, W., *The Principles of Moral and Political Philosophy* (2 vols, 10th edn, 1794).

Pellew, G., *The Life and Correspondence of the Right Hon. Henry Addington, 1st Viscount Sidmouth*, vols i–ii (1847).

Rosebery, A. (ed.), *Pitt and Wilberforce* (1897).

—— *Pitt* (1897).

Ross, C. (ed.), *The Correspondence of Charles, 1st Marquis Cornwallis*, vol. i (1859).

Russell, Lord John (ed.), *Memorials and Correspondence of Charles James Fox*, vols i–iii (1853–6).

Sichel, W. (ed.), *The Glenbervie Journals* (1910).

Smith, A., *The Wealth of Nations*, ed. K. Sutherland (Oxford: 1993).

Stanhope, G. and Gooch, G. P., *The Life of Charles, 3rd Earl Stanhope* (1914).

Stanhope, P. H., 5th Earl of (ed.), *Correspondence between the Right Hon. William Pitt and Charles, Duke of Rutland, Lord Lieutenant of Ireland 1781–1787* (1842).

—— *Life of the Right Hon. William Pitt*, vols i–iii (1861–2).

Thale, M. (ed.), *Selections from the Papers of the London Corresponding Society, 1792–1799* (Cambridge: 1983).

Tomline, George Pretyman, *Memoirs of the Life of the Right Honourable William Pitt* (2 vols, 1821).

Twiss, Horace, *The Public and Private Life of Lord Chancellor Eldon, with Selections from his Correspondence* (1844).

Ward, B., *The Dawn of the Catholic Revival in England, 1781–1802*, vol. i (1909).

Wickham, W. (ed.), *The Correspondence of the Rt. Hon. William Wickham*, vol. i (1870).

Wilberforce, A. M. (ed.), *Private Papers of William Wilberforce* (1897).

Wilberforce, R. G. (ed.), *Pitt and Wilberforce* (1892).

Wilberforce, R. I. and S. (eds), *The Correspondence of William Wilberforce*, vol. i (1840).

—— *The Life of William Wilberforce*, vols i–iii (1838).

Wyvill, C. (ed.), *Political Papers, chiefly Respecting the Attempt of the County of York ... to effect a Reformation of the Parliament of Great Britain*, vols i–iv (York: 1794–1800).

Index